CANADA'S
DIVERSE PEOPLES

Other Titles in
ABC-CLIO's
ETHNIC DIVERSITY WITHIN NATIONS
Series

The Former Yugoslavia's Diverse Peoples,
Matjaž Klemenčič and Mitja Žagar

Nigeria's Diverse Peoples, April A. Gordon

FORTHCOMING

Australia's Diverse Peoples, Andrew Wells and Julia Theresa Martínez

The Former Soviet Union's Diverse Peoples, James Minahan

CANADA'S
DIVERSE PEOPLES

A REFERENCE SOURCEBOOK

J. M. Bumsted

A B C ⬤ C L I O

Santa Barbara, California   Denver, Colorado   Oxford, England

Library of Congress Cataloging-in-Publication Data
Bumsted, J. M.
Canada's diverse peoples : a reference sourcebook / J. M. Bumsted.
p. cm. — (Ethnic diversity within nations)
Includes bibliographical references and index.
ISBN 1-57607-672-5 (hardcover : alk. paper) — 1-57607-673-3 (e-book)
1. Ethnology—Canada—History. 2. Canada—Emigration and
immigration—History. 3. Canada—Ethnic relations—History.
4. Canada—Race relations—History. I. Title. II. Series.
F1035.A1B86 2003
305.8'00971—dc21
2003011077

07 06 05 04 03 ❧ 10 9 8 7 6 5 4 3 2 1

This book is also available on the World Wide Web as an e-book.
Visit abc-clio.com for details.

ABC-CLIO, Inc.
130 Cremona Drive, P.O. Box 1911
Santa Barbara, California 93116-1911

This book is printed on acid-free paper.
Manufactured in the United States of America

TO MY MATERNAL GRANDPARENTS,

WHO CROSSED THE ATLANTIC IN 1905

Contents

THE FUTURE

Series Editor's Foreword

We think of the United States as a nation of peoples, with some describing it as a mosaic, a stew, an orchestra, and even yet as a melting pot. In the American vision of diversity the whole is perceived as greater than the sum of its parts—groups of peoples unify into a national identity. Not all Americans have shared that vision, or, to the extent that they initially did, they considered diversity as groups of people with shades of difference— such as shades of whiteness or variants of Protestantism. Many of the early newcomers would come to represent the core of an American society wherein distinctions were expected to fade by and large because a unity was anticipated that would be greater than any one homogeneous racial or ethnic national community. That unity would be forged through a common commitment to the American system of republicanism and a shared set of political principles and values—collectively, America's civic culture. For decades the diversity that was recognized (essentially in terms of religion and nationality) did not appear to be so formidable as to constitute a barrier to nationhood—as long as one did not look beyond the whiteness to the African and Native American (and later Latino and Asian) peoples. By rendering such groups invisible, if not beyond the pale, majority groups did not perceive them as representing a challenge to, or a denial of, the national unity. They were simply left out of the picture until, eventually, they would compel the majority to confront the nation's true composition and its internal contradictions. And, even before that more complex confrontation took place, streams of (mostly) European newcomers steadily stretched the boundaries of the nation's diversity, requiring a reexamination of the bonds of nationhood, the elements of nationality, and the core society and values. By World War II and in the ensuing two decades it became more and more difficult to ignore the impact of a dual development—the expanding Latino and Asian immigration and arrival of far more diverse groups of European newcomers. To secure their national vision, Americans had (albeit reluctantly and not without conflict) to make rather profound and fundamental adjustments to many of those components that had served as the nation's bonds, particularly the perception of America as a multicultural society and the belief that pluralism was a legitimate and inherent part of American society and culture.

To what extent has this scenario of a nation of peoples been present elsewhere in the world? Where have others struggled to overcome racial, religious, tribal, and nationality differences in order to construct—or to preserve—a nation? Perhaps one might even ask where, by the late twentieth century, had others *not* experienced such struggles? In how many of the principal nations has there long been present a homogeneity of people around which a nation could be molded and shaped with little danger of internal discord threatening the overall fabric of national unity? On the other hand, in how many countries has there been present a multiplicity of peoples, as in the United States, who have had to forge a nation out of a disparate array of peoples? Was that multiplicity the product of in-migrations joining a core society as it has been in the United States, or was there a historic mosaic of tribes, bands, and other more-or-less organized entities that eventually adhered together as their discovered commonalities outweighed their differences? Or, do we see invasions from without and unity imposed from above, or the emergence of one group gradually extending its dominance over the others—installing unity from below? Did any of these variations result in nation-states comparable to the United States—the so-called first new nation—and, if so, what have been the points of similarity and difference, the degrees of stability or unrest? Have their diversities endured, or have they been transmuted, absorbed, or suppressed? How much strain have those states experienced in trying to balance the competing demands among majority and minority populations? In other words, where nation-states have emerged by enveloping or embracing (or subjugating) diverse peoples, what have been the resulting histories in terms of intergroup relations and intergroup strains as well as the extent of effective foundations of national unity?

The challenges of coexistence (voluntarily or otherwise) remain the same whether two or twenty people are involved. The issue is what traditions, institutions, concepts, principles, and experiences enable particular combinations of peoples to successfully bond and what factors cause others to fall prey to periodic unrest and civil wars? Finally, many upheavals have taken place over the past 150 years, during which in-migrations have penetrated nations that were previously homogenous or were sending nations (experiencing more out-migration than in-migration) and were less prepared to address the rather novel diversities. Have theses nations had institutions, values, and traditions that enabled them to take on successfully such new challenges?

Examples abound beyond the borders of the United States that require us to examine the claims of American exceptionalism (that America's multiculturalism has been a unique phenomenon) or, at the very least, to understand it far better. Canada and Australia have had indigenous peoples but have also long been receiving nations for immigrants—however, usually far more selectively than has the United States. Brazil and Argentina were, for decades in the late nineteenth and early twentieth centuries, important immigrant-receiving nations, too, with long-term consequences for their societies. Long before there were Indian and Yugoslavian nation-states there were myriad peoples in those regions who struggled and competed and then, with considerable external pressures, strained to carve out a stable multiethnic unity based on tribal, religious, linguistic, or racial (often including groups labeled "racial" that are not actually racially different from their neighbors) differences. Nigeria, like other African countries, has had a history of multiple tribal populations that have competed and have endured colonialism and then suffered a lengthy, sometimes bloody, contest to cement those peoples into a stable nation-state. In the cases of South Africa and Russia there were a variety of native populations, too, but outsiders entered and eventually established their dominance and imposed a unity of sorts. Iran is representative of the Middle Eastern/Western Asian nations that have been for centuries the crossroads for many peoples who have migrated to the region, fought there, settled there, and been converted there, subsequently having to endure tumultuous histories that have included exceedingly complex struggles to devise workable national unities. In contrast, England and France have been tangling with about two generations of newly arrived diverse populations from the Asian subcontinent, the West Indies, and Africa that are particularly marked by racial and religious differences (apart from the historic populations that were previously wedded into those nation-states), while Germans and Poles have had minorities in their communities for centuries until wars and genocidal traumas took their toll, rendering those ethnic stories more history than on-going contemporary accounts—but significant nonetheless.

The point is that most nation-states in the modern world are not like Japan, with its 1 percent or so of non-Japanese citizens. Multiethnicity and multiculturalism have become more the rule than the exception, whether of ancient or more recent origins, with unity from below or from above. Moreover, as suggested, the successes and failures of these experiments in multiethnic nation-states compel us to consider what traditions, values, institutions, customs, political precedents, and historical encounters have contributed to those successes (including that of the United States) and failures. What can Americans learn from the realization that their own history—by no means without its own conflicts and dark times—has parallels elsewhere and, as well, numerous points of difference from the experiences of most other nations? Do we come away understanding the United States better? Hopefully.

An important objective of the Ethnic Diversity Within Nations series is to help readers in the United States and elsewhere better appreciate how societies in many parts of the world have struggled with the challenges of diversity and, by providing such an understanding, enable all of us to interact more effectively with each other. Thus, by helping students and other readers learn about these varied nations, our goal with this series is to see them become better-informed citizens that are better able to comprehend world events and act responsibly as voters, officeholders, teachers, public officials, and businesspersons, or simply when interacting and coexisting with diverse individuals, whatever the sources of that diversity.

Elliott Robert Barkan

Preface

When Elliott Barkan, the series editor for Ethnic Diversity Within Nations, approached me about contributing a volume to this series, I responded positively with considerable alacrity. My enthusiasm for the project was partly because of my eagerness to introduce the history of Canadian immigration and ethnicity to an American audience that had a parallel if not identical experience. The book was not intended to be a comparative study of the Canadian and American experiences with immigration and ethnicity, but American readers will be readily able to identify some of the significant similarities and differences. Canadians, of course, know much more about the United States than Americans know about Canada. Ironically, in terms of the history of American immigration and ethnicity, the Canadian understanding is often far too simplistic and stereotyped. Many Canadians perceive a much greater gulf between Canadian and American developments in these areas, especially in recent years, than is actually the case. One still hears Canadians talking of the profound distinction between the American "melting pot" and the Canadian "mosaic," for example.

If I was keen to write about immigration and ethnicity in Canada for a predominantly American audience, I was also fascinated by the opportunity to write a history that would combine an account of the development of policy and actuality for both immigration and ethnic groups. Canada has its fair share of historical studies of immigration and immigration policy, as well as a substantial number of works discussing ethnic policy or the ways in which the ethnic composition of the nation has been transformed over the years. These are listed in my bibliographies. But one can count on the fingers of one hand those studies that have made any serious attempt to combine all these various threads into one overarching and unified account. Thus, this work chronicles the gradual shifting of the origins of Canada's immigrants from a few countries in western Europe to the entire spectrum of the Third World. What seems to me to be the most important single point of the study is that Canada, which was once a profoundly racist and exclusionist country, is now far more accepting of racial, religious, and cultural differences than it once was. It seems pointless to attempt to identify which nation in the world is most tolerant, but Canada is high on any league table. This is not to suggest that racism and intolerance have been completely eradicated, but Canada has certainly come a fair distance in that direction and can face the future with some optimism.

Readers may be interested in my own background, both personal and professional. In personal terms, I am myself an immigrant to Canada and a proudly naturalized Canadian citizen. I was born in the United States to parents whose parents had themselves immigrated from Europe at the beginning of the twentieth century, and I came to Canada forty years ago as a young adult. I would not claim that an immigrant to Canada of European ancestry and American birth has experienced all the worst problems of immigrants to Canada, but I do come from an immigrant background, and my mother—as the daughter of German immigrants with a German name started school in Connecticut during World War I—was profoundly influenced by the hostile reactions she received from her schoolmates. My wife is also an immigrant to Canada, from Wales, and a third-language speaker, and I am grateful for all her advice and wisdom. In professional terms, I have spent much of my academic career studying Scottish immigration to Canada and Scottish ethnicity in Canada, particularly in the late eighteenth and early nineteenth centuries.

I am indebted to the Multiculturalism Program, the Department of the Secretary of State, and to the Social Sciences and Humanities Research Council of Canada for past subventions that have helped to make this book possible. I am also grateful to Elliott Barkan for his general editorial assistance. My family, as usual, helped keep me sane throughout the writing process.

List of Maps

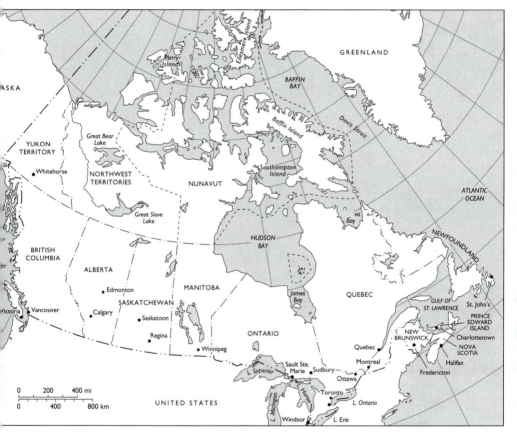

Map of Canada

CHAPTER ONE

The First Immigrants

The Aboriginal People before 1500

ORTH AMERICA has always been a place of immigration and movement. Yet, those Europeans who came to North America beginning in the late fifteenth century held the notions that they were the first to discover this land and the first to settle it. These ideas required, of course, that the European settlers ignore the people who already inhabited North America. They called the inhabitants of North America "Indians" in an extension of the misapprehension of Christopher Columbus that he had landed in "the Indies" in 1492, the lands of Asia east of the Indus River. The European settlers treated the aboriginal inhabitants as objects of debate, inquiry, and ultimate misapprehension. The initial debate questioned whether the local inhabitants were rational human beings capable of conversion to Christianity. The ultimate question, which arose when the visitors began to realize that there were hundreds of different aboriginal groups—speaking different languages and living in various forms of sociopolitical organization, stretching from the Arctic Ocean to the southern tip of South America—came over the origins of these peoples. Whence had they come?

Theories of Origins

Most native groups had legends about their beginnings, but none of the legends were in any real sense historical, and most were not acknowledged by the newcomers, who gave a variety of answers to the question of natives' origins. Some held that the natives were refugees from the Garden of Eden, driven out after the Fall. Others thought the natives were the descendents of people carried by Noah on his ark. A very popular explanation appears to have originated with a Dutch thinker named Fredericus

Lumnius in the 1560s. Lumnius noted the many similarities between European observations of the aboriginals and the characteristics one might expect of the scattered ten tribes of Hebrews referred to in the Old Testament in 2 Kings 17:6. This association between the Lost Tribes and the aboriginal Americans had a long currency and was basic to the *Book of Mormon* revealed to Joseph Smith in the nineteenth century.

Related to the Lost Tribes theory was another European conceit, that the inhabitants of America were the descendents of much earlier European peoples known only in legend, similar to the people of the lost continent of Atlantis. Other theorists preferred to speculate that the aboriginals had come from the ancient Phoenicians, or later, from the Welsh settlers led by Prince Madoc in the twelfth century. Most of the theories that placed the origins of human life in the Middle East or in Europe necessarily held that the aboriginals had not inhabited the New World for very long. The origins of the world could be precisely dated by biblical scholarship at 4004 B.C. The Phoenicians were contemporaries of the Greeks, and the Welsh had lived in the Middle Ages.

In 1589 Father José de Acosta speculated in his *Historia Natural y Moral de las Indias* that the native inhabitants of America were of Asiatic origin. They had probably wandered eastward, Acosta thought, via some land route as yet unknown and then had diffused across the continents. Although it is tempting to be impressed with Acosta's theories—they subsequently appeared similar to what would be learned of early human migration patterns through scientific investigation in the nineteenth and twentieth centuries—the truth is that he had no better factual handle on the origins of humankind in the New World than any of his contemporaries. What was needed was some hard evidence.

The speculative debate continued for several centuries, and it had several dimensions. One grew out of missionary activities and to some extent out of missionary ambivalences toward the aboriginals. Everyone could agree that the native inhabitants of North America were precivilized savages. The question was whether the aboriginals were "noble" in their very lack of civilization, exhibiting the true virtues of humankind before it was corrupted by modern values, or whether they were just plain backward. Another debate emerged over whether the observations of a growing number of Europeans who had tried to study the aboriginals indicated that they had a common background, suggested by the similarities of the many groups contacted, or a more complex one, suggested by an equal number of dissimilarities. The eighteenth century was an age of scientific classification rather more than of first theories, and the classifiers divided—as they usually do—into lumpers (those who sought to consolidate) and splitters (those who sought to subdivide). None of the North American peoples had a written language, and their oral history—although often collected by fur traders and missionaries—was not taken very seriously.

Further evidence was eventually provided by researchers working in the developing field of archaeology, who began to excavate the ruins and remains of the aboriginal peoples' ancestors in the early nineteenth century (Fagan, 1987). Historians like William Prescott were able to piece together information about conquered civilizations through evidence left by the conquerors, but given the absence of written records kept by the natives, could make only limited conclusions. The early archaeologists traveled all over the world. The civilizations of the ancient Assyrians, the Aztecs, and the Mayans were all uncovered in the 1840s and described in detail in a series of best-selling books. The archaeologists even uncovered pictographs and hieroglyphs from the Mayan civilization in the Yucatan peninsula, which, when eventually translated, would provide some insight into the origins of these cultures. The search for evidence, particularly for an association between human remains and those of extinct animals, continued throughout the nineteenth century. It became increasingly clear that there were no ancient caves or old tools to be found at the bottom of glacial deposits that would provide evidence of the origins of the North American people. By the end of the century, a debate emerged between scientists who insisted that North American natives had lived through the Stone Age (although this could not be proven) and scientists connected with the American government who insisted that the aboriginals were recent immigrants to North America, having come, at the most, a few centuries earlier than the Europeans. Viewing the Indians as relatively recent arrivals assuaged some of the guilt of conquest.

The first big breakthrough that dated the natives to the Stone Age came with a discovery in 1908 near Folsom, New Mexico, of a stone spear point in the bones of an extinct animal. This find led to further excavation near Folsom in 1926, which turned up more evidence of human occupation that went back at least 10,000 years. A further find was made at Clovis, New Mexico, in 1932. After World War II, the development of the technique of radiocarbon dating provided an independent test for determining the age of these and other finds. The results confirmed earlier estimates that the documented finds were more than 10,000 years old. To see the natives as recent arrivals became increasingly untenable. But how far back did human settlement in America extend, and how had the first settlers arrive?

The Beringia Controversy

Two obvious possibilities existed for the origins of aboriginal peoples in North America. One possible explanation was a passage by boat from somewhere that humans had resided before America was peopled. The other possibility was for a passage by land. The most obvious location for a land passage was across the Bering Strait between Siberia and Alaska, where scientists knew that at one point there had been a land bridge (which they called Beringia) between Asia and North America. The notion of a Siberian origin for aboriginal Americans gained credence from a variety of corroborative evidence, such as similarities of blood types and dental structure between American aboriginals and northern Siberians. Linguistic evidence also pointed to a similar pattern. Gradually a theory emerged, which gained strength by its seeming ability to explain all that a host of scientists—chiefly geologists, archaeologists, and climatologists— had discovered and were discovering about both the land and its people.

It is an axiom of science that the simplest explanation fitting the known facts is usually the most accurate one, and this theory was elegant in its relative simplicity, which was one of the greatest arguments in its favor. The theory was that sometime around 15,000 years ago, when Beringia provided a land connection between Asia and North America, human sojourners crossed into North America in search of food. The passage was not an easy one, and it probably took a long time for any individual or party to complete. Although the environment of the land bridge was relatively favorable to human life, the glaciers that then covered the northwestern part of the American continent were not. Some of the new arrivals headed north into the Arctic regions. Others straggled southward along a gap between the glacial ice sheets, making their way into the southwestern part of the continent (which was not covered with glaciers), where the earliest evidence of human presence has been detected. As the ice retreated and the climate changed in the northern part of the continent, more and more people were able to move into the southern regions and began to travel eastward across the continent, following the game animals.

The land bridge theory seemed appropriate for dealing with virtually all of the existing evidence. In order to explain relatively similar dates for surviving artifacts from one coast to the other, the theory had to postulate an extremely rapid extension of humankind across the continent in the postglacial period. Gradually the theory hardened into conventional wisdom. Although there were many skeptics and people who have preferred other explanations, their arguments have been hampered by the absence of any hard evidence that contradicted the standard view, particularly by the lack of indisputable evidence of an earlier occupation of the continent or of an alternate time sequence. Most mainstream scientists have insisted that all hard evidence of human habitation from this period (as opposed to such "soft" evidence as linguistic theory or literary legends) comes in the form of stone artifacts that cannot be dated earlier than 12,000 years. These scientists refused to entertain alternate theories so long as the "12,000-year barrier" remained intact. The mainstreamers have been particularly scathing in their criticism of those who advocate acceptance of one or more of the alternate theories of peopling, whether by refugees from the continent of Atlantis or by ancient space travelers.

Despite its elegance, the Beringian theory has in recent years come under increasing attack. Much of the critique has come from those who find it unlikely that the Americas could have remained free of any human habitation until only 12,000 years ago, especially given the increasingly great antiquity being uncovered for human/humanoid development elsewhere in the world (Stengel, 2000). There are also other arguments against the standard view of human arrival. One is that very few early human remains have been found in the northwestern part of the continent, where the first immigrants supposedly entered from Siberia, while many more remains, which are extremely old, have been uncovered on Canada's east coast, more than 4,000 miles from Beringia. Moreover, the few examples of early humans found in the northwest are not Mongoloid in appearance as people from Siberia would have been at that time. This was notably the case for Kennewick Man, found in Washington state in 1996. Another problem comes in terms of the development of languages, chiefly an insistence that 12,000 years is simply not sufficient to produce the levels of linguistic diversity found in the Americas (Greenberg, 1987). (Language complexities do not necessarily coincide with social complexities and can exist independently of them.) Recent studies of blood types and teeth across the Americas also suggest that a simple explanation of origin in Siberia will not work. The notion has recently gained ground that travel along the coasts by boat makes more sense than inland movement alongside glaciers (Gruhn, 1988).

There have long been alternative stories for the peopling of America (Sorensen and Raish, 1996). Perhaps more importantly, over the past few years there have been a number of archaeological finds that simply do not fit the standard pattern. Some finds in Chile, for example, have produced artifacts that date older than the Clovis find, an obvious conundrum for those who support the Beringia theory (Dillehay, 1997). A recent find in South Carolina has been uncovered that archaeologists say predates the most recent Ice Age, which ended about 10,000 years ago. What are we to make of the mounting evidence of scattered early human activity in the Americas that obviously does not relate to the older evidence? At this stage, it is unlikely that the Beringia theory will be totally overturned. There is simply too much genetic and linguistic evidence to support the view that America's "Indians" are mainly descended from Asian peoples. But there are clearly anomalies. It may be possible that this main wave of Siberians traveling swiftly across the Americas was entering a place previously settled by people who had reached their habitations from different places via different routes, or who had perhaps come from Siberia in a far earlier period than the present model allows. And it is also possible that new discoveries will force a paradigm shift for the archaeologists. Like most academic disciplines, archaeology is riddled with feuds and petty grievances that have been elevated over time into hardened ideologies.

More than academic reputations are at stake in the Beringia controversy. Because of the huge sums of money involved in litigation over compensation for tribal lands taken over by European interests, the ancient human history of the continent before European arrival is of new interest and takes on a high political significance. A North American continent on which aboriginal groups migrated constantly and took over the lands of neighbors, often by force, or on which the native inhabitants hunted birds and mammals to extinction, was hardly an Eden-like paradise of peace and respect for the environment. If it could be established that people of European origin had arrived on the continent long before 1492 and were displaced or absorbed by later cultures, this would add further weight to the notion that the European intrusion after 1500 was simply a continuation of developments occurring in all parts of the world—and certainly in America—since the world's human beginnings. At least one Canadian newspaper has already used recent academic revisionism as a basis to editorialize in opposition to any moral claim of native groups to "massive transfer payments and expensive government programs" (*National Post*, 2001, A19).

The sources for information about the early history of humans on the northern part of the North American continent (now the Dominion of Canada) are simultaneously extensive and limited. Material evidence consists chiefly of human artifacts—mainly of stone, which survives better than leather or wood—usually dug out of the ground by archaeologists. Dating these materials typically involves associating the artifacts with the geological remains in which they are found, a process that often does a better job of outlining a sequence of events than it does of providing precise dates for them. Scientific analysis such as radiocarbon dating can provide a rough notion of the date of an artifact. Given the absence of written records kept by any of the early inhabitants of northern North America, virtually the only way modern scientists can make human memory contribute to the record is by using the oral traditions and the languages of the various peoples. For many years, these oral traditions and linguistic remains were treated with considerable suspicion. They are now regarded as quite useful, but they extend only so far back in time.

Climate, Ecology, and Aboriginal Life

Although some scholars would push the record of humankind in North America back considerably further than 12,000 years—perhaps as much as another 50,000 years—we are still looking at a relatively recent occupation in terms of the total age of the earth. Humans are involved in only the most recent few long-term climate cycles, at most. The continent before human habitation has a history of millions of years, which need not concern us here. For the period in which humans have lived on the continent, at least, the dominant ecological factor in our lives has been the climate, the naturally occurring complexes of weather patterns found in meteorologically defined regions (Bryson and Wendland, 1967). These meteorologically defined patterns and regions coincide fairly closely to major biotic patterns and regions. Climatic conditions are not eternally fixed but are constantly shifting and changing, on both the macro and micro levels. During the period most often associated with human habitation—the past 12,000 years—temperatures have been getting warmer, glaciers have been retreating, and the land, previously covered with ice, has been reoccupied by flora and fauna. A period of rapid glacial retreat occurred from 11,000 B.C. to 8000 B.C. For some unknown reason, during this era around 200 species and at least 60 genera of major animals vanished from the Americas. It is possible that they were hunted to extinction. From 8000 to 5000 B.C. the climate turned warmer and drier. From 5000 B.C. to A.D. 500, the continent was extremely warm; forests reached their northernmost extension around 3000 B.C.

Since 500 B.C. climatic conditions have been relatively stable, with substantial shifts only along the borders between climatic zones. The period from 500 B.C. to A.D. 400 was one of extreme changes between winter and summer, and from A.D. 400 to 900 ameliorating conditions prevailed and the forest again extended northward. Between 1200 and 1500, the climate turned cooler and drier, again sending the northern forests into retreat. From 1550 to 1850 a still-colder period further reduced the growing season and sent the forests still further south. The coldest point of this period was reached in 1816, the famous "year without a summer," during which much of the Northern Hemisphere's population failed to harvest any crops. Since 1850 Canada has experienced slight warming trends within a stable climate, although conditions are thought to have been shifting again since the 1980s. Whether Canada's present warming trend is caused more by the "greenhouse effect" or by natural changes is still not completely certain, although increasing numbers of scientists attribute the trend to human-made causes.

Some of the basic assumptions in the diffusionist theories of the human occupation of the American continent involve the relationship between climate and people. The movement and subsequent cultural attributes of human beings are largely determined by climatic patterns. The early inhabitants of North America made little or no attempt to modify their environment. They either adapted to it or fled from it. Glaciers are assumed to retreat in postglacial periods, and, as the environment was in constant flux, so were the human cultures that had to adapt to it. Most of the changes occurred gradually over long periods of time, but occasionally change could be abrupt and swift, especially for those living on the borders of naturally determined climate zones and biotic ecosystems. As might be anticipated, the patterns of native response to the ecological environment varied. The most important factor was the nature and availability of food sources.

Aboriginal life was to a considerable extent environmentally controlled, although other factors besides environment increasingly governed the movement and culture of native communities, human relationships in particular. Native groups did have contact with one another. They traded and they learned new technology. They were extremely adaptable and adaptive. For instance, the speed with which the horse was assimilated into plains culture after its importation by Europeans around 1500 was quite astounding (Bryan, 1991, 179–184). Environmental changes, though, could force aboriginal groups to abandon their traditional territories, often setting off a chain reaction that might stretch over hundreds of miles. The northern environment—both the climate and the land itself—was not in most places particularly inviting for agriculture in the same way the subtropical and tropical regions farther south were. The northern climate was relatively harsh, particularly in the winter months. (It is important to note that the peoples of northern North America were, of course, not called Indians at the time of European intrusion. Most groups called themselves, in their own tongues, simply "the people," or by names describing the regions in which they lived.)

Cultural Variations

The stages of the development of human culture and methods of food acquisition varied from one region to another (Bryan, 1986). The earliest peoples for whom detailed evidence survives lived from 11,500 B.P. to 7500 B.P. The evidence is in the form of stone projectile points and other tools, and the items' makers have been labeled by archaeologists as the Paleo-Indians. Such tools have been found in sites from the west coast of modern Canada to central Nova Scotia. East of the Rocky Mountains, these people appear to have been big-game hunters, targeting bison on the plains and caribou in the eastern regions. On the Pacific slope, they had a more complex economy based principally upon salmon. Paleo-Eskimos entered the Canadian Arctic from Alaska in several successive waves beginning about 4,000 years ago. An Archaic people called the Pre-Dorset People moved into the region a few hundred years later, and gradually sophisticated into the Dorset People. The Paleo-Indians were succeeded in some regions by a people simply called "Archaic." Their lifestyle was one of hunting, fishing, and gathering. They lived chiefly in the eastern regions. Apparently few humans lived on the plains during much of the warmest period of the climatic cycle, but Archaic people appeared about 2200 B.P. Out of the Archaic culture came a woodland culture in eastern Canada. This culture began practicing horticulture borrowed from peoples to the south between A.D. 500 and 1000. Another whole culture, based upon new Japanese technology, entered the Arctic from Alaska around A.D. 900. Indeed, despite small numbers of people and a very harsh climate, the Arctic region has experienced an exceptionally complex history of immigration, caused chiefly by the need for large territories in which to gather food.

Not surprisingly, the native population of northern North America at the time of the arrival of the first Europeans (around 1500) presented quite a number of cultural variations in the regions, caused partly by differential responses to climatic change and partly by different historical origins. European first contact, although it began in the sixteenth century, did not occur everywhere in North America during that period. Instead, first contact situations in what is now Canada continued until well into the nineteenth century, as Europeans expanded westward across the continent. However, some of the consequences of contact, such as the arrival of new diseases or the reception by aboriginals of new technology, may have occurred well in advance of the actual meeting of aboriginals and Europeans.

The Eastern Maritime region, which was the one first contacted by Europeans, was populated by a hunting, fishing, and gathering population. In most areas, the population had stabilized well before the Europeans' arrival. The exception was in Newfoundland, where a Dorset Inuit people was replaced by the Beothuks around A.D. 600. Beothuks, who spoke a language distantly related to Algonquian, would become extinct by the early nineteenth century. The Micmacs inhabited most of what are now the Maritime provinces and the Gaspé peninsula in Quebec. They spoke Eastern Algonquian and inhabited a fairly rich region with varied resources. Thus, they were quite numerous in pre-European times, probably significantly greater in numbers than the first Europeans could appreciate. Considerable debate over their precontact numbers exists in the literature. The Malecites in the Saint John River Valley spoke a dialect of Algonquian and had begun the cultivation of corn by the time the Europeans arrived. These people did move their residences with the seasons, but they were not truly nomadic.

To the northwest of the Maritimes existed northern forests and subarctic tundra in what is now Labrador, Quebec, and northern Ontario. In today's northeastern Quebec and Labrador—stretching over to the Canadian Shield, that vast region of pre-Cambrian rock surrounding Hudson Bay—lived the Naskapi and Montagnais, both nomadic hunting peoples. These peoples were contacted by the French beginning in the sixteenth century (Bailey, 1969). To their west were the Algonquins, and to their west—out on the prairies—were the Ojibwa or Chippewa. The latter were more sophisticated food gatherers than the eastern peoples because of the availability of more usable vegetation in their territory, and they had therefore spread fairly widely. Nevertheless, this entire region consisted of seminomadic people who were mainly hunters.

To the south of this northern circle of hunters were the Iroquoian people of what is now southern Ontario, the Huron and Iroquois. These people had begun cultivating corn, having learned the technique through diffusion from the people of the Mississippi Valley. Horticulture permitted more permanent residence, greater social stability, and larger population densities than nomadic life did. Growing food also encouraged the development of pottery and complex trading patterns. The Huron lived in villages as large as 100 or more longhouses, with log buildings perhaps 8 meters wide and 30 meters long, inhabited by perhaps five families each. The principal Canadian corn growers were the Huron, who lived to the south of Georgian Bay. In adjacent New York State lived the Five Nations Confederacy of the Iroquois (the Mohawk, Oneida, Onondaga, Cayuga, and Seneca), who were also horticulturists. These two separate Iroquoian-speaking peoples (the Huron and the Confederacy) had coexisted for some centuries but, with the arrival of the Europeans, they would rapidly become rivals for the control of the fur trade.

On the central plains, the people were big-game hunters, particularly dependent on the bison, or buffalo. Before the introduction of the horse, which occurred in this region in about A.D. 1600, the hunters stalked their prey on foot, developing ingenious ways to slow down the animals, such as driving them into gullies and over cliffs. The horse arrived not long before the Europeans arrived in the region, but no observer could have guessed how recently the aboriginals had become mounted. The horse was ideally suited to the needs of a nomadic people, and it swiftly replaced the dog as a beast of burden. To the north of the prairies was a heavily forested zone of hills, lakes, rivers, and marshy sloughs. This parkland, not very usable by horses, extended westward from the Red River and ultimately into the Peace River country of modern British Columbia. Its inhabitants were hunter-gatherers, much like their eastern neighbors. Parkland patterns of horse usage moved east and west; prairie patterns of horse usage moved north and south.

The northern Pacific coast, with its rivers and coastal waters teeming with fish and marine life, was a special region unique to North America. Here the climate was temperate year-round, there were few accumulations of snow or ice, and the environment was rich with food sources. The result was a large population and the gradual emergence of complex social systems. The people here also developed large-scale woodworking using cedar, a very flexible and durable wood that encouraged decoration and aesthetic use. House joists were intricately carved, richly painted totem poles depicted ancestral symbols, and even canoes were embellished. Europeans did not arrive in this region until relatively late in the eighteenth century, and when they arrived they found a hierarchal society of nobles, commoners, and slaves, organized into clans and phatries. Linguistic development was particularly complex on the western mainland coast and offshore islands. In the interior of what is now British Columbia, between the coast and the prairies, was a mountainous region intersected by many lakes and river valleys. The people of this territory were hunters and gatherers but had some features of social organization—clans and hierarchies—probably borrowed from the coastal cultures.

In the subarctic areas of the continent, such as the basins of the Mackenzie and Yukon Rivers or the drainage basins of Hudson and James Bays, lived other groups of woodland peoples who were more nomadic hunters and fishers than gatherers. They constantly sought both big and small game. All were Athapaskan speakers, and their movement was southward away from the Barrens, that vast infertile stretch between northern Manitoba and the Arctic Ocean.

The Inuit (the word means "the people") lived in the high Arctic and subarctic coasts of northern Canada. Archaeological investigation of their habitat began only in the twentieth century and then quickly confirmed earlier suspicions that the first residents of the region (the Paleo-Eskimos or Pre-Dorset People) had come from Alaska about 2,000 B.C. Surprisingly enough, the arctic environment was extremely kind to artifacts, chiefly because it tended to "freeze-dry" and hence preserve them. The Paleo-Eskimos began as big-game hunters but gradually adapted to hunting the sea mammals of the coast as the climate began to cool around 500 B.C. Over time, the Paleo-Eskimos changed into a more settled lifestyle that has been called Dorset culture. The Dorset people built insulated houses of turf, boulders, and snow but left behind few signs of the standard features of more recent Inuit culture: the domed snow-hut, the dogsled, the kayak. These ingenious adaptations for living in an ice-bound world were apparently introduced from the western Arctic at a later date. The Dorsets did create a magnificent body of art, principally in bone and ivory, which carried on into the Inuit culture that succeeded them (McGhee, 1996).

Aboriginals at the Europeans' Arrival

Several points must be emphasized about the native peoples at the time when the Europeans arrived in North America. First, although any scholar would delight in being able to identify that definitive moment when a people was being observed totally uninfluenced and unaffected by a preceding European presence, such a moment rarely, if ever, occurred. As European penetration of the continent continued over several centuries, there were innumerable episodes of first contact. In the relatively isolated and fragile ecosystems of North America, the Europeans' influence spread

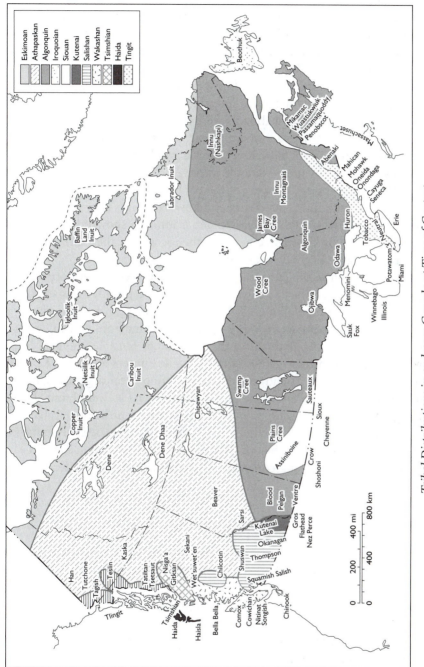

Tribal Distributions in and near Canada at Time of Contact

Source: Based on Dickason, Olive. Canada's First Nations: A History of Founding Peoples from Earliest Times.
(Toronto, ON: McClelland and Stewart, 1992), p. 453.

far in advance of the actual arrival of the first explorer—a point that the term *first contact* tends to obscure. For example, although the continent was not completely free of disease, it had far fewer incidences of communicable diseases than Europe, which translated into a lack of immunity on the Americans' part to illnesses that most Europeans took in stride. The result was a demographic disaster almost before the Europeans had even come ashore, as the epidemics were spread far ahead of the new arrivals.

Second, the indigenous inhabitants were the products of natural adaptation to the North American environment, and their technology, while not as showy as that of the newcomers, was a good deal more functional. The locals' birch-bark canoes were the ideal vehicles for gliding along the rivers and lakes of the eastern part of the continent, for example. The locals knew about vitamin C deficiency and how to cure it. They knew how to dress warmly for winter and how to get around on snowshoes. In the gradual exchange of knowledge between the locals and the newcomers, the aboriginals gave as good as they got.

Finally, although to the Europeans the indigenous peoples of northern North America looked very much alike, the native populations spoke more than fifty languages in literally hundreds of different dialects. Their hunting grounds spread across more than 4,000 miles from east to west and nearly 2,000 from north to south. In terms of lifestyle, the people ranged from simple hunter-gatherers to big-game hunters to salmon fishermen and full-time horticulturists. Their sociopolitical organizations, their religious practices, and their mythologies varied as well. From the very beginning of human settlement of this continent, one principal characteristic of the peoples of northern North America was sheer diversity. The land was a veritable patchwork quilt of peoples and tongues. The ultimate arrival of Europeans complicated, but did not really alter, this pattern.

Timeline

20,000–10,000 B.C.   Humans cross Siberian land bridge to North America.

12,000 B.C.   Clovis find in New Mexico given this date.

9000 B.C.   Appearance of fluted arrow points in North America. Emergence of salmon fishing culture on West Coast.

7000 B.C.   Gourds first grown in North America.

6500 B.C.   Appearance of first dogs in North America.

6000 B.C.   Land, climate, and sea levels stabilize in North America. Plano points, the ripple-flaked arrow points of a number of hunting peoples, appear.

3200 B.C.   Ceramics made in Peru; height of Sumerian civilization in the Middle East, with first known writing.

3000 B.C.   Hunting bison by drives becomes common on plains; North American forest reaches its northernmost extension.

2500 B.C.   First libraries established in Egypt; end of Stone Age in North America.

2000 B.C.   Inuit begin spreading from Alaska to Greenland.

1000 B.C.   Epic poems of Homer written.

500 B.C.   Height of the Greek city-states.

A.D. 500   Corn culture spreads to what is now Ontario.

A.D. 600   Dorset population disappears from North America; Europe invaded by "barbarians."

A.D. 1000   Tobacco and ceramic pots appear in what is now Ontario; Leif Eriksson and Vikings land on Vinland.

A.D. 1525   Horse introduced into North America.

Significant People, Places, and Events

ACOSTA, JOSÉ DE (1540–1600) Born in Medina del Campo, Spain, he joined the Jesuits and became a professor of theology in Lima, Peru. He was the author of *Historia Natural y Moral de las Indias*, published in 1590, the first work that speculated that the Amerindians had crossed into America from Asia across the Bering Strait.

ARCHAIC PERIOD A historical era in the development of humankind. In North America, the Archaic Period is regarded as extending from roughly 8500 to 600 B.C. The period is characterized by fishing; nomadic hunting of smaller game; and gathering of nuts, berries, and shellfish.

ARCTIC OCEAN A body of water stretching from the Labrador Sea in the east to the Beaufort Sea in the west, covered with ice for more than half the year.

AZTECS The Aztecs/Mexicas were the indigenous people who controlled northern Mexico at the time of Hernan Cortes, who conquered them in 1519. They were fierce warriors who founded the city of Tenochtitlan (now Mexico City) in 1325, from which they controlled a rich agricultural empire and trading system.

BEOTHUK The aboriginal inhabitants of Newfoundland, who became extinct at the beginning of the nineteenth century. Their disappearance (and the failure to preserve their language) has made study of them difficult. But they were a hunting and gathering people who lived in Newfoundland for many years before the arrival of the Europeans.

BERING STRAIT A body of water about 90 kilometers wide between Asia and North America connecting the Arctic Ocean and the Bering Sea. It is the point at which the two continents are closest together. At one time, the two continents were joined at this point by a land bridge.

BERINGIA The land bridge that at one time connected northern Siberia with Alaska. It is thought that the bridge was at one time almost 1,000 miles wide. This bridge provided a means for the migration of plants, animals, and people from Siberia to America and has been much studied in recent years.

CANADIAN SHIELD A region of Canada stretching northward from the Great Lakes to the Arctic Ocean and covering the middle section of Canada. It represents the world's largest area of exposed Archaean-age rock, formed in the pre-Cambrian era. Ice sheets and glaciers created lake basins in this region and removed much of the soil. It is a region of thick woodlands in the south and tundra in the north.

CLOVIS, NEW MEXICO The site of animal bone and human weapon remains found in 1932 and dated to around 12,000 B.C. These remains are still regarded by many archaeologists as the earliest evidence of human presence in the Americas.

COLUMBUS, CHRISTOPHER (1451–1506) An explorer born in Genoa, Italy. In 1492 he was appointed Admiral of the Ocean Sea and sailed westward from Spain. He eventually made a landfall in the West Indies and believed he had reached Asia.

DORSET CULTURE The term used to refer to the culture of the Arctic peoples from around 500 B.C. to A.D. 1500. The people lived in permanent habitations and probably were familiar with dogsleds and kayaks. They hunted sea mammals and were displaced by newcomers from Alaska beginning in A.D. 1000.

FOLSOM, NEW MEXICO Site of a discovery of bones in 1908 (although not recognized as important until 1926) on the Wild Horse Arroyo, among which fluted stone spear points were found. The bones were those of ancient bison that became extinct early in the Ice Age—thus demonstrating an early presence of humankind in North America.

HURON A confederacy of tribes who lived in what is now Simcoe County, Ontario, in the first part of the seventeenth century. They were horticulturists who lived in permanent villages. They were destroyed by disease and warfare in the middle years of the seventeenth century.

INUIT A term now preferred to the older term *Eskimo* to refer to the aboriginal people inhabiting the northern regions of Canada and speaking a common language known as Inuktitut, of which there are six distinct dialects. They probably did not emerge in the Arctic until well after A.D. 1000. The extent of possible influence among them by the Vikings remains uncertain.

IROQUOIS The five nations of the Iroquois Confederacy lived in upstate New York, although some Iroquoian speakers also lived in what is now Canada. The tribes consisted of the Mohawk, Seneca, Cayuga, Oneida, and Onondaga. In the early eighteenth century the Tuscarora also joined the confederacy. The Iroquois lived in longhouses and were extremely fierce warriors who became constant enemies of the French in Canada.

KENNEWICK MAN The name given to the human remains uncovered at Kennewick, Washington, in 1996 and analyzed in 1999 despite considerable opposition from some aboriginal groups. Examination determined that the remains were about 9,000 years old, and—perhaps most significantly—that the individual was of Caucasoid rather than Mongoloid descent.

LOST TRIBES OF ISRAEL The ten tribes of Israel that disappeared from the Near East in earliest Biblical times, ca. 800 B.C.E., speculated to have reappeared in America.

MADOC, PRINCE A legendary Welsh ruler who, according to bardic tales, sailed to America in the twelfth century (around A.D. 1170) and established a Welsh colony in the New World, perhaps in Ohio.

MALECITE (or Maliseet) The aboriginal Algonquian speakers who inhabited the St. John River Valley and northeastern Maine.

MAYA The indigenous people who controlled most of Central America at the time of European intrusion. They had their origins about 2,500 B.C. and began expanding around A.D. 325, reaching one cultural peak around A.D. 800 and then another between A.D. 900 and 1200 after mixing with the Toltec peoples. They had a highly developed numerical system, much astronomy knowledge, and hieroglyphic writing.

MICMACS The indigenous people who inhabited the coastal regions of the Gaspé peninsula and the present-day Maritime provinces of Canada east of the St. John River Valley. They spoke a dialect of eastern Algonquian and were a semisedentary people who were among the first aboriginals to encounter Europeans and to be affected by them.

MONTAGNAIS An Algonquian-speaking people who lived in eastern Canada north of the St. Lawrence River. They were often confused with the Naskapi, with whom they were closely related.

NASKAPI One of the Algonquian-speaking aboriginal people who inhabited eastern Canada from Labrador to the Canadian Shield but were found mainly in modern Quebec. They hunted caribou and moose, fished for salmon in the spring, and lived in wigwams covered with skins. They were among the earliest indigenous people to encounter Europeans and were greatly affected by the contact.

OJIBWA The aboriginal people who lived, at the time of European contact, between northeastern Georgian Bay and eastern Lake Superior. They later incorporated a number of related peoples and extended their territory. They were a hunting and gathering people who lived in birch-bark shelters and paddled birch-bark canoes. They were active in the North American fur trade.

PALEO-INDIAN A term used to describe a number of early human cultures in America characterized by the hunting of big game and the use of fluted projectile points. Paleo-Indian sites are spread across southern Canada as far as east as Debert, Nova Scotia. Most are places where large numbers of animal bones are found in association with projectile points.

PHOENICIANS A people also known as Canaanites, who lived on the Syrian coast and used their natural resources of timber and harbors to become famous seafarers. Their major towns were Byblos, Sidon, and Tyre. The Phoenicians traveled to Spain and Arabia in the years around 1000 B.C. and were incorporated into the Assyrian empire around 800 B.C.

PRE-DORSET CULTURE The culture of the Paleo-Eskimos, who first inhabited the Arctic regions of North America about 2000 B.C. Their technology was much simpler than that of the later Inuit and is often referred to as being a "small-tool" culture.

PREHISTORY An older and presently unfashionable term used to refer to human development in the period before the introduction of writing and written records by Europeans in the sixteenth century. It is currently disliked by many people, especially aboriginal groups, for its implication that history only began with the Europeans.

RADIOCARBON DATING A scientific method developed at the University of Chicago by a team of chemists headed by Professor Willard F. Libby. The radiocarbon method is based on measuring the constant rate of decay of the radioactive or unstable carbon-14 isotope. It remains the most widely applied dating technique for ancient remains.

SMITH, JOSEPH (1805–1844) Smith was born in Vermont. In 1827 he discovered a series of golden tablets, which he translated from some unknown language as the Book of Mormon with the aid of magic spectacles. Among the tablets' revelations was the story of the fate of the Ten Lost Tribes of Israel, which became part of the teachings of the Latter-Day Saints, the religion founded by Smith.

STONE AGE The period of human history when tools and weapons were being made from stone. In some parts of the world, the Stone Age began around 2 million years ago. In the Americas, the Stone Age started when humans first arrived on the continents, and it ended around 2500 B.C. at the earliest.

WOODLAND PERIOD A term developed in the 1930s to refer to a historical period falling between that of the Archaic hunters and gatherers and the later moundbuilders of the Mississippi River region. It generally is regarded as covering the years 2000 B.C. to A.D. 1000, with variations in different regions, although its basic characteristics do not represent so much a break with the Archaic Period as a further cultural development and sophistication of tools and techniques, such as ceramics and the elaboration of burial practices.

Documents

Where the First People Came from

So then, I shall tell another legend. I'll tell a story, the legend about ourselves, the people, as we are called. Also I shall tell the legend about where we came from and why we came . . . why we who are living now came to inhabit this land.

Now then, first I shall begin.

The other land was above, it is said. It was like this land which we dwell in, except that the life seems different; also it is different on account of its being cold and mild [here]. So then, this land where we are invariably tends to be cold.

So that is the land above which is talked about from which there came two people, one woman and one man . . . they dwelt in that land which was above. But it was certainly known that this world where we live was there.

Now then at one time someone spoke to them, while they were in that land of theirs where they were brought up. He said to them, "Do you want to go see yonder land which is below?

The very one about which they were spoken to is this one where we dwell.

"Yes," they said, "we will go there."

"The land," they were told, "is different, appears different from this one where we dwell in, which you dwell in now during your lifetime. But you will find it different there, should you go to see that land. It is cold yonder. And sometimes it is hot."

"It fluctuates considerably. If you wish to go there, however, you must go see the spider at the end of this land where you are. That is where he lives."

The spider, as he is called, that is the one who is the net-maker, who never exhausts his twine—so they went to see him, who is called the spider.

Then he asked them, "Where do you want to go? Do you want to go and see yonder land, the other one which is below?"

"Yes," they said.

"Very well," said the spider. "I shall make a line so that I may lower you."

So then, he made a line up to—working it around up to, up to the top.

"Not yet, not yet even half done," he said.

Then he spoke to them, telling them, better for him to let them down even before he finished it the length it should be.

Then he told them, "That land which you want to go and see is cold and sometimes mild. But there will certainly be someone there who will teach you, where you will find a living once you have reached it. He, he will tell you every thing so you will get along well."

So he made a place for them to sit as he lowered them, the man and the woman.

They got in together, into that thing which looked like a bag.

Then he instructed them what to do during their trip. "Only one must look," he said to them. "But one must not look until you have made contact with the earth. You may both look then."

So, meanwhile they went along, one looked. At last he caught sight of the land.

The one told the other, "Now the land is in sight."

The one told the other, "Now the rivers are in sight."

They had been told however, that "if one . . . if they both look together, before they come to the land, they will go into the great eagle-nest and they will never be able to get out and climb down from there."

That's where they will be. That's what they were told.

Then the one told the other, "Now the lakes are in sight. Now the grass."

Then they both looked before they arrived, as they were right at the top of the trees. Then they went sideways for a short while, then they went into the great eagle-nest. That's where they went in, having violated their instructions. . . .

Then the bear arrived.

So he said to them, . . . and they said to him, "Come and help us."

The bear didn't listen for long; but then he started to get up on his hind legs to go and see them. Also another one, the wolverine as he is called. They made one trip each as they brought them down.

But the bear was followed by those people.

That was the very thing which had been said to them, "You will have someone there who will teach you to survive."

This bear, he taught them everything about how to keep alive there.

It was there that these people began to multiply from one couple, the persons who had come from another land. They lived giving birth to their children generation after generation. That is us right up until today. That is why we are in this country.

And by-and-by the White People began to arrive as they began to reach us people, who live in this country.

That is as much as I shall tell.

Source: Elis, C. Douglas, ed. and trans., *Cree Legends and Narratives from the West Coast of James Bay* (Winnipeg: University of Manitoba Press, 1995), pp. 3–7.

The Implications of the Origins of North Americans

The following editorial appeared in the June 12, 2001 issue of the National Post, *one of Canada's largest-circulation newspapers with national coverage. The* National Post *is a conservative paper.*

The ancient myths of North America's natives are powerful to those who believe them, but nowhere near as powerful as their modern myths, at least not when it comes to shaping public policy. Stories of the Great Spirit or of the raven's role in creation have nothing on the notions that natives lived at peace with one another and in blissful harmony with nature before Europeans arrived, or even that natives are the continent's undisputed first peoples.

The respected journal *Science* has published two papers detailing how aboriginals in North America and Australia hunted many large mammal species and some birds to extinction long before the white man arrived. Next week, a U.S. federal judge will decide the fate of Kennewick Man, a Caucasoid (although not necessarily white-skinned) human who lived in eastern Washington state 9,500 years ago. Why are we mentioning these two news items in the same breath? Because, taken together, both conspire to undermine the myth that the population of pre-Columbian North America was a racially homogeneous group of environmentally responsible people who settled an unpopulated land en masse 15,000 years ago.

In fact, the Indian tribes that populated ancient North America, most expert[s] agree, were distinct groups that warred with one another, and frequently migrated from area to area as a result of conquest and defeat. The natives whom Europeans first encountered were not "First nations" as regards to the locations where contact was made. In many cases, they were third or fourth. It is easy to see why Kennewick Man makes some native groups nervous—for he is yet another piece in a growing body of evidence that suggests not all of North America's pre-Columbian settlers came over the Bering Strait. Roman-like artifacts have been discovered in Mexico, early European DNA in Ojibwa Indians and European linguistic markets in pre-Columbian native languages. Several archaeological dig sites, such as Cactus Hill in Virginia and Meadowcroft in Pennsylvania, point to the presence of European cultural influences thousands of years before the land bridge opened up to migration from Siberia.

All this ancient history has modern-day implications. If the people we now call "First nations" were not the continent's sole original inhabitants, what moral claim do they have to massive transfer payments and expensive government programs? And why should whites compensate the Huron, Mohawk or Cree any more than these native groups compensated the tribes whose lands they took before 1492? Tribal warfare and migrations are a fundamental theme of human history in all parts of the populated world. The arrival of Europeans in North America is often portrayed as the invasion of a red Eden by white warmongers. Seen in broad terms, however, European settlement was merely the perpetuation of the competitive North American status quo with more technologically advanced people.

Source: National Post, 12 June 2001, p. A19.

Bibliography

Bailey, A. G., *The Conflict of European and Eastern Algonkian Cultures 1504–1700: A Study in Civilization*, 2nd ed. (Toronto: University of Toronto Press, 1969).

Bryan, A., "The Prehistory of Canadian Indians," in R. Bruce Morrison and C. R. Wilson, eds., *Native Peoples: The Canadian Experience* (Toronto: McClelland and Stewart, 1986).

Bryan, Liz, *The Buffalo People: Prehistoric Archaeology on the Canadian Plains* (Edmonton, Alberta: University of Alberta Press, 1991).

Bryson, Reid A., and Wendland, Wayne M., "Tentative Climatic Patterns for Some Late Glacial and Post-Glacial Episodes in Central North America," in William J. Mayer-Oakes, ed., *Life, Land, and Water: Proceedings of the 1966 Conference on Environmental Studies of the Glacial Lake Agassiz Region* (Winnipeg, Manitoba: University of Manitoba Press, 1967), 271–298.

Dewar, Elaine, *Bones: Discovering the First Americans.* (Toronto: Random House Canada, 2001).

Dickason, Olive Patricia, *Canada's First Nations: A History of Founding Peoples from Earliest Times*, 3d ed. (Toronto: Oxford University Press, 2001).

Dillehay, Tom, *Monte Verde: A Late Pleistocene Settlement in Chile*, vol. II (Washington, DC: Smithsonian Institution Press, 1989).

———, *The Settlement of the Americas: New Prehistory* (New York: Basic Books, 2001).

Fagan, Brian, *The Great Journey: The Peopling of Ancient America* (New York: Thames and Hudson, 1987).

Greenberg, Joseph, *Language in the Americas* (Palo Alto, CA: Stanford University Press, 1987).

Gruhn, Ruth, "Linguistic Evidence in Support of the Coastal Route of Earliest Entry into the New World," *Man* 23 (1988), 22–100.

McGhee, Robert, *Ancient People of the Arctic* (Vancouver, British Columbia: University of British Columbia Press, 1996).

McMillan, Alan D., *Native Peoples and Cultures of Canada*, 2nd ed. (Vancouver, British Columbia: Douglas and McIntyre, 1995).

National Post, 12 June 2001, p. A19.

Ray, Arthur J., *I Have Lived Here since the World Began: An Illustrated History of Canada's Native People* (Toronto: Lester Publishing, 1996).

Sorensen, John, and Raish, Martin, eds., *Pre-Columbian Contact with the Americas across the Oceans*, rev. ed. (Provo, UT: Brigham Young University Press, 1996).

Stengel, Mark K., "The Diffusionists Have Landed," *Atlantic Monthly* 285:1 (January 2000), 33–43.

Wright, J. V., *A History of the Native Peoples of Canada* (3 vols.) (Ottawa: Canadian Museum of Civilization, 1995–2000).

CHAPTER TWO

The "Founding Peoples"

HE TWO EUROPEAN NATIONS whose arrival in northern North America eventually led to significant transplantations of populations there were the English and the French—whose military rivalry in the Old World went back to the eleventh century, when the Normans had successfully invaded England. John Cabot, an Italian-born Portuguese mariner sailing under the English flag, established an English claim to Newfoundland (and beyond) in 1497, and Jacques Cartier, sailing under the French flag, established a French claim to the St. Lawrence River valley through his expeditions there in the 1530s. (Vikings from Greenland had settled in Newfoundland around A.D. 1000. They had been driven off by the resident population and did not return.) The Portuguese took a brief interest in the northern Atlantic coast in the early sixteenth century and even planted a few early trading "colonies." The Portuguese today are remembered in Canada only by a number of place-names in the region, particularly in Newfoundland. Scotland, which in the early seventeenth century was a separate nation that shared a monarch (James VI of Scotland, a.k.a. James I) with England, attempted in the 1620s to establish colonies in Nova Scotia; these initiatives soon collapsed, however. A large number of "foreign Protestants" were brought by England to Nova Scotia in the early 1750s, although the colony was clearly intended to be predominantly English. By the 1750s, both England and France had well-established settlements, even colonies, in what is now Canada. In the 1960s, a Canadian royal commission would lead to the official labeling of the French and the English as the "founding peoples" of Canada, completely ignoring the previous presence of the aboriginals or the presence of a substantial population of mixed-bloods. Apart from this problem with the indigenous peoples, though, the royal commission's label fairly accurately reflected the historical reality of population growth in northern North America before the British conquest of New France in 1758.

Nova Scotia's John Cabot Park, located at the site where the explorer may have landed in 1497 (Corel Corporation)

The English

John Cabot (known in Italy as Giovanni Caboto and in Spain as Juan Caboto Montecalunya) sailed from Bristol, England, in mid-May 1497, and on 24 June 1497—as a later chronicle put it—"was Newfoundland fowend by Bristol men in a ship called the *Matthew*" (Firstbrook, 1997, p. 120). Apart from the date and the time (supplied much later by Cabot's son), no details survive for the 1497 landfall in Newfoundland. Cabot apparently went ashore briefly at some point, declared possession for England, and then continued sailing along the coast. He saw no native inhabitants and was most impressed by the great schools of fish observable from the deck of his tiny vessel. He did recognize what he had found as an island, and he died in 1498 or 1499 at sea on an informal follow-up expedition. The English did not formally follow up on Cabot's "discovery" until the next century: In 1576, on a voyage searching for the Northwest Passage, Martin Frobisher established an English claim to the Arctic, and two years later Sir Humphrey Gilbert projected a plan for taking possession of Newfoundland and colonizing it. In 1578 as well, Frobisher planted what would have been England's first colony in North America at Baffin Island, but he decided (it is not known why) to remove the settlers without allowing them to winter. The first real English attempt at settlement in what is now Canada, therefore, took place in 1597 at "Ramea," an ill-fated colony in the Magdalene Islands in the Gulf of St. Lawrence. Organized by religious dissenters who wished "to worship God as we are in conscience persuaded by his Word," the colonists were later driven off their island by an alliance of European fishermen and American aboriginals. After returning to London, some of the party joined compatriots in Amsterdam, where they became part of the Pilgrim people who came to America on board the *Mayflower* in 1620.

Apart from Ramea, the first major English colonization efforts came on the island of Newfoundland, where the London and Bristol Company for the Colonization of Newfoundland (founded in 1610) began a settlement on Conception Bay in July 1610. These first Newfoundland settlements—which predate most other English "plantations" in North America except the earlier Carolina ones associated with Sir Walter Raleigh, none of which survived—have been virtually forgotten, partly because they occurred outside the bounds of the United States, and partly because they did not lead in the short run to the creation of a formal colony with a proper colonial administration. But by 1650 a handful of permanent settlements had been established on Newfoundland, which has a claim to being England's second oldest colony in North America and the oldest in Canada. The big breakthrough came as a seasonal population gradually became a permanent one. New arrivals came on fishing boats and remained on the island after the boats went home at the end of the fishing season. A number of conditions were important for permanent residency. One of the most important was the transfer of property through the female because of the extent of male mortality at sea. Another was the English fear that the French would move into any settlement vacuum. Before 1700, most of the immigrants to Newfoundland came from the "West Country" seaports of Cornwall and Devon, and the Newfoundland fishery was an important component in the economy of these English seaports. These immigrants to Canada collected in more than thirty tiny settlements containing between one and twenty families each, all almost totally dependent upon fishing for their livelihood and existence. A typical pattern was a sort of dual residency, with families spending part of their time in England and part in Newfoundland. The island was not well suited to farming, and only occasional efforts at agriculture were made. After 1700, the English were joined by a substantial contingent of colonists from Ireland, mainly from the Cork area.

The tiny Newfoundland settlements were subject not only to considerable physical discomforts, but also to the vagaries of war. Especially between 1696 and 1708, the settlements were repeatedly attacked by French buccaneers acting under the authority of the French government, and they were virtually decimated. They had to be resettled throughout the eighteenth century. Newfoundland society during that period developed as a sharply bifurcated one, with English Anglicans on one side and Irish Catholics on the other. The British authorities allowed settlement to occur, but deferred to the West Country seaports by refusing to establish a year-round government in the colony. As a result, the substantial growth of a permanent population on the island continued to develop independently of any government policy or supervision. Permanent immigration was simply the product of the decisions of many fisherfolk (including women and children) to remain behind in Newfoundland rather than to return home to England with their vessels. Newfoundland's population grew to 3,500 by 1730 and to 7,300 by the 1750s. The percentage of permanent residents among the total summer population increased as well, from 15 percent in the 1670s to 30 percent in the 1730s to at least 50 percent by 1753. Both the Irish and English brought rich folk cultures with them, adding to this another rich ingredient from the fishery, and the mixture was preserved relatively unchanged by the island's relative isolation until almost the end of the twentieth century. Newfoundland thus became the home of a distinctive dialect of English and an equally distinctive folk culture like no other in Canada, especially in the fishing outports of the island.

On the mainland of northern North America, the first colonization under the auspices of the Crown of England was undertaken by Scots who were subjects of James I in his Scottish persona as James VI. Sir William Alexander received a patent for settlement in 1624 in a place called "New Scotland" or "Nova Scotia." Over the next few years, Alexander and several other Scottish noblemen sent ships with colonists to the areas around present-day Port Royal and the south coast of Cape Breton Island. These Scottish plantations were later the victims of Anglo-French warfare and of Charles I's need for subsidies from the French Crown to avoid calling Parliament to vote a proper revenue. In 1650, Oliver Cromwell seized the colony of Acadia from the French and claimed possession of it for England until 1670, when it was returned to France. But this early history provided the background for the eventual French cession of part of Acadia to the British—the parliaments of England and Scotland had been unified in 1707—at the Treaty of Utrecht in 1713.

From 1713 to 1755 the British, as administrative occupiers and colonial conquerors, governed the ceded territory, which they called Nova Scotia in remembrance of the older Scottish colony. At the time of the Utrecht treaty in 1713, the French residents of the colony had been given one year to remove to French territory or to become permanent British subjects. Most of the French chose to remain yet resolutely refused to give up their language, religion, or cultural heritage. The French residents also refused to take an oath of allegiance to their new country, always reserving the right to remain neutral in any military confrontation with their prior rulers, the French. The British were unable to enforce any policy of assimilation because of their relatively weak hold over the almost totally alien population of the colony. This failure of assimilation would become a familiar occurrence with minority groups in what would eventually become Canada. But the Acadian situation would have quite a different outcome than later, similar situations.

Before any final solution was attempted with the Acadians, the British decided to establish a non-Acadian presence in Nova Scotia. In 1749 the town of Halifax was founded as a destination for 2,500 settlers collected from the ports of England, mainly from among disbanded soldiers and sailors. Each transport that left England in May 1749 had its own Mess List (human inventory) of settlers aboard, totaling 1,174 heads of families, only 509 of whom were accompanied by their spouses. There were 414 children under the age of 16, and 420 servants, mainly males. Of the total heads of families, 654 were soldiers and sailors. The most numerous single civilian occupation listed was "farmer" (161 names), with 107 in the building trades; a vast assortment of other occupations was included in the list (Bates, 1973).

The town of Halifax in which they arrived—a town laid out by surveyors—was far from meeting its description in a contemporary English magazine of a "city . . . of 2,000 houses, disposed into fifty streets of different magnitudes," with in its center "a spacious square with an equestrian statue of His Majesty." The immediate reality was one of huts, tents, and primitive conditions. The new governor, Lord Edward Cornwallis (1713–1776), wrote home that "among these [settlers] the number of industrious active men proper to undertake and carry on a new settlement is very small—of soldiers there are only 100, of tradesman, sailors and others able to work, not above 200." The remainder, he claimed, "were poor idle worthless vagabonds that embraced the opportunity to get provisions for one year without labour, or sailors that only wanted a passage to New England. Many have as into a hospital to be cured, some of Venereal Disorders, some even Incurables" (Bell, 1961, p. 344n). The arrival of a garrison from Louisbourg, a fortress that had been returned to the French, further complicated matters by introducing a swarm of camp-followers who were mainly devoted to satisfying the thirst and the physical desires of the troops. Many settlers died over the first winter, and hundreds more left for New England. Persons who objected to assisting with the burying of corpses in St. Paul's Cemetery were struck off the ration list. Disbanded soldiers here, as elsewhere, proved to be unsatisfactory settlers. Although Charles Lawrence doubtless exaggerated, he had a point when he asserted in 1760: "every soldier that has come into the Province, since the establishment of Halifax, has either quitted it or become a dramseller [of spirits]" (Bell, 1961, p. 109n).

Most of the newcomers to Halifax either died or moved away to the American colonies (those in what would become the United States), and two years later the British moved in nearly 3,000 "foreign Protestants," settlers recruited in Switzerland and in the German principalities of the Hanoverian kings of Britain. This group of immigrants was composed of 40 percent adult men, 25 percent adult women, and 35 percent children; most of the adults were under the age of 40. As was typical of European immigrants to Canada throughout its history, those in family groups settled more easily than single individuals, especially than single males. The largest single occupational component—more than 60 percent—described themselves as farmers, but there were more than fifty other trades and professions represented, including carpenters, surgeons, watchmakers, schoolmasters, and clergymen. Few unskilled laborers appeared on the passenger rolls. The government intended to settle these newcomers in agricultural communities, chiefly on the Bay of Fundy, but most remained in Halifax because of the uncertainty over Acadian land titles. They did not like their shantytown. This experiment proved in many ways no more successful than the earlier establishment of Halifax, although more of the new settlers—mainly German speakers—did eventually take hold in communities to the southwest of Halifax. By the early 1750s, therefore, Nova Scotia had become very much a multicultural colony, with a French-speaking Catholic majority, two Protestant minorities—one English-speaking and one German-speaking—and a large number of Micmac aboriginals, also professing to be Catholic.

In 1755 the government of Nova Scotia—tired of Acadian recalcitrance, fearful of the French menace, and eager to distribute Acadian lands to more cooperative settlers—had a final confrontation with the Acadians that resulted in a decision to forcibly deport them from the colony. That deportation occurred late in 1755. More than 6,000 Acadians were rounded up and shipped to the American colonies to the south. Many Acadians escaped to French territory on Isle St. Jean and Cape Breton. In 1758, in the wake of the final capture of the French fortress of

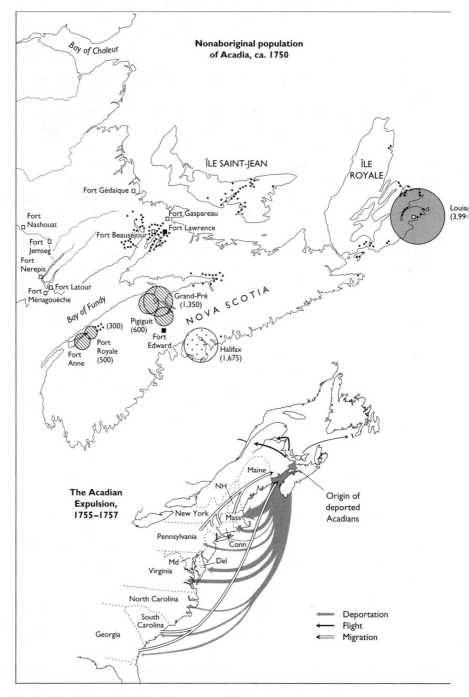

Nonaboriginal Population of Acadia, ca. 1750, The Acadian Expulsion, 1755–1757
Source: Buckner, P. A., and J. G. Reid, eds.
The Atlantic Region to Confederation: A History.
(Fredericton: Acadiensis Press, 1994), p. 157.

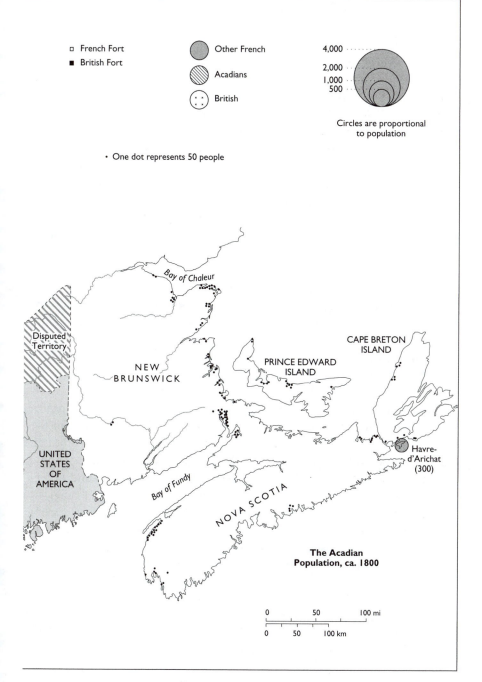

French Fort □
British Fort ■

Other French
Acadians
British

4,000
2,000
1,000
500

Circles are proportional
to population

· One dot represents 50 people

Bay of Chaleur

Disputed
Territory

NEW
BRUNSWICK

PRINCE EDWARD
ISLAND

CAPE BRETON
ISLAND

UNITED
STATES
OF
AMERICA

Bay of Fundy

NOVA SCOTIA

Havre-
d'Arichat
(300)

**The Acadian
Population, ca. 1800**

0   50   100 mi
0   50 100 km

The Acadian Population, ca. 1800
Source: Buckner, P. A., and J. G. Reid, eds.
The Atlantic Region to Confederation: A History.
(Fredericton: Acadiensis Press, 1994), p. 157.

Louisbourg on Cape Breton Island, another roundup of 6,000 Acadians was carried out by the British military. This time the Acadians were sent back to France; many, however, drowned when the ships transporting them were wrecked at sea by a series of storms. The draconian treatment of the Acadians made many in both Nova Scotia and Great Britain uncomfortable, and large-scale expulsion of recalcitrant minorities was never again attempted as a public policy in what is now Canada.

Beginning in 1758, the government of Nova Scotia began advertising in New England for settlers, attempting to lure them with promises of the establishment of a representative assembly, Acadian lands to be redistributed to newcomers, and substantial bounties for transportation and maintenance. Nova Scotia also offered a local government similar to that which the settlers enjoyed in their present homes in Connecticut, Rhode Island, and Massachusetts. By 1763, when the subsidies ran out, nearly 10,000 New England Yankees had been transplanted to Nova Scotia, providing yet another ethnic component to the population of the colony. Many of the New Englanders soon returned home, however, describing Nova Scotia as "Nova Scarcity."

Although it is tempting to characterize the New England from which the Nova Scotia settlers were drawn as a homogeneous society, this would be a mistake. The new arrivals were largely drawn from three colonies— Rhode Island, Connecticut, and Massachusetts Bay (which itself represented the annexation of two other colonies, Sagadahoc [Maine] in the early seventeenth century and the Plymouth Colony in 1690)—although some would come from northern New England as well. Each of these colonies had its own history and its own traditions, religious and otherwise. Rhode Island, for example, had always been the home of religious toleration, and Plymouth Colony had been far more tolerant of dissent than the Puritans of Massachusetts Bay. Connecticut and Massachusetts both had state-supported churches, but there the similarity ended; the nature of the church establishment was quite different in each colony. Furthermore, both established churches had begun to experience sectarian schism under the pressure of the great religious revival known as the Great Awakening. Such schism was extremely prevalent in isolated rural communities suffering from overcrowding, from which many of the Nova Scotia settlers were drawn. Moreover, the sorts of people for whom the offer of free land and subsidized settlement would be most compelling were the marginalized inhabitants of any region, those who had not played a leadership role in a society that put a considerable premium on the relationship between leadership and status.

New England settlement in Nova Scotia peopled three regions of the province. The first was the agricultural area formerly improved and inhabited by the Acadians, located mainly around the Minas Basin. This area was settled mainly by family groups, who quickly re-created their New England-style mixed farms in Nova Scotia. These settlers also brought various other aspects of their New England culture with them, such as their religions. Most of this group probably followed the Puritan religion. The most famous product of the farming communities was Henry Alline, the Nova Scotia evangelist and theologian, founder of the Freewill Baptists in the United States. Born in Newport, Rhode Island, Alline had come to Nova Scotia in childhood. Alline was forced to break both with Puritan orthodoxy and with his family responsibilities in order to begin his career of public preaching.

The second area was along the southwestern coast of the province. It was expected that townships in this region would be inhabited mainly by fishermen and traders, as the soil was not good for farming. As a result, the townships were extensive in area, as they did not need to be closely governed. Liverpool, for example, was a township of 100,000 acres—and the distribution of the land took considerably longer than in the Annapolis Valley. There were some substantial differences between the coastal settlements on the southwest coast and the settlements elsewhere in Nova Scotia. Perhaps the most important difference was demographic. The communities of the southwest coast, principally intended as fishing settlements, were initially settled by single young men rather than by families, who would come later. Many of the south shore people, at least initially, moved to Nova Scotia only for the summer fishing season. Simeon Perkins, who had been born in Norwich, Connecticut, in 1735, probably commuted from Liverpool to Norwich during the 1760s; he certainly spent a year and a half in Connecticut from late 1767 to mid 1769. Perkins had married in 1760 and had one son. But he was always less interested in land and farming than in commercial activity and lumbering, as the diary that he kept for most of the period from 1766 to his death in 1812 well demonstrates. Perkins became a magistrate soon after his arrival in Liverpool, and his diary makes clear that the court on which he sat was an integral part of local government, seemingly far more active than a town meeting.

The third main area for New England settlement in Nova Scotia was in the St. John River Valley in what is now New Brunswick. These settlements were made after the initial negotiations between the settlers and the Nova Scotia government in 1759–1760. Maugerville was created by

TABLE 2.1   CENSUS OF NOVA SCOTIA, 1767

| | Nationality | | | | | |
Place	English	Irish	Scottish	American	German	Acadian
Nova Scotia	686	1,831	143	5,799	1,862	650
Cape Breton	70	169	6	170	21	271
North (NB)	25	53	17	874	60	147
St. John	130	112	7	70	3	197
Total	911	2,165	173	6,913	1,946	1,265

SOURCE: Census of Canada 1665–1871, volume iv of 1871 Census of Canada (Ottawa, 1876), p. 71.

Massachusetts people in 1762, the grant divided into 101 freehold lots of 500 acres each extending along the riverbank for 12.5 miles. Being far from Halifax, it received little supervision and managed its own affairs through the church and the town meeting. Maugerville was so successful that in 1774 it attracted a New England-born clergyman in the person of Seth Noble. When the American Revolution began, Noble became one of the principal spokesmen for it in his community, and he was eventually forced to leave to return to the United States when Maugerville remained British.

At the mouth of the river, a group of American-born merchants including William Hazen set up a trading partnership. Other land grants in the valley were given to a variety of applicants, mainly from Nova Scotia and Great Britain, who were seeking to establish agricultural estates based upon tenantry. Such a principle was alien to most of the Americans who settled in Nova Scotia before the American Revolution. The largest grant, 400,000 acres, was made to 68 proprietors of the St. John River Society, who combined notions of speculative advantage with dreams of new landed estates. A few of the Society's proprietors brought New Englanders to settle at the villages of Gagetown and Burton.

A census of Nova Scotia taken in 1767 demonstrated just how culturally complex was the mixture of those among its resident and immigrant populations, including as the census did separate columns for English, Scots, Irish, Americans, Germans, and Acadians. This census (See table 2.1) included neither aboriginals, of whom there were nearly 1,000 in the region being enumerated, nor blacks, of whom there were several hundred.

The French

Early History

France entered the "exploration of America sweepstakes" through the activities of an Italian named Giovanni da Verrazano (c. 1485–c.1528), who persuaded the French king to sponsor a voyage of exploration in 1523. On this voyage, da Verrazano established definitively that the American continent was not Asia, but he did not find the Northwest Passage he was looking for, or any natural resources to exploit. In 1534, a native-born Frenchman, Jacques Cartier (1491–1557), was sent by his monarch to uncover new lands "where it is said that a great

Italian explorer Giovanni da Verrazano (c. 1485–c.1528) convinced the French government to sponsor his exploration of the American continent. (Library of Congress)

quantity of gold, and other precious things, are to be found" (Cook, 1993, p. xii). Cartier eventually made three voyages: one to find a new region to investigate; a second to locate some mineral resource there that would attract investors and the royal court; and a final large-scale settlement effort that ended in failure.

The new regions examined by Cartier were the Gulf of St. Lawrence (on the first voyage) and the St. Lawrence River Valley (on the second voyage). On his initial visit, Cartier made the first contact with aboriginal people described in any detail. On his second visit, he traveled inland as far as a native village called Hochelaga, on the present site of Montreal, but wintered at another village to the east called Stadacona. From the natives there Cartier learned of a fabulously rich civilization farther inland, where—he was told—people lived who "possessing no anus, never eat nor digest, but simply make water through the penis." His news was exciting enough to convince the French Crown to mount a major expedition, which colonized on the St. Lawrence in the 1540s but found no real mineral wealth nor any exotic civilization.

French explorer Jacques Cartier ascends the St. Lawrence River in Canada. Cartier's voyages from June 1534 to May 1536 were the beginning of France's efforts to explore Canada. (Library of Congress)

Following this early failure, the French produced only trading factories in the north Atlantic region of North America until the early years of the seventeenth century. After several abortive French attempts at settlement, Pierre Du Gua de Monts (1558?–1628) and his young assistant Samuel de Champlain (c. 1570–1635) planted a colony at Île Saint-Croix, at the mouth of the Saint Croix River (now Maine) and then moved it in 1605 to Port-Royal in the Annapolis Basin of Nova Scotia. After a few years, the early French colony at Port-Royal was wiped out by an English buccaneer, and the years between 1624 and 1650 turned into a confusing period of struggles between individual families seeking to control the fishing and fur trading resources of Nova Scotia, all complicated by the arrival of the Scots in the late 1620s. Nova Scotia was captured by the English in 1650 and held until 1670, when it was briefly conquered by the Dutch and then returned to French hands.

As for Samuel de Champlain, he moved on from Port-Royal in 1608 to found a trading post-cum-colony on the St. Lawrence River. Champlain managed to work his way into the major fur trading network of the aboriginals, and, beginning in 1618, started to advocate a full-scale settlement venture in the St. Lawrence region. In 1627 Cardinal Richelieu responded to Champlain's promotional efforts by founding the Company of One Hundred Associates, which spent a fortune raised from courtiers and French merchants in the late 1620s on colonization efforts but accomplished virtually nothing. Champlain's settlement was captured and evacuated by an Anglo-Scottish armed expedition in 1629 and was not reestablished until 1632. Little interest had been shown before this time in missionary activity to the aboriginal peoples, but now the French became committed to bringing Christianity to the natives. The Jesuits were sent to the St. Lawrence, and the famous *Jesuit Relations* began to be published.

At Champlain's death in 1635, the number of French in Canada, as his colony was called, was still fewer than 200. The religious devout in France sent money, settlers, and male and female missionaries in considerable numbers to the St. Lawrence. The colony was economically dependent upon the fur trade and found itself under attack from the Iroquois Confederacy based in New York, which had sought to usurp the Hurons' role as middlemen with the northern aboriginals by destroying the Huron people (they attacked the French because the French supported the Huron). Victims of European colonization and missionary activities, the

Huron were virtually destroyed by 1650. Throughout the 1650s, the French settlements were under constant attack from the Iroquois.

Since 1647 Canada had been governed by a central council and a group of elected representatives from the major districts. It had a population of just over 3,000 people in 1663, when the French Crown decided to take control of it and turn it into a royal colony. This population originated chiefly in west-central France. It was composed about half of urban folk, and half of rural. The three chief cities of the region were Paris, La Rochelle, and Rouen. Few of the early immigrants had substantial agricultural experience, and most were artisans. In this sense, the early settlers were not representative of French society, although most elements of that society were represented in Canada's population. Most of the arrivals before 1663 came in family groups.

The royal takeover in 1663 certainly rejuvenated the colony. The French Crown moved immediately to quell the Iroquois by sending out a regular regiment of soldiers (the Carignan-Salières regiment). It also began increasing the population by sending over the *filles du roi*—orphan girls raised at the king's expense. Not surprisingly given France's emphasis on sending over soldiers and orphan girls, the vast majority of the post-1663 arrivals came as single individuals. In addition to sending these separate groups of gendered settlers, the French reorganized the government of Canada, introducing a military governor and a civilian "intendant" who was responsible for the administration of French affairs in America. Both officials worked under the watchful eye of the minister of marine, Jean-Baptiste Colbert. Before the royal takeover, a contemporary observer might have predicted that the French would lose a war of attrition to the aboriginals, who boasted that the French "were not able to goe over a door to pisse" in safety. This observer might also have argued that the English would inherit the continent, almost by default. By 1670, however, the situation had been quite reversed. The English, under the later Stuarts (Charles II, James II), withdrew from the northern parts of the continent, and the French infused a new energy into their land possessions. Shortly afterward, the French government attempted to establish a foothold in Newfoundland and regained control over Acadia. Although success would contain the seeds of destruction, the French in 1670 seemed to be on the eve of what would later be almost a century of expansion and dominance in North America. New France would become the overall name given to the French possessions in America, which stretched from Newfoundland on the east to the Mississippi River on the west to Louisiana in the south.

New France, 1670–1759

New France was always a complex collection of colonies and peoples, hardly homogeneous in any sense. It never really enjoyed a single period when it was at its fullest extent, as Acadia and Newfoundland were turned over for European reasons to the British just at the high point of French hegemony in North America. Nonetheless, four colonial regions (not all of them formal colonies) made up continental New France. In the east, there was Acadia, part of which was ceded to the British in 1713 to become Nova Scotia and the remainder of which was divided after 1713 into Ile St. Jean (Prince Edward Island) and Ile Royale (Cape Breton Island, home of the great fortress of Louisbourg). Canada was the largest colony, situated along the St. Lawrence River. To the southwest of Canada was the *"pays d'en haut,"* the backcountry fur trade region inhabited chiefly by aboriginals and a growing population of mixed-bloods, stretching from Detroit to the lower reaches of the Mississippi River, where Louisiana was established in 1700.

Acadia

No one was ever entirely certain of what territory was included in Acadia, as the French and the British discovered in 1713 when Acadia to its "ancient limits"—apart from Cape Breton Island and the Island of St. John—was ceded by the French to the British. What the French claimed as Acadia, although they had neither fully settled nor really governed it all, was what is now New Brunswick and Nova Scotia. The French fishing settlements on Newfoundland, particularly around Placentia, were not regarded as part of Acadia proper yet did not belong to any other colony in New France; they too were given up in 1713.

Between 1670 and 1713, the regions of Nova Scotia around the Annapolis Basin, the Minas Basin, Cobequid, and Chignecto Bay were all settled by descendants of the handful of French residents who had survived the complicated occupations of the mid-seventeenth century. Nearly all of the surnames in the region had origins before 1670. By 1710 there were probably around 2,000 francophone inhabitants of this region, most of them born in North America. The bulk of the expansion of Acadian population was carried out by members of a younger generation seeking new land. The bulk of the settlement was located in the tidal lowlands of the Bay of Fundy, where the construction of dikes enabled the inhabitants to control the tides and enrich the soil. Although the farms there were small in size, the land was extremely fertile and harvests were considerable. The Acadians raised livestock and grew fruit, which they traded with Yankee merchants from the south. A few fishing settlements also flourished on the south coast of Nova Scotia.

Government sat lightly on the Acadians before 1713, for neither France nor Canada attempted to exercise any real administrative control. Canada worked instead through missionary priests, who brought military instructions to the region to be carried out mainly by the aboriginal followers of the missionaries. Most of Acadia's people came from a relatively small area of southwestern France (the provinces of Vienne, Poitus, Aunis, and Saintonge) and spoke a southwestern dialect of French, which only became more distinctive in the New World environment. The Acadians were agricultural peasants of separate cultural and political development from Canada. The family ("le clan") and the local community were the important units, well designed to provide for survival under difficult conditions.

After the transfer of part of Acadia to the British in 1713, its new masters were no more able to exercise administrative dominance over the population than had been the French. The Acadians continued to expand, seeking the free pursuit of their religion and the right to remain apart from any military conflicts in the region. France had previously expanded its presence in the region through the construction of a major military fortress at Louisbourg on the southeastern coast of Cape Breton Island and through the beginnings of settlement on the Island of Saint John, and the French had continually put pressure on the Acadians to support their military endeavors. After taking over the region, the British eventually managed to induce the Acadians to take conditional oaths of allegiance but conceded to them the right of neutrality. The fortress/town of Louisbourg was attacked by an Anglo-American military expedition in 1745 and fell to the invaders fairly easily. It was returned to France in 1748 to be reinforced and refortified. These military activities had highlighted for the British the dangers of a population not fully loyal. The British government of Nova Scotia gave the Acadians one more chance to become full citizens (which included military responsibilities), then decided to expel them. Many Acadians escaped to what is now northern New Brunswick or to the Island of Saint John, where they became part of a second deportation in 1758. Some 2,000 Acadians sought refuge in Canada, where they blended themselves into the Canadian population.

Despite two expulsions, the British were never really able to eliminate the Acadians from the Maritime region. Some Acadians escaped deportation by hiding in remote parts, and others who had been forcibly removed made their way back into the region and joined their compatriots in new communities. Even as early as 1767, in the incomplete census taken of Nova Scotia, more than 1,200 Acadians were counted.

Canada

The major colony of New France was always Canada, a long, thin strip of inhabited territory stretching several hundred miles along the St. Lawrence River and its tributaries. By the mid-eighteenth century, the Swedish visitor Peter Kalm was able to describe the heartland of Canada as "a village beginning at Montreal and ending at Quebec, which is a distance of more than one hundred and eight miles, for the farmhouses are never above five arpents [293 meters] and sometimes but three apart, a few places excepted" (Benson, 1927, vol. 2, pp. 416–417). From its earliest foundation, one of the principal difficulties for Canada was attracting European settlers. Unlike the English colonies to the south, which welcomed hundreds of thousands of immigrants from the British Isles, Canada never experienced a long-term, large-scale influx of population, and a substantial percentage of those who did come (usually because of indenture, military service, or subsidy) subsequently went back to the mother country. The extent of coercion in the migration of population to Canada was always substantial. Very few immigrants, perhaps only five percent of the total, ever came voluntarily. (The figures in the English colonies to the south ran at around 50 percent voluntary arrivals). The numbers of immigrants were larger than the numbers of usually counted because of the high rate of return to the mother country.

The French government never really promoted a mass movement to North America, partly because it wanted its population at home to serve in the military. As Colbert wrote in 1666, "It would not be prudent [for the King] to depopulate his Kingdom as would be necessary in order to populate Canada" (Charbonneau et al., 1993, p. 24). For their part, the ordinary people of France saw Canada as a cold wasteland inhabited by fierce aboriginals, a place of exile to be avoided at all costs. It was hard to get to and very isolated once one was there. Thus, despite famine, unemployment, and general oppression, the French were reluctant to emigrate. The French attempted to make up the resulting labor shortage in Canada with slaves culled from among the blacks of the West Indies and the aboriginals of western North America, but although household slavery flourished, field slavery did not. The French also adopted into their families a substantial number of young English people taken as captives in the constant warfare between those two nations.

The bulk of the 15,000 seventeenth-century immigrants to Canada arrived before 1680. Such a flow averaged about 160 immigrants per year and represented only a miniscule percentage of the population of the mother country. More than two-thirds either returned quickly to France or died in the colony while still unmarried. Prospects for marriage were bad, particularly due to the surplus of marriageable men. Nevertheless, nearly 4,000 immigrants—almost all born in France west of a north-south Bordeaux-Soissons line—did settle in the St. Lawrence Valley to serve as the basis of the French Canadian population. The pioneer immigrants were almost entirely young, single individuals traveling alone. Many of the subsequent marriages were between younger women and considerably older men. A disproportionate number of the younger women, especially the *filles du roi,* came from the Paris region, which helps account for the gradual adoption of the Parisian dialect of French as the dominant one in Canada. Despite a reputation for large families and many children, the Canadians initially appear to have lagged behind their French counterparts in fertility. By the eighteenth century, however, birth rates ran to more than 50 per 1,000 inhabitants, and women bore an average of 7 children. Couples statistically had 5.65 children surviving infancy, while in France the average was 4.5. Despite the cold climate and harsh physical environment, the people of New France (the term used to denote all the French possessions in North America—Acadia, Canada, the *pays d'un haut,* and Louisiana) were considerably longer-lived than those in France. This low mortality can be attributed partly to the selection of healthy immigrants and to a relatively epidemic-free environment.

Almost from the beginning, Canada suffered from a demographic problem, especially in comparison with the English colonies to the south. In 1706, an anonymous French writer observed, "If anyone gives considered attention to the progress the English have made in the case of their New England colonies, he will have good reason to tremble for our colony in Canada. There is no single year but sees more children born in New England than there are men in the whole of Canada" (Innis, 1940, pp. 136–137). Part of the problem was the size of the initial group of immigrants. By 1660 the French could count only 3,215 people in Canada, but the English had several hundred thousand in their continental colonies. After a concerted effort by the French government between 1665 and 1680, immigration fell to a very low level from 1680 to 1740, and throughout the entire period after 1680, the number of female immigrants was very small, less than 500 in total. Moreover, the shortage of females helped encourage young males to head west into the fur trade. Perhaps as many as 25 percent of able-bodied Canadian males were involved in the western trade at some point in their lives. Some came back to the St. Lawrence to settle down, but many took aboriginal wives and remained in the backcountry. By 1754 there were perhaps 60,000 people in Canada and nearly 2 million in England's continental colonies.

As befitted a colony operated by an absolutist monarch, Canada's government was structured from the top down in strictly hierarchical fashion. Its vocabulary and visible social structure was that of the mother country; its law code the "Coûtume de Paris" (law code of Paris). Canada's French origins provided institutions, a terminology with which to express them, and a set of assumptions about how society ought to operate. The several social orders were to stay in their places and subordinate themselves to the good of the whole, as defined by the Crown. Moreover, Canada did not attempt simply to replicate the Old World in the New, but to reform some old institutions, particularly by eliminating centuries of traditions that decentralized power and limited royal authority. The most important official in Canada was not the governor, who was a military man. Rather, it was the intendant, who was a civilian career civil servant. Canada refracted the concept of the metropolis through the dual prisms of deliberate royal reform and North American reality. What at first glance sounded familiar to the European observer turned out to be quite different in practice.

Although the society of Canada was predominantly rural and agricultural, there was also a substantial urban presence, containing nearly one-quarter of the region's total population. The two major towns were Quebec and Montreal, which were the centers of government, economic activity, and the Church. French Canadians were universally regarded as bad farmers, preferring extensive wheat cultivation and a move to new soil when the old, unfertilized land was worn out to the fertilization and crop rotation common in Europe. This lack of farming acumen may have partly reflected the nonagricultural origins of many of the early settlers, but it was also fairly typical of North American agriculture in general. There was a small yet active merchant class in Canada as well. The military was always a strong presence in the colony, and virtually every adult male was considered eligible for militia duty. The male residents expected to be called into service—and often were.

The culture of Canada was perhaps the region's most distinguishing characteristic. From the beginning this culture was predominantly oral, based upon its language, which came to be the French of the Paris region, spoken extremely well. "All are of the opinion," wrote Peter Kalm, "that in Canada the ordinary man speaks a purer French than in any province in France, yes, that in this respect it can vie with Paris itself" (Benson, 1927, vol. 2, p. 554). Canada had no newspapers or printers, but it had an artistic and aesthetic life that was based on the ritualistic requirements of the Church. It also had a powerful literary culture in its folk tales and songs, to which were added a strong musical voice. Moreover, the culture of ordinary *Canadiens* was expressed through the activities of daily life, perhaps the hardest form of culture to eliminate or transform.

French Canada was well equipped to survive and even flourish after a military conquest and change of rulers at the top. The basic institutions of language, religion, landholding, and law were well entrenched and functioned effectively. The French language was distinctive in North America and culturally important to it. French Canadians were pious and orthodox Catholics. There were too few clerics for the region to be regarded as priest-ridden, but much of the life of the colony revolved around the Church, which patronized art, music, and architecture. Everyday existence revolved around the sacraments and holy days of the Church. Even in the rural districts, the church building was the center of every community. The rural districts were dominated by a river-lot pattern, with narrow holdings positioned along the rivers and extending several miles inland, as well as by a seigneurial system in which the land was held by seigneurs (both lay individuals and the Church) and distributed to tenants in return for the payment of certain obligations. Under the French regime the seigneurial system did not produce a feudal society, chiefly because land was too easy to obtain. Still, it did mean that most land was not held in freehold tenure (in which the owner and his or her heirs unconditionally possessed the property without reference to any other possessors, such as a landlord or the Crown). The legal and judicial systems of the colony were based on the civil law of the Coûtume de Paris. The courts were not adversarial, and there were no trained or paid lawyers in the colony. Justice was generally even-handed and fairly administered.

The Pays d'en Haut

From the earliest years of settlement in the seventeenth century, the fur trade had been essential to the economy of Canada. The quest for fresh sources of furs forced the Canadians to work together with the aboriginal inhabitants and also pressed them constantly westward. The French government did its best to reduce Canada's dependence on the fur trade and to limit the western expansion, which exposed New France to military threats along a vast frontier. Nevertheless, by the 1670s the Canadians had made their way into the Mississippi–Missouri river systems, which would take them to the Gulf of Mexico. In the region to the south of the Great Lakes, the French employed subtle diplomacy based on ritual gift exchanges to deal with the many aboriginal inhabitants of the region, many of whom had only recently migrated there as part of the fallout from the fierce struggle for control of the fur trade farther east among the Dutch, French, and English. The French constructed forts that also served as the centers of local trading, and their liaisons with native women began to produce a mixed-blood population that rapidly assumed a dominant role in the fur trade. Along the rivers of the region, a number of trading communities developed that were inhabited mainly by mixed-bloods, of which Kaskaskia was probably the largest and best known. The *pays d'en haut* served as the original spawning ground for the ethnogenesis of the Métis people, who would become so important in the development of the Canadian West.

Louisiana

Beginning in the early 1680s, the Canadians began attempting to colonize at the mouth of the Mississippi River under René-Robert Cavalier de La Salle (1643–1687). These early efforts were relatively unsuccessful, but in 1700 the French government decided to take over the colonization efforts. The formal establishment of Louisiana as a colony in 1701 was part of complicated French policies that had to do mainly with events in Europe, but it committed France and New France to an extension of territorial control from Newfoundland westward across half the continent and south to the Gulf of Mexico. Instead of opposing expansion, the French Crown became positively committed to it. Eventually, the ring of French territory surrounding the British colonies forced Great Britain to make a major commitment of its own, and the end result would be the total surrender by the French of all its North American territory, with most of it going to the British (see upcoming sections of this book for more details).

The Aboriginals

The arrival of Europeans on the shores of North America was ultimately a disaster for the indigenous peoples of the continent. Much of the disaster was inadvertent, the result of conditions over which none of those involved had any control. No Europeans of the time understood very much about infectious disease and immunity, certainly not enough to know that casual contact could spread germs that were, given the aboriginals' lack of built-up resistance to them, fatal on a large scale. The Jesuit missionaries did not know that they brought deadly diseases with them when they first entered an aboriginal community, nor were they aware that by suddenly undermining the natives' traditional religion, which was an integral part of their symbiotic relationship with their environment, they were greatly weakening the aboriginals' cultural ability to survive in that environment. The Europeans probably had only a slightly better understanding of the impact their intrusion would have on the fur trading patterns and military relations of the aboriginals. The notion that providing the natives with an "improved" technology could have disastrous consequences for the natives would have been difficult to explain to the Europeans.

Moreover, despite our appreciation of the ultimate result, we in the modern world must not make too much of the lack of parity between the local residents and the newcomers, at least not the way it was for the first several centuries. Unlike the Spaniards to the south, neither the French nor the English initially sought to exert direct political power over the natives; the Europeans claimed sovereignty, but not ownership, of "their" various territories. The aboriginals were bound by European laws and brought under the European imperium only in areas inhabited by the Europeans. In this sense, they were never "conquered." Both France and England recognized that the natives were entitled to their own government and their own laws in their own territories. Although the natives were dispossessed of considerable prime land for settlement, most of the continent remained effectively in aboriginal control until well beyond 1763. The aboriginals may not have understood clearly the distinction Europeans made between sovereignty and land ownership, but both the French and English made it. The natives had experienced considerable difficulty in unifying in opposition to European expansion, but the years after the middle of the eighteenth century saw the beginnings of a movement of aboriginal unification, especially in the Great Lakes region. These years were also characterized by a willingness on the part of the major imperial powers (mainly Great Britain, after 1763) to formally recognize the natives' right to hold their own territory free of European settlement. This notion was the basis of the first attempt at an overall imperial policy by the Europeans in the Proclamation of 1763.

Culturally, the aboriginals contributed at least as much to the Europeans as they received in return. They knew how to cultivate corn. They knew how to walk on top the snow in the winter and how to cure scurvy.

Peter Kalm noted even more European borrowings from the natives, observing that the French "use the tobacco pipes, shoes, garters, and girdles of the Indians. They follow the Indian way of waging war exactly; they mix the same things with tobacco; they make use of the Indian bark boats and row them in the Indian way; they wrap a square piece of cloth around their feet, instead of stockings" (Benson, 1927, vol. 1, p. 511). As early as 1685, Canada's Governor Denonville argued that instead of the Europeans civilizing the aboriginals, the very opposite had occurred and that, for the children of the settlers, "having no means of subsistence except the woods because not being accustomed to wield the axe or pick or guide the plow their only recourse is to the rifle" (Bumsted, 1969, p. 23). The population spent its life in the woods, insisted the governor, "where there are neither priests to trouble them, nor fathers nor Governors to constrain them."

Conclusion

Homogeneity and diversity are both relative terms. Although the "founding peoples" of Canada came initially from only two practically adjacent nations in Western Europe and joined the aboriginal peoples in taking up residence in North America, that generalization disguises more than it reveals. In truth, the combination of the regional characteristics of the incomers and the regional differences in their adaptation to the North American environment—as well as the influences of the natives—produced a quite varied and culturally complex society in early Canada. That complexity would only grow and become more extreme as time went on.

Timeline

1497   John Cabot makes landfall on "newfoundeland."
1534   First voyage of Jacques Cartier.
1576   First voyage of Martin Frobisher to Baffin Island.
1597   Colony of Ramea founded.
1605   Port-Royal established by Pierre Du Gua de Monts and Samuel Champlain.
1608   Champlain builds "habitation" at Quebec in Canada.
1610   First Newfoundland settlement at Cupid's Cove.
1624   Sir William Alexander gets grant for New Scotland.
1630   Quebec sacked by British buccaneers.

1640   First Acadian dykes built.
1642   Montreal founded.
1663   French crown takes over Canada.
1670   Hudson's Bay Company founded; Acadia restored to France.
1682   LaSalle reaches mouth of Mississippi River.
1685   "Code noir" clarifies legal status of slaves in Canada.
1701   Peace Treaty with Iroquois.
1713   Treaty of Utrecht; Acadia surrendered to British.
1718   Louisbourg begun.
1749   Founding of Halifax.
1755   First Acadian Expulsion.
1758   Second Acadian Expulsion; first legislative assembly summoned in Nova Scotia; invitation to New England Yankees to settle in Nova Scotia.
1759   Battle of Quebec.
1763   New France transferred to British by treaty of Paris.

Significant People, Places, and Events

Acadia The name given to the francophone settlements in the Maritime region of what is now Canada.

Acadian Deportations (or Expulsions) The forcible removal of the Acadian population from Nova Scotia by the British, first in 1755 and then in 1758.

Alexander, William, Earl of Stirling (1577–1640) Born at Menstrie, Scotland, he was given a grant of territory in North America in 1621, which he named Nova Scotia. He financed colonization there by selling knight-baronetcies beginning in 1624. His son briefly established two settlements there in the late 1620s.

Alline, Henry (1748[49]–1784) Born in Rhode Island, Alline grew up in Falmouth, Nova Scotia. He developed a unique theology that he preached during the years of the American Revolution, which he resolutely ignored.

Baffin Island The largest island in the Canadian Arctic, 1500 kilometers long and 200–700 kilometers wide, it was discovered by Martin Frobisher, who hoped to establish a mining industry there in the late 1570s.

Bay of Fundy A body of water located between modern Maine, New Brunswick, and Nova Scotia. It has the highest tides in the world, which in the colonial period made possible the natural fertilizing of large areas of marshland through diking. Many of the earliest French and English settlements in North America were established along its coastline.

CABOT, JOHN (c. 1449[50]–1498[99]) An explorer born in Genoa. His voyage from Bristol, England in 1497 resulted in the first recorded landfall in North America since that of the Vikings. He died on a follow-up voyage in 1498 or 1499.

CARIGNAN-SALIÈRES REGIMENT A unit of French regular troops sent to Canada in 1665 to quell the Iroquois. The regiment never actually fought the natives in open battle before their recall in 1667, but it did leave many soldiers behind as colonists.

CARTIER, JACQUES (1491–1557) Born in St.-Malo, France, he was the first European to chart the St. Lawrence River and the first to attempt to establish a French claim to the region. His encounter with aboriginals is probably the first recorded in any detail since those of the Vikings.

CHAMPLAIN, SAMUEL DE (c. 1570–1635) Born at Brouage, France, he first traveled in North America in 1603 and published an account of his voyage. In 1604 he sailed with Pierre Du Gua de Monts, helped establish Port-Royal in 1605, and established a settlement at Quebec in 1608. For nearly thirty years he led the French settlement on the St. Lawrence River.

COLBERT, JEAN-BAPTISTE (1619–1683) Born in Rheims, he entered the service of Cardinal Mazarin in 1651 and became the chief minister of Louis XIV in 1661. He reorganized the French state, the French military, and the French colonies, always with the aim of strengthening the monarchy and the nation with which it was associated.

DONNACONNA (d. 1539) A headman of an Iroquoian-speaking group of natives resident in the St. Lawrence River region, he was the first aboriginal in what is now Canada for whom we have a name. He was taken to France and died there.

FOREIGN PROTESTANTS A term used to refer to European settlers of Protestant religion who lived in France, Germany, and Switzerland. They were mainly German speakers and were recruited by the British to settle Nova Scotia in the early 1750s.

FORT BEAUSÉJOUR A fort built between 1751 and 1755 on the west bank of the Missaguash River near modern Sackville, New Brunswick. When it was captured by the British in 1755 it was found to contain many Acadians, leading the British to believe that the Acadians were supporting the French in large numbers.

FROBISHER, MARTIN (1539–1594) While searching west of Greenland for a passage to Asia, he found what was later named Frobisher Bay and also found rocks that he thought contained rich ore deposits. He made several follow-up voyages in 1577 and 1578 that hauled back tons of rock before assayers determined that it was worthless. In 1578 he planted the first English colony in North America at Baffin Island, but returned the settlers to England that same year.

HALIFAX A town established by the British on Chebucto Bay in Nova Scotia in 1749. It became the capital of Nova Scotia.

ISLAND OF SAINT JOHN (ISLE DE SAINT-JEAN) A large island off the coast of Nova Scotia and modern-day New Brunswick, settled by the French in the early eighteenth century.

JAMES VI (OF SCOTLAND, JAMES I OF ENGLAND) (1566–1625) The only son of Mary, Queen of Scots, he ascended to the throne in 1567. In 1603 he also became king of England. As Scots ruler he supported the colonization plans of Sir William Alexander (q.v.).

JESUIT RELATIONS A series of annual letters and documents compiled by Jesuit missionaries in Quebec and sent to France by the Society of Jesus beginning in 1632. This material was published, and it served as publicity for the missionary venture in North America, simultaneously raising money and repelling colonists.

KALM, PETER (1716–1779) Born in Sweden, he was a botanist who was recommended by Linnaeus for an expedition to North America to search for and collect new plants hardy enough to survive in Sweden's northern climate. He published a journal of travels in Sweden in 1753, which was translated into English in 1770. He was one of the few contemporary observers of both the English and French colonies who could view them from a neutral perspective.

KASKASKIA A trading town on the Illinois River established in 1721 and inhabited by merchants, mixed-bloods, and black slaves.

LA SALLE, RENÉ ROBERT CAVELIER DE (1643–1687) Born in Rouen, he came to New France in 1659 and won a reputation as an explorer. In 1682 he traveled down the Mississippi River to its mouth, claiming the region for the French Crown. He subsequently attempted to establish a settlement on the Gulf of Mexico, but was murdered by a colleague in 1687.

LONDON AND BRISTOL COMPANY FOR THE COLONIZATION OF NEWFOUNDLAND A company founded in 1610 by English merchants to settle Newfoundland, in order to have an advantage in access to the fishery of the island. Its first settlement was at Cupid's Cove on Conception Bay, established in 1610.

LOUISBOURG A fortified town established by the French on the southeastern shore of Cape Breton Island (Ile Royale) in 1713. It functioned as a separate colony and was captured in 1745 by a joint Anglo-American military expedition, returned to France in 1748, and retaken in 1758. Today it is the site of major historical reconstruction undertaken by the government of Canada.

MINAS BASIN The broadest part of the southeastern head of the Bay of Fundy, its south shore was mainly low and permitted extensive diking for agricultural purposes. This shore was the center of early Acadian agricultural settlement in North America in the seventeenth and early eighteenth centuries.

NEWFOUNDLAND A large island off the eastern coast of North America, first settled by the Vikings in the early eleventh century, landed upon (probably) by John Cabot in 1497, and settled again by the English beginning in 1610.

NOBLE, SETH (1743–1807) Born in Massachusetts, Noble served as minister of the Maugerville Congregational Church from 1772. He was the leading spokesman for the pro-American party in the St. John River Valley during the American Revolution, and was forced to leave in 1776.

NOVA SCOTIA (NEW SCOTLAND) A territorial designation originally used to refer to the colonies of Scotland established on the peninsula of Nova Scotia and later used to refer to the entire peninsula, as well as to the land to the north of the Bay of Fundy as far as the St. Lawrence River.

PERKINS, SIMEON (1734[35]–1812) Born in Connecticut, Perkins became the leading citizen of Liverpool, Nova Scotia, a fishing community on the southwest coast of the province. He remained loyal to the Crown during the American Revolution.

PORT-ROYAL A settlement established in 1605 by the Pierre Du Gua de Monts (and Samuel de Champlain) on the north shore of the Annapolis Basin near the mouth of the Annapolis River. It was abandoned in 1607, reestablished in 1610, and destroyed in 1613. Sir William Alexander put a settlement there in 1628, but the French reasserted control of it in 1632. Port-Royal claims to be the earliest permanent settlement north of Florida.

RAMEA A settlement on the Magdalene Islands in the Gulf of St. Lawrence established by English Puritan dissenters in 1597. They were driven off by aboriginals and Basque fishermen.

RICHELIEU, ARMAND JEAN DUPLESSIS, CARDINAL, DUC DE (1585–1642) Minister to Louis XIII starting in 1624, he organized the Company of One Hundred Associates in 1627 to colonize New France.

SEIGNEURIAL SYSTEM An institutional arrangement of land distribution and settlement begun in New France in 1627 and abolished in 1854. It was based on a French system with its roots in feudalism but had its own realities in North America. Under this system, all land in the colony was allocated as fiefs to seigneurs, who were obliged to redistribute the land to tenants. Most seigneuries were partitioned into narrow rectangular strips fronting on a river.

UTRECHT, TREATY OF The treaty ending the War of the Spanish Succession (King William's War in the American colonies) in 1713. By the treaty, the French relinquished their colonies in Newfoundland and Acadia, although they retained Ile St. Jean and Ile Royale (Cape Breton Island).

VERRAZANO, GIOVANNI DA (c. 1485–c. 1528) Born in Italy, he sailed for America under the French flag in 1523 and was probably the first European explorer to recognize that the mainland of North America was a distinct continent, separate from the West Indies and Asia.

VIKINGS A seafaring warrior people originating in Scandinavia. They reached Iceland in the ninth century and Greenland in the tenth century, and sent several ships farther west to establish colonies on the coasts of North America.

Documents

Journal of the Jesuit Fathers, in the Years 1662 and 1663

Beginning in 1632 Father Paul Le Jeune (1591–1664) began sending from Canada back to France the first of the annual reports, the famous Jesuit Relations, *that were forwarded until 1791 to the Provincial Father of the Society of Jesus in Paris. The* "Relations" *soon became public documents, consciously intended to explain and promote the missionaries' efforts in the mother country. They combined a wealth of detail about life in New France.*

1662, January

In the morning, a Drummer came to give a Serenade in our Corridor, in honor of Monseigneur the Bishop. We did not Deem it advisable to send him away. He was asked on whose behalf he came, and he said that it was on his own, for monseigneur the Bishop and for the Superior. We gave him a silver écu. Perhaps it will be necessary to prevent this when Monseigneur the Bishop ceases to lodge with us.

As Monsieur d'Avaugour, the Governor, is not a man of Ceremony, I contented myself with going to the fort alone after I had said mass at the Ursulines'; but I found that he had already gone out to hear mass, at the end of which he forestalled us. Vespers, sermon, benediction, and procession from the parish church, as last year.

I had prepared something on the evening before to give to ours, but the presence of Monseigneur the Bishop, who wished to be at the distribution of sentences, prevented me. I sent to each of our fathers half a dozen pieces of Citron-peel, a considerable quantity of which had come by the last ships. . . . There was much talk respecting the permission to sell liquor to the savages, that was given by Monsieur the Governor; we used every effort, except Excommunication, to oppose it. . . .

1662, December

There was some disorder in connection with the drink of the singers or Children of our seminary. In addition to their beer, I had a pot of Wine given them on the eve; and on the Day itself, the churchwardens also gave them some, without our knowing it. This made Amador so hoarse that he could not sing any more on the feasts; the same happened to the other musicians, François d'Anger and others.

1663, January

On the eve, as new-year's gifts to ours, the father Minister carried to the rooms of our Fathers 3 pieces of Citron-peel and a coil of wax taper for each, and to our brethren a coil of wax taper; to Monsieur garnier, two pieces of Citron-peel and a coil of wax taper. At the sentences I gave each one a Picture on Vellum, and another representing the holy handkerchief. . . .

1663, February

Item, during Shrove-tide. This time was remarkable, among other things, for a frightful and sudden Earthquake. It began half an hour after the close of benediction on Monday, the 5th of february, the feast of our holy martyrs of Japan, namely at about 5 ½ o'clock, and lasted about the length of 2 *misereres.* It took place again at night, and was repeated many times on the following Days and nights, sometimes more and sometimes less violently. It injured some chimneys and caused other slight losses and damages, but did a great deal of good to souls; for on shrove tuesday and Ash wednesday one would have said that it was eastern Sunday, so many Confessions and Communions were there, and all devotions were frequented. This lasted until the 15th of march, or thereabout, quite perceptibly. . . .

1663, April

Sowing began on the 15th. . . .

1663, May

On the 29th, father simon started with Jaques Aubry for 3 rivers, in Monsieur de la poterie's shallop. On the same Day, at about 9 or 10 o'clock in the evening, sieur de beaulieu was burned to death in his own house at the Island of orleans with one of his valets in a fire that had broken out by accident. . . .

1663, June

It turned out that the fire which had caught in the house of sieur de beaulieu had not occurred by accident but through the malice of a valet, after he had killed his master and another valet, his comrade. He was convicted and sentenced to have his *hand cut off, and to be hanged and then burned*. Monsieur the governor was contented that he should die upon the scafford; after having been tormented thereon by the executioner, he was shot on the 8th of June.

Source: Gold Thwaites, Reuben, ed., *The Jesuit Relations and Allied Documents: Travels and Explorations of the Jesuit Missionaries in New France 1610–1791*, vol. 46 (Lower Canada, Ottawa, Canadian Interior: 1659–1661) (Cleveland: Burrows Brothers, 1896), pp. 273–274, 295–305.

Jacques-René Brisay de Denonville to the French Minister of Marine

13 November 1685

It seems to me that this is the place, Monseigneur, that we have to take into account the disorders which occur not only in the woods but also in our settlements. These disorders have come to the Youth of this country only through the laziness of the children, and the great liberty which the light control of fathers and mothers and Governors have exercised over youth in allowing them to go into the woods on pretext of hunting or trading. This has reached the extremity, Monseigneur, that as soon as the children can shoulder a rifle the fathers can no longer restrain them and do not dare to make them angry. You may judge what evils may ensue from such a manner of living. These disorders, Monseigneur, are greater among the families of those who are *gentilshommes*, or those who have set themselves up to be such, because of idleness or vanity, having no means of subsistence except the woods because not being accustomed to wield the axe or pick or guide the plow their only recourse is the rifle. They have to pass their lives in the woods, where there are neither priests to trouble them, nor fathers nor Governors to constrain them. There are, Monseigneur, among those men some who distinguish themselves above others in these disorders and against whom I have promised to employ the authority which the King has entrusted to me to punish them severely. I am persuaded, Monseigneur, that you will acknowledge and will approve that I do not amuse myself with a formality of justice which would tend only to subtlety in order to hide the vice and leave the disorders unpunished. Convincing proof not always being readily established I believe, Monseigneur, that military justice in this case is more suitable than any *arrêt* of a judge.

Mr. De la Barre has suppressed a certain order of *chevaliers*, but he has not taken away its manners or disorders. A way of dressing up like savages, stark naked, not only on carnival days but on all days of feasting and debauchery, has been treated as a nice action and joke. These manners tend only to maintain the young people in the spirit of living like savages and to communicate with them and to be eternally profligate like them, I could not express sufficiently to you Monseigneur the attraction that this savage life of doing nothing, of being constrained by nothing, of following every whim and being beyond correction, has for the young men.

It was believed for a long time that approaching the savages to our settlements was a very considerable means of accustoming these people to live like us and to be instructed in our religion. I perceive, Monseigneur, that the very opposite has occurred because instead of training them to our laws, I assure you that they communicate very much to us everything that is meanest in them, and themselves take on only what is bad and vicious in us. I have been somewhat lengthy, Monseigneur, in giving you the details of all these matters so that you may provide the remedies by the orders you give me.

Source: Bumsted, J. M., ed., *Documentary Problems in Canadian History,* vol. 1 (Georgetown, Ontario: Irwin-Dorsey Press, 1969), p. 23.

Bibliography

Bates, George T., "The Great Exodus of 1749, or the Cornwallis Settlers Who Didn't," in *Collections of the Nova Scotia Historical Society,* vol. 38 (1973), 27–62.

Bell, Winthrop Pickard, The "Foreign Protestants" and the Settlement of Nova Scotia: The History of a Piece of Arrested British Colonial Policy in the Eighteenth Century (Toronto: University of Toronto Press, 1961).

Benson, Adolph, ed., The America of 1750: Peter Kalm's Travels in North America, 2 vol. (New York: Dover, 1927).

Bumsted, J. M., ed., Documentary Problems in Canadian History, vol. 1 (Georgetown, Ontario: Irwin-Dorsey Press, 1969).

Charbonneau, Hubert et al., The First French-Canadians: Pioneers in the St. Lawrence Valley (Newark, DE: University of Delaware Press, 1993).

Choquette, Leslie, Frenchmen into Peasants: Modernity and Tradition in the Peopling of French Canada (Cambridge, MA: Harvard University Press, 1997).

Clark, Andrew Hill, Acadia: The Geography of Early Nova Scotia to 1760 (Madison, WI: University of Wisconsin Press, 1968).

Cook, Ramsay, ed., The Voyages of Jacques Cartier (Toronto: University of Toronto Press, 1993).

Eccles, W. J., France in America (Markham, Ontario: Fitzhenry & Whiteside, 1990).

Firstbrook, Peter, The Voyage of the Matthew: John Cabot and the Discovery of America (Toronto: McClelland and Stewart, 1997).

Griffiths, Naomi, The Acadians: The Creation of a People (Toronto: McGraw-Hill Ryerson, 1973).

Handcock, W. Gordon, "Soe long as there comes noe women': Origins of English Settlement in Newfoundland (St. John's, Newfoundland: Breakwater Press, 1989).

Innis, H. A., The Cod Fisheries: The History of an International Economy (Toronto: University of Toronto Press, 1940).

Moogk, Peter, La Nouvelle France: The Making of French Canada—A Cultural History (East Lansing, MI: Michigan State University Press, 2000).

Reid, John, Acadia, Maine, and New Scotland: Marginal Colonies in the Seventeenth Century (Toronto: University of Toronto Press, 1981).

Trudel, Marcel, The Beginnings of New France, 1524–1663 (Toronto: McClelland and Stewart, 1963).

White, Richard D., The Middle Ground: Indians, Empires, and Republics in the Great Lakes Region, 1650–1815 (Cambridge, MA: Harvard University Press, 1991).

CHAPTER THREE

French Canadians, Acadians, Métis, and First Nations, 1760–1815

I N 1763, the British permanently acquired almost all of France's North American Empire, with very few commitments to the indigenous populations of those territories. Indeed, the Acadians in the Maritimes had already been physically expelled from their homelands, and the British government could at that point have been capable of overwhelming the French Canadians in Quebec with English-speaking Protestants. In 1763, England intended to resettle most of the new territories with loyal Britons, with the exception of the First Nations lands south of the Great Lakes and west of the Appalachian Mountains, which would be set aside as an aboriginal preserve. By 1815 these intentions had been totally defeated by a long series of interrelated events. As a result, by 1815 the Acadians had returned to the Maritimes; Quebec (now called Lower Canada) was a thriving province inhabited by French Canadians, whose religious, legal, and civil rights were guaranteed; and the trans-Appalachian west was in United States hands.

The French Canadians under the Capitulation

In early September of 1760, the French garrison at Montreal surrendered to a large British army led by General Jeffrey Amherst (1717–1797). The fifty-five articles of capitulation drawn up at this point would govern the British occupation of Canada until the final peace treaty in 1763 and would give hints of British policy beyond that date should the victors decide to keep their conquest—which was not at all certain in 1760. The inhabitants of Canada were readily given freedom of worship, security of property, and the right to remain in their own homes. However, Amherst's response to their request for neutrality and the continuation of customary law was: "They become Subjects of the King." The capitulation immediately forced French royal officials to depart the colony, and many of the colony's merchant and landed elite would leave as well. But during the three years of British occupation of Canada, the three military administrators of the colony, all Britons who spoke French and who accepted it as the "language of the country," ruled the French Canadians with a relatively light hand.

From the capitulations of Montreal to the final conclusion of peace with the French, the British public had been bombarded with literature about French America (the British name for New France) and the relative merits of Britain's keeping it. The great debate over the peace—whether or not to keep Canada—was conducted in the context of an international conflict, and the chief issue in London was the need to balance British territorial gains against the widespread need for peace. Nevertheless, French America, and especially Canada, had figured prominently both in the public discussions and in those conducted within the British government's corridors of power. Most Britons held that French America should be retained, partly for its economic potential but mainly in order to eliminate the long-standing military threat it had posed to Britain's American colonies to the south. An important minority in England, however, argued that the French menace in North America was the principal protection for Britain against the potential independence of those very same colonies to the south. Also, many of those involved in the debate worried about the potential problems in governing 70,000 francophone Roman Catholics who had long been living by French law and French customs.

Although not everyone in the mother country could agree on the value of retaining Canada and other French possessions in North America, far greater consensus prevailed on what policies should be pursued in the wake of that retention. The recent war with France had highlighted the extent to which the American colonists had slipped into assumptions of political and constitutional autonomy. The Americans would have to be returned to a "due subordination." Also, the First Nations in the Ohio country had been promised security from European settlers' encroachment on their lands, which only the military could accomplish. As for the new French subjects, they would require a military contingent to keep them in hand, at least in the short run. The Americans would also have to share, at least symbolically, the burden and expenses of administering the new North American empire. All these considerations pointed to the need for both a standing British army in North America and new revenue measures to help support that army, as part of the far-reaching reassertions of the power of Parliament on that continent. This kind of thinking among the Britons would, of course, lead straight to rebellion by the American colonists.

The Proclamation of 1763

The British government produced its first statement of policy in the wake of the Treaty of Paris through the notorious Proclamation of 7 October 1763. In it, Britain's "extensive and valuable acquisitions in America" were organized into four new governments (Quebec, East and West Florida, and Granada). Quebec was reduced in size to the agricultural settlements along the St. Lawrence River; Newfoundland was given the fishing islands in the Gulf of St. Lawrence; and Nova Scotia acquired Ile St. Jean (now the Island of St. John) and Ile Royale (now Cape Breton Island). Military men who had served in North America were entitled to apply for wilderness land grants "without fee or reward." No settlement was to occur in the region beyond the rivers flowing into the Atlantic Ocean. This territory—as far west as the Hudson's Bay Company's fur preserve of Rupert's Land and as far south as the Floridas—was reserved for the First Nations and was to be administered by the Crown, which would grant licenses for trade under close military supervision. Quebec and the other new provinces, almost as an afterthought, were guaranteed "the benefit of the laws . . . of England" immediately and were promised elected assemblies as soon as possible.

Three points must be made about this imperial policy. First, no particular accommodations had been made for the newly acquired French territory or for its francophone population. Indeed, the absence of distinctive treatment was the principal characteristic of the policy. The British had hardly accepted French Canada as a "distinctive society," but rather planned to administer it according to the general rules of the existing Empire. Quebec would achieve full provincial status (including an elected assembly) as soon as its population had either acquired a large British component or had assimilated sufficiently to deserve such status. Second, the British government anticipated a flood of American colonists to the new territory, partly because the American colonists were known to be land-hungry and partly because they were being deliberately shut out of the interior of the continent. Finally, while the British sought to pacify the First Nations, they had little notion of how to deal with these people in ways that would be understood or accepted.

Quebec under the Proclamation of 1763

The civil government of Quebec was not inaugurated until August of 1764. The commission and instructions to General James Murray, who was named civil governor at that time, elaborated on the new arrangements for that province, which thoroughly exposed the problems that the British would face in governing it. The British were caught in a catch-22 situation: A government based on a thorough accommodation of the existing French Canadian population in Quebec—recognizing and accepting, for example, the French language, religion, law, and customs of the country—was hardly likely to attract those anglophone and Protestant British colonists who were supposed to, over time, outnumber the French Canadians. But a government designed to appeal to new arrivals, who had not yet appeared in any real numbers, would literally revolutionize the colony and was hardly likely in the short run either to satisfy the French Canadians or to make them docile subjects.

The result was an obvious administrative schizophrenia. The governor's commission prohibited office holding to anyone but those prepared to take oaths against the papacy, thus depriving virtually the whole of the French population of the opportunity to hold public office in the colony. The instructions given to Murray created a governor's council and warned that, without an assembly of that council, "nothing be passed or done that shall in any ways tend to affect the life, limb or liberty of the subject, or to the imposing of any duties or taxes." Religious toleration was confirmed, although the Church of England would be established by law as the official religion of the colony and the instructions specified that the inhabitants of the colony should be "by degrees . . . induced to embrace the Protestant religion." The ecclesiastical jurisdiction of Rome was positively forbidden. Complex provisions for land granting were advanced in anticipation of a rush of settlers to be produced by a governor's proclamation publicizing the country's many advantages. The land granting policy followed general guidelines of the time: Land was to be surveyed into 20,000-acre townships (8,000 hectares), with typical grants of 100 acres (40 hectares) per head of family and 50 (20 hectares) for each dependent. Grantees would pay quitrents (small annual rentals in lieu of services) to the Crown of at least two shillings per acre.

Simply put, British policy for Quebec was unrealistic and hence destined not to work. American colonists did not flock there as they were expected to, for a number of reasons. Settling wilderness land in a northern climate would at the best of times have proved attractive only with substantial financial inducements for the new pioneers, and in the years after 1763, such financial assistance would come only from private entrepreneurs. The failure (or inability) of the Quebec government to eliminate the seigneurial system made the province even less attractive to restless Americans, who were already suspicious of the climate, the prevalence of a foreign culture and religion, and the absence of familiar political institutions. Moreover, the administrators of Quebec could not operate in total disregard of the mounting crisis involving the American colonies to the south. Some balance had to be struck between the needs of the dominant French Canadian population and the demands of a small but vociferous British one, recently arrived since 1759 to take over control of most of the commercial activity of the province. Concessions to the Canadians ran the risk of incensing the British minority in the colony, or the Americans to the south of it. But nevertheless, the overall dynamic in Quebec was a simple one, moving gradually but inexorably from a province intended to become British to one accepted as being French. The principal debates there occurred over the nature of government, law, and religion.

For James Murray, who had to make the transition from military to civil government in 1764, there was nothing but grief. Murray was sympathetic to the problems of the Canadians and very conscious of the obstacles he faced, writing, "It is by military force we are to govern this lately conquered Province, in which there does not exist above 50 Protestant subjects exclusive of the troops and by my instructions of these 50 Protestants must be composed the Magistracy." As such comments suggested, Murray was in no hurry to establish an assembly, much less a judiciary, and he initially governed through a council he was instructed to create made up entirely of Protestant newcomers. He and the council soon ran up against the thorny problems of adapting English and Anglo-British practice to Quebec's conditions. The administration faced increasing hostility from a slowly enlarging body of anglophone merchants who wanted the terms of the Proclamation of 1763 fulfilled and were less than appreciative of accommodations being made to the French population, such as permitting French Canadians' participation in the inferior courts.

The fundamental problem was that the Proclamation of 1763 had been distinctly unfair, not only to the conquered population but to Britain's First Nations allies as well. Quebec's integration into the British Empire could not be based upon a simplistic imposition of new systems from without, particularly in view of the terms of the surrender of 1760, which guaranteed French rights, and of the transfer by France in 1763. The situation was a nightmare for any governor and a challenge to the best legal minds of the age. In 1760 Canadians had been guaranteed their property, which precluded any wholesale change in property law, the central cornerstone of any jurisdiction's civil law. They had only been guaranteed freedom of worship "so far as the laws of Great Britain permit," which was hardly much of a concession, as Catholicism was legally proscribed in Britain. But to limit too greatly the Roman Catholic Church would mock existing realities in the colony, and to deny political rights to Catholics would disenfranchise virtually an entire population. Murray managed to pass the first religious hurdle successfully, encouraging a priest named Jean-Olivier Briand to become consecrated in France as a bishop to govern a hitherto bishopless Catholic Church in Quebec. The willingness of the London authorities to turn a blind eye to their own laws, accommodating the religion of the Canadians by allowing Rome to consecrate a bishop, says a good deal about the temper of the victors. But Murray's legal ordinance of 1764, which introduced English law while not eliminating the old Canadian codes, upset everyone by being too confusing and ultimately got the governor recalled.

The effect upon the habitants of all the policy maneuvering is now difficult to assess. The Conquest has for more than two centuries been viewed by historians as a turning point in Canadian historical development. By and large, historians writing from the British perspective have emphasized the difficulties of the administrative problems and the relative generosity of the victors. Those writing from the Canadian point of view have been gradually moving away from interpretations that concentrated on the sharp break with the French regime, although there remains the insistence that for the "conquered," the new situation was traumatic and psychologically damaging. Evidence for psychological damage is not easy to provide in standard documentable form. However, the average Canadian of the time did not articulate a reaction to either the transfer to Britain or the subsequent integration of Quebec into the British Empire. The average habitant in the 1760s, as in the 1770s, lived in a world of oral culture and did not often produce written statements on anything. As a result, what we now have, for the most part, are written comments by elite observers, who usually saw what they wanted to see.

James Murray quickly fell victim to the complications of British policy. He had done reasonably well under difficult circumstances but could not satisfy either the vociferous British merchant group in Montreal or the law officers in London. The former protested his "arbitrary" government; the latter, his attempt to meld the existing French judicial system with English common law. He was replaced in 1766 with Colonel Guy Carleton, who did not arrive in Quebec until 1768. Carleton found, in addition to Murray's earlier problems, a new need to defend Quebec in case of a rupture between the American colonies and Britain. French Canadian loyalty had become essential. He saw little possibility of substantial British immigration, arguing that "barring a catastrophe shocking to think of this country must to the end of time be peopled by the Canadian race. . . ." (*Dictionary of Canadian Biography,* 1983, p. 143). Like most colonial administrators of people and systems different from their own experience, Carleton elevated his own needs into a policy, finding potential local allies within the ranks of the former seigneurial class and the Roman Catholic Church. The seigneurs had never enjoyed much local influence under the French, but Carleton saw them as English country gentlemen who could be co-opted into the system. He also saw the value of the support of the Church and allowed Bishop Briand considerable autonomy to deal with ecclesiastical matters. As for the merchants, he allowed them to trade directly and without licenses with the First Nations, both in the Ohio Valley and to the north of the Great Lakes.

The Quebec Act of 1774

In 1770 Carleton went back to London to regularize "a more effectual provision for the province of Quebec." In 1774, his lobbying finally produced the Quebec Act, which, as one historian has observed, was "based almost exclusively on the wishes of Canadians as interpreted by Guy Carleton" (Neatby, 1972). The Quebec Act was not intended to deal with the American colonies, but rather with the unsettled condition of Canada. The American colonists interpreted sinister motives in four features of the legislation: the reinstitution of feudalism; the recognition of the rights of the Catholic Church; the withdrawal of the earlier promise of a legislative assembly; and the extension of the boundaries of Quebec into the Ohio Valley. All these provisions had been anticipated by earlier imperial decisions that were now regularized through parliamentary legislation, however. The pacification of Quebec was indirectly connected with the American troubles, of course, as a discontented colony would be difficult to defend in the event of war. But the principles of that pacification were inherent in the internal affairs of the colony, although probably less popular with the bulk of the population than Carleton and the British may have believed at the time.

The Quebec Act came in 1774 because, in large measure, the Proclamation of 1763 had proved unworkable. The French Canadians had not become assimilated, a wave of anglophone settlers had not come, and the army necessary to administer the policy on interaction with the western natives had not materialized. Thus, Quebec's boundaries were reextended to their historical limits both east and west. Roman Catholicism was legally recognized in two senses: the oath of allegiance was reframed so that Catholics in Quebec could take it and thus hold office; and the clergy could now legally collect a tithe from its own adherents. New instructions to the governor put the bishop and the clergy under government control, but these provisions were in practice neglected during the upcoming emergency. The promise of an assembly was positively revoked and the size of the executive council nearly doubled. Governor and council were given legislative authority but not the power to levy general taxation; a separate statute, the Quebec Revenue Act, provided revenue through duties, license fees, and the old feudal payments that had been used in the French regime. The Quebec Act provided the colony with English criminal law (although not with habeas corpus) and the old French civil law, including the property provisions of the seigneurial system. At least implicitly in all the provisions of the Act, the French language had also been accepted as the language of the people.

The Quebec Act now stands for quite different things in different national histories. For American historians, it has long represented British repression. For Canadian historians, as historian A. L. Burt pointed out more than half a century ago, for all its limitations, the Quebec Act "embodied a new sovereign principle of the British Empire: the liberty of non-English peoples to be themselves" (Burt, 1968, pp. 180–181). From the British perspective, Philip Lawson has added, the most contented and most novel part of the Quebec Act was its extension of religious toleration to Roman Catholics.

Once concessions had been extended to the people of French Canada, of course, there would be no turning back. The British had now recognized the French Canadian language, religion, and culture as legitimate expressions of the population of Quebec. The British Crown had not yet, however, extended the "rights of Englishmen" to the French Canadian people. That would take another whole series of political decisions and actions over many more years. What is important to this discussion, however, is that the gradual process by which French Canada became an equal partner in a bilingual state was chiefly a political one.

Troops under the command of Benedict Arnold make their way through Skowhegan Falls, Maine, en route to attack Quebec during the American Revolution. Arnold's mission was to rendezvous with General Richard Montgomery's forces to capture Canada in late 1775, but by June 1776 the invasion was abandoned and Montgomery was dead. (Library of Congress)

The American Invasion of Quebec

Not long after the passage of the Quebec Act, which was passed by the British Parliament at the same time as the "Intolerable Acts" of 1774, American colonial delegates meeting at a Continental Congress in Philadelphia accepted the logic of separation from Britain. Once the shooting had started for the American Revolution in April 1775, the Americans immediately thought about Canada. There were two reasons for this. One was that Canada, now in British hands, had for a century posed a military threat to the American colonies. It might well do so again if not prevented by a preemptive strike. The other reason, not quite contradictory, was the belief in many rebel quarters that the Canadians, now suffering under the burden of British tyranny, were ripe for liberation from their oppressors as a "fourteenth colony." The British managed to hold the city of Quebec against a desperate American attack on New Year's Eve in 1775. The Yankee army remained in the region of Quebec until May of 1776, but its behavior during this occupation—the soldiers lived off the land, paying for food with almost-worthless American paper money—was not designed to win over the bulk of French Canadians to the cause of independence.

A few hundred Canadian *habitants* took the American government's offer of money and formed a French Canadian regiment under the command of the American-born Moses Hazen, but this contingent was forced to join the American army when Quebec was evacuated by the American army in the spring. When the British reinforced their army in 1776, Quebec became a northern military center, as the Americans had feared. Quebec became the staging ground for the invasion of the United States under Burgoyne in 1777, which led to the disaster at Saratoga in which an entire British army surrendered to the Americans. Quebec subsequently served as the base for Loyalist contingents engaged in guerrilla warfare against the Americans in upstate New York. Guy Carleton's earlier policy of alliance with the church and the seigneurs may have had some positive effect during this period, as the habitants remained quiescent for the remainder of the war, no doubt influenced by the hard currency the British paid them for provisions. Virtually no hard evidence survives to this day of their feelings in the matter.

The Coming of the Loyalists and the Constitutional Act of 1791

The thirteen colonies of the mainland of North America became independent as the United States of America and were given the fur trading territory south of the Great Lakes by the peace treaty between Britain and the United States in 1783. By 1791, the northern assortment of jurisdictions, added piecemeal to Nova Scotia, Newfoundland, and an ill-defined fur trade territory in the Hudson Bay drainage basin, had become five full-fledged British provinces complete with legislative assemblies (Upper Canada, Lower Canada, Nova Scotia, New Brunswick, and Prince Edward Island). There were also two additional colonies (Cape Breton and Newfoundland) without representative government but moving toward it, and a still ill-defined western fur trade territory north of the Great Lakes. These provinces and colonies, now known as British North America, repelled attacks from the United States during the War of 1812 and managed to keep their territory intact.

If the impending American Revolution during the 1770s had forced the British to pacify the French Canadians by recognizing their language and unique institutions, such concessions were hardly the same thing as extending to the people of Quebec the common rights of Englishmen to representative government and habeas corpus (see the Significant People, Places, and Events section at the end of this chapter). Within the internal politics of Quebec, the Quebec Act did not appear to be a liberal act but a retrogressive one, essentially denying the extension of English rights to the province. The impetus for the further extension of rights was the coming of the Loyalist refugees from the American Revolution and the settlement of Quebec by anglophone colonials during the 1780s. These newcomers added their voices to the long-standing complaints of the English merchants, still such a small minority within the province.

The official government party in the Quebec legislative council attempted to interpret the Quebec Act as a "precious charter" through which the Canadians "will in a short time be indissolubly incorporated into the British nation." But radicals in the council denied that the Quebec Act was a charter, much less a sacred one, because it deprived citizens of Quebec of their liberty. This debate continued throughout the 1780s, although it was somewhat altered in spirit by the reappointment of Guy Carleton (now Lord Dorchester) as governor of the province in 1785. Dorchester brought with him a new chief justice in the person of William Smith, who had been one of the most brilliant legal minds among the Loyalists of New York. Smith came to Quebec committed to reunifying the British Empire by turning the province into a model of superior government. The British government itself, however, wanted reforms that allowed the anglophone merchants and loyalists a share of the government without totally alienating the French Canadians, a quite different matter. Smith sought to anglicize the province's legal system in order to encourage American immigration, but he ran into a hornet's nest of opposition in the council. Any action seemed quite impossible to take.

In 1789 in London, William Wyndham Grenville, the new Home Secretary, drew up a new proposal for reform, based on the principle of dividing Quebec into two distinct provinces, with most of the Loyalists in one province and the French Canadians in the other. This plan cut the Gordian knot. Great Britain had determined that the most important principles were to bring each of the two provinces' constitutions into conformity with the British one, and to enable each province to levy taxes. Under the new plan, Upper and Lower Canada would each receive their own governors, councils, and legislative assemblies. French Canadians would be allowed to vote for and sit in the assembly for Lower Canada. In theory the governor-general in Quebec City, who was also the governor of Lower Canada, was superior to the head of Upper Canada, who was only a lieutenant governor, but in practice the two provinces operated independently. The plan was put into effect by Parliament in 1791 and has always been called the Constitutional Act of 1791.

Quebec Politics under the Constitutional Act

Lower Canada began its separate legislative existence with its politics divided along class lines. The earlier political divisions in Canada were replaced by new ones. The "French Party" consisted chiefly of Canadian seigneurs supported by the clergy and a few English officials. They wanted the French civil law restored and retained. The bulk of the French Canadian population was not yet integrated into the political system. The opposition, mainly English merchants, wanted the introduction of English commercial law, radical constitutional changes, and habeas corpus. Over the next few years, the French Revolution and its controversies gradually made their way to Canada, often assisted by deliberate propaganda and subversion from France via the United States. In 1796–1797, the French government actually developed a plan to invade Canada from Vermont, although it had little public support. The English official elite in Lower Canada overreacted to the French threat, exaggerating the colony's importance to France and the disloyalty (or potential disloyalty) of the Canadien (French Canadian) people. The British elite acted as though the colony was constantly faced with insurrection, and they engaged in repressive tactics. In 1794, the assembly, opposed by only a few Canadien members, passed an Alien Act that suspended habeas corpus, not only in cases of treason but also in cases of sedition. The legislation was used to conduct a witch-hunt and to jail many without bail.

As the French Canadian population became more experienced at electoral politics—and their experience grew rapidly, as "An Early Election in Lower Canada, 1792" at the end of this chapter suggests—they inevitably reacted to the suspicions and repressive tactics of the official elite. By 1796, the Canadiens won a majority of seats in the assembly. Official Lower Canada saw this election as a victory for treason and a revolt of the

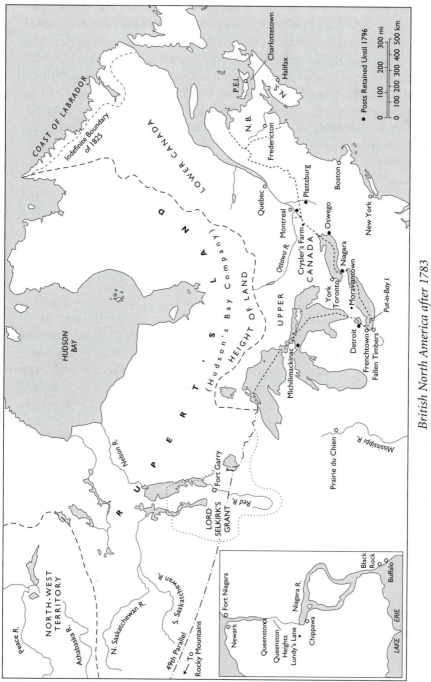

British North America after 1783

Source: *Based on Morton, W. L. The Kingdom of Canada: A General History from Earliest Times. (Toronto: McClellan and Stewart, 1963), p. 203.*

Canadien lower orders. The ethnic division was quickly made more permanent by the authorities' insistence on viewing the French Canadians as being determined to turn the colony over to the French *sans culottes* (who had brought on the French Revolution). The ethnic division also ended any possibility of reform of the government created by the Constitutional Act of 1791. The *Canadiens* continued to favor reform, while the former anglophone reformers now allied with the English officials to form the "English Party," devoted to preservation of the status quo. Virtually the only immigrants from France to Lower Canada during this period were clergymen, refugees from the anticlericalism of the French Revolution who were hardly likely to preach revolution to their flocks.

By the end of the eighteenth century, the ethnic division between the British and the French was probably irreparable, and it only got more entrenched in the years before the War of 1812. The English party continued to fear an imminent French invasion that would be warmly supported by the Canadiens. Such fears were encouraged by the deterioration of relations between the United States and Great Britain and by the increased pressure of the "Parti Canadien" (as it came to be called) for a constitutional change that the English elite was certain represented the start of rebellion. Partisanship reached a new height during the 1810 elections, in which Governor Lieutenant-General Sir James Henry Craig seized newspaper printing presses and jailed both printers and leaders of the "Parti Canadien," an act that became a symbol of British tyranny. For their part, the French Canadians had quickly adopted the tactics of a popular party in a British-style legislature. But they had been forced to do more: They had also turned their popular party into one committed to the preservation of French Canadian values and even the perpetuation of French Canadian nationalism.

The Return of the Acadians

Despite the best efforts of the British to eliminate the Acadian population from the Maritime region in the 1750s, their campaign was not completely effective. Historians do not completely understand the process by which the Acadians regrouped in the region, as most of the movement occurred outside of official record keeping and beyond the reach of central authority. What is know, however, is that after the Treaty of Paris of 1763, British policy permitted Acadian resettlement, provided that oaths of allegiance were taken and that the population moved to designated places in small numbers. Throughout the Maritime region, Acadians gradually returned to farm and fish, usually in remote districts far from existing settlements and often on marginal land. The governments in the region made no attempt to assist them or to fully accept them, but they were tolerated and left to create their own institutions. Those institutions were dominated, as they always had been, by the nuclear family, kinship, and to a much lesser extent by the Church. The scattered Acadians, many of whom had some aboriginal ancestry, had great difficulty in finding priests, especially French-speaking ones, from the Quebec Church, which claimed it had few priests to spare for missionary service. As a result, the Acadians became accustomed to a religion dominated by laymen and supplemented by the arrival of occasional missionaries. Many of the regulations of the Church, including those on marriage, were not enforced, and parochial organizations were slow to develop. Despite these problems, by 1803 a religious census showed nearly 4,000 Acadians in Nova Scotia, nearly 4,000 in New Brunswick, and nearly 700 in Prince Edward Island.

The process of the Acadians' survival is perhaps best understood on the Island of Saint John/Prince Edward Island. According to the Bishop of Quebec, who visited the Island in 1812 and spoke with many Acadians, "Most of them abandoned their lands for two or three years; others only came back after the peace of 1763. Still others, having settled elsewhere, forget their former homeland and never returned" (Arsenault, 1989, p. 51). As early as 1764, surveyor Samuel Holland reported that about thirty families of Acadians lived in the woods on the Island, where "they lived on the fish they have cured in the summer, and game which they frequently kill" (Arsenault, 1989, p. 51). A few years later, another surveyor found more than 200 Acadians in residence, all engaged in fishing for British employers. All these people took an oath of allegiance to the Crown. By the end of the century, nearly 700 Acadians were located in three communities. Another major administration of the oath of allegiance to Acadians took place in Rustico in 1794. Although most of the increase in population was natural (that is, through reproduction), some Acadians had immigrated to the Island from New Brunswick, Nova Scotia, the Magdalene Islands, and the Island of Miquelon. For these people, fishing was initially more important than farming, and they were indifferent agriculturalists until well into the nineteenth century.

Since the entire Island of Saint John had been distributed to British proprietors in 1767, most Acadians "squatted" on lands without holding proper title to them and were often dispossessed when new British settlers appeared looking for land. Even those Acadians who paid rentals to landlords frequently did not have documentable titles and were eventually evicted. Many Saint John Island Acadians left for Cape Breton Island in the early years of the nineteenth century, and others left their homes and established farms on uninhabited lands rather than come to disadvantageous terms with the legal owners of the land they lived on. One group of Acadians who did deal with a proprietor bought 6,000 acres of land for 625 pounds in 1816, and others who had abandoned their farms would eventually be forced to come to terms with the farms' landlords. Ironically, the Acadians of Prince Edward Island had difficulty in developing a permanent institutional presence until well into the nineteenth century, when they were no longer able to move to wilderness land. The first Acadian school was not opened in Rustico until 1815, and educational facilities for Acadians did not become common until after 1830, when the government helped subsidize education in the colony.

Although the Acadians had much in common culturally with the French-speaking people of Quebec, their history and their sense of identity—as well as the way they spoke French—would prove to be quite different and distinctive.

The Métis in the West

If the Acadians were a resurrected culture, the mixed-bloods of the Red River region represented a striking example of an emergent one. Racial mixing began in North America virtually from the first moment of European contact with the aboriginals. A good deal more of it probably occurred in the early years in territory controlled by the French than in territory controlled by the English, if only because the French dominated a greater extent of heavily populated land and—through the fur trade—spent more time living or dealing with the First Nations. But, it must be added, the French also insisted on racial mixing as a matter of policy. When Champlain said, "Our young men will marry your daughters, and we shall be one people," he was expressing a general French approach to racial relations in North America (Dickason, 1985, p. 23). Always short on population, especially in comparison with the English, the French fully supported miscegenation. After 1680 the state provided dowries of fifty livres for First Nations girls who married Frenchmen, but few ever claimed the prize. Nevertheless, there was probably an extensive population of mixed-blood people in New France, never recognized nor identified in the colonial population. One Quebec scientist calculated in 1970 that nearly half of French Canadians had one First Nations ancestor, and French historian Rameau de Saint-Père a century earlier (1889) had actually attempted to assess numbers of mixed-bloods in his study of Acadia. But for the most part, historians of French Canada have generally ignored the matters of intermarriage and the offspring that resulted, presumably because their readers may have been offended to learn the extent of the mixing. The general assumption has been that mixed-blood children tended to stay with their mothers—that is, to become cultural Amerindians themselves—and there is considerable evidence that this is what happened in the early western fur trade country, where large numbers of First Nations leaders in the late seventeenth and eighteenth centuries are known to have been mixed-bloods. A similar process occurred in Acadia. But historians simply do not know about the extent to which those children of intermarriage have assimilated into the European populations of Canada and Acadia.

The situation in the west of the continent was somewhat different, not least because the rivalry between French and English in the fur trade prevented the alliances between French and First Nations from ever becoming regularized—it was always possible to outbid one's rival—and because the British, who took over control of the Old Northwest (eventually the states of Ohio, Indiana, Illinois, Wisconsin, and Michigan) after 1763, had a different and less favorable official attitude toward intermarriage and miscegenation. Moreover, in the Old Northwest there really was no European society within which mixed-bloods could disappear. The result was that western mixed-bloods from the mid-eighteenth century tended to think of themselves as a separate people. By the end of the eighteenth century, there was a distinctive people that lived in a number of Great Lakes trading communities, including Detroit, Michilimackanic, "Frenchtown" on the Rivière Raisin, Green Bay, and Sault Ste. Marie. At this point, a major development occurred: An American population from what would become the United States appeared to settle the Old Northwest, and it took over fairly rapidly. These new settlers provided a different population into which the mixed-bloods could assimilate, and many quickly disappeared in the early years of the nineteenth century. Some of those who did not choose to become cultural Europeans or Americans— mainly francophones—headed further west, first to Sault Ste. Marie and later to the western plains, where they joined the children of fur-trade alliances and formed a distinctive population.

The area around the Red River was, by the second decade of the nineteenth century, the center of a complex trade war between two rival fur trading companies, the Hudson's Bay Company and the North West Company. The latter company assisted the district's mixed-bloods, those individuals with aboriginal or mixed-blood mothers and European fathers, to assert their claim to the territory as inheritors of aboriginal rights to the land. Many of these mixed-bloods came from the fur trade. Their fathers were mainly French Canadian voyageurs, although quite a few of their fathers were Scotsmen in the fur trade. But other mixed-bloods represented refugee people who had been driven out of the Great Lakes region by the arrival of new settlers. In response to the fur trade war, the mixed-bloods (not yet usually called Métis but more frequently "half-breeds" or "bois-brûlés") declared themselves "a New Nation" and even created a "halfbreed flag," about "4 ½ feet square, red and in the middle a large figure of Eight horizontally of a different colour" (Bumsted, 1991, pp. 389–390). This "nation" overreached itself in 1817 when it killed a large number of European settlers at the Battle of Seven Oaks (as a result of an unexpected confrontation), but it served as the basis for a new people who came to inhabit the Red River Area. Missionary activity by the Quebec Catholic Church beginning in 1818 organized this people—the Métis—who were fervently Catholic as well as francophone, but nonetheless quite distinctive from the French Canadians. The people of Red River developed their own language (called mitchif, a blend of French, Gaelic, and native languages, mainly Cree), customs, and folklore. Red River served as the center of the Métis people for more than fifty years, although after 1820 they moved south into the United States and, after 1870, west into Saskatchewan.

First Nations

The British elimination of the French from North America was a negative turning point for the First Nations in several ways. First, the new regime no longer left the aboriginals with any bargaining power and cut them off from most gift giving (presents accompanying treaty negotiations). Second, the British approached First Nations–European relations in a much more legalistic way than the French had, insisting on formal peace treaties and land purchases that moved the Amerindians further to the margins of North American society. Finally, the British were settlers, and despite the attempt of the British Crown to safeguard the trans-Appalachian west and to honor article 40 of the articles of capitulation of Montreal—which guaranteed protection for First Nations lands—they were unable to control their colonial governments, which in turn were unable to control their citizens, if they ever sought to do so. Instead of ending a flow of white people's depredations, the British conquest only increased it.

In the west, the period after 1760 was one of considerable turmoil. The First Nations had attempted to assert some control over their future by rising in arms against the British, but "Pontiac's Rebellion," as this uprising was called, gradually fizzled out with no concrete results. The rebellion had sought to harness a spiritual movement among the Amerindians that advocated a return to the traditions of their ancestors and the unification of all native peoples. Although Pontiac was a real person, he was probably less important as a leader than prophets like Neolin, who told his people, "if you allow the English among you, you are dead; maladies, smallpox, and their poison will destroy you totally" (Dickason, 2002, p. 158). Aboriginal land claims should have provided a worthy challenge to the best legal minds of the day, equal to that of accommodating the French Canadians without giving in to them. But the land claims were not dealt with because the British did not really take the First Nations seriously at all. The Proclamation of 1763 really fell short for the indigenous peoples. The British understood that their dealings with the First Nations required a policy, but one that prohibited European settlement in the West was only half of what was required. The Proclamation of 1763 did not guarantee the natives title to their lands, much less provide them with any sort of political control over the territory that they claimed. The British never regarded the issue of aboriginals' sovereignty to be a real problem worth resolving, although Europe had plenty of examples of land arrangements in which both the ultimate sovereignty of the Crown and the immediate autonomy of the territory were preserved. But, in British eyes, the First Nations were not a people entitled to much attention.

Any official British attempts to limit settler intrusions were ended by the American colonies' assumption of independence. For the duration of the Revolutionary War, the First Nations once again found some opportunity to maneuver between conflicting powers, although for the most part the war was a painful experience for everyone. The Americans sought to keep the aboriginals neutral, but the British wanted their active military assistance. In the west during the war, small armies of American settlers roamed around and fought with the aboriginals. The Treaty of Paris in 1783 totally ignored the First Nations. Their lands in the west were transferred to the United States, and no provision was made for their protection. Native leader Joseph Brant was beside himself with anger at the British betrayal, and it was no solace to him that other natives loyal to the

Crown would be treated in exactly the same way. Brant and his people would later accept land in the Grand Valley of Ontario that had been taken by the British government from another native tribe. Although after the war the British would prove reluctant to evacuate their posts in the west, holding most of them until Jay's Treaty in 1794, the aboriginals were now at the mercy of punitive American military expeditions and advancing settlement. Many of the more militant First Nations leaders (such as Tecumseh) would eventually support the British as being less obnoxious than the Americans in the War of 1812, taking little joy out of the eventual military stalemate.

Apart from the trans-Appalachian west, the British assumed after 1763 that in most eastern places the First Nations were a declining people who needed to be integrated into the European population as quickly as possible. Those Amerindians who insisted on maintaining their old ways were quickly shoved to the margins of society and, at least in Newfoundland, driven to extinction. The situation was different in Upper Canada and in the vast northwestern regions of the continent. The core of British policy toward the natives in this region since 1763 had been the notion of an orderly frontier. In theory this involved a legal procedure for the orderly purchase of lands, the reservation to the natives of sufficient land on which to make a living, and, in Upper Canada, the full application of legal rights under the law wherever possible. This approach was taken partly for the purpose of symbolically distinguishing Canada from the United States. It involved the application of the common law to everybody, including the aboriginals, both because the common law was a bulwark of Tory ideology and because it provided a framework for good government. The law-centered approach was meant to avoid unnecessary violence and warfare and to reeducate aboriginal people into the new order. It worked better in theory than in practice. One of the assumptions of the law-centered approach was that the First Nations would not become a part of society until they were thoroughly integrated into Europe's hierarchies and authority structures.

Conclusion

Although the British government after 1763 was officially committed to the assimilation of all francophones in its territory, Whitehall was continually forced to make concessions for the realities of North America. The British government consciously acquiesced in decisions that ultimately resulted in the acceptance of French-speaking Roman Catholic as full-fledged members of the body politic and also eventually accepted that French civil law and the seigneurial system would continue in Quebec. The British government also tacitly accepted the return of many Acadians and tolerated Acadian communities throughout the Maritime region. Moreover, the British also permitted the Métis in Rupert's Land to establish themselves as a distinctive people. As for the First Nations, they found themselves legally recognized and placed (at least potentially) in the context of European society. Whatever their official policy, however, by 1815 the British had unofficially recognized the full political rights of the French Canadian people and the right of existence to the Acadians and the Métis. The British had also extended the right of existence to the First Nations, although entirely in European terms.

Timeline

1759   Battle of Quebec.
1760   French garrison at Montreal surrenders to British.
1761–1762   "Canada-Guadeloupe" debate in Britain.
1763   Treaty of Paris; Pontiac's Rebellion in west; Proclamation of 1763 issued; Acadians allowed to resettle.
1764   Civil government inaugurated in Quebec under General James Murray.
1766   Governor Murray recalled, is replaced with Colonel Guy Carleton.
1768   Carleton finally arrives in Quebec.
1770   Carleton returns to London to lobby for new legislation on Quebec.
1774   Quebec Act passed at the same time as the "Intolerable Acts."
1775   Americans invade Quebec.
1776   Americans retreat from Quebec.
1785   Carleton returns to Quebec as Lord Dorchester, accompanied by William Smith.
1791   Constitutional Act of 1791 passed.
1794   Lower Canada's assembly passes Alien Act.
1796   Fears of French invasion from Vermont; new assembly elections result in French Canadian majority.
1803   Religious census of Maritime provinces shows nearly 10,000 Acadians.
1810   Sir James Craig's "Reign of Terror."

1815   Métis in Red River display a "halfbreed flag."
1817   Battle of Seven Oaks.

Significant People, Places, and Events

AMHERST, GENERAL JEFFREY (1717–1797) Born in England, Amherst was the British general who eventually conquered Canada. Commander-in-chief of the British army in 1763, he failed to handle well the First Nations rebellion of that year.

BATTLE OF SEVEN OAKS (1817) A military confrontation in June 1817 between a small band from the Red River Settlement, led by its Governor, Robert Semple, and a larger group of mounted Métis. Most of the settlers were killed.

BRIAND, JEAN-OLIVIER (1715–1794) Born in France, he came to Quebec in 1741. After the Seven Years' War, Briand served the Canadian church as vicar-general and was selected by his colleagues (with support of the colonial government) to return to France to be consecrated as bishop of Quebec.

CANADA-GUADELOUPE DEBATE A great public debate, carried on in newspapers and pamphlets in England from 1760 to 1763, over British policy at the peace negotiations ending the Seven Years' War. The chief questions revolved around what territory Britain should retain in the peace treaty.

CAPITULATION, ARTICLES OF The fifty-five clauses of the terms of surrender of the French army to the British in Montreal in September of 1760. The articles were intended to deal only with immediate circumstances, but many French Canadians came to regard these terms as a British commitment for the future.

CARLETON, GUY, FIRST BARON DORCHESTER (1724–1808) Born in Ireland, he served as governor of Quebec 1768–1778, then went on to become British commander-in-chief at New York, returning as Baron Dorchester to govern Quebec again 1786–1795. Carleton was largely responsible for the Quebec Act and for the British evacuation of the Loyalists from New York in 1782 and 1783.

CONSTITUTIONAL ACT OF 1791 Parliamentary legislation in 1791 that separated Quebec into two provinces and provided each with a full colonial government.

CRAIG, SIR JAMES HENRY (1748–1812) Born in Gibraltar of Scottish origins, he served in the British army in North America and in Cape

Colony, becoming governor in South Africa 1795–1797. In 1807 he was appointed governor of Quebec, although seriously ill, and during his regime he allowed his officials to carry on a repressive policy against French Canadians in the province.

ENGLISH PARTY Active during the 1760s and 1770s, the English Party consisted of a small group of English merchants and officials outside the government who sought to gain full British constitutional privileges for the colony in Quebec. Gradually this group became larger, acquired a wing in the general assembly, and by the 1790s had become virtually synonymous with the administration of Lower Canada.

GRENVILLE, WILLIAM WYNDHAM (1759–1834) Foreign secretary of Britain 1791–1801, he was responsible for drafting and passing the Constitutional Act of 1791.

HABEAS CORPUS One of the longstanding principles of English common law, it literally means "produce the body." It is usually embodied into a writ that commands that the authorities produce for appropriate legal action an individual they have been holding without charge.

HAZEN, MOSES (1733–1803) Born in Massachusetts, Hazen served in the British army in the Seven Years' War and subsequently took up a land grant in Quebec. In 1775 he recruited a regiment among the habitants to support the Americans in their invasion of Quebec.

LOWER CANADA A new British province carved out of the eastern part of Quebec by the Constitutional Act of 1791.

LOYALISTS The various categories of individuals who went into exile from the American Colonies after the end of the American Revolutionary War. Many came to Canada and received land grants there.

MURRAY, JAMES (1721[22]–1794) Born in Scotland, Murray served as an officer in the British army. He was appointed military governor of Quebec in 1759, serving until he was appointed civil governor in 1764. He was recalled in 1766 amid charges that his administration was entirely too sympathetic to the French Canadians.

ORDERLY SETTLEMENT The informal name for a First Nations policy adopted by the British government in North America after 1791, which insisted on the rule of law and the proper transfer of native title to the Crown through treaties.

PARTI CANADIEN The political party opposed to the English Party in Quebec from the 1790s. It usually had a majority of seats in the legislative assembly, was led by French Canadian professionals, and was committed to the preservation and extension of French Canadian power and nationality in the province.

PONTIAC'S REBELLION A First Nations uprising that began near Detroit in 1763 and continued sporadically until 1766, when Sir William Johnson negotiated a peace with the Shawnee, who were the leading rebels.

PROCLAMATION OF 1763 A public proclamation in October 1763 that set forth the terms under which the newly acquired territories formerly belonging to France were to be governed by the British. It created four new governments (East and West Florida, Quebec, and Granada), set up an aboriginals' territory west of the Appalachian Mountains in which European settlement was barred, and provided for land grants for former soldiers.

QUEBEC ACT An Act of Parliament in 1774 that revised British policy for Quebec by accepting far more of the laws and customs by which Quebec had previously been governed under the French Regime.

REIGN OF TERROR A policy of repression of press and freedom of expression carried out by the administration of Quebec in 1810.

SMITH, WILLIAM (1728–1791) Born in New York, Smith was a highly successful lawyer who remained loyal to the Crown during the American Revolution. He was appointed chief justice of Quebec in 1786 and was expected by the British to help settle the question of how to govern Quebec.

TECUMSEH (1766?–1813) A chief of the Shawnee people, he led the opposition to American policy in the Old Northwest. In the War of 1812, Tecumseh became a brigadier general in the British Army and led a large contingent of First Nations. He was killed at the Battle of the Thames in 1813.

UPPER CANADA A new British province created by the Constitutional Act of 1791, its boundaries roughly conforming to the southern region of what is now Ontario

Documents

The Religious Provisions of the Quebec Act, 1774

After a preamble describing the boundaries of the province of Quebec and declaring the former provisions of the Proclamation of 1763 void after 1 May 1775, the legislation turned to religion.

And for the more perfect Security and Ease of the Minds of the Inhabitants of the said Province, it is hereby declared, That His Majesty's Subjects, professing the Religion of the Church of *Rome* of and in the said Province of *Quebec,* may have, hold, and enjoy, the free Exercise of the Religion of the Church of *Rome,* subject to the King's Supremacy, declared and established by an Act, made in the First Year of the Reign of Queen *Elizabeth,* over all the Dominions and Countries which then did, or thereafter should belong, to the Imperial Crown of this Realm; and that the Clergy of the said Church may hold, receive, and enjoy, their accustomed Dues and Rights, with respect to such Persons only as shall profess the said Religion.

Provided nevertheless, That it shall be lawful for His Majesty, His Heirs or Successors, to make such Provision out of the rest of the accustomed Dues and Rights, for the Encouragement of the Protestant Religion, and for the Maintenance and Support of a Protestant Clergy within the said Province, as he or they shall, from Time to Time, think necessary and expedient.

Provided allways, and be it enacted, That no Person, professing the Religion of the Church of *Rome,* and residing in the said Province, shall be obliged to take the Oath required by the said Statute passed in the First Year of the Reign of Queen *Elizabeth,* or any other Oaths substituted by any other Act in the Place thereof; but that every such Person who, by the said Statute is required to take the Oath therein mentioned, shall be obliged, and is hereby required, to take and subscribe the following Oath before the Governor, or such other Person in such Court of Record as His Majesty shall appoint, who are hereby authorized to administer the same; *videlicet,*

I, A. B., do sincerely promise and swear, That I will be faithful, and bear true Allegiance to His Majesty King GEORGE, *and him will defend to the utmost of my Power, against all traiterous Conspiracies, and Attempts whatsoever, which shall be made against His Person, Crown, and Dignity; and I will do my utmost Endeavour to disclose and make known to His Majesty, His Heirs and Successors, all Treasons and traiterous Conspiracies and Attempts, which I shall know to be against Him, or any of Them; and all this I do swear without any Equivocation, mental Evasion, or secret Reservation, and renouncing all Pardons and Dispensations from any Power or Person whomsoever to the Contrary.* so help me god.

Source: Shortt, Adam, and Doughty, Arthur G., eds., *Documents Relating to the Constitutional History of Canada 1759–1791* (Ottawa, Ontario: King's Printers, 1907), pp. 401–405.

An Early Election in Lower Canada, 1792

This electoral protest from a French Canadian candidate for the assembly in the 1792 election in Lower Canada, the first held after the Constitutional Act of 1791, shows how quickly the French Canadians had accepted the politics of representational government.

TO THOSE ELECTORS OF THE COUNTY OF QUEBEC

Who have voted, and those who were prevented from voting in my favour the 25th, 26th, 27th June last:

The more obstacles you have surmounted, you have shown the greatest wisdom and firmness, in a country where liberty is but just dawning; for the general good and at the same time of esteem for myself, in thinking me worthy of being a representative, penetrated like yourselves with patriotism and gratitude for so distinguished a degree of your confidence, I entreat you to accept my sincere thanks and to be persuaded that I will neglect nothing for the accomplishment of your wishes and to obtain the justice due to us.

I cannot help observing on the silence kept by the *Quebec Gazette*, with respect to the extraordinary circumstances of the Upper and Lower town of the County of Quebec, particularly on the abstract and mysterious turn that the *Quebec Gazette* of Thursday last has given to what passed at Charlebourg during the election for the County of Quebec, doubtless the author of that paragraph is one of those who heretofore have been so much fatigued themselves to write, print, and vaguely cry against the laws of this country, against the Honourable profession of Advocate, and who have employed such low means as those known to the public, but who have found no advantage in publishing the true facts arising from the Constitution; I shall not, however, undertake to establish them in this paper, the election for the County of Quebec being intended to be a subject of examination and I hope of just censure in the House of Assembly, I confine myself at present to inform the public of the state of the poll,

Salaberry, Esq. 515
Lynd, Esq. 462
Berthelot, Advocate. 436

It is evident that I find myself the lowest by 26 votes, but the public cannot be ignorant how many are to be deducted from the other two candidates of persons who are neither proprietors nor naturalized; I might depend on this point alone or contest the election altogether, by the means contained in my protest signified by two Notaries when the poll was unexpectedly closed. 62 Voters more on the spot presented themselves in my favor and formally protested even in the building where the election was held, from which they were chased by some gentlemen who demolished it by force, but they continued their protest and finished it in the neighbourhood.

I hope that the country and the truth will not fail to direct *resources*, and that no personal influence will deprive my fellow countrymen of the advantages of our Constitution, which is in itself so good that the elections have made known the good subjects in this country, as well as the intentions and cabals of some others who have preached up union and non-distinction of birth, while they would secretly favourize a certain class of men who alone are neither able to effect the welfare or the peace of this colony.

Bethelot Bartigny

Source: *Quebec Gazette*, 5 July 1792.

Bibliography

Aresenault, Georges, *The Island Acadians* (Charlottetown, Prince Edward Island: Ragweed Press, 1989).

Bumsted, J. M., "The Cultural Landscape of Early Canada," in Bernard Bailyn and Philip D. Morgan, eds., *Strangers within the Realm: Cultural Margins of the First British Empire* (Chapel Hill: University of North Carolina Press, 1991), 363–392.

Burt, A. L., *The Old Province of Quebec* (c. 1933; reprint, New York: Russell & Russell, 1970).

Dickason, Olive Patricia, "From 'One Nation' in the Northeast to 'New Nation' in the Northwest: A Look At the Emergence of the Métis," in Jennifer Brown and Jacqueline Peterson, eds., *The New Peoples: Being and Becoming Métis in North America* (Winnipeg, Manitoba: University of Manitoba Press, 1985), 23.

———, *Canada's First Nations: A History of Founding Peoples from Earliest Times* (Toronto: Oxford University Press, 2002), 158.

Dictionary of Canadian Biography, vol. 5 (Toronto: University of Toronto Press, 1983), 143.

Dowd, Gregory Evans, *A Spirited Resistance: The North American Indian Struggle for Unity, 1745–1815* (Baltimore, MD and London, U.K.: Johns Hopkins University Press, 1992).

Everest, Allan S., *Moses Hazen and the Canadian Refugees in the American Revolution* (Syracuse, NY: Syracuse University Press, 1976).

Graymont, Barbara, *The Iroquois in the American Revolution* (Syracuse, NY: Syracuse University Press, 1972).

Greenwood, F. Murray, *Legacies of Fear: Law and Politics in Quebec in the Era of the French Revolution* (Toronto: University of Toronto Press, 1993).

Lawson, Philip, *The Imperial Challenge: Quebec and Britain in the Age of the American Revolution* (Montreal, Quebec and Kingston, Ontario: McGill-Queen's University Press, 1990).

Neatby, Hilda, *Quebec 1760–1791* (Toronto: McClelland and Stewart, 1966).

————, ed., *The Quebec Act: Protest and Policy* (Scarborough, Ontario: Prentice-Hall, 1972).

Stanley, George, *Canada Invaded 1775–1776* (Toronto: Hakkert, 1973).

CHAPTER FOUR

Yankees, Loyalists, and Highland Scots, 1759–1815

RIVING THE FRENCH from North America by force of arms did not produce for British North America the anticipated benefits. In the 1750s, the British government decided to make an all-out effort to eliminate the French from North America, and British military power was successful in doing the job. Within a dozen years of the peace treaty, though, Britain's American colonists had risen in armed rebellion, seeking an independence they would achieve successfully by 1783. Britain was forced to regroup, reconstructing an American Empire out of the remains of its North American possessions. Although the British managed in the 1780s to reconstitute British North America, it was a far different collection of colonies from the earlier one. A major difference was in the inability of the British to enforce a cultural hegemony to match their seeming political and military supremacy. Instead of hegemony, diversity and cultural difference in small, segregated communities seemed the dominant pattern.

Demographic Change

In the years between 1759 and 1815, the nature of the population of what was known in 1815 as British North America changed rather substantially. About 10,000 American settlers came to Nova Scotia and Quebec between 1759 and 1775, a number of previously expelled Acadians chose to return to their ancient territories in these years, and there was not only the beginning of immigration from Scotland (mainly the Highlands) but also the resumption of immigration from Ireland. During and immediately after the end of the fighting of the American Revolutionary War, moreover, thousands of American residents and British soldiers (black,

white, and native) chose to leave the United States and resettle in the remaining British provinces, although some of the refugees ultimately decided to return to their homeland. Following the Treaty of Paris in 1783,
many Britons (especially Scots Highlanders and Irish) and more Americans decided to begin their lives anew in British North America.
Throughout the entire period, moreover, the French-speaking population
of Quebec managed to protect much of its ancient culture and heritage
from attempts at forcible assimilation into the anglophone culture of
North America.

Population Movements, 1759–1774

Nova Scotia and the Atlantic Region

With the two removals of the Acadians in 1755 and 1758, the British had
opened much of the Atlantic region for settlement. Beginning in 1759, a
number of American-born settlers, mainly from the overpopulated
southern New England colonies of Massachusetts Bay, Connecticut, and
Rhode Island, were encouraged by transportation subsidies and liberal
land policies to take up residence in Nova Scotia. These "Yankees" settled
in three regions: the agricultural lands of the St. John River Valley in what
is now New Brunswick; the rich agricultural lands formerly inhabited by
the Acadians in the Minas Basin-Annapolis Valley region of the colony;
and the southwestern shore of Nova Scotia, with its access to the fishery of
the Bay of Fundy. The new settlers joined the colony's official and merchant classes (also largely American) in Halifax and the German-speaking
population of the south shore.

The so-called Yankee Planters who were attracted to Nova Scotia—between 7,000 and 8,000 in number—were drawn by the promise of the fertile lands vacated by the Acadians and access to the rich fishing grounds of
the Nova Scotia coast. Both agricultural and fishing communities were established, the former dominated by families and the latter by single men
(much as in Newfoundland). The Minas Basin-Annapolis Valley townships were founded using the same procedures of land allotment and the
same form of local government that had characterized New England settlements for more than a century. The result was small, equitably allocated freeholdings. The Halifax government, however, did not like Yankee
institutions of democracy and worked to replace them with a more traditional political and economic structure modeled on Virginia and Europe.

Most of the new arrivals were desperately short of capital, and when subsidies ended in the early 1760s, the newcomers quickly discovered that Nova Scotia was no bargain; many returned to New England. Rates of turnover were very high. Nevertheless, the Planter communities took root, and a version of the frontier society of northern New England gradually developed. It was characterized by a propensity to sectarian revivalism, especially during the Great Awakening led by the New Light preacher Henry Alline. Planter society should have become more dominant than it did in Nova Scotia, but the Yankees were not sufficiently numerous to control more than a few circumscribed regions of the colony. In those districts, visitors often commented that the settlers were a poorer version of New Englanders, nowhere more so than in their wheeling and dealing over land.

The Yankees' small freeholdings were not the only form of landholding pattern in Nova Scotia or the Atlantic region. From the first removal of the Acadians, many landholders hoped to recreate European estates based on more traditional landlord–tenant relationships—and in some cases on black slavery. These landholders received large grants of land from the government and proceeded to populate these grants with resettled Acadians or recently arrived European immigrants; after 1770 many of the latter were from Wales and the Highlands of Scotland. The entire Island of St. John was divided in advance of settlement into 67 township lots of 20,000 acres each, and these lots were distributed in 1767 to important military and colonial officials as well as to some British politicians. The Island lots had a considerable quitrent payment attached to them, and the Island would become the last jurisdiction in British North America in which quitrents were assessed and collected.

By the eve of the American rebellion, two collateral trends were at work in the Atlantic region. One was a substantial decline in the proportion of settlers of American origin as numbers of returned Acadians and British immigrants moved into the region. Some of the British arrivals, reported Governor Francis Legge, "come to purchase, others perhaps, to become Tenants & some to Labour." The immigration from Britain began in the late 1760s and was fueled by unfavorable economic conditions in the British Isles and the acquisition of large land grants by former soldiers and speculators. This led to the second trend, which was the establishment of European-style estates peopled by tenants rather than freeholders. Three of the major new landlords were Captain William Owen on Campobello Island, John MacDonald on the Island of St. John, and J. F. W. DesBarres in Nova Scotia. Many of the new tenants were Gaelic-speaking

Roman Catholics from the western Highlands and islands of Scotland. The Maritime provinces became the principal northern destination of the Highland Scots; the Island of St. John was particularly attractive to these newcomers. Acadians also settled as tenants during this period, often on their old lands, which were now in the hands of British entrepreneurs. In Newfoundland, newcomers—mainly Irish—were neither freeholders nor tenants, but instead were perched precariously on the seacoasts on land to which they held no titles, where they fished for cod.

Two early communal settlements of Highland Scots arrived in the Maritimes during the early 1770s, to become subsequently celebrated as the beginnings of Highlander settlement in what would become Canada. One group arrived aboard the *Alexander* on the Island of St. John in 1772. It consisted of Roman Catholic MacDonalds from the western Highlands and islands, who became tenants on the Island of St. John. A few of these people were fleeing religious persecution and landlord abuse, although most were simply seeking better economic opportunities than were available at home. The other group landed at Pictou on the north coast of Nova Scotia on the Northumberland Strait aboard the *Hector* in 1773. They were coming from lands administered by the Board of Forfeited Estates, one of the most progressive landlords in the Highlands. Both groups of Highlanders, for the most part, had chosen to emigrate and had sufficient resources to pay for their own passage.

Quebec

After the conquest of Canada by the British, some American traders and merchants did move into the newly acquired French-speaking territory. The merchants established themselves mainly in Montreal, always the center of the French fur trade, and some began to move into the western wilderness as wintering traders, replacing the French in this role. Some Americans also entered the timber business in the upper Richelieu Valley and obtained seigneuries in the region. A few parties of Highland Scots, mainly Gaelic-speaking Catholics, came to Quebec. As was the case in the Maritimes, the Highlanders tended to emigrate in extended family groupings aboard chartered vessels that took them straight to isolated destinations, permitting them to replicate their Old World communities in North America. There was also frequent movement of settlers between Quebec and the disputed territory that would eventually become Vermont.

The Coming of the Loyalists

Hostilities between Britain and its American colonies turned to open warfare in 1775. From the onset of fighting, some Americans who opposed their countrymen's fight for independence had chosen, or were forced, to go into exile. Originally known as Tories, the supporters of the Crown soon acquired the more attractive label of Loyalists, which has stuck with them over the centuries. In the early years of the conflict, most Americans who fled the United States for political reasons were members of the elite—usually office holders, large merchants, and Anglican clergymen—singled out by the rebels for harassment and proscription. Most of these early exiles went to Britain, but there was also a constant trickle into Halifax, Nova Scotia, and Quebec. Later in the war, as the British finally encouraged its supporters to organize militarily, larger numbers of people were branded with the Loyalist mark. Perhaps as many as one-half million Americans of European origin (20 percent of the colonies' European population) supported the British cause. The British had also encouraged both free and slave blacks to oppose the Americans and forced the aboriginals along the frontiers to choose sides as well.

The British lost the military struggle in 1781 when Lord Cornwallis and his army surrendered at Yorktown. The British government began the process of extricating itself from a lost cause by negotiating a peace treaty with the United States. In the process, the British sacrificed most of their earlier commitments to their American supporters. While negotiations dragged on in Europe, Loyalist refugees and soldiers were drawn to New York City, now the major center of British authority and military power on the eastern seaboard, already the wartime home of thousands of pro-British people. The Loyalists waited anxiously for word about the outcome of the peace negotiations and for an announcement of the ultimate policy for those who had supported the mother country. In the meantime, agents fanned out across Britain's remaining North American empire, from Nova Scotia and Quebec to the Caribbean to Florida, investigating land and political conditions in the event of the independence of the American colonies.

By the autumn of 1782 it was clear that the Americans were not likely to forgive and forget—nor were the British likely to remain firmly committed to their supporters—and Sir Guy Carleton (who had been transferred from Quebec to New York earlier in the war) began arranging for the movement of large groups of Loyalists to Nova Scotia. There, Governor John Parr had been warned to reserve as much land as possible for

Sir Guy Carleton,
the British commander in New York
in 1783, organized the relocation of
thousands of Loyalists to Nova Scotia.
(National Archives of Canada)

their arrival. The Island of St. John, Cape Breton, and Newfoundland had no land readily available, and hence were not destinations for the primary migrations of 1782 and 1783.

Moving and compensating the Loyalists would be an expensive business, representing a major act of support for resettlement, arguably the largest ever executed by the British government in its history. The ultimate cost of Loyalist resettlement ran into the millions of pounds and made the earlier expenditures on colonizing Nova Scotia appear puny. Not all of the colonies in the remaining North American Empire benefited equally from British generosity, though. Newfoundland received no Loyalists, and Cape Breton and the Island of Saint John (the latter very indirectly) received about 1,000 each. About 35,000 arrived in Nova Scotia, and about 10,000 sought refuge in the colony of Quebec. Other Loyalists moved south into Florida and the Caribbean area. Under emergency conditions, the loyal colonies of the North American Empire received a publicly subsidized injection of much-desired anglophone settlers.

Deciding who was entitled to Loyalist largesse would have been a difficult matter had the British attempted to make careful distinctions. Instead, in the short run, they treated everyone who wanted land and assistance as eligible. Britain would later be more discriminating in its compensation policy, so that only a few thousand elite were actually awarded compensation or pensions for losses they had suffered during the rebellion. The British colonies, however, allowed Americans to claim land as Loyalists until the end of the eighteenth century, and many later arrivals who came to British America mainly for land or for religious refuge were included under the Loyalist umbrella. Those who were dealt with under the Loyalist banner were a fairly polyglot selection of refugees. The traditional Canadian historical view has been that the Loyalists represented the cream of American society, but that view is now no longer tenable. Military settlers were mixed in with the civilian refugees, and the British army was quite varied in its ethnic composition, including many German mercenaries. Many of the incoming "Loyalists" were aboriginals or blacks, and among those of European origin there was a rich ethnic mixture from the British Isles, especially of Highland Scots and Irish, as well as a number of Mennonites. Many of these exiles had arrived only recently in the American colonies from the British Isles or Europe. Rather than being the elite, the Loyalists tended to be the least assimilated part of the American population. Further complicating matters, many of the newcomers returned silently to the United States as soon as the political situation calmed down.

The great migration of Loyalist refugees to Nova Scotia took place in 1783, with troop transport ships bringing thousands of newcomers to the region. There were two principal destinations in the spring of 1783: the mouth of the Saint John River and Port Roseway (renamed Shelburne) on the southwest shore of Nova Scotia. Two instant cities sprang up as the transports disgorged their passengers. Shelburne was surrounded by some of the most marginal agricultural land in the region, and its 10,000 people quickly dispersed. But Saint John had a rich agricultural hinterland up the Saint John River, where hundreds of newcomers went, and it managed to survive as an urban center. The city witnessed a fierce struggle between the old Tory elite, who were attempting to reestablish their authority in the new land, and an equally ambitious new Loyalist middle class, mainly artisans and shopkeepers. With the aid of the colonial authorities, the old elite would eventually emerge triumphant.

The "spring fleets" brought civilian refugees, but they were joined later in the year by Loyalist soldiers and their families as well as by merchants attracted by the promise of good trading connections within the Empire. The disbanded soldiers scattered around the region, some being attracted to the Island of Saint John or to Cape Breton. Battalions often stayed together under the leadership of former officers. Civilian refugees quickly became dissatisfied with their initial locations (especially around Shelburne) because of remoteness and lack of decent soil, and moved on.

Also among the new arrivals were 3,000 freed blacks, whose names were recorded in a special book; but they would not be well treated by the authorities. They received only small allotments of marginal land and

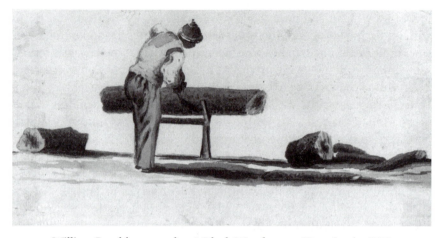

William Booth's watercolor, A Black Woodcutter, *Nova Scotia, 1788*
(National Archives of Canada)

found themselves subject to considerable racial discrimination. A major disability for the blacks was a lack of leadership. Of the more than 3,000 black Loyalists transported to Nova Scotia, only 1,155 actually received land grants, for a total acreage of 12,015.5 acres, or less than 11 acres per grant. Black Loyalists suffered other disabilities as well. Although many paid taxes, they were not entitled to trial by jury and in what became New Brunswick were not allowed to vote. Blacks brought to British North America as slaves by Loyalist masters continued in this status until the start of the nineteenth century, when local courts ruled slavery out of existence by extending English laws to the colonies. The courts treated freed blacks more harshly than they treated whites convicted of the same or similar crimes. Nearly half of these freed blacks would become part of an exodus from Nova Scotia to Sierra Leone in the early 1790s.

Smaller contingents of Loyalists made their way into Quebec, with some 2,000 remaining along the St. Lawrence (Sorel was a noted Loyalist center), and 7,500 journeyed into the Mississauga country on the frontier. Concentrations gathered in what is now southeastern Ontario (Glengarry County), at Cataraqui (later Kingston), and in the Niagara peninsula. Many from the Niagara contingent had taken refuge around Fort Niagara in the last days of the fierce guerrilla fighting in New York state, often being associated with irregular units such as Butler's Rangers. The Cataraqui people had each served in one of three other provincial corps (the King's Royal Regiment, Jessup's Loyal Rangers, and Rogers' King's Rangers) based in Quebec, which had been active in the New York fighting during the Revolutionary War. They were joined by several hundred Associated Loyalists, who came north from New York City. By late summer 1784, some 4,400 Loyalists (and, by 1786, 5,800 Loyalists) resided west and southwest of the Ottawa River, mainly in the Bay of Quinte area. Another 1,200 were at Niagara, and a few hundred more were near Detroit. These settlers brought about 500 black slaves with them. In addition, some 1,800 Iroquois from northern New York and 300 to 400 aboriginals from northwestern native tribes sought refuge from American persecution in western districts of what was then Quebec, especially around the Brantford area, where Joseph Brant became an acknowledged aboriginal leader. As with the blacks, the aboriginal Loyalists never received their full entitlements of land and were prevented by the British government of Upper Canada from selling their grants to European settlers.

By the mid-1780s, the Loyalist migration proper was ended, although Americans claiming to be loyal subjects of the Crown—and receiving treatment as such—continued arriving in British North America until the end of the eighteenth century. Many of the latecomers were German-speaking Mennonites seeking freedom from assimilationist pressures in the United States. Of the thousands of immigrants, only 3,225 actually presented Loyalist claims to the British government. Of these claimants, 468 were females. Women suffered particularly in this first American "civil war," although the nature of the war was seldom acknowledged as such in the United States. Exile was especially difficult for women, as unlike their male counterparts, the women had difficulty in reestablishing relationships in the new land. Most had not been consulted about political decisions in their households, and they found themselves and their needs sacrificed in favor of their men's principal loyalty, which was to the Crown.

The three largest groups of Loyalist exiles from New York settled in three "instant towns" in Nova Scotia and Quebec: Port Roseway (later renamed Shelburne) on the southwest coast of the Nova Scotia peninsula; Saint John at the mouth of the Saint John River in what would soon become the Province of New Brunswick; and Cataraqui (later Kingston) on the eastern shores of Lake Ontario. (Loyalist newcomers also swelled the population of Charlottetown on the Island of Saint John and founded Sydney on Cape Breton Island.) The two Nova Scotia "instant" communities (Port Roseway and Cataraqui) quickly, if only temporarily, replicated the relative urbanity of New York itself. Although initially all these new communities experienced boom-time conditions based on the current availability and future promise of British generosity, their long-term success depended on becoming the centers of some kind of economic activity in their regions. Consequently, Shelburne, located in some of the poorest agricultural land in Nova Scotia and lacking any exploitable resource except fish, quickly declined as a major community. Its failure was assisted by the many problems with land granting in the area, including long delays in surveying. Saint John would find some economic viability through the rich agricultural hinterland of the Saint John River Valley and through the seemingly inexhaustible timber resources of the province. Kingston would struggle on as an administrative center, but with little economic vitality until well into the nineteenth century. Kingston served briefly as a provincial capital, but the other two Loyalist cities were isolated from political power in their respective provinces.

Perhaps half of the Loyalist arrivals first settled in urban surroundings, although many would gradually fan out into the countryside. Loyalist military units tended to settle together. In every province of loyal British North America, Loyalists had difficulty in obtaining the agricultural land they wanted. Surveying land quickly enough in advance of a settlement that was relatively unexpected was not easy, particularly given a shortage of qualified surveyors. Because of the small European population in most of British North America, one might have expected that large quantities of land could be put quickly at the disposal of the Loyalists. But much of this land had been previously granted to large landholders or was claimed by native peoples. The native claims proved not to be much of an obstacle except west of Lake Ontario, but in Nova Scotia much of the land intended for the Loyalists had to be recovered legally from individuals to whom it had been cavalierly granted in large tracts before the Revolution. On the Island of Saint John, land assigned to Loyalists was the center of a fierce legal dispute over ownership. Some of the most attractive land in what would become New Brunswick was peopled by Acadians who held no formal title to it and had to be forcibly evicted.

The difficulties involved in obtaining good land—despite, ironically, the apparent absence of a legitimate resident population—probably helped account for one of the most characteristic features of Loyalist settlement: the extent of the transiency or mobility of the population. Few of the newcomers stayed where they initially settled. The best record of permanence was among the previously mentioned Loyalist military units (The King's Royal Rangers of New York, Jessup's Rangers, Roger's Rangers) that settled in eastern Ontario. In general, Loyalist military groups led by their own officers and united by similar ethnic backgrounds provided an element of coherence otherwise absent in much Loyalist set-

tlement. Other than in these three groups, though, a mobile quest for better land was encouraged by the governments' failure to provide proper
land grants and titles. The American-born tended to become more
quickly dissatisfied with their situations. Recent immigrants to North
America from overseas settled more readily in their new homes than did
those immigrants from other parts of the continent, perhaps because the
overseas immigrants had some prior experience at resettlement (they had
done it before in coming from overseas). The most stable newcomers
were members of the office holding elite, who tended to cluster in the
provincial capitals. In any case, the 1780s saw continual Loyalist relocation, sometimes within the colony of original settlement, sometimes to
another colony of greater promise, and often eventually back to the
United States after subsidies ran out and initial hostility to the Loyalists in
that country had died down. Nobody is certain about the number of Loyalists who ultimately returned to the United States, but it was a considerable number, perhaps as much as half of the initial total.

    If the Loyalists were by and large a restless population in a geographical
sense, they were also a discontented and highly vocal one in political
terms. Although only a fraction of the new arrivals would be formally
compensated for lost property in the United States, all felt that they had
suffered for their allegiance to the Crown and that they were highly de-
serving of both land and government assistance. Moreover, as most of the
Loyalists had lived in the American colonies, they were accustomed to certain levels of participation in the political process. Many ordinary Americans (including some Loyalists) had supported colonial criticisms of
British policy, at least up to the point of the open break with the mother
country, and they did not like arbitrary or oligarchic government and de-
tested any landholding principles (such as leaseholding or the seigneurial
system) except freehold tenure.

    Loyalist political activity in what would become Canada occurred on
different levels simultaneously. On one level, there were the Loyalists' demands to be allowed to share in government. Quebec Loyalists complained bitterly about the absence of a representative assembly in the
province, and Nova Scotia Loyalists complained about the domination of
the government by the older inhabitants. On another level, Loyalists were
often divided among themselves politically. There were two chief internal
divisions: One was between the old colonial office holding American elite
(much of which had gone into exile in England or Nova Scotia during the
war) and a new one that had emerged in the future United States, chiefly
in the junior officer ranks of Loyalist regiments during the course of the

fighting. Many current officers, like James Moody or Justus Sherwood, had not been leaders before the war.

The other division was between the elite and the more articulate among the rank-and-file, who sought a more democratic and open future. The most public example of this latter conflict occurred in the town of Saint John. In the summer of 1783, fifty-five leading Loyalists—men of "the most respectable Characters" by their own assertion—petitioned Governor Sir Guy Carleton for 5,000-acre grants in Nova Scotia in order to regain their old standing. Such grants, the petitioners argued, would be "highly Advantageous (to the colony) in diffusing and supporting a Spirit of Attachment to the British Constitution" (Bell, 1983, p. 240). A counter-petition, organized among several hundred people at a meeting at Roubelet's Tavern in Saint John, argued that the government's acceptance of such requests would produce an exclusion of themselves from the good lands and thus keep them in a subordinate position. A combination of British policy and the ultimate scattering of the Loyalists limited the success of these critics of the ruling elite, at least in the short run. But from time to time such sentiments would reappear in post-Revolution politics.

The Loyalist migration remade British North America in a variety of ways. For one, it led to considerable political readjustments to Quebec and Nova Scotia. Quebec was ultimately divided in 1791 by Parliament into a francophone colony to be called Lower Canada and an anglophone colony to be called Upper Canada. Also, Northern Nova Scotia was separated off from the rest of the province in 1784 and made into the province of New Brunswick, to provide worthy Loyalists with offices and a government of their own. These four colonies all ended up with their own legislative assemblies, in which local politics could be acted out. The newcomers also brought with them strong traditions of political partisanship in the context of representative government; not many Americans in the eighteenth century were true democrats who believed in a sound state in which all had equal rights, although some of the artisan groups among the Loyalists had such values. The Loyalist migration also arrested the prewar tendency to large land grants and the growth of tenancy on landed estates. Most Loyalists received decent-sized but not enormous freehold grants, and the principle and practice of freehold tenure received a substantial boost. Compensation and pensions for Loyalists represented a substantial injection of cash into the local economies (not the government coffers).

Finally, the Loyalists made a substantial contribution to the cultural ethos of British North America. They helped ensure that, in the English-speaking areas of British North America, the language spoken would be American English rather than English with some form of British accent and vocabulary. Patrick Campbell, speaking on the Grand River in Upper Canada in 1792, was answered by a man "in a twang peculiar to the New Englanders": "I viow niew you may depen I's just a-comin." When asked how far, the response was, "I viow niew I guess I do'no,—I guess niew I do'no—I sear niew I guess it is three miles" (Campbell, 1937, p.157). The Loyalists also brought with them American models of domestic housing styles, particularly wood framing construction techniques. In all these respects, the so-called Late Loyalists, who arrived after the mid-1780s in British North America—especially in Upper and Lower Canada—were probably critical. Some of the later arrivals, it should be added, were from pietistic and pacifistic religious sectarian communities (usually of German origin), who came to British North America in search of the right to be left alone to worship and believe as they chose. Certainly, at the time of the War of 1812, the English-speaking colonies of British North America were more American than they had ever been before—or would be afterward.

Highland Immigration

Part of the Loyalist migration, especially to Quebec, involved the movement north of several communities of Highland Scots, communities that had been settled in the American colonies (especially in upstate New York) in the years immediately preceding the American rebellion. One such community, Glengarry, on the north bank of the St. Lawrence River west of Montreal, was peopled by Highlanders who had immigrated to New York from Skye in 1773. The leaders of the prewar emigration were Roman Catholic MacDonalds (or Macdonells), members of Clan Glengarry. Originally settled in the Mohawk Valley under the protection of Superintendent of Indian Affairs William Johnson, these Highlanders actively supported the British cause during the war and could not remain in New York after it. In 1784 an intrepid former Jacobite officer, Captain John Macdonell, led these Scots northwards. The story was later told of his response to a comparison of his expedition with that of Moses. Banging down his cane, Macdonell (by then an old man) exploded: "Damn it, sir, Moses lost half his charges in the Red Sea, and I brought all these folk through without losing a man, woman, or child" (Dumbrille, 1954, p. 7). And he had.

A few parties of Highlanders left Scotland for British North America in 1790 and 1791, but the real outpouring of emigrants from Highland Scotland began only in 1801. Although contemporaries regarded the Highland region as being overpopulated and in need of socioeconomic reform, most of the emigrants of these years did not come from regions where people were being removed from their traditional homes. Many of them came instead from the kelping regions of the western Highlands and islands, where social and economic conditions were in a transitional phase not particularly favorable to the tenants of the region. Harvesting kelp from the seacoasts was an economic activity rendered temporarily profitable by wartime shortages of alternative alkaline substances. It was a labor intensive business, involving working for long hours in freezing waters, and the landlords in the kelping areas were quite fearful of losing their labor force to emigration at the same time as they sought as high a production as possible at the lowest possible cost. One of the few alternatives to exploitation for the discontented small tenant was to sell his livestock and take passage for British North America, and thousands did so at the beginning of the nineteenth century. However, these people were not "cleared" from their lands; indeed, the kelping landlords fought desperately to staunch the human flow of population from the region. In 1803, the kelping lobby encouraged the British Parliament to pass legislation regulating the transatlantic passage of emigrants to the American continent, ostensibly in the name of improved conditions but mainly to raise the cost of passage out of the reach of the average prospective emigrant.

Parliament was responding to a new type of Scottish emigration, one not involving organization by local community leaders but operated by individuals acting as emigrant contractors in the hope of making a profit. This form of contracting became prevalent in the first years of the nineteenth century. The nascent timber trade was already providing vessels sailing to North America without cargo, and after the closure of the Baltic by Napoleon in 1807, the upsurge in the timber trade with British North America provided increasing numbers of vessels that could carry immigrant passengers. Until well into the nineteenth century, the association between timbering and British immigration would be close. The vessels provided relatively cheap transport, sailed to British North America rather than to the United States, and dropped their passengers either in important timber ports or at important timbering regions (such as the Miramichi in northeastern New Brunswick), thus influencing the patterns of settlement. As little assisted passage was available before 1815, most of the immigrants of this period had some capital with which to purchase transportation, but many arrived in British North America without money to obtain land.

The emigration from the Highlands to British North America during these years—undertaken by between 6,000 and 10,000 people—was terminated less by official opposition than by the resumption of the Napoleonic war in 1803, which interrupted transatlantic transportation until 1815. Most of the emigrants from Scotland headed for either a Maritime province destination or for Upper Canada. By 1815, Gaelic was the third most common European language spoken in British North America, extremely prevalent in Prince Edward Island, parts of Nova Scotia and Cape Breton Island, and eastern Upper Canada. One of the few individuals who persisted in assisting Highland emigrants after 1803 was the Earl of Selkirk, who, in a famous book published in 1805—*Observations on the Present State of the Highlands of Scotland, with a View of the Causes and Probable Consequences of Emigration*—insisted that a redundant agrarian population from the Highlands had the right to relocate itself to land-rich North America, where it might be able to preserve its traditional customs and way of life. Selkirk established Highland communities in Prince Edward Island, in Upper Canada, and on the Red River in Rupert's Land in what is now the province of Manitoba. The Highland settlement in Red River later came into open conflict with a resident Métis population composed of the children of francophone fur traders and aboriginal women.

Characteristics of the New Immigration and Settlement

The new immigration confirmed the tendency of the non-French population of British North America to diverge from the officially supported Church of England in the directions both of Protestant dissent and of Roman Catholicism. Unlike the thirteen American colonies, where the Church of England was dominant in some colonies, Anglicanism in early British North America was outnumbered not simply by Protestant dissent but, more importantly, by Roman Catholics. Indeed, Catholics were in the overwhelming majority in Lower Canada, were a majority in Newfoundland and Rupert's Land, and were the largest single denomination in Cape Breton and Prince Edward Island by the end of the eighteenth century. By the 1780s the British authorities had given up attempting to enforce positive proscriptions against Catholics in the various provinces.

But official tolerance of Roman Catholicism, even the right to hold land, was not the same as full acceptance. The situation was complex. By the end of the eighteenth century, Catholics were enfranchised only in the Canadas (by the Constitutional Act of 1791) and in Nova Scotia (by a 1789 legislative enactment). New Brunswick withdrew Catholic enfranchisement after its first elections and did not restore it until 1810. Prince Edward Island did not allow Catholics to vote until 1830. Newfoundland, Cape Breton, and Rupert's Land had no popularly elected political bodies—in the first two colonies partly because of the Catholic presence. Moreover, until 1830 the Canadas alone allowed Catholics to sit on the legislative bodies for which they could vote. These discriminations against Catholics encouraged British North Americans who were Catholic—especially those Catholics residing elsewhere than Lower Canada—to think of themselves as outsiders and thus to view their communities as distinctive cultural units.

Few of the new immigrants made their way into the Canadas before 1815. Lower Canada remained dominantly French Canadian, and Upper Canada was largely American and ethnic Loyalist. Almost everywhere in the region, the cultural landscape of early British North America was far more complex than a single concept of biculturalism could describe. In addition to the British and the French Canadian cultures, a variety of emergent vernacular cultures, most with French or British roots, flourished. Only the French in Lower Canada had a reasonably mature and well-developed culture, dominating throughout most of the province even though it was governed by men with an alternative set of cultural values and assumptions. Even in colonies where the French did not predominate, outside the major urban areas there was a cultural complexity. There existed American culture, mixtures of American and regional British culture, isolated regional British culture (particularly Irish and Highland Scots), and even resurgent Acadian culture.

In the years before 1815 the politically dominant British had proved unable to create a cultural hegemony. This was partly because of the presence of the French in Lower Canada. But in the absence of national institutions, the French in Canada had little influence on policy elsewhere in British North America. Nevertheless, the British seemed unable or unwilling to find ways to transmit and impose their official culture upon the divergent vernacular ones. Absolutely critical in limiting cultural hegemony was the absence of a common and unifying traumatic experience, such as the war of national liberation experienced by the American colonies. Unlike in the United States, which was also ethnically complex, British North America had no powerful fusing force of a national revolution and no development of a pervasive national political and sociocultural ideology. The War of 1812 was seriously felt only by Upper Canada and to a lesser extent by Lower Canada, while passing virtually unacknowledged in the Atlantic region. Perhaps significantly, the War of 1812 did provide a unifying experience and mythology for many Upper Canadians, but not one that could be extended elsewhere in the British colonies. And the Upper Canadian experience was to some extent itself limited by the fact that, in its insistence on extreme commitment to British loyalty, it cut against the grain of the still-dominant American population of the province.

Timeline

1758   Conquest of Louisbourg.

1759   Battle of Quebec (Plains of Abraham); beginning of Yankee migration to Nova Scotia.

1763   Treaty of Paris; Proclamation of 1763; end of Yankee migration.

1767   Island of Saint John distributed to proprietors by lottery.

1772   Arrival of *Alexander* on Island of Saint John with Highland Scots settlers.

1773   Arrival of *Hector* with Highland Scots settlers on north coast of Nova Scotia; other Highland Scots settle in New York.

1774   Western territory restored to Quebec.

1775   Beginning of American Revolutionary War.

1781   Surrender of Lord Cornwallis and end of Revolutionary War fighting.

1782   Guy Carleton sketches out policy for Loyalist relocation.

1783   Great migration of Loyalists to Nova Scotia; Treaty of Paris confirms American independence, cedes Ohio Valley to the United States.

1784   Creation of New Brunswick; Glengarry Scots led northward to Quebec.

1789   Catholics enfranchised in Nova Scotia.

1790   Migration of Highland Scots to British North America resumes.

1791   Constitutional Act of 1791 divides Quebec into Upper and Lower Canada.

1801   Treaty of Amiens reopens Atlantic Ocean for Highland Scots' emigration to British North America.

1803   Passenger Vessel Act passed to regulate immigrant traffic; war with Napoleon resumes.

1807 Closure of the Baltic.
1812 War of 1812 begins with American invasion of Upper Canada.
1815 War of 1812 ends with neither side victorious in North America.

Significant People, Places, and Events

ALEXANDER Chartered vessel that carried the first large contingent of Highland Scots (from the Highlands and islands) to the Island of Saint John in 1772. These Scots were MacDonalds and were led by their traditional elite.

ALLINE, HENRY (1784–1784) Rhode Island-born resident of Nova Scotia, who led a great religious revival in the colony during the years of the American Revolution.

AMIENS, PEACE OF A two-year break, 1801–1803, in the lengthy Napoleonic Wars, which enabled emigrants from the north of Scotland to make their way to British North America.

"BOOK OF NEGROES" A book in which was kept the names of blacks in New York who were allowed to accompany the Loyalist vessels to Nova Scotia in 1783.

BRANT, JOSEPH (1742–1807) A mixed-blood Mohawk warrior who became the military leader of the loyal Iroquois during the American Revolution. He later led his people to the Grand River Valley and established Brantford, which was named for him.

CAMPBELL, PATRICK (fl. 1759–1824) A Scotsman who traveled through the North American colonies in the 1790s and reported on the customs of the residents.

CARLETON, SIR GUY (1724–1808) The British commander in New York in 1783, he was responsible for organizing the transport to Nova Scotia of the thousands of Loyalists in the city.

DESBARRES, J. F. W. (1721–1824) A Swiss-born marine surveyor, DesBarres was governor of Cape Breton Island and Prince Edward Island after the American Revolution. Before the war, he had established a large estate at Tatamagouche on the north shore of Nova Scotia, peopling it with Acadian tenants.

GLENGARRY A Scots Highland community in eastern Upper Canada, famed as the center of Gaelic culture in the province.

HECTOR The vessel that brought Highland settlers to the shores of northern Nova Scotia in 1773. It and its passengers have been mythologized as the first party of Highlanders to immigrate to Nova Scotia.

JOHNSON, SIR WILLIAM (c. 1715–1774) A British Indian agent, he parlayed his influence with the Six Nations in the Mohawk Valley into an estate of several hundred thousand acres, which he peopled with settlers from the Scottish Highlands (most of whom become Loyalists) in the years before the American Revolution.

LOYALISTS The term preferred by those who supported the Crown during the American Revolution. Many went into exile from the United States after the war, and more than 30,000 resettled in what is now Canada.

MACDONALD, JOHN (1742–1810) Led a party of Catholic MacDonalds to the Island of Saint John in 1772 and established them as tenants on land he had obtained. He later served as a captain in the British Army.

MOHAWK VALLEY REGION An area of upstate New York along the Mohawk River that was settled by Scots Highlanders in the 1770s. During the American Revolution it was the scene of bitter guerrilla fighting between rebels and those loyal to the Crown, including a substantial number of aboriginals.

OWEN, CAPTAIN WILLIAM (1737–1778) A Welsh naval officer, he received a large grant of land on Campobello Island in 1769 as "lord of the soil." In 1770 he led a party of colonists to the island and settled them as tenants.

PLAINS OF ABRAHAM (Battle of Quebec) The high plateau outside Quebec where the French and the English armies fought the decisive battle of the Seven Years' War—won by the English—in September of 1759.

SELKIRK, THOMAS DOUGLAS, FIFTH EARL OF (1771–1820) A Scots nobleman who established a number of settlements in British North America (in Prince Edward Island, Upper Canada, and Red River) between 1803 and 1812. He was the leading British proponent of North American immigration in the years before the War of 1812.

SIERRA LEONE An African colony established by British humanitarians in the 1790s, with most of the colonists consisting of discontented black Loyalists resident from Nova Scotia.

TREATY OF PARIS (1763) The treaty that concluded the Seven Years' War. By its terms, France surrendered all of its North American territory, Britain kept Florida and acquired Canada and Acadia, and France compensated Spain for its losses by ceding to it the western half of Louisiana and the port of New Orleans.

TREATY OF PARIS (1783) The treaty that confirmed the independence of the United States from Great Britain. The Americans set the terms of the treaty, refusing to guarantee compensation for Britain's losses and insisting on the transfer of the Ohio region from the British.

WAR OF 1812 A war begun by the United States in 1812 with an invasion of Canada, which the Americans had always coveted. The war, fought mainly in Upper Canada, on the Great Lakes, and on the high seas, came to an inconclusive end, with both sides agreeing to return to the prewar status quo. Both sides claimed the victory at the time, and each still has its own version of events.

YANKEE PLANTERS The 8,000 to 10,000 American settlers who came from New England to Nova Scotia between 1759 and 1763. Many ultimately returned to their original homes.

Documents

Robinson and Rispin on the People of Nova Scotia

In the early 1770s, two Yorkshiremen visited Nova Scotia with a view to obtaining land there. They published an account of the colony in England in 1774.

The New Englanders are a stout, tall, well-made people, extremely fluent of speech, and are remarkably courteous to strangers. Indeed, the inhabitants, in general, poor as well as rich, possess much complacence and good manners, with which they treat each other as well as foreigners. To the honour of this country, we may say, that abusive language, swearing and profaneness, is hardly known amongst them, which is the great scandal and reproach of Britain.

The Sabbath is most religiously observed; none of them will do any business, or travel, on that day; and all kinds of sports, plays and revels, are strictly prohibited. They take great care to educate their children in the fear of the Lord, and early to implant in them a right notion of religion, and the great duty they owe to God and their parents. The children have a very engaging address, and always accompany their answers with "Yes, Sir"; or "No, Sir;" or, "Yes, Ma'am"; or "No, Ma'am," to any questions that are asked them; and, on passing their superiors, always move the hat and foot.

The men wear their hair queu'd, and their cloathing, except on Sundays, is generally home-made, with checked shirts; and in winter, they wear linsey-woolsey shirts, also breeches, stockings and shoes: instead of which, in summer, they have long trowsers, that reach down to their feet. They dress exceedingly gay on a Sunday, and then wear the finest cloth and linen. Many of them wear ruffled shirts, who, during the rest of the week, go without shoes and stockings; and there is so great a difference in their dress, that you would scarce know them to be the same people.

The women, in general (except on Sundays) wear woolseys both for petticoats and aprons; and instead of stays, they wear a loose jacket, like a bedgown. It is owing to the high price of stays, and not to any dislike they have to them, that they are not worn in common. The few that are used, are imported either from New or Old England, as they have not any stay-makers amongst them. The women, in summer, in imitation of the men, usually go without stockings or shoes, and many without caps. They take much pain with their hair, which they tie in their necks, and fix it to the crown of their heads. Nor are they on the Sabbath less gay than the men, dressing for the most part in silks and callicoes, with long ruffles; their hair dressed high, and many without caps. When at Church, or Meeting, from the mistress to the scullion girl, they have all their fans. We even thought, in the article of dress, they outdid the good women of England.

. . . . Such of the New Englanders, into whose manners and characters we particularly inspected, appeared to us to be a lazy indolent people. In general, they continue in bed till seven or eight o'clock in the morning; and the first thing they do, after quitting it, is to get a glass of rum, after which they prepare for breakfast, before they go out to work, and return to dinner by eleven: They go out again about two, and at four return to tea. Sometimes they work an hour, or two after, and then return home, both masters and their servants, amongst whom there seems to be no distinction; and you scarce can know one from the other.

Source: Robinson, John, and Rispin, Thomas, *A Journey through Nova-Scotia, Containing a Particular Account of the Country and Its Inhabitants* (York, 1774), pp. 54–56.

Thomas Halliday on His Hard Life on Prince Edward Island

In this letter to Lord Selkirk, the Edinburgh-born stonemason Thomas Halliday described his experiences as a settler on Prince Edward Island, typical ones for early Scots in the Atlantic region. The spelling and capitalization are reproduced as Halliday wrote them.

Thomas Halliday to Lord Selkirk, Cape Bear, 28 October 1815 . . . .

I Resolved for to go the Island and Settle the farm. . . . When we got to Wood Islands I got a Lodging for my famley and the night that I Got them there Mrs. Halliday had a miscarriage and no person with us but the Childring. There was not a Woman that could Speak to her nearer than Wood Islands and that was 5 Miles. But through the Blessing of God she got better again. Then I set tow clear Land for to plant in the Spring of the Year but I had all our provitions to Carry from the Wood Islands on my back in the Winter Lame as I was for I could not put on Shoes but only Moggisons a kind of Large Brougs made of untaned Leather. But I keept good heart thinking that I would not Be to Dow the Same nixt year. But My Money got all spent, then I had to Sell Sugar and Tea and Coffie that we Brought from Hallifax for the mor nessary things to keep my life in and the Lives of My familey. Then in the spring of the year I applied to Mr. Williams and he Trusted Me with forty Bushels of potatoes to plant. But the Land Being so bad I did not get then at the time of Digging. Then the Winter Cuming on I engaged with the people of Wood Islands for to keep School for five Months for the Some of Ten pounds and to take any kind of produce that they chused to give. I was also to have bed and Bord and to go to my own house every Saterday and Return on the Monday in time for the School. Bujt such a five months I nevour had since I knew the Worald, for they have no beds but Share and they all to a man have the itch and Lousy. Evary night that I Went to My own house I was to be over-haled before that I could cume near a Bed. But I shall only teil you that I only had Bread twice in all the five Months. Nothing but potatoes and Rotten Stinking herring and to ly on the floor on Straw in there Lousy itchy Blanckets, so that with all our Care Both my Wife and my Self got the Highland Scabb and when the Spring of the year did cum I had to gett sumthing from a Docter Mcally for to get clear of it. Again this year Sowed a Bushel and a half of wheat and so much barly and planted plenty of Potatoes and the first year I cleared a half acer of Land of all the Stumps of the treas for a Garden and Burnt forty Bushels of shels into Lime for it. Brought Sea weed and kelp from the shoe for it, but for all my truball it has not payed me for the mice has Destroyed Both it and all my Crops so that for provitions we ar no Better then at first and for Clothing A Great Deal worse for the Land is indeed very Bad.

Source: Bumsted, J. M., ed., "Thomas Halliday, Mary Cochrane, The Earl of Selkirk, and the Island," *The Island Magazine,* no. 19 (spring/summer 1986), p. 31.

Bibliography

Bailyn, Bernard, and Philip D. Morgan, eds., *Strangers Within the Realm: Cultural Margins of the First British Empire* (Durham: University of North Carolina Press, 1991).

Bell, David G., *Early Loyalist Saint John: The Origin of New Brunswick Politics, 1783–1786* (Fredericton, New Brunswick: New Ireland Press, 1983).

Brebner, John Bartlet, *The Neutral Yankees of Nova Scotia: A Marginal Colony during the Revolutionary Years* (reprint, Toronto: McClelland and Stewart, 1969).

Brown, Wallace, *The Good Americans: The Loyalists in the American Revolution* (New York: Morrow, 1969).

Bumsted, J. M., *The People's Clearance: Highland Emigration to British North America 1770–1815* (Edinburgh, Scotland: University of Edinburgh Press, 1982).

Campbell, Patrick, *Travels in the Interior Inhabited Parts of North America in the Years 1791 and 1792*, ed. H. H. Langton (Toronto: Champlain Society, 1937), 157.

Conrad, Margaret, ed., *Intimate Relations: Family and Community in Planter Nova Scotia 1759–1800* (Fredericton, New Brunswick: Acadiensis Press, 1995).

Dumbrille, Dorothy, *Up and Down the Glens* (Toronto: Ryerson Press, 1954).

Johnston, C. M., ed., *Valley of the Six Nations: A Collection of Documents on the Indian Lands of the Grand River* (Toronto: Champlain Society, 1964).

MacDonald, M. A., *Rebels and Royalists: The Lives and Material Culture of New Brunswick Early English-Speaking Settlers* (Fredericton, New Brunswick: New Ireland Press, 1990).

Mathews, Hazel C., *The Mark of Honour* (Toronto: University of Toronto Press, 1965).

Walker, James W. St. G., *The Black Loyalists: The Search for the Promised Land in Nova Scotia and Sierra Leone, 1783–1870* (New York: Africana Publishing Co., 1976).

Immigration to British North America, 1815–1867

ETWEEN 1815 AND THE EARLY 1860S, the population of the British colonies in North America grew from 600,000 to more than 3,500,000. This sixfold population expansion contributed to the beginning of serious discussions over the unification of British North America, as well as to a growing interest in westward expansion from coast to coast on the northern half of the continent. Although much of the growth in numbers of people resulted from natural increase, especially in French Canada, a good deal was also the product of a substantial movement of people, mainly from Europe—and particularly from the British Isles—to British North America during these years. They helped transform British North America from a collection of colonies in which more than half of the population of European origin spoke French to one in which English predominated in all provinces, including United Canada, by 1850. In several provinces, notably Prince Edward Island and the Cape Breton part of Nova Scotia, more people spoke Gaelic than French.

After the end of the Napoleonic Wars, the British government and the British ruling/landlord classes became convinced that the British Isles were overpopulated. They increasingly saw emigration as a preferable alternative to public assistance for the poor and underemployed, as well as an outlet for superfluous farmers in an era of agricultural transformation. "Shovelling out paupers" became standard practice for municipal authorities with large numbers on the poor rates (the local taxes used to support the impoverished). Nearly 2 million residents of the British Isles sailed westward to destinations in British North America between 1815 and the 1860s; these were part of a larger exodus of people from the British Isles to the United States and other British settlement colonies (in South Africa, Australia, and New Zealand). After 1849 some even set out on the Pacific Ocean to settle on the West Coast of British North America. However, not all of the 2 million coming to British North America settled permanently there—perhaps as many as half moved on to the United States, and some unknown number returned to Britain. Nor was the traffic coming solely from one direction. In 1853, for example, Canada West (see Significant People, Places, and Events) was the seventh most popular destination of immigrants arriving at New York. In any event, a good many immigrants did put down new roots in British North America during this period.

Much of the folk memory of this great movement includes tales of great suffering endured by those involved in the process. They were driven from their homes and taken advantage of by unscrupulous ship captains, then they landed destitute in howling wildernesses. Although the nature of the tales varies with the amount of wealth and education of the emigrants, even the better-off classes felt that they had suffered substantially. No shortage of abuse existed, in truth, but many of the problems occurred—particularly with the wealthier arrivals—because the British had a very idealized picture of the wilderness and did not take advantage of the good advice they were given. Although there was some exaggeration of how favorable the conditions were in British North America, literally hundreds of emigration pamphlets and manuals (as well as letters home from previous emigrants) emphasized that the climate was different from what they were used to, that clearing a farm from the wilderness was expensive and labor-intensive, and that amenities were in short supply in most parts of the colonies. Almost to a person, however, the emigrants believed that such strictures would not apply to them, and most suffered as a result.

All other events in British North America—including the Rebellions of 1837, the Union of the Canadas in 1841, and the Gold Rush on the Pacific Slope in the late 1850s and early 1860s—took place against the backdrop of the massive movement of migration and resettlement during these years. The importance of immigration is demonstrated in the pages of the *Dictionary of Canadian Biography*. Of the 538 persons given entries in volume 7 of that work, covering those who died between 1835 and 1850—and including much of the leadership of British North America in the first half of the nineteenth century—fewer than 200 were born in the colonies, and most of those were born in Lower Canada. The remainder came almost entirely from the British Isles and the United States.

Patterns and Problems

Detailed public record keeping was only in its infancy in the first half of the nineteenth century, as was public regulation of the movement of people, even across oceans and borders. As a result, the statistical data available for this emigration/immigration on either side of the Atlantic are extremely limited. The various provinces of British North America maintained no overall control or data on the numbers arriving. Counting of arrivals was done most systematically—after 1829—by the port of Quebec, which was probably the single most important official port of arrival for immigrants in British North America. But immigrants also arrived at dozens of other ports, and some ships dropped off their human cargoes on remote beaches, where no counting or processing was ever done. On the British side, some attempt was made to record numbers of people departing, but the best single series of records of annual emigration to British North America (published by the British Parliament) relies far too heavily on the Quebec records and thus substantially underrecords the total flow. It is probably more useful at presenting the relationship of British North American numbers to the numbers of people departing for the United States and to other British colonies, such as Australia. No control at all over the movement of people existed on either side of the border between the United States and British North America in this period. As a result, historians have really no idea of how many people came to British North America from the United States in these years or how many recently arrived British emigrants passed on into the United States.

If the total numbers of emigrants from the British Isles to North America is fairly problematic, the proportions of people departing from the various constituent parts of the United Kingdom can only be estimated on the broadest terms. Arrivals at the Port of Quebec, 1829–1859, suggest that emigration from Ireland represented more than half the total flow, that from England about one third, and that from Scotland the remainder. According to one study, the Irish percentage of total immigration to British North America was 68.5 percent in 1825–1829, 64.2 percent 1830–1839, 64.2 percent 1840–1849, 41.1 percent 1850–1859, and 22.4 percent in 1860–1869. But even if such proportions are relatively accurate, they obscure the realities of movement from the various regions of Britain, which were quite distinctive. Emigration from the northern part of Ireland was quite a different matter from emigration from southern Ireland, particularly in the timing and the characteristics of the emigrants. Emigration from the Highlands of Scotland operated independ-

*This illustration of Irish emigrants leaving the seaport of Cork in Ireland
en route to North America first appeared in the* Illustrated London News
on 10 May 1851. (National Archives of Canada)

ently of emigration from the Lowlands of Scotland, and again, the characteristics of the emigrants were quite different. Moreover, in this period,
emigration from Wales was lumped together in the records with that from
England. The largest port of departure from Britain was undoubtedly Liverpool, which enjoyed a disproportionate number of regular sailings on
passenger vessels, most of which headed for ports in the United States. Arrivals in Quebec embarked from more than seventy other ports in England, Scotland, and Ireland, however, and many vessels collected passengers outside the ports as well.

What is known about the numbers suggests that Scottish emigration
remained relatively steady throughout the period at 10–15 percent of the
total flow, although a far higher proportion of Highlanders than Lowlan-
ders departed in these years. Irish emigration varied annually from 30–70
percent of the total numbers, with Irish movement to North America before the 1840s dominated by people (mainly Protestants) from the north
of Ireland. The Irish emigrants began only in the mid-1840s to include
huge numbers of Catholic southerners. As a result, the whole nature of
Irish emigration to British North America was quite different from Irish
emigration to the United States. British North America received far more

Irish immigrants in the early period than did the United States. Also, the Irish flow to what is now Canada included far more Protestants and Orangists (a political sect) than did that to the United States, which was composed almost exclusively of Catholics from the south. The proportion of immigrants to British North America from England (and Wales) increased substantially after 1850. Although the number of Welsh was never calculated, it probably represented about 10 percent of the English total in the later years of the period.

The national and regional complexity of the population in the British Isles produces several interesting questions and problems. It is tempting from a twenty-first-century perspective, for example, to assume that the British emigrants were a relatively homogeneous group of people, although on many levels nothing could be further from the truth. Each of the historic nations of Britain continued in the nineteenth century to preserve its own cultures and its own histories. There was no homogeneity of either language or religion. Many of the Irish, especially in the south, spoke the Irish tongue, and almost all Scots from north of the Highland fault spoke Gaelic as a first language, but those in the Lowlands spoke a Scottish variant of English. Dialects and linguistic variants were also extensive in England and Wales. In Wales, there was a north-south language division paralleling those in Ireland and Scotland. In both Wales and Scotland, the northerners were more likely to speak non-English tongues, but in Ireland the northerners far more commonly spoke English.

At the same time as these immigrations, the nineteenth century saw considerable growth of a common Britishness that to various extents overcame regional distinctions in British North America. On the other hand, people's acceptance of the concepts of Great Britain and "Britishness" were quite variable. Many of the southern Irish, for example, would not have agreed either that they were British or were willing subjects of the British Crown. As a result, American immigration history tends to regard the Irish emigration as separate from the "British" one. Although this may reflect American realities, it does not work so well for British North America, where a far larger proportion of the Irish emigrants were from the Ulster counties, which were proudly loyal to the British monarchy.

Another difference between immigration to the United States and that to British North America was in nature of the vessels employed in the transatlantic passage, which had certain ramifications for the sorts of emigrants who departed for each of the countries. Traffic to the United States tended to occur, especially after 1840, in large vessels specifically designed to carry passengers, but the voyage to British North America was usually executed in smaller vessels designed for the timber trade. These timber vessels sailed to Britain and then carried passengers on the return voyage in makeshift accommodations in lieu of sailing in ballast. The result of this difference was that the cost of the passage to British North America was considerably cheaper than that to the United States. When these substantial differences in cost were combined with the much shorter duration of the passage from the British Isles to the eastern seaports of British North America (which meant that fewer provisions were required for the journey), the result was probably that far more of the immigrants to British North America sailed on extremely limited budgets and without much capital in reserve than those who went to the United States. It is hard to generalize, however, because the rates for passengers varied substantially from time to time. One Belfast advertisement from 1820 put the charge for a family of husband, wife, and six children to the United States at eighty guineas, for example, and the cost of the same family to New Brunswick at twenty-four guineas. Such rates meant that only those with considerable capital could afford to sail at all in 1820. Rates by mid-century were much lower, though. Many of those arriving in British North American ports without capital may have intended to move on to the United States when they had managed to accumulate the means, but how many actually managed to do so is another matter entirely. Large numbers of those arriving with little or no capital were already in debt to friends or relatives at home. They had borrowed the price of steerage passage and were bound to repay the debt out of their first earnings.

Both costs and geography also meant that, throughout the period, British North America rather than the United States received the vast bulk of the emigrants from the Highlands of Scotland. As immigrants, many of these Highlanders arrived virtually destitute in British North America and could not afford to continue on to the United States. Sufficient numbers of Gaelic-speakers from Highland Scotland arrived in various parts of British North America (notably parts of Upper Canada, the eastern townships of Lower Canada, Cape Breton Island, and Prince Edward Island) to make the language an important medium of communication in these areas in ways that simply did not exist in the United States, where newcomers were much more encouraged to assimilate to the dominant society.

The Atlantic Passage

From the middle of the eighteenth century, the Atlantic Passage had been notorious for the horrible conditions under which ordinary emigrants had suffered on their way to North America. The passage by sailing vessel took a minimum of eight weeks at sea; there were no standards for ships or provisions and no health inspections; and little medical attention was given to emigrants. The British landholding classes, who were basically opposed to emigration before 1815, took advantage of the many well-publicized horror stories to pass legislation beginning in 1803 that regulated the passage, ostensibly to protect the emigrants but also to make emigration more difficult. After 1815, however, when emigration from Britain seemed a good solution to the perceived problem of superfluous population, efforts to regulate the passage became more concerned with the welfare of the passengers. This became a matter of extreme public interest during the Irish famine years of the 1840s, when the exodus from Ireland and Scotland reached its peak. Those who could afford first-class passage seldom suffered excessively in terms of conditions and accommodations. First-class passengers ate and drank well. Companionship was convivial, and most vessels had well-stocked wine cellars and libraries.

Those attempting to cross the Atlantic at minimal expense were less well treated, however, especially on the timber vessels (almost all sailing ships) that carried most of the steerage passengers to British North America in improvised accommodations below deck. Parliament made a series of efforts to close legal loopholes and improve conditions on the passage, and the various provinces of British North America acted to protect themselves from the dangers of mass emigration by taxing new arrivals to pay for the establishment of quarantine stations—which ended up serving as further incubation centers for contagious disease.

A series of related concerns bedeviled the passage. One was the unsanitary and unhealthy conditions in steerage, with passengers crammed together in communal facilities and kept below deck for weeks on end, eating bad food, drinking fetid water, and sleeping in overcrowded quarters. One European passenger wrote:

The weak and the ill would have preferred the gruel promised in the advertised menu, but it was available only once or twice during the crossing and then not in sufficient quantities. Half of the applicants were turned down when they held up their tin cups to the distributor of soup. During meals the mess hall looked like a pigsty, but what else could be expected when five-six hundred people were thronged together in a limited space and were weaving in and out to get their rations? . . . In addition, you should try to imagine the uninhibited disgorging of the seasick before the eyes of the diners, and you have some notion of the delights of the table in steerage. (Overland, 1989, p. 65)

Most reformers insisted that the slavers were treating slaves on the passage considerably better than many ship owners treated their steerage passengers. Related to shipboard conditions was the incidence of contagious disease being brought aboard vessels by emigrants who were not given even minimal health inspections before embarkation. Another whole dimension of the passage was the criminal mistreatment and abuse of emigrants in the various ports of embarkation in the British Isles, especially the larger and busier ones. Stories of the horrors of mistreatment by landlords in Britain merged together with those of the transatlantic passage to create a folk memory for many of the British ethnic groups in British North America who peopled it in the first half of the nineteenth century.

Patterns of Emigration and Immigration

Although many variations were possible in the ways Britons travelled across the Atlantic and resettled in British North America, the arrangement of the passage and of the resettlement were typically separate and independent actions dominated by different variables. The literature on emigration has been dominated by the passage, while the literature on immigration has dealt mainly with land policy and settlement. Overall, however, four basic patterns prevailed: assisted emigration and settlement; unassisted individual emigration and assisted settlement; communal or assisted emigration and unassisted settlement; and unassisted emigration and unassisted settlement.

Assisted Passage and Resettlement

A package of assistance on the passage and aid in resettlement most frequently involved governments, often more than one government acting in concert on either side of the border. For example, government on the British side would provide assistance in passage, the colonial governments would provide land, and one government or the other would offer tools and subsistence to colonists while they were getting established. Such schemes frequently involved disbanded soldiers and sailors, especially after the War of 1812, or poor artisans in the 1820s, often from Scotland or Ireland. The two private parties who attempted to offer such a package were Lord Selkirk (whose schemes were mostly before 1815) and the Earl of Egremont, working in collaboration with local parish committees and private emigration societies in Sussex in the 1830s in a scheme usually called the Petworth Project. Petworth immigrants arrived in Quebec and traveled up the St. Lawrence in open boats to destinations in Upper Canada. (These immigrants had been promised a journey up the Rideau Canal, but although the canal was officially open, it was never really usable in the 1830s.) Although these settlers traveled on well-supplied ships to cross the Atlantic, they found the inland run very intimidating, particularly as the promised journey on the Rideau Canal never materialized. Some immigrants settled in the Peterborough area, but most went on to Toronto or beyond to the western districts. In Toronto they became part of the thousands of immigrants passing through the town in the 1830s. The Petworth immigration of 1832–1837 demonstrated that it was possible to reduce the unpleasantness of the transatlantic passage with careful planning, by spending a little more money, and by regulating matters more carefully. This immigration also proved that some sponsors and some immigrants were prepared to pay a little more for additional comfort and safety in crossing the Atlantic. The real problem, as it transpired, was in the inability to improve the inland passage.

The various government experiments with assisted resettlement demonstrated that the cost of the process was extremely high. The parliamentary undersecretary at the Colonial Office in Britain, Robert John Wilmot-Horton, was an advocate of government sponsorship to rid the country of unwanted paupers. But a series of parliamentary committees in the later 1820s demonstrated that even with the greatest economy possible, the cost to the public of removing a family of five from Britain and placing them on land in British North America would be a minimum of 60 pounds per family. Local taxpayers understandably objected to footing the bill at this level of expenditure, however much Wilmot-Horton insisted that the price was cheaper than continued assistance under the "poor laws." Reports from Upper Canada, moreover, suggested that only the poorest settlers would remain in the bush for any amount of time.

Unassisted Passage and Assisted Resettlement

One of the major reasons that Wilmot-Horton's schemes were never fully implemented was that an alternative (and less expensive) solution emerged in the late 1820s. It was advocated by Edward Gibbon Wakefield, who concentrated less on the passage than on the disposal of colonial land. Unlike Wilmot-Horton's ideas, attacked as "shovelling out paupers," Wakefield's approach concentrated on land policy. In place of attempting to give the land away to newcomers, Wakefield favored charging a "sufficient price" that would ensure revenue for colonial improvements and help guarantee that those acquiring land began with some capital.

In the earlier period of immigration, land had been freely distributed to proprietors who would agree to develop the land and sponsor emigrants to settle on it. The Island of Saint John (Prince Edward Island) was a perfect example of such an arrangement. On the Island, the proprietors offered to rent small properties to newcomers, which meant that immigrants could obtain land without capital or local connections. A similar policy was followed by Colonel Thomas Talbot in Upper Canada. The chief problem with such proprietary arrangements was that most landlords were not eager to spend money to develop their lands. The Wakefield plan involved the creation of privately funded land companies—which could raise large amounts of capital for development—utilizing public lands in the colonies for which they paid annual revenue. This scheme was basically one that privatized organized settlement. Three large land companies gradually emerged: the Canada Company in Upper Canada; the British American Land Company in Lower Canada; and the New Brunswick and Nova Scotia Land Company. The Canada Company was the first and most active of these companies.

The Transatlantic Contractors

The owners and captains of timber vessels provided yet another dimension to the emigration process. These vessels were either chartered to people who collected passengers or were filled through advertisements in distressed areas. The story of the brig *Albion* is fairly representative. The *Albion* was built for a Welsh merchant family in 1815. Her owner turned to the distressed farmers of Cardiganshire to provide a human cargo to North America. He found 180 people in 1819 who responded to his advertisements in English and Welsh and were willing to take passage to New Brunswick. They paid considerable sums of money to purchase their passage. After a transatlantic voyage in the overcrowded vessel, the *Albion's* passengers disembarked at Saint John with little money and no local connections. The ship owner felt no obligation to the passengers once they were on shore, and it was only thanks to the assistance of local inhabitants (who raised several pledges of money in Saint John and Fredericton to assist them) that the people of the *Albion* were able to survive and ultimately flourish. An element of luck helped as well. The new surveyor-general of New Brunswick, Anthony Lockwood, took the strangely clad newcomers under his wing. He quickly visited and surveyed a potential settlement site not far from Fredericton, about 100 kilometers up the Saint John River. Lockwood moved the immigrants to what would become known as the Cardigan Settlement. Ninety-eight immigrants in all, including eighteen men, eighteen women, thirty-three boys, and twenty-nine girls, were brought to the site in the autumn of 1819. According to contemporary accounts from the time, the Welsh were totally unfamiliar with work in the woods but were willing to learn. At the same time, they were unable to build the types of houses they needed because of their inexperience, and their first winter was very difficult. Many returned to the towns, although some stuck it out and would eventually settle in.

Like many of the timber vessels, the *Albion* filled its hold with people drawn from a single area. They knew one another and all spoke the same language, which in the case of the *Albion* passengers was Welsh. The mutual support of such a group was undoubtedly useful to them in their time of trial. The same was true of Scots Highlanders, often Gaelic-speakers, whose passage was paid by lairds (lords) seeking to remove redundant population, particularly from the islands of the Hebrides. The Highlanders were particularly victimized on the passage. The Hebrides landlords often chartered vessels to transport their tenants but seldom provided the passengers with any assistance except their passage. Such emigrants arrived in North America almost totally destitute, requiring massive amounts of charity just to survive. As a result, the Hebridean landlords understandably acquired reputations as the cruelest of men. Other vessels loaded up at large seaports (like Liverpool or Glasgow or Dublin) with individual emigrants and emigrant families who had little in common except their passage. When they were deposited at docks in British North America, many of these folk faced a far more uncertain future and often far more public hostility. Those with capital may have been able to obtain land, but many poor emigrants who came with the transatlantic contractors ended up in the city in which they arrived, desperately seeking work as unskilled laborers. When the work was available, all was well. But British North America had both a seasonal and a cyclical economy, and not everyone could be employed.

The Unassisted Immigrants

Most new arrivals in British North America had sailed at their own expense and had arrived alone or in small family units. Often they were forced to endure weeks of quarantine before finally being allowed to seek their fortune. Some of these immigrants paid their own costs out of modest capital, usually acquired by selling off their lands and their possessions back home. Others had borrowed the cost of passage from friends and neighbors. In some communities there were organized emigration societies that collected membership dues and sent members to the New World. If the money for the passage was borrowed, it had to be repaid out of the early earnings of the immigrant, thus providing another hurdle the newcomer had to overcome.

Besides good health and capital, the other important ingredient for success in the New World was undoubtedly kin and family connections. A typical pattern for unassisted emigrants was for one family member to come to North America and establish himself or herself in a community (often with financial assistance from kin at home). If the person prospered, he or she would write home for other members of the family to follow. Letters home were undoubtedly the most useful way for publicizing the colonies, and connections between families in particular districts were extremely common. Family connections were one of the factors that led immigrants to cluster together in communities in the New World.

Not all immigrants were assisted by family, however. In 1876 a tiny volume appeared in Toronto entitled *Life and Adventures of Wilson Benson, Written by Himself.* This little memoir represents one account of what happened to an ordinary immigrant. Benson was born in Belfast in 1821, had spent some time working in Scotland, and with his young wife had departed for Quebec in early 1841. The couple arrived in Canada with two sovereigns in cash—a relatively small amount—and a chest containing a few personal possessions. These were stolen from them as they made their way to Brockville by barge. They went to Brockville for no better reason than because they had heard it was a promising place. Mrs. Benson hired out as a live-in housekeeper while Wilson hunted desperately for employment. Over the next few years he held a variety of jobs, each on a temporary basis. Not until 1851 were he and his wife able to obtain some land, but it was the death of his father in Ulster that probably provided the money.

Wilson Benson had changed his district of residence eleven times (six in Ireland and Scotland between 1836 and 1838 and five in Canada West between 1838 and 1851) before finally settling on his Grey County farm at the age of thirty. He had shifted occupation twenty-nine times and apprenticed to at least six different trades in the 1830s and early 1840s. Even after acquiring his farm, he also kept a store in the community. Although perhaps on the extreme end of occupational and physical mobility, Benson's life suggests the extent of change with which immigrants had to deal. Like some (but not all) successful immigrants, Benson was pleased with his ultimate fate, writing "it is a source of extreme gratification to me, as it no doubt will be to all pioneers of my early days, that their sacrifices of worldly comforts and exposure to toil and suffering have so largely contributed to their development of our country and the welfare of succeeding generations." Benson had a point. Any progress made by either the immigrants or their host country had been purchased on the backs of the newcomers. Unfortunately, there seemed no real way to avoid the suffering.

The Rise of New Ethnic Tensions

From the first arrival of Europeans in North America, tension among races, cultures, and peoples had been characteristic of the continent's development. The European newcomers had fought with the aboriginal residents and then with one another as the various empires attempted to establish themselves in the New World. During the colonial wars, the conflict had been particularly sharp between Catholic French Canada and Puritan New England, between Acadian and British. After 1763, ethnic tension in much of the part of British North America that would become Canada declined substantially. The elimination of the French government from North America contributed to the decline, although the major cause was segregation of the various ethnic groups into separate settlement enclaves, a process made possible by the sheer amount of wilderness available in the northern colonies. Aboriginals were separated from Europeans, and Europeans of distinct ethnic backgrounds were able to live in their distinctive communities. The Foreign Protestants in Nova Scotia had been removed to Lunenburg County; the Acadians had been forced to escape to the frontiers. Quebec was split into Upper and Lower Canada in order to produce two ethnically distinct provinces. At the beginning of the nineteenth century, the most striking feature of British North America was the presence of a series of relatively isolated ethnic enclaves, often speaking distinctive languages and preserving distinctive cultures and heritages.

After 1815, the ethnic isolations of British North America steadily deteriorated. A number of factors were responsible for the change. For one, a major increase in population was accompanied by the steady settlement of previously uninhabited lands. As early as 1850 in the eastern colonies, most prime agricultural land had been settled and brought under the plough, and ethnic enclaves found it much more difficult to exist in isolation from one another. Also accompanying the rise in population was the rapid growth in the size of cities. Urbanization forced people of various ethnic origins together into one social and economic space. The relatively small physical size of cities in British North America before 1865 meant that residential segregation was relatively difficult. Urban dwellers did not always live together in harmony, but they also could not always live apart in ethnic compartments. There was also a tendency toward a reduction of ethnic hostility as the various groups from the British Isles turned into British North Americans, loyal to their new homeland as well as to a common Empire and monarchy. Although the various nationalities of people perpetuated their old identities—all British North Americans were well aware of the national origins of their neighbors—they also intermarried and attended church together.

On the other hand, an increase of certain forms of ethnic conflict in the British Isles was imported into British North America. Ireland was a major arena for such conflict, as Protestants and Catholics in that country became constantly more aware of their antipathies to one another. Irish ethnic problems spilled over into both England and Scotland, as large Irish populations in cities like Liverpool and Glasgow came into conflict with local English and Scottish populations. Then, as Irish immigration turned into a flood—especially when the potato famine drove hundreds of thousands of impoverished and bitter Irish Catholics across the Atlantic—the Irish groups were increasingly forced into contact with one another and with other national groups in North America. Irish ethnic differences were not simply confessional or historical. They were also class-driven. In most places, the Catholic Irish were both the most recent and the poorest arrivals, forced to take the worst lands (often as tenants) in the countryside or the worst jobs in the cities. The Irish were looked down at, and often responded with anger to their treatment.

The Irish also had a longstanding tradition of parades and public events to celebrate their major ethnic holidays, a tradition that they brought to British North America. The northern Irish also had the Orange Order. Founded in Ireland at the end of the eighteenth century to honor the victory of William of Orange at the Battle of the Boyne in 1690, the Orange Order quickly became an unofficial collaborator with the British in the suppression of the Irish rebellion of 1798. It later migrated to British North America with the Ulster immigrants. The Grand Lodge of British North America was founded in 1830 in Brockville, Ontario, and it rapidly spread across the colonies. It was a combination of fraternal order (with a Masonic-style ritual) and ethnic–patriotic organization, committed to loyalty to Britain and Protestantism, and obviously opposed to Catholicism (especially of the southern Irish variety). The organization flourished in the 1840s and 1850s, especially in regions such as New Brunswick and the Ottawa Valley, which experienced large Catholic Irish migrations. In places where Ulsterites were thin on the ground, Scots and English served as the membership base, partly for fraternal reasons and partly to express their British loyalty and anti-Catholicism. The Orange Order was involved in a number of outbreaks of rioting and violence, usually associated with public demonstrations on key Irish holidays. A notorious example occurred in Woodstock, New Brunswick, on 12 July 1847. It became renowned in song and story throughout the region.

When the Prince of Wales toured British North America in 1860, in most places he was greeted with great expressions and demonstrations of loyalty to Great Britain and to the British monarchy, which suggested some decline in earlier ethnic identifications. During his visit, however, the Orange Order in Canada marred the general outpouring of sentiment for the British monarchy by attempting to leash the monarchy to Orangist goals; Orange bands and demonstrators did their best to lead the parades in the towns and cities of the province, and the Prince's retinue was forced to threaten to avoid visiting certain places if the Order was not kept out of the limelight.

Other European Immigrants

Although the huge influx of immigrants from the British Isles was the major development in British North America in the period between 1815 and the 1860s, other ethnic groups also began to make their appearance. A small number of newcomers from Germany and central Europe—often described in censuses as either Swiss or Germans—had trickled into British North America beginning in the 1750s, frequently as mercenary soldiers in the British army or as refugees from religious persecution, and subsequently as Mennonite Loyalists. Lord Selkirk hired a contingent of disbanded Swiss mercenaries in 1815 as a private army to defend his Red

River Settlement. The Selkirk estate subsequently brought a party of 200 German-speaking Swiss settlers to Red River in 1821. They helped make Red River one of the most ethnically diverse places in British North America, populated by Métis, Scots, Canadians, Norwegians, and Swiss. French, English, Gaelic, German, Norwegian, and several aboriginal tongues, as well as pidgin languages (bungee and mitchif) were spoken on the banks of the Red River. However, most of the Europeans left Red River in 1826 after a great flood and moved into the United States.

Perhaps the best known of the early central European immigrants was Casimir Gzowski, a Polish engineer who migrated to Canada in 1841 and became a well-known engineer, businessman, and community leader, knighted by Queen Victoria. Most of the Germans who came to the Canadas between 1820 and 1870 were on their way to the United States, via either the route from Quebec City along the St. Lawrence or from New York to Detroit via Lake Ontario. Most of the thousands of Germans who arrived in Quebec in the 1850s were on their way to the United States Midwest. Using either route, the newcomers passed through Upper Canada, where they were often surprised to find German-speakers, mainly Mennonite farmers, along the way. After a major famine that started in 1847, the German states of southwestern Germany—Baden, Hesse, and Wurttemberg began to send excess population—the British government called them the "refuse of foreign pauperism"—at public expense to New Brunswick and Canada; many ended up in Waterloo County, Ontario, where they settled a number of townships in the county, including Berlin and Freiberg. Larger numbers of Germans and Poles began to settle in Canada in the later 1850s and 1860s, having been deliberately recruited by the Canadian government, which had agents in the German states between 1857 and 1866 directing potential immigrants away from the United States. By the first Canadian census in 1871, there were 202,991 persons of German ethnic origin in the dominion of Canada. The presence of such a large number of Germans has been one of the best-kept secrets of the ethnic history of British North America. One of the reasons the Germans are not better recognized is because two world wars against Germany led them to suppress their ethnic origins. In the Great War (World War I) particularly, the Germans anglicized the names of many of their communities.

Other nations of Europe began to provide settlers, particularly to Canada West, after 1850. For the most part, these people, such as the Swedes and Norwegians, were immigrants crossing Canada on their way to the midwestern United States. In 1863 a Norwegian farmer named Johan

Schroeder was encouraged by Norwegian shipping interests (who found immigrants preferable to ballast on the western voyage to North America) to tour Canada with a view to publicizing immigration. Schroeder was not impressed with Canada at all. In his various published reports, Schroeder found Canada preferable to Norway, Sweden, and Denmark in its availability of cheap land of good quality combined with a liberal government, but in the end he insisted that the United States was by far the preferable destination.

The Visible Minorities

The occasional representative of a visible minority (apart from the First Nations) had appeared from the earliest days of settlement; usually these visible minority members were blacks. The years after 1815, though, saw the appearance of another visible minority other than the blacks and the establishment of sizeable minority communities in various provinces, especially Upper Canada and Vancouver Island.

The Blacks

The unheralded ethnics—at least until recent years—in British North America before Confederation have been the visible minorities, especially the blacks. Most of the free black Loyalists had departed Nova Scotia in the 1790s for Sierra Leone. Another contingent of blacks—who had taken shelter with the British during the War of 1812—were transported to Nova Scotia and New Brunswick at the end of the war. Like the earlier Loyalists, these were treated as settlers but were given only small amounts of inferior land (to which they were denied title) and were subject to much racial hostility.

The bulk of black immigration to British North America after 1815 came into Upper Canada, the result of American blacks fleeing slavery or racial discrimination and hoping that the British colonies would serve as a sanctuary. As one contemporary popular song had it,

> I'm on my way to Canada
> That cold and distant land
> The dire effects of slavery
> I can no longer stand—

> Farewell, old master,
> Don't come after me,
> I'm on my way to Canada
> Where coloured men are free.

According to another song supposedly sung by fugitives crossing into Canada at Niagara Falls,

> Oh, I heard Queen Victoria say,
> That if we would forsake,
> Our native land of slavery,
> And come across de lake,
> Dat she was standing on de shore,
> Wid arms extended wide,
> To give us all a peaceful home,
> Beyond de rolling tide.

Not all the newly arrived blacks were fugitives, though, and indeed a majority probably were not. Many from the northern cities were relatively prosperous freedmen, eager to escape racial discrimination. But British North America was much better at providing refuge than in eliminating racism.

Three distinct periods of black migration to Canada occurred. In the first, before 1830, a handful of disorganized individual blacks crossed the United States border. In the second, between 1830 and 1850, an increasing level of organization accompanied the exodus. One key development of the period was the Underground Railroad, which was not a railroad at all, but a complex network of ad hoc human individuals and groups that smuggled blacks northwards. It had a mystique of well-orchestrated secrecy not entirely deserved. This period also saw the beginning of the active involvement of white abolitionists on both sides of the border in the migration process. In the final period, beginning in 1850, all forms of activity intensified in response to the passage in that year of the American Fugitive Slave Act, which provided that the identity of a fugitive slave could be determined by the affirmation of the owner or his agent. An example of the workings of the Fugitive Slave Act could be seen in May of 1850, when a Virginia slave named Frederick Wilkins escaped from his master in Norfolk, Virginia and headed for Boston, Massachusetts. The master learned of his former slave's whereabouts and sent a "slave catcher" to Boston to bring the miscreant home. The slave catcher

Caroline Bucknall Estcourt's water-color, The Good Woman of Colour of Lundy's Lane, *Upper Canada, 1839 (National Archives of Canada)*

obtained a Boston warrant, had Wilkins arrested, and brought him before a federal commissioner. A large group of blacks intervened, freeing him and removing him from the courtroom. Six days later, on 20 February 1851, the fugitive reached the city of Montreal in Canada East via the recently opened Vermont Central Railroad. He had crossed open ice twice, once for a distance of 9 miles. In Montreal the former slave renamed himself Shadrach Minkins, received a warm welcome from the community, and soon was working as a barber. A later visitor reported that Minkins "feels what he never felt previous to his residence in Canada, that he owns himself, and is perfectly safe from the impious clutch of the manhunter" (Collison, 1997, p. 188).

Blacks' migration to the north also expanded to the Pacific Coast, where several thousand blacks left California for Vancouver Island and British Columbia, driven from California by state efforts to legalize slavery. They were initially cordially received, and a charitable society collected $2,500 to help them settle, mostly in Victoria and on Saltspring Island. The black community in the colony was led in the 1860s by Mifflin Gibbs, who was a city alderman and often was acting mayor in Victoria before his eventual return to the United States. Everything was not always completely amicable, however. In 1864 a corps of "African Rifles"—founded in 1860 and consisting of three officers and forty-four men, with blue uniforms and orange facings—was ordered to be disbanded by the government; apparently they were the victims of jealousy from the white

Vancouver Island Volunteer Rifles, founded in 1861. This began a campaign in Victoria of attempts to segregate the blacks, which led eventually to the dispersal of the black community, mainly back to the United States.

As many as 50,000 blacks came to Canada and British North America before the American Civil War and were protected legally by the courts, which provided freedom and legal security from extradition, as well as important civil rights, for blacks. But there was much informal racism in Canadian society; one black refugee insisted: "Canadian Negro Hate is incomparably MEANER than the Yankee article" (Collison, 1997, p. 182).

The Chinese

China was opened to visitation from Europe in the first half of the nineteenth century, and some of its enormous population was recruited as contract laborers by visiting merchantmen. Some Chinese people began arriving in British Columbia from California in the late 1850s, and others were brought in from China to work in the mines and at other menial occupations. The new arrivals were overwhelmingly male, chiefly from rural districts in south China in the province of Guangdong. They were unskilled and spoke little or no English. Many came as "sojourners," temporary workers seeking to earn enough money to retire in their villages. The Chinese represented the first substantial population of "guest workers" to British North America, although after Confederation the numbers of such sojourners would increase substantially. The Chinese were extremely unpopular in British Columbia. Once there, they dropped much of their traditional reliance on extended families in favor of a new dependence on voluntary organizations, often secret ones. The first such organization, a chapter of the Chinese society the Zhi Gong Tang, was formed in the mining community of Barkerville, probably in 1862. The secret societies in Canada were chiefly intended as mutual help organizations, but they quickly acquired a reputation among British Columbians as the centers of all sorts of imaginable vice and intimidation. The Chinese were regarded as unassimilable, the importers of every social evil imaginable, from dope to slavery for prostitution, and they were blamed as causing unfair competition for employment. As early as 1860 the colonies of Vancouver Island and British Columbia contained as many as 7,000 Chinese people, although these numbers were not yet sufficient to make them social pariahs and objects of the intense racial hostilities they would later face.

These men from the Mohawk nation at Kahnawake (Quebec) were the Canadian lacrosse champions in 1869. (National Archives of Canada)

The First Nations

The years after 1815 saw a substantial deterioration of the position and condition of the aboriginal peoples, particularly in the eastern part of British North America. The enormous increase in population and areas of settlement increasingly pushed the First Nations to the margins. The march of settlement was usually accompanied by incidents of violence between Europeans and First Nations. The British government assumed that aboriginal numbers were declining. Whether this decline in numbers facilitated dispossession and marginalization or whether dispossession and marginalization reduced the population has never been entirely clear. In any case, the result was the same. The British also believed that, in order to survive, First Nations needed to be integrated into European society as quickly as possible by becoming educated and "civilized" by missionaries who would turn them into farmers. At the same time, the British also began to assume that until aboriginals were fully integrated they were not really part of the fabric of British North America. Thus the First Nations were simultaneously entitled to their own laws and were not full citizens with voting rights. From the standpoint of the colonial governments, the ideal solution was to take over aboriginal land for the Crown (by treaty negotiations) and then to grant to the natives reserves in remote districts, where they could retain their own laws and culture if they insisted.

Conclusion

British immigration after 1815, combined with British policy after the suppression of a series of ill-organized rebellions by the colonists in the Canadas in 1837 and 1838, finally resulted in the production of an anglophone majority in Canada, the province formed by the merger of Upper and Lower Canada in 1841. (The merger, recommended by Lord Durham, was intended eventually to assimilate the French Canadians.) At the time of this union, the French Canadians were still a majority of the population, but by 1850 the anglophones had become more numerous and were demanding a representation reflecting the numbers. The political position of French Canada in the union, especially after 1850, was a curious one. Canada was a legislative union, in which legal and cultural matters were administered by separate departments along linguistic lines, thus preserving the earlier concessions made to French Canada.

The introduction of responsible government—by which the executive of the government of the colonies was chosen by a majority of the colonial assemblies—in the late 1840s had brought new problems. A variety of political conventions were advocated, especially by the French Canadians, that would maintain a substantial French Canadian presence in any government. One was the "double majority," under which any government had to have the support of a majority of both linguistic groups. More workable was government by coalition between the two sections. Fully parallel political parties could not develop in French and English Canada, chiefly because the anglophones had produced one party, the liberal "Clear Grits," which was committed to Protestantism, religious voluntaryism (as opposed to having an official state church), and to general hostility to the French language and French Canada. As a result, government of Canada during this period tended to be by unstable coalitions of Tories. Both English and French Canadians tended to chafe under the constraints of working together in one province, and one of the principal impetuses for a larger confederation was the opportunity to give French Canada its own province (with protection for its language, religion, laws, and culture) within the context of a larger English-speaking union.

Timeline

1815   End of Napoleonic Wars.
1819   Voyage of the *Albion* to New Brunswick.
1821   Selkirk estate brings 200 Swiss settlers to Red River.
1826   Canada Company formed.
1828   Wilmot-Horton brings his emigration scheme before Parliament.
1830   Grand Lodge of Orange Order founded in Brockville, Upper Canada.
1831   New Brunswick and Nova Scotia Land Company formed.
1834   British American Land Company formed.
1840   Union of the Canadas.
1841   Wilson Benson and his wife arrive in Canada; Casimir Gzowski arrives in Canada.
1845   Potato famine in Ireland and Scotland.
1847   Famine spreads to Europe.
1847   Woodstock riot.
1848   Clear Grits formed.
1851   Canadian census shows anglophones outnumber francophones in Canada.
1857   Canadian government begins recruiting immigrants in German states; Gold Rush begins in British Columbia; Chinese begin arriving in British Columbia.
1860   Tour of British North America by the Prince of Wales.
1867   Canadian Confederation formed.

Significant People, Places, and Events

ACT OF UNION Parliamentary legislation in 1840 that, at the recommendation of Lord Durham, amalgamated Upper and Lower Canada into one province called Canada.

ALBION A sailing vessel built in 1815. She had one deck, two masts, and was 75 feet long. This tiny vessel made a number of voyages to British North America carrying Welsh immigrants.

BENSON, WILSON (b. 1821) Author of an autobiography that represents one of few surviving accounts of the adventures of an immigrant to Canada who was not of the elite class.

BRITISH COLUMBIA Colony formed on the Pacific Coast in 1858 when gold was discovered in its interior regions. Its capital was at New Westminster. It was joined with Vancouver Island in 1866 to become the province of British Columbia, with its capital at Victoria.

British American Land Company Incorporated in 1834 to develop the Eastern Townships of Quebec southeast of Montreal.

British Isles A geographical label used to refer to the island group off the northwest coast of Europe. The largest island contains England, Wales, and Scotland, and the next largest contains Ireland and Northern Ireland.

Canada Company Formed in 1826 to purchase the Crown reserves and half of the clergy reserves—land set aside for the support of the Crown and the clergy, respectively—of Upper Canada, it helped develop large sections of the colony and provided a revenue for it until the early 1840s.

Canada East An unofficial term used to refer to what had, before the Act of Union of 1840, been Lower Canada.

Canada West An unofficial term used to refer to what had, before the Act of Union of 1840, been Upper Canada.

Cholera The most devastating of several communicable diseases that often turned into epidemics in British North America. It was often brought to North America by immigrants.

Clear Grits A term used to refer to the radical wing of the reform party of Canada West after the late 1840s. The Clear Grits were committed to Protestantism and voluntaryism and were hostile to French Canada.

Gzowski, Sir Casimir (1813–1898) An engineer, businessman, and soldier who was born in St. Petersburg and came to Canada in 1841. He was the best known of immigrants from eastern Europe before Confederation.

Liverpool An English port that was the most popular point of departure for North American immigrants during 1815–1865. It was notorious for its corruption and ill treatment of those leaving the British Isles.

Minkins, Shadrach A Virginia slave, formerly named Fredrick Wilkins, who was assisted in escaping to Montreal, where he assumed the name Shadrach Minkins and became a successful barber.

New Brunswick and Nova Scotia Land Company Formed in 1831 to settle several large tracts of land in New Brunswick.

Orange Order A fraternal and ethnic organization formed in the northern part of Ireland in 1798 to promote loyalty to the Protestant succession in Britain.

Petworth Project An assisted immigration scheme of 1832–1837 headed by the Earl of Egremont, which brought several thousand farming families from Sussex, England to Upper Canada.

PRINCE OF WALES, TOUR OF BRITISH NORTH AMERICA A famous tour in 1860 by the heir to the British throne, during which British North Americans demonstrated their enthusiasm for the British royal family.

SOJOURNERS An earlier term for those who come to work in a foreign country but who have little intention of remaining there permanently.

TALBOT, COLONEL THOMAS (1771–1853) An Irish-born landholder in Upper Canada who developed large tracts of land and settled immigrants on them.

ULSTER The six northern and predominantly Protestant counties of the north of Ireland.

UNDERGROUND RAILROAD An informal network of individuals and organizations committed to helping smuggle black refugees out of the American South, often into Canada.

VANCOUVER ISLAND A British colony on the west coast of North America organized by the British government in 1849.

VOLUNTARYISM The term used in Canada to refer to commitment to the separation of church and state (called voluntarism in the United States).

WAKEFIELD, EDWARD GIBBON (1796–1862) An English colonial theorist who developed colonization schemes based on charging a "sufficient price" for land.

WILMOT-HORTON, ROBERT JOHN (1784–1841) An English politician and Colonial Office official who advocated public assistance to enable those who might become public charges to emigrate to British North America.

Documents

John & Magret Evans to Owen Thomas, 1820

Frederickton
January 13th, 1820

My dear Brother & Sister,
    I have received your letter on the 29th of December and we was very glad to have it and we was very glad to hear that you are all well when you write that letter we have and we have take our liberty to write to you few lines in hopes that they may find you in good Estate in the same that we are at present. We are all well in health I and my wife and children and

James my Brother, and his wife and children are all well at present. I am settle in our land and in a new house since the beginning of the winter and James my brother is near to me in his own house and we are all well please in our Settlement. We have a very good land but is full of woods, but we are begin to clear it now to set a crop the next Spring in hope that we will find our provision on the land. Sir, I have sent to you if you are a mind to come here to America, if you do come I beg on you not to go to New York, because it is very dead on every trade. I have hear from a letter that taken out from the post on the same time that I have that letter I have from you, from the brother in law of Ann of Benbulied. That is in New York since the last Spring Twelve Months and is gone worse ther every month and he is willing if he cold have an emploiment to spend the spare of his time under the British Government. Remember me and James Evans my brother to Samuel Evans my brother and my uncle William and his children and William Phillips and his wife and children, and I am very sorry to hear the news I have heard of you. We have every family a grant of land 200 Acres for Nothing but we must pay sum quantity of Money in space of Three Years for the agreement and if you can come here you can get more Money in one Month than you can get there in Twelve Months. This I send to my brother is very good wages to a labourer, five or six Shillings a day, and from Five to Six pounds a month, and is a very good place to everyman to get Money here and a good place in Saint John and Frederickton to a carpenter and every trade can get from £2 to £2 and Five shillings a week. The cost prices of the Cows from £9 to £10 and a pair of oxen is from 25 to 30 pound and a pair of horses from 20 to 25 pound and the bread is very cheap and the Cheese and the Butter and the Pork is very dear. I have no more to send you at present but I hope that you are all be good estate and the Lord God Almighty be with you all Amen.

This is from your obedient servant.
John & Magret Evans

Direct to Mr. John Evans, Cardigan settlement, to the care of Mr. Brunner, Saint John, New Brunswick, N.A. I let you know that William John the father Evan John of Cardigan is remember me to my son that we are all well at present.

Source: Thomas, Peter, *Strangers from a Secret Land* (Toronto: University of Toronto Press, 1986), pp. 181–182.

Nathaniel Carrothers to His Brother

Westminster [Canada West], January the 29th 1866

Dear brother

I once again take up my pen to write to you hoping that thse few lines may find you and famely in good health as the lave me and famely at present thank god for all his goodnes; with the ecception of my second son Joseph who has been in a state of bed health for two years and dont seem to get beter it is a liver and stomack complaint that eals [ails] him, he has tried three docters and none of them seem to do him any good. Last spring we got every thing ready to send him to Ireland for two or three months in the summer, and when we told the doctor who is a Scochman he would not hear of it; he said the climate in Ireland was to cold and damp for his complaint and that it was sure to make him worse but he advised us to send him north on our freshwater lakes a voiage [voyage]; so we sent him; he was a way two months and felt better when a way but since he has come home I see no improvement in him. I see by your letter to Joseph that times is better with youes, and youes are all hard at work to make money for your land lords; this is all write so long as your family stick together and is content. . . . We had a young man a Mr. Armstrong son to Willey of the woods who came to see this country make us a visit last winter, he stopt a week with me, he could tel me a good dale [deal] about my old friends and acquaintance a bought Green-hil, and he lived this country so well that the whole famely has come out this harvest, they have bought a farm of two hundred acres with a good breck [brick] house and other suitible buildings on it for seven thousand Dollalrs. I went to see them after the came the distance of 16 miels and we had jouvel [jovial] time of it. They were stoping at the house of my old friend and acquaintence Mr James Armstrong of Latin, the are all de-lighted with this country. I have bought since I last wroute to you two hundred more acres of land for John and Joseph my two eldest sones, there is one of them 75 acres cleared and on the other 50 acres. John is maried and is living on his, the other I have rented to a man at 100 Dolars a year. The cost four thousand dolars which is something more than eight hundred of your pounds; so I have got 100 acres for each of my sones so that may liv comfertible with out toiling all their dayes to make the rent. I have been talking to a good many that lives on rented farms hear and the say that the woud rather live on one in this country than there; ther is a scoch man living on a rented farm near me and he has saved as much money as has bought him self a farm last year; I have been thinking had you come to this country when you were thinking of it with such a famely of sons how wel of you woud have been and how well it would have been for them besides toiling all their dayes in Ireland. If you would send one of the boyes out to this country to see their friends and the country how the woud like it before the go renting a farm there and be no likin to live here and wishing to return, I will pay his passage home a gain and I am shure he wil be much the wiser after it; I have had strong nosions of going back to see the old country and you in times that are past, put I suppose that I never shal now. There has been deaths and mariges a mong the friends hear since I wrout last. Brother Thomas has beried his wife and is maried a gain to a scoch woman, but I suppose Brother Joseph has sent you al perticulars. . . .

Source: Houston, Cecil J., and Smyth, William J., *Irish Emigration and Canadian Settlement: Patterns, Links, & Letters* (Toronto: University of Toronto Press, 1990), pp. 262–263.

Bibliography

Akenson, Donald, *The Irish in Ontario: A Study in Rural History* (Montreal, Quebec and Kingston, Ontario: McGill-Queen's University Press, 1984).

Cameron, Wendy, and Mary Maude McDougall, *Assisting Emigration to Upper Canada: The Petworth Project 1832–1837* (Montreal, Quebec and Kingston, Ontario: McGill-Queen's University Press, 2000).

Collison, Gary, *Shadrach Minkins: From Fugitive Slave to Citizen* (Cambridge, MA: Harvard University Press, 1997).

Cowan, Helen I., *British Emigration to British North America: The First Hundred Years,* rev. ed. (Toronto: University of Toronto Press, 1961).

Craig, David, *On the Crofters' Trail: In Search of the Clearance Highlanders* (London, U.K.: Jonathan Cape, 1990).

Elliott, Bruce S., *Irish Migrants in the Canadas: A New Approach* (Montreal, Quebec and Kingston, Ontario: McGill-Queen's University Press, 1988).

Guillet, Edwin C., *The Great Migration: The Atlantic Crossing by Sailing-Ship 1770–1860,* 2nd ed. (Toronto: University of Toronto Press, 1963).

Houston, Cecil J., and William J. Smyth, *Irish Emigration and Canadian Settlement: Patterns, Links, & Letters* (Toronto: University of Toronto Press, 1990).

Johnston, H. J. M., *British Emigration Policy, 1815–1830: "Shovelling Out Paupers"* (Oxford, U.K.: Clarendon Press, 1972).

Magosci, Robert Paul, ed., *Encyclopedia of Canada's Peoples* (Toronto: University of Toronto Press, 1999).

Overland, Orm, ed., *Johan Schroder's Travels in Canada, 1863* (Montreal, Quebec and Kingston, Ontario: McGill-Queen's University Press, 1989), 65.

Thomas, Peter, *Strangers from a Secret Land: The Voyages of the Brig* Albion *and the Founding of the First Welsh Settlements in Canada* (Toronto: University of Toronto Press, 1986).

CHAPTER SIX

Immigration and Immigration Policy, 1867–1914

In 1867, three provinces of British North America (Canada, Nova Scotia, and New Brunswick) became unified as Canada, a nation initially consisting of four provinces (Ontario, Quebec, Nova Scotia, and New Brunswick) under a constitution, the British North America Act, which was a piece of legislation created by the British Parliament. The new nation quickly added three new provinces—Manitoba (1870), British Columbia (1871), and Prince Edward Island (1873)—as well as a vast western territory that would, in 1905, become Alberta and Saskatchewan. The reasons for the 1867 confederation were complex but were dominated by the perceived political instability of Canada, which was attempting to work with the dual cultures of the French and English. Other factors included military fears of the United States, the desire for an expanded market, and the ambition to annex vast western territories by purchase from the Hudson's Bay Company.

Before the unification of Canada in 1867, immigration policy had been the responsibility of individual provinces, most of which did not actively attempt either to attract newcomers or to screen those who arrived, except in terms of the most obvious of health requirements. After 1867, Canada implemented (or more often failed to implement) a variety of intentions and prejudices. Somewhat paradoxically, between 1867 and 1914 the national origins of Canada's immigrants were greatly expanded geographically, at the same time that specific national limitations on immigrants were also greatly increased. On one level, immigration policy up until World War I (called at the time the Great War) was dominated by the acquisition of the Canadian west, which, it was thought, required development and settlement. Everyone could agree on the need for hard-working immigrants, especially farmers, to settle the west, and this was first translated into homestead legislation beginning in 1868, which provided free

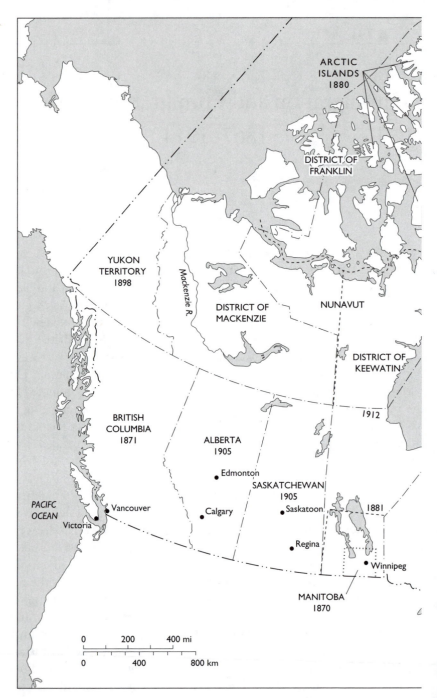

ARCTIC
ISLANDS
1880

DISTRICT OF
FRANKLIN

YUKON
TERRITORY
1898

Mackenzie R.

DISTRICT OF
MACKENZIE

NUNAVUT

DISTRICT OF
KEEWATIN

1912

BRITISH
COLUMBIA
1871

ALBERTA
1905

Edmonton

SASKATCHEWAN
1905

PACIFC
OCEAN

Vancouver

Calgary

Saskatoon

1881

Victoria

Regina

Winnipeg

MANITOBA
1870

0   200   400 mi

0   400   800 km

The Political Divisions of Canada since 1867
Source: Based on Morton, W. L. The Kingdom of Canada: A General History
from Earliest Times. *(Toronto: McClellan and Stewart, 1963), p. 404.*

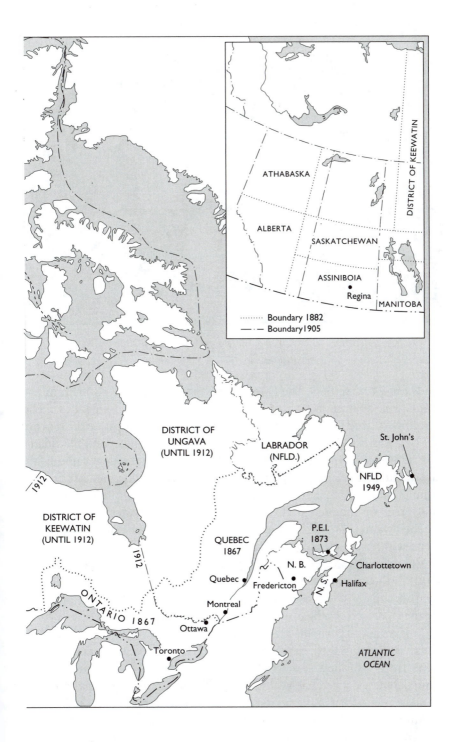

ATHABASKA

ALBERTA

SASKATCHEWAN

ASSINIBOIA

Regina

MANITOBA

DISTRICT OF KEEWATIN

.... Boundary 1882
—·— Boundary 1905

DISTRICT OF
UNGAVA
(UNTIL 1912)

LABRADOR
(NFLD.)

St. John's

NFLD
1949

1912

DISTRICT OF
KEEWATIN
(UNTIL 1912)

P.E.I.
1873

QUEBEC
1867

1912

N. B.

Quebec

Fredericton

Charlottetown

Halifax

N.S.

ONTARIO 1867

Montreal

Ottawa

Toronto

ATLANTIC
OCEAN

Three generations of Croatian settlers, Kenaston, Saskatchewan, ca. 1910
(National Archives of Canada)

lands for actual settlers. The Dominion Lands Act of 1872 entitled immigrants to a quarter section of land (160 acres) free of charge. But most newcomers were not experienced farmers, and developing a working farm out of a wasteland was an expensive proposition, often beyond the financial resources of the average settler. Moreover, most settlers came from Great Britain, and the British government preferred to export its "excess" population rather than its most industrious people. Also, almost everyone else agreed on the preferability of farmers from the United Kingdom, but Quebec wanted farmers from France and advertised extensively to get them, without much success.

Many immigrants came increasingly from farther and farther east and south in the continent of Europe. Some, like the Mennonites, were even pacifists and conscientious objectors who wanted guarantees of toleration for their particular religious beliefs. Some newcomers were not wanted at all, at least not as permanent residents. Americans were always accepted, if not always encouraged. Newcomers that were regarded as "unassimilable" came from Asia and some from within the black community in the United States. Canada had considerable difficulty in producing a coherent immigration policy in the period between Confederation and the 1890s.

After the mid-1890s, Canada continued to encourage the immigration of farmers, shifting increasingly from recruiting them from Great Britain

Jewish settlers Samuel and Hanna Schwartz with daughter Simma and her husband outside their farm home in the Lipton district of Saskatchewan, ca. 1903 (Courtesy of the Saskatchewan Archives Board)

Group of Jewish immigrant women, Toronto, 1910. Montreal immigrants tried to escape the economic depression of 1907–1908 by moving to Toronto and other cities. For these same reasons Jewish immigrants came to Montreal. (Archives of Ontario)

From Canada, The Granary of the World *published in 1903, this cartoon titled "Now Then, All Together!" depicts representatives of various nationalities singing "The Maple Leaf Forever." (Courtesy of the Saskatchewan Archives Board)*

to recruiting them from eastern Europe and the United States. This eastern European and American flow has been emphasized in much of the literature on the history of Canadian immigration. Curiously enough, however, probably more Britons (especially British farmers) arrived in Canada between 1896 and 1914 than ever before. Despite the emphasis on Americans and "men in sheepskin coats," the bulk of the prewar immigration to Canada continued to come from the British Isles. Moreover, though agricultural immigration has always been stressed in the histories, Canada also actively encouraged the arrival of industrial laborers after 1896, often on a contract basis. Also after 1896, Canada became increasingly exclusionist, writing new legislation that kept out immigrants for various health reasons and fighting hard to prevent "undesirable" and "unassimilable" racial minorities from entering the country.

Acquiring the West

As early as the 1850s, the province of Canada regarded the vast western territories administered by the Hudson's Bay Company as part of its natural living space. One argument was that Canada had inherited the west as part of the *pays d'en haut* of New France when it had been transferred from Great Britain in 1763. A parliamentary commission in 1857 agreed with Canada that most of Rupert's Land would eventually become part of Canada, although in the short run it was left under the administration of the Hudson's Bay Company (HBC) to protect the aboriginal inhabitants of the region. The Northwest, as it was often called, was conceived to contain thousands of square miles of rich, arable farmland, the settlement of which would turn Canada into a great country.

One of the major reasons for the unification of British North America in the 1860s was to create a state suitable for expansion, and one of the first actions of the newly confederated Canada was to pass, in late 1867, resolutions preliminary to negotiating with the HBC for the transfer of the western territory into Canadian hands. In 1868 a ministerial delegation was sent to London, U.K. to arrange the transfer of the Northwest to Canada, finally working out a deal with the HBC by which the Canadian government paid 300,000 pounds and agreed to substantial land grants for the company in the newly acquired territory. Perhaps not surprisingly, no one thought to consult with the residents of the Northwest, either the Métis in Red River or the First Nations beyond, about the transfer. The takeover was scheduled to take place on 1 December 1869, with Canada planning to administer the new territory in traditional colonial terms under an appointed council consisting chiefly of outsider officers.

Not surprisingly, the Métis and mixed-bloods of Red River were extremely suspicious of the Canadians' intentions. A Canadian party building a road from Lake of the Woods to the settlement had already been involved in a number of racist incidents. Another Canadian party surveying the land in advance of takeover was employing the standard square patterns of Ontario (and the United States), although Métis lands in Red River were laid out in long, narrow strips along the rivers. Canada would later claim that it had intended to honor existing property holdings in the settlement, but in this as in other matters, it had never communicated with the local inhabitants. A Métis leader emerged in the person of Louis Riel (1844–1885), a member of a respected family in the community. The young Riel spoke out publicly against the surveys, and in October 1869, while the surveyors were running their lines south of the Assiniboine River, Riel led a group who stood on the surveying chains and told the surveyors to stop.

Meanwhile, one William McDougall (1822–1905) traveled through the United States to assume the office of first lieutenant-governor of the

Northwest. A newly organized "National Committee of the Métis" decided that McDougall should not be allowed into the Northwest and ordered him to keep out unless he had its permission to enter. The warning was signed "Louis Riel, Secretary." The local authorities of the Red River Settlement were unable to convince Riel to stop his opposition. He insisted that he and his people were "simply acting in defence of their own liberty" in insisting that they not admit a new governor until they had negotiated "the terms and conditions under which they would acknowledge him." In early November Riel and a large party of armed Métis horsemen occupied HBC's fort at Upper Fort Garry, and thus took over military control of the settlement. One major question was whether Riel's Métis—francophone Roman Catholics who represented slightly more than half of the mixed-bloods of Red River settlement—would be able to persuade their English-speaking (and Protestant) fellow countrymen to join them in their resistance. The anglophones were at this time fairly sanguine about a Canadian takeover and unwilling to divide the settlement in a way that might lead to a possible civil war. Riel managed to obtain passive anglophone acceptance of his resistance, and in early December he issued a "Declaration of the People" establishing a provisional government that would negotiate with Canada on the terms for Red River's entry into the Confederation.

Over the winter of 1869–1870, Riel masterfully orchestrated the settlement's opposition to Canada. In February 1870, a convention of forty representatives divided equally between the two language groups prepared and debated a "List of Rights," which embodied the major demands of the settlement, subsequently appointing three delegates to go to Ottawa to negotiate provincial status for Red River within the Confederation. Riel had succeeded in suppressing several armed oppositions to his provisional government and imprisoning their leaders in Upper Fort Garry. Unfortunately, Riel allowed his men to vent their anger on one of the prisoners, a Northern Irishman named Thomas Scott. A Métis jury summarily sentenced Scott to death in early March, and Riel accepted the sentence, commenting, "We must make Canada respect us." Scott was indeed executed before the walls of Fort Garry on 4 March 1870. It happened that Thomas Scott had been a member of the notorious Orange Lodge, however, and his execution would have enormous implications in Protestant Ontario, which was searching desperately for an excuse to condemn the Red River resistance, which they saw as being composed of upstart Catholic "half-breeds."

While Riel's delegates went to Ottawa with its List of Rights, a small group of lobbyists who called themselves Canada First managed to raise high emotions in Ontario over the "murder" of Scott. The situation was complicated by the insistence of the British government that it would support a military expedition to Red River only if the Canadian government satisfied the legitimate conditions of the local residents. The Red River delegation thus gained a number of important concessions for the inhabitants of Red River. At what the Canadian government of Sir John A. Macdonald (he was knighted in 1867) always regarded as the point of a gun, the Métis managed to get the Manitoba Act of 1870 passed; this Act granted provincial status to what would now be called Manitoba (a name favored by Riel), a province of only 1,000 square miles, with 1,400,000 acres set aside for the Métis and with bilingualism guaranteed. What the delegates did not succeed in wresting from the Canadians was a commitment in writing that provided for an amnesty for the leaders of the resistance for any illegal acts carried out by them, including, of course, the killing of Thomas Scott. The delegates knew that they were under no circumstances to negotiate with Canada without assurances of an amnesty, but they allowed themselves to be persuaded by informal promises that the Canadians had no intention of honoring. The Canadian government's duplicity would prove symptomatic of its treatment of Métis and aboriginals over the ensuing years.

In May 1870 the Canadian government sent a so-called peaceful military expedition to Red River, made up of imperial troops and Canadian militia units that included many Orangemen eager to kill Riel. A few hours before their arrival at Fort Garry, Riel and several of his associates fled into exile. After the postage-stamp-sized province called Manitoba was taken over, the remainder of the territory transferred to Canada by HBC—the Northwest Territories—was initially administered under the original legislation passed by the Canadian Parliament in 1869. The natural resources of the Northwest, as well as its ungranted lands or wastelands, were under the exclusive control of the "government of Canada for the purposes of the Dominion." The lieutenant-governor of Manitoba also served as the lieutenant-governor of the Territories. The temporary legislation of 1869 was renewed without change in 1871. The Territories were actually given an appointed council consisting of eleven members, only two of whom resided there, in 1872. The other nine lived in or near Winnipeg, and initial meetings of the council were held in that city. Provincial status was finally granted to the Territories, which became Saskatchewan and Alberta, in 1905.

Not until the question of Rupert's Land dragged to its conclusion was the Canadian government able to act on an earlier request from British

Columbia—to which Vancouver Island had been annexed in 1866—for admission to the new union. The negotiations between British Columbia and Canada took place shortly after the passage of the Manitoba Act. The Canadians were generous to a fault, meeting all of the Pacific province's demands, especially that of a rail link with Canada—which was to be begun within two years and completed within fifteen. Canada already knew that it needed a transcontinental railroad to match the lines rapidly being constructed across the United States. On 20 July 1871 British Columbia joined the Confederation as the sixth province, and the Dominion of Canada was a coast-to-coast nation that had completed its "manifest destiny" just as surely as had its American neighbors to the south.

Developing the West to 1885

The crucible for the new Canada would be in the vast expanse of territory west of the Great Lakes. Here, the many problems faced by the nation would become clearly apparent. From the beginning, it was not at all clear how the tiny province of Manitoba would turn out. The Roman Catholic Church did its best to supplement the existing Métis population with well-educated French Canadian professionals in an effort to keep the French Catholic contingent alive and well in the province. Unfortunately, the transplanted easterners did not get along well with the Métis, and their disagreements allowed the anglophones to dominate the province politically within a few years. The refusal of the federal government to allow the Métis to receive their promised land in concentrated blocks helped encourage many Métis to sell off, pack up, and move farther west to the Qu'Appelle Valley. At the same time, Canada was quite happy to negotiate block settlement with new settlers from various parts of Europe.

The Aboriginal Residents: The interests of the Canadian government in the Northwest, especially under Sir John A. Macdonald, were focused on rapid agricultural settlement. Such settlement would provide an outlet for excess eastern population and a means of developing a transcontinental nation that could take advantage of the new railroad that was being built at great expense. In the process, the First Nations inhabitants of the region were pushed aside as rapidly as possible. Canada appreciated that native title to land in the Northwest would have to be extinguished, and it did so through a series of numbered treaties negotiated with the First Nations in which the aboriginals surrendered their land in exchange for reserves on the most marginal and least attractive land and in exchange for vague

The interior of a Canada Pacific Railway colonist railway car,
drawn by Melton Prior for the Illustrated London News, *24 November 1888*
(Courtesy Glenbow Museum of Alberta, Canada)

promises of assistance in the transition from a hunting to an agricultural lifestyle. Most of the great First Nations leaders of this era understood full well that the end of the era of the great bison herds was upon them and that natives who did not adapt to the new ways would soon disappear. In August 1876, for example, the First Nations of central Saskatchewan gathered at Fort Carlton to consider the terms of the government's Treaty no. 6. The Plains Cree chief, Poundmaker, objected to Canada's offer, saying that the government was not doing enough to train the natives as farmers and to assist them in other ways after the buffalo disappeared. For its part, the government was suspicious that the First Nations would become life-long welfare recipients and was hesitant to make long-term promises. Poundmaker signed the treaty, and three years later accepted a reserve on the Battle River. Another important Plains Cree chief, Big Bear, held out for six years, but signed in 1882 when his people were starving.

The First Nations got nowhere near enough assistance from the Canadian government to make a smooth transition from hunting to farming.

Canada was extremely short on funds to develop the west and spent much of its available capital on the construction of the Canadian Pacific Railway. Worse, the inadequate amounts of money made available to local native agents were administered by individuals who were often unsympathetic to the natives' plight. The problem was complicated by bad growing conditions in the early 1880s. In a spiraling emergency, the First Nations' inability to grow enough food to feed themselves—and the federal government's failure to supplement the shortfall—exposed the aboriginals to malnutrition, which in turn led to a reduced resistance to epidemic disease. The result was a series of local epidemics in the early 1880s.

The Mennonites

In its eagerness to bring population to the prairies, Canada was not satisfied with the migration west of its own eastern population, mainly from Ontario; people from Quebec never headed west in great numbers, despite the efforts of the government and the Roman Catholic Church throughout the nineteenth century. In addition to its normal homestead and settlement policy, Canada sought to encourage the settlement of various ethnic communities from Europe, usually through promises to emigrant leaders to provide them with blocks of land for self-contained ethnic settlement. There were certainly large numbers of candidates in Europe for such block settlements. The first successful negotiations along this line were carried out with Russian Mennonites beginning in 1872 and 1873. These Mennonites were European Quakers who had originated in Prussia and Poland in the sixteenth century and were driven out of their homes by threats of military conscription in the eighteenth century. They found an asylum in Russia, where Catherine II offered them generous conditions of resettlement, including land, freedom of religion, their own schools, and permanent exemption from military service. By the 1870s, though, the Mennonites were again being threatened, this time by rising Russian nationalism. The Canadian government offered similar inducements to the earlier Russian ones: exemption from military service, religious liberty, control of education, free homesteads of 160 acres, and the right to purchase additional land at one dollar per acre. Canada set aside two blocks of townships for the Mennonites in southern Manitoba: one block of eight townships was on the east side of the Red River southeast of Winnipeg, and another block of twelve townships ("the West Reserve") was along the international boundary west of the Red River. The blocks of reserves made clear to the Mennonites that they could live in their own village communities (and hold land in common) apart from their neighbors, and about 8,000 Mennonites settled in 1874 in southern Manitoba.

The Icelanders

The second major ethnic group allowed by the Canadian government to establish itself as an autonomous community was that of the Icelanders. People from Iceland had begun coming to Canada in substantial numbers beginning in the early 1870s, motivated both by volcanic eruptions and grassland shortages in their homeland and a general population excess that pressed on available resources. The first immigrants settled in Ontario and Quebec but were dissatisfied with their conditions. In the spring of 1875 a party of Icelanders traveled west to find satisfactory land for a block settlement that had been promised them by the Canadian government. The land they chose was on the west side of Lake Winnipeg, stretching from present-day Selkirk to Hecla Island and including the modern town of Gimli. This territory was north of the boundary of the province of Manitoba and was thus in the relatively ungoverned Northwest Territories of Canada, where the newcomers were able to create the Republic of New Iceland, an autonomous settlement with its own laws and judicial system. The Canadian government accepted a provisional council set up by the Icelanders and allowed them to produce a fully articulated system of self-government with four districts *(byggdir)*, each governed by a council of five people headed by a reeve, culminating in a governing council *(Thing)*. This republic became part of Manitoba when the boundaries of the province were expanded in 1881, but self-government remained in effect until 1887.

Although the territory chosen for New Iceland was ideal for access to fishing on Lake Winnipeg, it was in some of the poorest agricultural land in the region. Moreover, the Icelanders experienced considerable calamities in their new home. A devastating smallpox epidemic arrived late in 1876, transmitted from aboriginal peoples to Icelanders (who also lacked immunity to the disease), and Lake Winnipeg experienced spring flooding between 1876 and 1880. Completing the problems, a major religious dispute among the settlers emerged in the later 1870s. The result was that outward migration from New Iceland began in the early 1880s, and many inhabitants went either to North Dakota or to the burgeoning city of

Winnipeg, where they settled in the West End of the city. Immigration from Iceland to the territory picked up again by the mid-1880s, though, and by 1900 the population of New Iceland had recovered to 2,500. Most of those made a living by fishing on Lake Winnipeg for fish to sell as dried fish (hardfiskur) in markets in the United States. Icelanders were generally well educated and committed to the preservation of their language. Schools were established in New Iceland only months after the arrival of the immigrants, with instruction being conducted in Icelandic. Although fluency in Icelandic gradually declined in Manitoba, the community produced a number of poets and writers who wrote in the native language.

The Métis

Like the First Nations, the Métis systematically drifted to the margins of the new country of Canada. Sir John A. Macdonald's government had created Manitoba as a province only under duress, and the Prime Minister regarded the mixed-bloods as a people to be "kept down by a strong hand until they are swamped by the influx of settlers" (Sprague, 1986, p. 4). And swamped they were. As thousands of new settlers, mainly from Ontario but including a number of Mennonites, arrived in the province, guarantees of land rights to the Métis were gradually whittled down, and much of the land itself—about 2 million of the 2 ½ million acres promised to the Métis in 1870—ended up in the hands of speculators. By 1885, Ontario-born settlers outnumbered Métis 5 to 1 in Manitoba, and only 7 percent of the population of the province was of mixed-blood origin. The extent to which deliberate government policy was responsible for the plight of the Métis has been one of the most bitterly fought historical controversies ever seen in Canadian historiography, and the last word has not yet been written on the subject.

Many Métis headed farther west, often to the Saskatchewan Valley, where they formed several mission settlements, including Qu'Appelle, Batoche, and Duck Lake (Lee, 1989). But the buffalo they needed for their sustenance were becoming scarce. French, English, and Scottish mixed-bloods in the region demanded grants similar to those given to the mixed-bloods under the Manitoba Act. Government surveyors caused uncertainty and fear, as they had done in Red River a decade earlier, as to whether the river lot holdings of the Métis would be allowed to survive in a square survey system. Part of the problem was that the surveying was not happening fast enough, not just for the Métis (who sought exemptions from it), but for the European settlers as well. By the early 1880s, the Europeans in the Northwest were becoming as restive as the aboriginals and the Métis, although for somewhat different reasons. The Europeans' concerns were more political. In March of 1883, the Qu'Appelle Settlers' Rights Association passed resolutions calling for parliamentary representation, land law reform, proper legislation for settlers, and government assistance for immigrants. In December of that year, a Manitoba and Northwest Farmers' Union was organized in Winnipeg. A motion for repeal of Canada's constitution, the British North America Act, and the formation of a "new confederacy of the North-West Provinces and British Columbia" was only barely defeated. A Bill of Rights was drawn up, which was summarily rejected in Ottawa. In 1884, with the approval of the European settlers of the region, the Métis invited Louis Riel to return to Canada and lead a peaceful demand for an improved Canadian policy toward the West.

The peaceful protest ended early in 1885 with armed conflict between the Northwest Mounted Police and the Métis, who were quickly abandoned by their European settler allies. The Canadians quickly moved a military force into the region, utilizing the recently completed Canadian Pacific Railway to move troops from Winnipeg to the Qu'Appelle Valley. A number of aboriginal bands joined the Métis in the uprising, acting out of their own sense of grievances against the Canadian federal government, and "massacres" of European settlers occurred at several places. The uprising was quickly suppressed. Canada focused its legal response against the Métis on Louis Riel, who was quickly tried, convicted of treason, and hanged. His followers were dealt with relatively leniently, and most were amnestied within a few years. When the government had finished with the trials of aboriginals at Regina and Battleford, nine had been hanged and another fifty sentenced to penitentiary terms for their parts in the uprising. The trials, particularly at Battleford, were most improper, conducted without full translation against people who understood little English and less of the law being employed. Few of the defendants were properly represented in court. Most First Nations people and their leaders had tried to remain clear of the Métis uprising, but this did not save them from a subsequent campaign of repression by Assistant Indian Commissioner Hayter Reed, who insisted that the rebellion had abrogated the treaties and who introduced a series of policies that made the First Nations totally dependent on the largesse of Canada. As for the Métis, their will was broken by the swift suppression of the rebellion, and they would not again be a major force in the settlement of the West.

The Chinese

Some Chinese people had arrived in British Columbia with the Gold Rush in 1858, and others were brought to the province by mine owners in the 1860s and 1870s as contracted laborers. But a major immigration of Chinese did not begin until the early 1880s, when Andrew Onderdonk, the contractor responsible for the construction of the British Columbia section of the Canadian Pacific Railway (CPR), began importing Chinese workers to perform heavy labor on what was generally agreed was the most difficult part of the building of the CPR. The workers were transported to railway camps along the rail line at Yale, Port Moody, and Savona. It has been estimated that approximately half of the 15,701 Chinese workers who entered Canada between 1881 and 1884 were employed directly on labor crews for the CPR, and a number of the others worked in industries that supported the construction. Sir John A. Macdonald protected the Chinese during the building of the CPR, telling the Canadian House of Commons in 1883 that "It will be all very well to exclude Chinese labour, when we can replace it with white labour, but until that is done, it is better to have Chinese labour than no labour at all" (Magosci, 1999, p. 359). As soon as the railroad construction was completed, Macdonald gave in to pressures from British Columbia and elsewhere to "do something" about the Chinese, who were regarded as the source of a variety of social and economic evils. A royal commission on Chinese immigration in 1885 recommended restrictions on the Chinese workers, and Macdonald instituted a head tax of fifty dollars on every Chinese person entering the country. The law also restricted the number of Chinese people who could be carried on individual vessels entering Canadian ports. This federal legislation joined numerous provincial statutes limiting the rights of the Chinese in Canada.

Immigration after 1885: Larger Numbers and Increasing Exclusionism

In 1882, the Canadian government had begun the policy of granting large blocks of prairie land to the CPR. These blocks joined those given to the HBC in 1870 and other lands purchased by private land companies with the intent of providing a private enterprise alternative to the acquisition of homestead land by incoming immigrants in the west. Most settlers preferred private land, especially railroad land, to government land, because government land was not usually located in places likely to be developed.

Immigrants in front of Winnipeg Station, ca. 1900
(Courtesy of the United Church of Canada/Victoria University)

Until the last years of the nineteenth century, these private land entrepreneurs had not been forced to select their promised land allocations, which meant that much of the west was not really open to settlement. Moreover, up to the mid-1890s, Canadian immigration authorities concentrated on recruiting farmers in the United Kingdom without a good deal of success. The Prairie provinces had less than 300,000 inhabitants in 1896, and in the previous twenty years—especially between 1881 and 1891—more people from Canada had departed for the United States than had come to Canada from abroad. Part of the problem was that the American West was simply more attractive than its Canadian equivalent, but the difficulty of obtaining people with agricultural experience from the United Kingdom also contributed to the population shortfall.

In 1896, a new Minister of the Interior (with responsibility for immigration) took office. Clifford Sifton was an Ontario-born Manitoban who believed in massive agricultural immigration as the key to Canadian development. The trick, he felt, was to find the immigrants and to get them onto the land. Sifton decided to take his farmers from wherever in the world he could find them, rather than concentrating on recruitment in

*Mr. and Mrs. Luite Visscher, New Holland, Alberta, 1915
(Courtesy Glenbow Museum of Alberta, Canada)*

the United Kingdom. He was prepared to recruit in eastern Europe, especially on the steppes of Russia where grain cultivation was important, and in the United States as well. Sifton saw the quality immigrant as a "stalwart peasant in a sheep-skin coat born on the soil, whose fore-fathers have been farmers for ten generations, with a stout wife and a half-dozen children" (Petryshyn, 1985, p. 21). Changing conditions both in Russia and in the United States would work to Canada's advantage after 1896. Sifton was willing to centralize and simplify land distribution policy as well as to force the private land companies to select their lands and make more agricultural land available for settlement. Furthermore, Sifton was also prepared to restrict the admission of people whom he did not think were suitable for agriculture—or for Canada. Such restrictions would be taken even further by Sifton's successor, Frank Oliver, between 1905 and 1911.

The Ukrainians

The Ukraine was a vast territory on the central and southern steppes of eastern Europe, mainly during the later nineteenth century period of the Russian (85 percent) and Austrian Empires (15 percent). The first settlers from the Ukraine to Canada had come in the early 1890s, and they joined

Mennonites and Hungarians as early arrivals from these two vast empires. In 1895, Dr. Joseph Oleskiw, a Ukrainian academic who taught agriculture, visited Canada and proposed an extensive Ukrainian immigration to the Canadian west, which Clifford Sifton did his best to implement. Between 1896 and 1914, about 170,000 Ukrainians—chiefly from the overpopulated Austrian provinces of Galicia and Bukovyna—had entered Canada, settling mainly in the prairie region. In their homeland, these peasants had been experiencing increasing subdivision of their land and declining productivity because of lack of capital caused chiefly by heavy taxation. By 1900, half of the landholdings in the provinces of Galicia and Bukovyna were less than 2 hectares in extent, and many small landholders were heavily in debt. These conditions, not appreciably different from those of Scottish crofters of the same period, were a ready-made incentive for immigration to North America. The Ukrainians would have probably preferred the United States, but they faced increasing immigration restrictions and an often hostile reception from the Americans, who no longer had any unsettled agricultural land to distribute to newcomers. Many of the newcomers came to Canada because of a secret agreement between the Canadian government and the North Atlantic Trading Company, which directed immigrants to Canada in return for under-the-table payments on a per capita basis. Indeed, steamship and railway companies were probably more active recruiters of agricultural immigrants outside of the British Isles than was the Canadian government.

Canada may have been a second choice, but at least it encouraged Ukrainian immigration and could make land available to the immigrants. Most Ukrainian immigrants were poor but not destitute. They had sold their land and possessions to purchase their passage. Like all immigrants of this period, they found the transatlantic passage in steerage to be a difficult experience. As their own historians have emphasized, the situation the Ukrainians entered in Canada was little different from that at home: bare survival on the land and an early death for those who failed. But they were stubborn and hopeful. Many new arrivals found the quarter-section homestead concept—160 acres or one-fourth of a square-mile township, the standard survey unit in the West—to be beyond their comprehension, partly because there was too much land, and partly because the size of the homestead meant there could be no compact village communities like the ones they had at home. The first Ukrainians typically emigrated without many of their natural leaders, especially parish clergymen, and were assisted by men like Joseph Oleskiw, Kyrolo Genik, and the Reverend Nestor Dmytriw, who were members of the Ukrainian intelligentsia employed by the Canadian government as "overseers" and advisors. These three men produced a substantial body of writing to assist the new arrivals. This advice emphasized the need for capital to establish a farm, the adoption of Western styles of dress, and the acquisition of free land. Canadian society received the Ukrainians with considerable suspicion, chiefly because they were obviously non-British "foreigners" who spoke an alien language and practiced different customs. Those who settled in the cities (especially Winnipeg's North End) in ethnic slum communities were most visible. But the willingness of most new arrivals to work hard was in their favor, at least before the onset of the Great War. After 1914, though, Austria-Hungary joined Germany as the enemy, and many Ukrainians in Canada came to be regarded as enemy aliens.

Usually considered as separate from the Ukrainians—although originating in the Ukraine—were the Doukhobors, a sectarian movement that broke away from the Russian Orthodox Church in the eighteenth century. The Doukhobors (the term means "spirit wrestlers") in the nineteenth century became a Quaker-like pacifist group that emphasized the brotherhood and sisterhood of all men and women and the validation of their group's beliefs not in books but in the "book of life." With the aid of Russian novelist Leo Tolstoy, the Doukhobors went to western Canada in search of refuge from Russian persecution. They were granted recognition as conscientious objectors by the Canadian government on 6 December 1898. Over the next few years, more than 7,500 Doukhobors arrived in Canada to settle on tracts reserved for them in what would become

Doukhobor Women, 1899 (National Archives of Canada)

Saskatchewan and Alberta. They were joined by their leader Peter Verigin (1859–1924) in 1903. In 1907 the Canadian government backed away from an earlier promise that the Doukhobors could live and work communally, insisting instead on individual homesteading and an oath of allegiance. As a result, under the leadership of Verigin, communal-living Doukhobors bought land in the interior of British Columbia and moved into the Kootenay region. Many of the Doukhobors subsequently struggled with the Canadian authorities over the issue of compulsory education, oaths of allegiance, and participation in the body politic.

The Americans

Although the Canadian press would occasionally complain about the "Americanization" of the west, most Americans had always been regarded as desirable settlers who "understand the ways of this continent and its institutions" (Troper, 1972, p. 12). Many Americans, of course, had at one time resided in British North America. Some exceptions to the favorable attitude toward Americans existed, however. Many Canadians objected to the pluralistic marriage practices of the Mormons, who were one of the earliest groups of immigrants into Alberta in the 1880s, and few Canadians showed any enthusiasm for the admission into their country of American blacks. In addition to the Mormons, a few American cattle and sheep ranchers arrived before the 1890s. But after the well-publicized "closing of

*Settlers from Colorado arriving by special train at Bassano, Alberta, March 1914
(Courtesy Glenbow Museum of Alberta, Canada)*

the frontier" in the United States after 1896, the Canadian government made a real effort to recruit American farmers of European origin for what became known as The Last Best West. Canadian agents openly sought wealthy immigrants, and the most common form of recruitment was through personal correspondence from existing settlers. Much of the settlement in Alberta and Saskatchewan occurred in the so-called Palliser's Triangle, a dry-belt region with marginal rainfall. American farmers were alleged to be the best settlers of such land, as they were familiar with techniques of dry farming. In a series of land rushes, thousands of American farmers settled the dry-belt in the years between 1906 and 1914. They prospered because there was adequate rainfall during this period. When the region's normal drought conditions resumed, beginning during the Great War, the Americans rapidly abandoned the region and returned to the United States.

The British "Home Children"

Canadians were generally more willing to accept immigrants from the British Isles than from any other place, although there was some resentment against those Britons who looked down their noses at their "colonial cousins." On the other hand, some Canadians objected to the activities of British philanthropists and philanthropic institutions in using Canada as a dumping ground for unwanted children of the urban poor. These children were recruited as cheap labor, chiefly for Canadian farms. The majority were young boys, but there was a substantial minority of girls as well. More than 50,000 of these "home children" were imported into Canada before the Great War, most of them recruited in British slums. Many were encouraged to go by their parents; others were literally seized from parents and sent overseas "for their own good." The results were rather mixed, with the worst experiences suffered by children of both genders who were sent into rural homes, where they were often treated cruelly by their supposed benefactors.

Perhaps the most colorful of the philanthropists involved in this child "rescue" venture was the Dublin-born Thomas John Barnardo (1845–1900), who was personally responsible for sending more than 30,000 youngsters to Canada. Rejected for missionary service in China because of his idiosyncrasies, he poured his energy into child saving near his mission house in East End London, according to legend sending his first boy to Ontario in 1871. Barnardo, always known as "Doctor" Barnardo, actually scoured the streets of London for waifs and collected thousands of pounds from the British public for his charity work. He did not use the money to improve existing care, but instead used it to constantly expand his activities. In 1877, Barnardo's Homes for Destitute Girls and Boys were formally vindicated from accusations of abuse and mistreatment brought against them by a blue-ribbon committee of charity leaders after a summer of hearings. A few years later, in 1882, he decided to concentrate on sending the children to Canada, and in 1884 he established a huge (14 square miles) Industrial Farm at Russell, Manitoba and an urban residence in Toronto. Despite a continuing low level of complaints of abuse and victimization, he carried on with his work until his death in 1900.

Other New Arrivals

European Contract Workers

Despite the emphasis on agricultural settlement and the concerns about assimilability of new immigrants, a number of Canadian corporations insisted on the need for willing workers. For these companies, headed by the railroads, British and other western European immigrants were not desirable because they complained about wages and working conditions; farmers were unsuitable because they left their industrial jobs at harvest

Italian railway workers in British Columbia, 1907
(Courtesy of the Multicultural History Society of Ontario)

time. The CPR turned increasingly after 1901 to contract workers, often Italians supplied by labor agents working in Europe who could "live for a year on the wages they earn in six months" (Avery, 1995, p. 30). The railroads also liked Bulgarians and Poles because they worked hard and lived simply. For the same reasons, they liked Italians, claiming they were "peculiarly suited for the work." A massive national railway construction program between 1900 and 1914 by the Canadian Pacific, Grand Trunk Pacific, and Canadian Northern Railways was basically sustained by between 50,000 and 70,000 immigrant navvies (construction workers) per year. Mining corporations were equally attracted by Slavic and Italian workers. By 1913, more than 300 labor agencies were recruiting more than 200,000 per year workers from abroad for labor in Canada. The majority of these workers were construction navvies. Several foreign governments protested the treatment of their nationals by labor agencies and Canadian employers, claiming that workers were being exploited by high agency fees and kickbacks, as well as by bad working conditions in construction camps. Undoubtedly more Asian workers would have been recruited, except for the extent of the public's hostility at that time toward Asians. Both organized labor and nativist groups opposed the contract laborers as being scabs, and these groups put enormous pressures on the Canadian government for exclusionist policies.

The Lebanese

The Chinese were not the only visible minority to come to Canada in the years before the Great War. Japanese people began arriving in small numbers in the 1880s, and a small but constant stream of other immigrants also arrived from the Near East after 1900. Most came from Lebanon, which was officially under Turkish rule as a part of Syria before 1920. Thus, these people usually appear designated as "Syrians" in the early official records. The overall Lebanese diaspora was a substantial one, with more than 15,000 people per year departing the country in the early years of the twentieth century for a variety of foreign destinations, including Canada, the United States, and Australia. The bulk of the Lebanese emigrants were Coptic Christians and Eastern Orthodox Christians who felt persecuted by the Ottoman Muslim authorities in their home country. These people were also searching for better economic opportunities. Those who came to Canada, at the rate of a few hundred a year, settled mainly in small numbers across the Canadian provinces. Many did not choose to come to Canada, but instead were transported there by immigrant contractors who chose people's destinations in term of the availability of ships. One of the curious footnotes to the sinking of the *Titanic* in 1912 was that the bulk of Canadian-bound steerage passengers on board the ill-fated liner were "Syrians." Once Lebanese immigrants had established themselves in a destination, they wrote home for their relatives to come and join them. In Canada, the newcomers tended to become small businessmen. Many began their careers as itinerant peddlers pushing wheelbarrows and worked their way up into small stores. Because there were not enough people or clergymen to establish Coptic or Orthodox churches, most of the arrivals gravitated to the churches with rituals closest to their familiar ones. For Coptic Christians this was often the Anglican Church; for Eastern Orthodox Christians, frequently the Catholic one. The 1921 Canadian census showed 4,134 persons in Canada who had been born in Syria, distributed as follows:

Prince Edward Island	27
Nova Scotia	419
New Brunswick	233
Quebec	1,416
Ontario	1,467
Manitoba	122
Saskatchewan	227
Alberta	146
British Columbia	82

The Syrians were one of the few visible minorities that did not congregate in British Columbia.

The Sikhs

East Indians, however, did mostly go to British Columbia. Substantial East Indian immigration to British Columbia did not begin in any frequency until the early years of the twentieth century. It occurred against the background of a growing movement for "Oriental" exclusion in the province, with repercussions across the nation of Canada and indeed across the continent. However, the East Indian diaspora, although in Canadian terms directed chiefly to British Columbia, was both a continental and an international phenomenon. Economic conditions in India were leading large numbers of Indian workers to seek new sources of employment, and political conditions in India were leading a smaller but active number of Indian nationalists to look both for political refuge and a new audience for their critique of the Raj (Barrier and Dusenbery, 1989).

Most of the early East Indian immigrants to British Columbia were male Sikhs from the Jat Sikh community in rural Punjab, chiefly from six districts of the central Punjab: Hoshiarpur, Guraspur, Jullundur, Ferozepur, Amritsar and Ludhiana. As was usually the case with other immigrant groups as well, the trailblazers among this group of immigrants came from a community that was energetic and where the people were well prepared as peasant landholders for a highly calculated immigration. The males came to Canada as sojourners, seeking employment and intending to return to the Punjab when the remittances sent home from their labor had sufficiently improved the economic status of their families. Most were between the ages of twenty and twenty-nine. According to official Canadian statistics, the number of East Indian adult females entering Canada in 1904–1907 was fourteen, and the number of children twenty-two. This initial sojourning pattern was typical for immigration to Canada from Asia and was quite common among immigrants from other places, such as Italy and the Balkans.

By the 1890s, the Sikhs had begun spreading through the British Empire in search of employment. Their spread was to some extent facilitated by the British Empire itself, which employed Sikhs as ceremonial troops. One contingent of Sikh soldiers travelled via Vancouver to and from the coronation of Edward VII in 1902. Whether or not this incident publicized British Columbia as a possible destination, large numbers of Sikhs began arriving in the province beginning in 1904. Sikh immigration was given a double boost by the introduction of a new Canadian head tax of $500 in 1904 on Chinese immigrants. By reducing the numbers of Chinese immigrants, the head tax both increased the job prospects for Sikhs and made available an increased carrying capacity aboard vessels from Asia that had previously dealt mainly with the Chinese. Local employers found Sikhs to be "energetic workmen with a keen desire to learn." Soon the white workers of British Columbia became concerned about the Sikhs, who readily found employment with lumber companies and railway contractors at wages substantially lower than that demanded by the whites.

More than 5,000 immigrants from India arrived in British Columbia in the years between 1904 and 1907, mainly in 1906 and 1907. American evidence suggests that almost without exception, Indians arriving in the

United States in this period paid their own way. There is no reason to doubt that the situation in Canada was any different. Immigrating East Indians, therefore, were among the most prosperous members of their communities. At the same time that the Canadian government was moving firmly toward exclusion of other groups, the East Indian community was beginning to become both organized and articulate. The Khalsa Diwan Society, a fraternal organization with nationalist overtones, was organized in Vancouver in 1907. A Committee for the Management of Sikh Gurdwaras and Temples was established by well-educated East Indians—not all of them Sikhs—soon afterward. Such organizations aided community solidarity and identity. Equally important, Indian revolutionary agitators had begun their work, mainly in the United States initially, but soon extending to Canada. Separating the activities of Indian nationalists into those directed at abuses at home and those concerned with treatment of immigrants abroad is not easy and is perhaps futile. An inability to rouse the local Sikhs was characteristic of the agitators, who often complained of the subservience or apathy of the immigrant community. But in the emergence of even the threat of violence from the agitators involving the immigrant community, the Sikhs had introduced something new into Canada: For the most part, immigrants before this had left their domestic agitations behind with them when they came to Canada, but not so the Sikhs.

The Swadesh Sevak Home was begun by Guran Dittar Kumar in Vancouver in 1909. It was alleged to be a rendezvous and residence for revolutionaries. Kumar's periodical, *Swadesh Sevak*, published in Vancouver, was banned by the Indian government. The United India House was opened in Vancouver in 1910; its leaders *were* interested in protesting the new immigration regulations limiting the passage from India to vessels engaged in a continuous voyage. The Vancouver Sikh temple agreed in 1912 to send a deputation to Victoria, Ottawa, London, and India to take up the case of the discrimination against Indians in Canada. This delegation presented its arguments to the Indian National Congress, India's nationalist political party, and when the group returned to Vancouver, the Canadian government attempted unsuccessfully to deport them. The battle, for Canadian Sikhs, had become part of the Indian nationalist agitation. Much of our knowledge about the nationalists comes from information collected by police undercover agents, such as William Charles Hopkinson in Vancouver, and must be understood in this context. Hopkinson was convinced that the leading revolutionaries were advocates of violence, prepared to employ terrorism in support of their goals. He was responsible for the attention given by government to the revolutionary agitator Har Dayal in 1913.

The Restrictions

Canada's first serious efforts to restrict immigration had come in 1872, when criminals and other "vicious classes" were denied entry by federal legislation. For the most part, though, immigration restriction was executed by discretionary means. In 1879, a federal order in council (a law passed by the cabinet) prohibited the entrance of paupers and other destitute immigrants, adding to the list of undesirable immigrants the physically and mentally challenged. The first serious attempt by the Dominion to limit the admission of a national group had come in 1885, when a federal head tax of fifty dollars was imposed on Chinese immigrants. Additional harassment of Chinese people came from the province of British Columbia, which, beginning in 1875, passed legislation limiting the rights of Chinese residents in the province. Although the years after 1885 saw the admission to Canada of millions of immigrants and contract workers, the period of 1885–1914 also saw increasing restrictions on immigrants in three quite separate senses. One was an insistence on the good health, good character, and resources of the individual immigrant as he or she entered the country. Another was an equally strong insistence on preventing group immigration by certain undesirable nationalities, usually labeled nonassimilable, a list headed by those from the continent of Asia but also including American-born blacks. The third involved provincial legislation (mainly from British Columbia) to limit the rights of unwanted residents.

The administrative apparatus of federal immigration increased substantially under Clifford Sifton, although immigration policy was not substantially altered in a formal way. However, in informal senses Sifton was prepared to close the door to "unwanted" immigrants, such as Italian workers, Chinese "coolies," or black farmers. Nevertheless, the Immigration Act of 1906, passed under Sifton's successor Frank Oliver, marked a new departure. The Act consolidated previous legislation and spelled out broad categories of unacceptable newcomers, ranging from prostitutes to the mentally challenged to those with contagious diseases to the hearing impaired, speech impaired, visually impaired, and generally infirm. It also established a functional immigration service, put in place in 1908 at thirty-eight particular United States border crossings, and provided for the deportation of "undesirable immigrants" who had become a public charge or had become the inmates of a jail, hospital, or asylum. Racial violence in Vancouver in 1907 led Prime Minister Sir Wilfrid Laurier's deputy minister of labor to go to London to deal with the Sikh and Chinese situations. A clause in the Indian Emigration Act of 1885 prohibiting emigration under contract was dug out of mothballs to be enforced. And two imperial orders in council issued by the British cabinet (1) excluded immigration by any route except directly to Canada from point of origin, and (2) denied entry to immigrants from Asia who did not have $200 in cash in their pockets. These exclusionary measures were subsequently incorporated into a new Canadian immigration law in 1910, which allowed the Canadian federal cabinet discretionary power to regulate the admission of immigrants to Canada. The 1910 Act also permitted deportation of immigrants for moral or political reasons (including the advocacy of the overthrow by force or violence of any government.) It also introduced a $25 head tax on all immigrants except the Japanese; the head tax on Japanese immigrants having been increased to $500 in 1903.

Efforts at a broader exclusionary practice involving specific national groups, mainly from Asia, also increased after 1896. These efforts involved bilateral negotiations with foreign nations to restrict the departure of their nationals, such as the exclusionary agreement with Japan in 1907, which followed after anti-Asian riots in Vancouver of that year. In 1908, an amendment to the Immigration Act provided that all immigration to Canada had to come via a continuous journey on a through ticket from the country of origin. This "continuous journey" requirement was intended to make it more difficult for immigrants to Canada to evade emigration restrictions placed by the governments of their homelands.

In May of 1914 the Japanese vessel *Komagata Maru* arrived in Vancouver harbor with 376 passengers aboard. Of these, 165 had boarded at Hong Kong, 111 at Shanghai, 86 at Moji, and 14 at Yokohama. Of the ship's passengers, 340 were Sikhs. The expedition had originated with a Punjabi-born contractor, Baba Gurdit Singh, supported by Indian nationalists from Hong Kong. It was motivated by a mixture of humanitarianism, profit making, and nationalism. The Canadian regulations to which Indian immigration were subject were patently exclusionist and inequitable. The head tax did not apply to European immigrants, and the "continuous voyage" requirement could not ever be met, as no vessels sailed directly from India to Canada. Singh expected that the Canadians would overlook the continuous voyage requirement when the ship was actually at the dock in Vancouver, and he thought that the local East

Indian community would raise the money for the head tax and for the ship's charter. He was right on the second count but wrong on the first.

The voyage across the Pacific of the *Komagata Maru* (almost no modern historians call the vessel by the name given it by Gurdit Singh—*Guru Nanak Jahaz*) was long and difficult. The Canadian government—backed by Vancouver municipal authorities and the British Columbia government, which both became quite hysterical over the entire business—refused to allow most of the passengers to land; conditions on board the ship deteriorated rapidly, and the incident quickly became an international one. The Canadian government seriously contemplated kidnapping the passengers to return them to India, while the passengers equally seriously contemplated a mass escape into Vancouver. The local courts refused to hear a test case, and Singh refused to order the vessel to depart. Canadian immigration authorities attempted to storm the ship by force, but they failed abysmally. Eventually the vessel sailed out of Vancouver harbor under naval escort and headed to India, a graphic symbol of a Canadian racial exclusionist policy, which is still very powerful today.

The *Komagata Maru* has quietly entered into the textbooks and reference works in Canadian history over the past few years, becoming an incident familiar to at least some Canadians. But there are two significant incidents resulting from the affair that are almost totally unknown among Canadians at large. These are the riots at Budge Budge in India in 1914 and the execution of Mewa Singh in 1915. The Budge Budge affair appears to have originated in a heavy-handed attempt by the Raj government of Bengal to force the passengers of the *Komagata Maru* against their will back to their villages, where they would have found no employment. A committee of inquiry laid all the blame for the riots on Gurdit Singh and the passengers, who were said to be heavily armed. The inquiry did provide a good deal of further evidence on the composition of the passengers, a subject hitherto shrouded in much mystery. The riots themselves provided a set of Indian martyrs to the oppression during the British rule of India.

As for the execution in Canada of Mewa Singh, it came at the end of a long and complicated series of events. A police informer named Bela Singh was arrested in September 1914 for shooting several Sikhs. While he was awaiting trial, fellow police informer William Hopkinson was shot in the provincial courthouse by a man named Mewa Singh, who immediately surrendered to police and confessed his guilt, saying that he had taken Hopkinson's life in order to publicize the spy's behavior. Although

Canadian officials doubted that Singh had acted on his own, he was summarily tried within ten days of the shooting and easily found guilty; there was no defense. Soon afterwards, Bela Singh was acquitted by a judge and jury, but Mewa Singh was hanged on 11 January 1915. The date of his death was for many years commemorated in the Indian community of British Columbia. The events of 1914 in one sense provided their own closure, but they were also quickly subsumed in the War to End All Wars (as World War I was sometimes called). In any event, the death of Mewa Singh can be seen both as ending the first period of East Indian immigration to Canada and as exemplifying the ways in which the Sikh history in Canada was intertwined with violence.

Not only was federal action involved with restrictions against the visible minorities from Asia, however. Provincial governments—especially in British Columbia—also introduced their own restrictions. As early as 1884, Chinese people were prohibited from acquiring Crown lands. In 1890 they were prevented from working underground in mines, and in 1897 were prevented from being hired on public works. By 1907, the British Columbia legislature had disenfranchised nationals of China, Japan, and Imperial India. This effectively prevented such nationals from serving in municipal office, on school boards, and on juries, as such service was based on the provincial voters' lists. These restrictions were generally reaffirmed in 1920.

Conclusion

The Canadian record on immigration was, to say the least, a mixed one between 1867 and 1914. Millions of newcomers were allowed into the country, mainly from the British Isles but also from a variety of other nations in Europe and Asia. For some peoples there was an "open door" policy. But a tension always existed between the nation's need for immigrants to help develop the country and serve as a source for labor, and the nation's reluctance to accept immigrants without reference to their background or circumstances. Almost all Canadians wanted immigration, but few wanted to deal with immigrants whose language was strange, whose customs were different, whose education was seen as deficient—and whose skin colour was not the same as that of the vast majority. British Columbia and Quebec led the way in opposing the open admission of large numbers of immigrants. Even J. S. Woodsworth, one of the major

All People's Mission, Winnipeg, 1904
(Courtesy of the Provincial Archives of Manitoba)

champions of a warm welcome for *Strangers within Our Gates*—as his 1909 study of immigration policy was called—insisted on the exclusion of "essentially non-assimilable elements."

Timeline

1868   Federal-provincial conference sorts out spheres of influence on immigration: federal government to appoint agents in Great Britain and Europe; provinces can recruit anywhere. First Free Grants and Homestead Act passed; transfer of Hudson's Bay Territory to Canada negotiated.

1869   Louis Riel proclaims provisional government at Red River.

1870   Manitoba Act passed by Canadian Parliament.

1871   British Columbia admitted to Canada as sixth province.

1872   Federal legislation prohibits entry of criminals and other "vicious classes" into Canada; Dominion Lands Act passed; Dominion begins extensive advertising in Europe and introduces passenger warrant system by which passage costs are reduced for approved emigrants.

1874 First Mennonites arrive on prairies.

1875 Icelanders found Republic of Iceland at Gimli.

1876 Treaty no. 6 signed with First Nations at Fort Carlton.

1878 Sir John A. Macdonald takes Interior portfolio.

1879 Federal order in council prohibits paupers and destitute immigrants.

1881 ff More than 15,000 Chinese immigrants admitted to work on railway.

1882 Two hundred forty Jews leave London for Manitoba and Northwest; CPR begins selling large land blocks to settlers.

1885 Northwest Rebellion suppressed; Métis and First Nations moved to the margins of the country; Chinese immigration restricted and regulated(stiff head tax of $50 would later be raised).

1887 Small community of Mormons led by Charles Card comes to Alberta; Emigrants' Information Office established in London under control of Colonial Office.

1888 Passenger warrant system discontinued; first Scots crofter settlers arrive under crofter settlement schemes.

1892 Federal immigration, previously under jurisdiction of Department of Agriculture, transferred to Department of Interior until 1917.

1896 Clifford Sifton appointed minister of immigration.

1898 Sifton orders Italian laborers deported; Doukhobor immigration agents arrive in Canada.

1899 North Atlantic Trading Company (a syndicate of steamship agents based in Antwerp) organized to send agricultural settlers from Europe to Canada; bloc settlements encouraged in Canada; 7,500 Doukhobors arrive between January and July.

1900 Sifton moves to encourage American farmers to migrate; Japanese immigrants begin to arrive in northern British Columbia; organized labor opposes inundation by non-English-speaking aliens.

1901 CPR imports Italian workers through Montreal-based agent Antonio Cordasco; British Columbia mining companies import Italian strikebreakers.

1902 Salvation Army immigration office opened in London. Barr colonists organized in Britain to come to Saskatchewan.

1903 Federal Immigration Office opened in London.

1904 Sikhs arrive in British Columbia.

1905   Frank Oliver appointed minister of immigration; Canadian immigration policy becomes more selective (eastern Canadians, Brits, and Americans preferred; other nationalities not desired).

1906   Immigration Act of 1906 consolidates immigration legislation, barring large categories of people; North Atlantic Trading Company contract cancelled; bonuses raised for British immigrants.

1907   One hundred immigration agents appointed for Britain, to receive $2 bonus for every farm laborer recruited; Vancouver Branch of Asiatic Exclusion League organized; Asians riot in British Columbia; pressure for immigrant navvies mounts for railroad construction; Canada reaches agreement with Japan that all immigrants can come but the Japanese government will limit laborers to 400 per year.

1908   Continuous journey regulation introduced; border inspection service established on U.S. border.

1909   J. S. Woodsworth publishes *Strangers within Our Gates.*

1910   A restrictive Immigration Act passed; subsequent orders in council imposed $200 head tax on Asian immigrants and various amounts on other immigrants.

1911   Petitions against blacks lead to order in council prohibiting black immigration.

1914   *Komagata Maru* incident.

Significant People, Places, and Events

BARNARDO, "DR." THOMAS JOHN (1845–1900) A London evangelist and child-saver who founded the Barnardo Home for Destitute Boys and Girls, first in Britain and, after 1884, in Canada.

BARR COLONY Settlement organized in Britain in 1902 by Isaac Barr, a British clergyman and utopian.

BRITISH COLUMBIA A British colony created by joining Vancouver Island and British Columbia together in 1866, it joined the Dominion of Canada in 1871 when Canada promised the completion of a transcontinental railroad within ten years.

CANADIAN PACIFIC RAILWAY Created from the merging of several railroads in 1881 to complete a transcontinental railroad between eastern Canada and British Columbia, the railway received generous subsidies in cash and land. The line was completed in 1885.

COPTIC CHRISTIANS A sect to which many of the Syrian immigrants to Canada belonged. The Coptic Church was a descendant of the early Christian Church in the Near East.

DOMINION LANDS ACT OF 1872 Based on American legislation, this statute described the method by which homestead lands in western Canada were to be supplied to incoming settlers. Each settler was to receive one 160-acre quarter section of land in return for a small registry fee and performance of certain requirements, such as the building of a habitation on the premises.

JAPANESE EXCLUSION An agreement between Canada and the Japanese government in 1907, by which Japan would limit the number of male immigrants to 400 per year, (reduced in 1928 to 150 people per year).

KOMAGATA MARU AFFAIR In 1914 a group of people from the Punjab, chiefly Sikhs, chartered a Japanese freighter (the *Komagata Maru*) in order to meet the Canadian requirement that immigrants from India to Canada could come only by a continuous passage. When the ship arrived in Vancouver harbor, the Canadian immigration authorities used force to prevent the immigrants from landing.

MANITOBA ACT The 1870 act of Parliament that created Manitoba as a province of Canada and set aside 1,400,000 acres of land for Métis children.

MENNONITES A Protestant religious group of Anabaptist origins that left Russia in the 1870s to settle in Manitoba, the Northwest Territories, and the United States. The Mennonites were pacifists who believed in communal ownership of property.

MÉTIS The mixed-blood residents of western Canada, most often speaking the French language and belonging to the Roman Catholic Church.

MORMONS A religious community that originated in the nineteenth-century United States and began immigrating to the Northwest Territories under the leadership of Charles Ora Card in 1887.

NEW ICELAND An autonomous community of Icelandic inhabitants established on the west shore of Lake Winnipeg in 1875 in the Northwest Territories. It became part of Manitoba in 1881.

NORTH ATLANTIC TRADING COMPANY A cartel of shipping agents and shipping firms that had a secret agreement with the government between 1901 and 1906 to supply contract laborers for Canada.

NORTHWEST MOUNTED POLICE A paramilitary police force based on the Irish constabulary, organized in 1873 to keep law and order in the Northwest Territories of Canada.

OLESKIW, DR. JOSEPH (1860–1903) A professor of agriculture at the teacher's seminar at Lviv, Oleskiw was sent to Canada by the Prosvita Society to investigate the possibility of Ukrainian immigration to Canada. Upon his return, he published a number of pamphlets in Ukrainian providing information about Canada and immigration there.

OLIVER, FRANK (1853–1933) Minister of the interior and superintendent of Indian affairs 1905–1911. Although he continued the immigration policies of Clifford Sifton, he was also responsible for more formal immigration restriction.

PALLISER'S TRIANGLE A dry-belt region of southwestern Saskatchewan and southern Alberta, it was settled by American farmers (1908–1914) during a period of decent moisture and was later (1921–1935) abandoned by most of its residents.

POUNDMAKER (1842–1886) Chief of the Cree people, he reluctantly accepted Treaty no. 6 (see below). During the Northwest Rebellion, some of his people attacked Battleford. He was subsequently sentenced to three years in the federal penitentiary for felony treason.

RIEL, LOUIS (1844–1885) Leader of the Métis people of Red River, he succeeded in securing the region's admission to Canada as a distinct province, although he was outlawed for his resistance. In 1885 he sparked another Métis uprising in Saskatchewan against Canada, which was easily suppressed by the government. He was tried and convicted of high treason and was executed in November of 1885. Riel would become the symbol of resistance to Canada's racial exclusionism.

ROYAL COMMISSION ON CHINESE IMMIGRATION Established in 1885, its hearings led to recommendations that the Canadian government restrict Chinese immigration by levying a head tax on new arrivals from China.

SIFTON, CLIFFORD (1861–1929) Minister of the interior and superintendent-general of Indian affairs in the government of Sir Wilfrid Laurier from 1896 to 1905, Sifton promoted immigration from outside the preferred regions of the British Isles and northwestern Europe.

TREATY NO. 6 One of a series of numbered treaties (1–9) by which First Nations surrendered land claims to the Canadian government in the 1870s. Treaty no. 6 was negotiated at Fort Carleton in 1876 with the Cree.

UKRAINE A wheat-growing region on the steppes of central Europe and Asia, the Ukraine was partly composed of the provinces of Galicia and Bukovyna in the Austro-Hungarian Empire and of the Ukraine in the

Russian Empire. This was the homeland of more than 170,000 immigrants to Canada before World War I.

VERIGIN, PETER (1859–1924) Leader of the Doukhobor sect starting in 1886 and exiled to Siberia, he joined his people in Canada in 1903, encouraging them to oppose attempts by the Canadian authorities to impose on them education, oaths of allegiance, and restrictions on communal ownership of land.

Bibliography

Avery, Donald, *Reluctant Host: Canada's Response to Immigrant Workers, 1896–1994* (Toronto: McClelland and Stewart, 1995).

Barrier, N. Gerald and Verne A. Dusenbery, eds., *The Sikh Diaspora: Migration and the Experience beyond Punjab* (Delhi: Chanakya Publications, 1989).

Epp, Frank, *Mennonites in Canada, 1786–1920: The History of a Separate People* (Toronto: Macmillan of Canada, 1974).

Johnston, Hugh, *The Voyage of the* Komagata Maru: *The Sikh Challenge to Canada's Colour Bar* (Delhi: Oxford University Press, 1979).

Knowles, Valerie, *Strangers at Our Gates: Canadian Immigration and Immigration Policy, 1540–1997*, rev. ed. (Toronto, Ontario and Oxford, U.K.: Dundurn Press, 1997).

Kristjanson, Wilhelm, *The Icelandic People of Manitoba: A Manitoba Saga* (1965, reprinted 1990, Winnipeg: Wallingford Press).

Lee, David, "The Métis: Militant Rebels of 1885," *Canadian Ethnic Studies* 21:3 (1989), 1–19.

Macdonald, Norman, *Canada: Immigration and Colonization 1841–1903* (Toronto: Macmillan of Canada, 1970).

Magosci, Paul Robert, ed., *Encyclopedia of Canada's Peoples* (Toronto: University of Toronto Press, 1999).

Petryshyn, Jaroslav, *Peasants in the Promised Land: Canada and the Ukrainians, 1891–1914* (Toronto: James Lorimer, 1985).

St. Germain, Jill, *Indian Treaty-Making Policy in the United States and Canada 1867–1877* (Toronto: University of Toronto Press, 2001).

Singh, Narindar, *Canadian Sikhs: History, Religion, and Culture of Sikhs in North America* (Ottawa: Canadian Sikhs' Studies Institute, 1994).

Sprague, D. N., "The Manitoba Land Question, 1870–1882," in J. M. Bumsted, ed., *Interpreting Canada's Past*, vol. 2 (Toronto: Oxford University Press, 1986).

Troper, Harold Martin, *Only Farmers Need Apply: Official Canadian Government Encouragement of Immigration from the United States, 1896–1911* (Toronto: Griffin House, 1972).

CHAPTER SEVEN

Two Wars and a Depression, 1914–1945

LTHOUGH THE PERIOD between 1914 and 1945, which included
two world wars and a major depression, has never been celebrated
for its immigration to Canada, these years saw the admission of
more than 1,700,000 newcomers, representing an average of nearly 60,000
per year, with more than 1,166,000 arriving between 1921 and 1931. Even
wartime immigration during the Great War had been larger than might
have been expected, with 247,000 immigrants entering Canada between
1914 and 1919. The numbers were much smaller from 1931 to 1941—
with only 140,000 immigrants for that entire decade—and between 1942
and 1945, with 50,000 new arrivals in that period. Nevertheless, especially
before 1931, immigration during these two decades had been substantial.
At the same time, probably the most important feature of this entire period was the mounting negative attitude on the part of the Canadian authorities and citizens toward extensive immigration and toward many
immigrants and immigrant groups. Exclusionary policies seemed increasingly in vogue. The main task of the Immigration Department seemed to
be to figure out ways to keep immigrants out, rather to develop ways of
allowing productive immigrants to enter the country. This exclusionism
was similar to attitudes and policies in the United States, probably less in
imitation of the Americans than a response to similar international conditions of war and depression.

The Enemy Alien Problem, 1914–1920

Like every other participant, Canada entered the Great War in 1914 with
no conception of its ultimate length, intensity, or futile savagery. The nation allowed itself to become a combatant on the strength of the British

Bishop Budka and parishioners in front of a church in Borschiw, Alberta, 1916
(National Archives of Canada)

Empire's involvement. At least initially, the enthusiasm of English-speaking Canadians for the war was considerable, although the war ran against the grain of French Canadian attitudes toward Europe and the British Empire. Almost forgotten at the outset were the implications of the presence in Canada of a large population whose roots were in the countries of the enemy. Canada in 1914 contained nearly 400,000 Germans, 129,000 from the Austro-Hungarian Empire, almost 4,000 from the Turkish Empire, and some from Bulgaria. At least one of the leaders of the Austrians in Canada, Bishop Nykyta Budka of Winnipeg, had, before the war began, reminded his people of their obligation "to go to the defence of our threatened Fatherland" (Avery, 1995, p. 66). From the beginning of the war, the War Measures Act allowed the Governor-in-Council (the Canadian federal cabinet) a free hand with enemy aliens. Gradually, aliens were prohibited from possessing guns and were placed under close police surveillance. Nearly 80,000 aliens were registered and more than 8,000 were interned as potential threats against the nation, mainly in Vernon, British Columbia, and Kapuskasing, Ontario.

Although the bulk of the enemy aliens were of German origin, most of those persecuted and detained were citizens of the Austro-Hungarian Empire, chiefly people of Ukrainian origin. German-speakers were typically placed into a "first-class" category and confined in comfortable camps. Those described as "Austrian," "Galician," or "Ruthenian" were sent to work sites where they engaged in heavy construction activities and worked on parole for private companies. In 1917, every Ukrainian immigrant who had arrived in Canada after March 1902 was disenfranchised. Few incidents of sabotage or espionage involving the Austro-Ukrainians actually occurred, but there were many public calls for government activity against them. The situation was made more severe after 1917 by the activities of a number of radical ethnic organizations and newspapers that responded with enthusiasm to the Russian Revolution. The Winnipeg-based newspaper *Robotchny Narod,* for example, supported a strike by construction workers and began to be critical of the Dominion government's policy of compulsory military service. Canadian capitalists were easily persuaded that the Ukrainian community was the center of Bolshevism in Canada, although the most successful radical labor organization, the International Workers of the World (IWW), was not led by either Communists or Ukrainians. As the war ground to an end, a special investigation into activity among the foreign-born community in Canada reported that there was a conspiracy developing among this group, led by the "Bolsheviki faction of Russia." As a result, two orders-in-council (regulations passed by the Canadian cabinet with the force of law) suppressed the foreign language press and most socialist/anarchist organizations in the autumn of 1918.

At the end of the war, the Canadian government and some of the country's population began sparring over public policy. The government, a coalition "Union" government of Conservatives and English-speaking Liberals, still ran the country as if it were at war, increasingly fearful of a social upheaval in Canada comparable to that in Russia. The opposition, headed by the labor unions, insisted that the government was repressing legitimate dissent. The growing national controversy erupted into open confrontation in Winnipeg in May of 1919, when a large body of workers voted to close down the city's services and declared a "General Strike." As usual, the Canadian authorities responded with alacrity to anything that smacked of popular discontent, especially if associated with immigrants. The strike was actually organized and led mainly by Canadian- and British-born workers and trade unionists, but both the general public and returning soldiers were easily persuaded that what was needed was to "clean the aliens out of this community and ship them back to their happy homes in Europe which vomited them forth a decade ago" (quoted in Bumsted, 1994, p. 66). The strike was broken by arresting its leaders (six of British background and four "foreigners"). The leaders of British background were accused of sedition, and the "foreigners" were summarily shipped to an internment camp and ultimately secretly deported. The police magistrate who had ordered the men interned commented, "As

Alberta internment camp, 1915 (Courtesy Glenbow Museum of Alberta, Canada)

Police Magistrate I have seen to what a large extent Bolsheviki ideas are held by the Ruthenian, Russian and Polish people, whom we have in our midst. . . . it is absolutely necessary that an example should be made. . . . If the Government persists in the course that it is now adopting [of wholesale deportations] the foreign element here will soon be as gentle and easily controlled as a lot of sheep" (quoted in Bumsted, 1994, p. 67). The Canadian government's repression of foreign radicalism continued throughout the 1920s and into the 1930s, when the Communist Party of Canada was suppressed as an alien political force advocating the violent overthrow of the nation's legitimate rulers. Political considerations had become an important part of Canadian immigration policy.

Many leaders of the returned veterans became convinced, along with Dr. A. M. Forbes, vice president of the Great War Veterans' Association, that "among the most important [national issues] are the settlement of our agricultural lands and the pressing problem of the alien population of Canada" (Fedorowich, 1995, p. 71). This linking of settlement (often by veterans) and the alien question was common in the years immediately after the war.

Soldier Settlement, 1918–1939

To conceive of a war involving Canada that did not end with some effort to resettle soldiers on the land was almost impossible, because the Anglo-Canadian tradition had always been to reward soldiers with free land.

There was no reason to think that the Great War would be different. Prime Minister Sir Robert Borden assured Canadian soldiers that his government would "prove to the returned man just and due appreciation of the inestimable value of the services rendered to the country and empire" (Fedorowich, 1995, p. 46). To provide returning veterans with land had a variety of advantages, not the least of which would be to dampen threats to political stability while favoring the basic building block of the nation: the agricultural community. "No nation can be regarded as unhealthy when a virile peasantry, contented with rural employments . . . exists on its soil," wrote one publicist (Fedorowich, 1995, p. 72).

Unfortunately, Canada would experience substantial agricultural difficulties after the Great War. These were caused partly by overexpansion during the prosperous days of the war. Farmers had borrowed money during the war to increase the amount of arable land under cultivation and to purchase farm machinery. After the war, the bottom fell out of the market, and farmers were left repaying boom-time borrowings with non-boom earnings. Moreover, a shift in weather and climate (chiefly drought and lack of rainfall) during the 1920s exposed many farmers in dry-belt areas to years of bad crops.

Given prewar concerns over rural depopulation, soldier settlement was an obvious policy to implement. It was begun by the provinces before the war was over, and in 1917 the Soldier Settlement Act provided for supplying returning veterans with a homestead while increasing the country's agricultural production. The Act established a Soldier Settlement Board (SSB), which could make loans up to $2,500 available at 5 percent for twenty years for land, livestock, and farm machinery. The returning soldier could apply the loans to property he already possessed or to lands he wished to obtain by purchase or homestead. Unfortunately, only about 2,000 veterans took advantage of this program between 1917 and 1919, chiefly because it was difficult to find large quantities of productive and accessible land on short notice.

The program was revamped in May of 1919 to expand the amount of land available and to provide a more generous supply of credit. Much of the new public land available in the west was to be taken from underutilized Indian reserves, although the most important provision was the opportunity to buy private land with government support. From the beginning, critics complained that the land program was not based on sound business principles. More than 100,000 Canadians, including 25,000 ex-soldiers, were placed on the land by 1920, but there were many problems. One was that normal requirements of guarantees of repayment were waived. Even more significantly, the soldiers had bought while prices for land, stock, and equipment were still high, and they soon had to face the collapse of Canadian markets in 1920. Moreover, much of the land put under cultivation (with the enthusiastic support of provincial governments) proved to be only marginally arable.

With some reluctance, Canada agreed to allow British ex-servicemen and women an opportunity to farm under the aegis of the SSB. While it accepted the offer of the British government of grants of free passage for British veterans, Canada insisted that those eligible had to have some capital to qualify for SSB assistance. It was understandably difficult to guarantee that those given free passage would actually become farmers, and a number of destitute and unemployed ex-imperial soldiers surfaced in Canada in 1920, especially in Ontario and British Columbia. Canadian veterans' organizations complained that the ex-imperials were making it difficult for Canada's own soldiers to be reabsorbed into the economy. The Canadian government and the Colonial Office were soon at loggerheads over the free passage scheme. The limited statistics available for the 26,095 who came to Canada with free passage suggest that few were actually farmers.

Although soldier settlement had temporarily expanded the agricultural sector in Canada immediately after the war, it did so at the expense of long-term prosperity. When the markets for grain and livestock collapsed in 1920 and 1921, many of the new arrivals were hung out to dry. By 1923 the failure rate among soldier-settlers was 21.5 percent. Nevertheless, many soldier settlers did remain on the land and become successful farmers. One of the major problems with soldier settlement, however, was that it absorbed a disproportionate amount of the money spent on veterans' benefits by the Canadian government: About 4 percent of the total number of able-bodied Canadian veterans got about 14 percent of the money spent on benefits.

Empire Settlement

The response of many Canadians to the Great War was to insist on both the importance of maintaining British values in Canadian society and on the need to do something to recompense the soldiers who had fought in the trenches. Both these goals could seemingly be met by Empire Settlement, in which former soldiers and other British people could serve as the basis of large state-assisted settlement schemes in the various dominions of the British Empire. As previous chapters of this book have shown, most Canadian immigration officials were not from the beginning very enthusiastic about such ideas. Their experiences over the years with publicly assisted emigration from the United Kingdom had on the whole been disappointing. As one official commented, such proposals "would produce a great many settlers who are not likely to make a success on the land and who would give our country a black eye" (Constantine, 1990, p. 151). Large-scale emigration schemes had never worked. Canada remained convinced that only experienced farmers could be successful western pioneers, and Empire Settlement was at worst a dumping scheme for unemployed British workers. Leo S. Amery, the leading parliamentary spokesman for the scheme, insisted that the potential emigrants deserved a chance to "make good citizens and good workers on the land." Canada's experiences with free passage for British veterans in 1920 and 1921 had not been favorable, and although the Dominion reluctantly agreed to participate in Empire settlement in 1923, it earmarked only small amounts for the program and confined assistance to household workers, agricultural workers named by established Canadian farmers, and children between ages eight and fourteen sponsored by a recognized voluntary society. What little Canadian involvement there was in the scheme perpetuated earlier Canadian programs, most of which had failed as badly as it was predicted Empire Settlement would.

Increased needs for labor beginning in 1924 and evidence that Canadians were leaving for the United States led to some greater enthusiasm for new arrivals of British stock. But despite the expenditure of considerable sums of money on training and settlement schemes, none of the various initiatives undertaken in the 1920s proved particularly successful. A variety of factors contributed to the doom of each program. Some failed because they were badly conceived, others because they required substantial provincial contributions, and almost all failed because Ottawa was not really very enthusiastic about the concept of settlement by British citizens. Dominion officials remained persuaded that most of those being recruited were "defectives" being sent out of Britain by those "anxious to rid the country of people who are a burden to the community" (Constantine, 1990, p. 166). The enthusiasts insisted, of course, that a new chance in a new country would reinvigorate many, but most Canadians remained suspicious of the quality of those on offer. (Canada would move quickly to terminate assisted settlement in 1930, at virtually the first sign of the Depression.)

In 1925 Canada came up with a new program to utilize land it had obtained for soldier settlement but had not used. It offered the land to 3,000

British families, who, if they possessed £25 pounds upon their arrival in Canada, could obtain up to £300 pounds in loans and advances as well as other assistance. The 3,000 Families program recruited particularly heavily in the Outer Hebrides of Scotland and was regarded in that region as quite successful among crofter families. According to one fifteen-year-old participant from Lanarkshire, her family heard nothing but positive accounts of the scheme. The families recruited "wrote of the hearty welcome which they had received on arrival, of the pleasant farms they had been placed upon, and the exceptional kindness shown them by their neighbours, and seemed by the hopeful tone of their letters to be fully assured of future prosperity" (Harper, 1998, p. 132). By 1928, however, Canadians had turned against all assisted emigration. The government refused to expand the 3,000 Families operation, and it rejected schemes for unemployed miners to be brought to Canada to help with the harvest, as well as a program for juveniles.

Although Empire Settlement brought more than 100,000 British immigrants to Canada between 1922 and 1935, especially under three general categories—female domestics (20,000); young people intending to be farmers (10,000); and British farm families (3,500)—it was a failure in terms of the expectations of its proponents. Most observers recognized that assisted settlement did not work chiefly because the Canadian government—and the Canadian people—were not really supportive of it. At the same time, it should be added that Empire Settlement did not work well anywhere in the British dominions.

Exclusionary and Nonexclusionary Policies of the 1920s

Canada's ambivalence about foreigners—even British-born immigrants if they did not fit the country's needs—was only enhanced in the 1920s by a new immigration policy in the United States. President Warren Harding signed the Emergency Immigration Quota Act in 1921, and by 1924 a permanent quota system was put in place, based on the numbers in the American population from any particular country in the 1920 census. This quota system had the effect of enhancing the numbers of the older preferred immigrant groups in the United States and working against eastern and southern Europeans. Numbers of Asian immigrants were limited by an Exclusion Act. At the same time, the Americans also exempted Canada and most of the Western Hemisphere from the quota restrictions, thus encouraging nearly one-half million Canadians to move to the United States between 1925 and 1932.

Hostility in Canada to Asian immigration only grew during the interwar period—especially, but not exclusively, in British Columbia—partly because it became clear that the numbers of Asians was increasing through natural increase despite the best efforts of the Dominion and the province toward exclusion. The 1920s saw a surprising success for the Vancouver Asiatic Exclusion League, which claimed more than 20,000 members and sought to end Asian immigration, to deport Asian criminals and "illegals," and to do whatever else was required "to preserve white domination and control" (Ward, 1990, p. 129). The tightening of laws within the control of the provinces was of limited effect, and most of the pressure to act was placed on the federal government. In 1923 a new Chinese Immigration Act was passed by the Dominion Parliament. It abolished the head tax and simply limited the entry of Chinese people to a few categories involving a handful of immigrants. Prime Minister William Lyon Mackenzie King defended the legislation as producing a system similar to that in effect for the Japanese. Canada opened further negotiations on immigration with the Japanese in 1925, and in 1928 the Japanese agreed to restrict further the number of their nationals going to Canada to 150 per year and to put a stop to the so-called Picture Brides: Japanese women coming to Canada to marry Canadian Japanese men whom they had never met.

Not all was unabashed exclusionism during the 1920s, however. Although Jewish immigrants were not quite welcomed with open arms, more than 200 Jewish war orphans were allowed entrance in 1920, and the Jewish Colonization Association subsequently succeeded in gaining admission to Canada for more than 3,000 Jewish refugees from the Ukraine who had been received and then expelled by Rumania. Over the period 1920–1930 nearly 50,000 Jews gained admission to Canada, almost 4 percent of the total immigrants for the decade. At the same time, in an unprecedented move in 1925, the government of William Lyon Mackenzie King responded to boom conditions across the nation—and an increased demand for labor—by signing an agreement with Canada's two major railroads. Both companies ran colonization departments and had long complained of obstacles thrown in their way by the immigration authorities. The Dominion now agreed that the railroads could recruit genuine European agriculturalists until 1928 from previously "non-preferred" parts of Europe. Not surprisingly, the Canadian business community favored the arrangement, but labor and the churches opposed it. Over the next half-decade, nearly 200,000 immigrants from central and eastern Europe were admitted to Canada, normally by coopera-

Canadian Pacific Railway festival, 1928
(Courtesy of the Provincial Archives of Manitoba)

tive arrangements between the railroads, their colonization companies, and various ethnic and religious organizations in Canada, such as the Hungarian Slovak Colonization Board. The CPR even gave preference for employment with the company to new immigrants who had come on CPR ships.

Nonetheless, the immigration authorities constantly complained of abuses of the railroad concessions, and opposition to the railroad activities among farmers and others grew in western Canada. Professor A. R. M. Lower of Wesley College distinguished between "cheap" labor (the immigrants) and "dear" labor (native Canadians) and insisted that a sort of Gresham's law (by which the bad drove out the good) prevailed on the farm. "The gradual displacement of the English speaking farmers from the small farms and soils by Central Europeans who demand less from life is an illustration of the principle of the 'cheap' and 'dear' man," Lower insisted (Avery, 1995, p. 103). But such arguments were unable to halt the flow of newcomers until the arrival of the Depression cut into the numbers.

Canada and the Armenian Genocide

In 1908 the government of the Ottoman Empire was taken over by the so-called Young Turks, a nationalist movement that was firmly committed to a homogeneous state and the eradication of all who did not satisfy majority standards. The new Turkey was to be ethnically Turkish and religiously Muslim. These policies were strenuously resisted by the Christian Armenians in the Ottoman Empire. In 1915 the Turkish government began its practice of removing these recalcitrant elements, ordering all Armenian soldiers in the Turkish army to be shot. The government then disarmed the civilian Armenians, imprisoned their leaders, and began expelling, dispersing, and massacring thousands of Armenians. The people of Canada were quite affected by news of this mistreatment, and in 1920 they raised hundreds of thousands of dollars to assist the refugee survivors of this genocidal policy. At the same time, Canada did not step forward to provide refuge for the surviving Armenians.

In a foreshadowing of the later Canadian policy toward the Jewish refugees from Nazi Germany, the Canadian immigration authorities managed to combine and employ two different standards for exclusion—refugee status and racial classification—to keep the number of Armenians allowed into Canada to a mere 1,200 during a period when 23,000 Armenians were admitted to the United States and another 80,000 allowed into France. The first Canadian regulation of which the Armenians ran afoul was the passport one: All immigrants (except Britons and Americans) had to possess a valid passport and a visa issued overseas by a Canadian immigration official or a British official. Most Armenians lacked passports and were unable to get them from their local authorities, who were trying to destroy the passports. Canada resolutely refused to recognize the special identity certificate developed by the League of Nations High Commission for Refugees.

The Canadian Immigration service also insisted on treating the Armenians as Asians—while admitting they were not—which brought all of the Canadian regulations designed for the people of Asia to bear on the Armenians. They were required to have $250 in cash in their possession, to come to Canada via a continuous journey, and to meet Canada's occupational requirements as farmers. Even trained agriculturalists were discouraged from applying for entrance on the grounds that "the style of farming to which they are accustomed is so different to the farming in this country that they cannot be looked upon as having any experience of much value to them" (Kaprielian-Churchill, 1990, p. 96). Although these tactics were executed by civil servants, they were at least tacitly supported by the politicians, who could have overridden what was being done at any point. A few Armenian orphan boys were accepted in 1923 by ministerial prerogative, but this was not a typical exemption. Jewish and Mennonite refugees also faced considerable difficulty gaining admission to Canada in the 1920s, but they at least had the advantage of being classified as Europeans and had strong lobbies working on their behalf.

The "Red Scare" of the Early 1930s

As already noted, by the 1920s, the Communist Party of Canada (CPC) was regarded by the authorities as a major threat to the Canadian way of life. The CPC was considered dangerous both because it was thought to seek the overthrow of the incumbent government and because it recruited so successfully among ethnic workers. Unlike the One Big Union (OBU) and the International Workers of the World (IWW), both contemporary radical organizations in Canada, the CPC got most of its support from foreign-born workers, especially militant Finns and Ukrainians. The CPC did not really compete with the OBU and the IWW, as their memberships were relatively different. Because the CPC was one of the few labor organizations that were prepared to adopt a militant attitude toward government policy in the early years of the Depression, it made substantial popular gains. By early 1931 CPC demonstrations in the larger cities became larger and more aggressive. Fortunately for the Canadian authorities, the CPC had experienced considerable division within its ranks in the later 1920s. One of the major problems was the insistence of the Communist International (the Comintern) upon the Bolshevization of all national Communist parties, thus turning the Canadian CPC into an ideological puppet of the Soviet Union.

In 1931 the major CPC leaders were arrested and charged under section 98 of the Criminal Code of being seditious members of an illegal organization. The leading Toronto CPC members (the "Toronto Eight," which included Tim Buck) were convicted and sent to federal prison, and most of the foreign-born among the CPC leaders were deported under section 41 of the Immigration Act. Similar treatment was given to labor leaders of other radical organizations that remained independent of the CPC. The party fought back through the Canadian Labour Defence League (CLDL), which had organized 123 branches by 1931 and had created a special division called "The Defence of the Foreign Born." The government's repressive tactics actually substantially increased the membership of the CLDL. The continued association in the public mind of the CPC with the foreign workers, of course, worked to the disadvantage of both the CPC and the workers, who could be branded as opponents of the "Canadian Way of Life."

Canadian Response to the Coming of World War II

In 1930, at the start of the Great Depression, the Canadian cabinet passed an order-in-council that suspended European immigration to Canada. Pursuing earlier policies, the order-in-council confined admission to Canada to those who had capital to establish farms or who were the dependents of those already in Canada. A year later, Order-in-Council P.C. 695 established a new Canadian policy, hardly much broader than that of 1930, for the duration of the Depression. Under this policy, only British and American citizens with capital, farmers able to become farm proprietors, and those who were guaranteed employment in mining or timbering—as well as dependents of males currently residing in Canada—would be permitted to enter the country. Once having established such an exclusionary policy, Canada chose to stick to it, however much international conditions changed over the decade. It was certainly the case that much of Europe would have been pleased to allow Canada to become the destination of as many of its "undesirables" as it was prepared to admit, so the dilemma for Canada seemed fairly clear-cut. It could allow its immigration policy to be controlled by European events totally beyond its control, in the process making life potentially more difficult for its own people, or it could continue to hold the line on denying access to refugees unwanted in Europe.

Jewish Refugees

From Adolph Hitler's assumption of the office of German chancellor in 1933, it was clear that the relatively small Jewish population of Germany was going to be a target for persecution. The numbers of Jews at risk from Nazi policy were increased in two ways: first, by an extension of the definition of Jew to include anyone with one Jewish (or partially Jewish) grandparent; and second, by the German takeover and subsequent military conquest of much of central Europe, home of millions of Jews. From the beginning of Nazi rule, those Jews who could escape did so, although most Jews were unable to respond swiftly enough to the German annexations of the Rhineland, Austria, and Czechoslovakia. Most of the European countries that sheltered the refugees made it clear that they were providing only a temporary refuge, and when approached, Canada initially agreed to accept a very small number. Upon further reflection, however, the Canadian authorities decided against accepting even a tiny

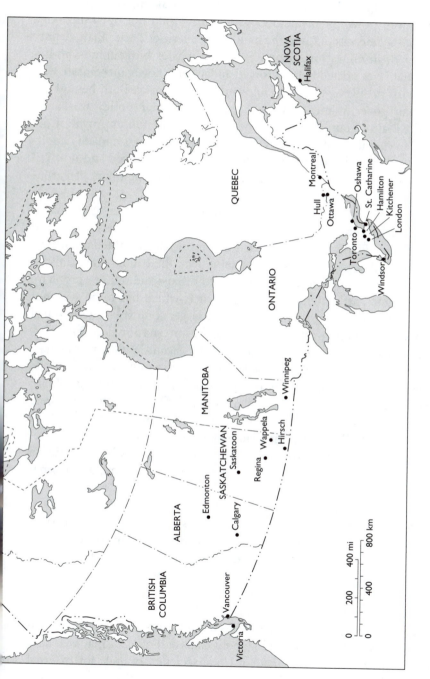

Canada's Cities with Jewish Communities

Source: Smith, MacKay L. The Jews of Montreal and Their Judaisms: A Voyage of Discovery. (Montreal: Aaron Communications, 1997), p. 19.

trickle of refugees. The numbers of refugees and unemployed persons in Europe was growing daily, and Canada felt it could not open its doors. Holding the line was put into the hands of Frederick Charles Blair, deputy minister of immigration. Blair was both a master bureaucrat who believed that rules existed to be enforced and a well-known anti-Semite who saw Jewish people as unassimilable and conspiratorial. Both he and the Canadian government, however, denied that their policy was anti-Semitic. Blair certainly enforced the rules with the full approval of the Canadian cabinet. Unfortunately, Jewish organizations in Canada had little political clout in the 1930s, as they were badly financed and not well organized. After 1935 there were only three Jewish members of Parliament, hardly much of a lobby.

Until 1938, a few Jews were admitted to Canada under the terms of various agricultural settlement schemes. This route was effectively closed in 1938 when Frederick Blair decided that most Jews admitted as farmers were not really agriculturalists. That same year, the United States invited thirty nations to meet at Evian, France, to discuss the refugee problem. Canada reluctantly attended this conference, which has to be seen not simply in the context of refugees but in the larger context of international policy and Canadian attitudes toward the international community. Canada was a nation with large amounts of vacant land. It routinely—and quite accurately—feared that the world community would be quite happy to resolve its economic and political problems by dumping them in Canada's lap. In the larger sense, many Canadians in the late 1930s were thorough isolationists, convinced that there was no reason for Canada to involve itself in a European mess not of its own making. And, no part of Canada was more isolationist than Quebec, which was both hostile to Canadian involvement in Europe and opposed to all immigration, especially of Jews.

The handful of Jewish M.P.s, with the support of J. S. Woodsworth of the Co-Operative Commonwealth Federation, a left-wing political party, proposed to the Canadian cabinet that Canada offer at this conference to admit 5,000 Jewish refugees over four years, with all costs to be assumed by Jews already in Canada, including guarantees that the newcomers would not become charity cases. The Canadian Cabinet rejected this suggestion, chiefly on the grounds that it represented the tip of the iceberg. By 1938, of course, 5,000 was a mere trifle when there were at least a million refugees to be dealt with. Canadian politicians and officials may well have believed in 1938 that—as Canadian Undersecretary of State for External Affairs O. D. Skelton told the Americans—"governments with unwanted minorities must equally not be encouraged to think that harsh treatment at home is the key that will open the doors to immigration abroad. It is axiomatic that no state should be allowed to throw upon other countries the responsibility of solving its internal difficulties" (Abella and Troper, 1991, p. 27). This position was perhaps defensible in 1938, before the full understanding of the meaning of the Holocaust was known, but it would be increasingly feeble as events continued to unfold. The 1938 conference at Evian proved to be less of a problem than Canada had assumed. All nations attending agreed that they were "not willing to undertake any obligations toward financing involuntary immigration" (Abella and Troper, 1991, p. 32). From the Nazi perspective, the conference demonstrated the lack of international support available for the Jews.

Public support in Canada for some humanitarian gesture toward the Jewish refugees grew in the wake of the "Kristallnacht" pogrom of late November 1938, but the Canadian government still refused to yield. As the European situation worsened, Canada's Jews mounted a desperate series of public demonstrations to arouse support for a change of policy. On 23 November 1938 a delegation of Jews met with William Lyon Mackenzie King and T. A. Crerar, the immigration minister, to plead for the admission of 10,000 refugees at no expense to the government (the Jewish community again offered to finance the admissions). The Jews were rebuffed. On the other hand, mounting pressure on the government led to some internal discussion among the officials, one writing: "We don't want to take too many Jews, but, in the present circumstances particularly, we don't want to say so" (Abella and Troper, 1991, p. 34). On 13 December 1938, the cabinet agreed to keep existing immigration regulations but to interpret them "as liberally as possible." Since the existing system encouraged the immigration of only farmers with capital, such a concession was not very significant. Immigration officials were themselves convinced that few Jews wanted to farm. They were equally persuaded that refugees would say anything to be admitted, and they systematically rejected highly skilled professionals and intellectuals (including doctors, scientists, and musicians) as "inadmissible" applicants.

Not only did Canada refuse to admit refugees who were not farmers, but it was prepared to expel any Jews in Canada with tourist status, even though the authorities were told that such an action might send those involved to their deaths. In May of 1939, nearly 1,000 German Jews left Hamburg on a luxury liner, the *St. Louis,* some with entrance visas for Cuba. The Cubans refused to take most of them, and when Canada joined other North American nations in its lack of sympathy, the passengers were forced to return to Europe. Some editorial opinion in English-speaking Canada had turned by the summer of 1939. The *Winnipeg Free Press* insisted that circumstances had changed and, by keeping productive people out of Canada, "We are cutting off our nose to spite our face" (Abella and Troper, 1991, p. 65). But when war began, only the Americans seemed to have any inclination to be concerned about refugees. Canada refused throughout the war to open its doors. The most that can be said for the official Canadian attitude toward the Jewish refugees was that it was consistent with past national policy. Canada's immigration policy had never been strongly influenced by humanitarian considerations, and Canadian authorities had always been obsessed by the need for what they saw as assimilable newcomers.

For a nation as limited in world-renowned scientific, intellectual, and cultural talent as Canada was, the result was a cruel—if totally deserved—shortfall. Other countries, particularly the United States and Great Britain, benefited greatly from admitting Jewish refugees in fields as diverse as physics, medicine, theater, music, and education. Canada did not. Even in the crassest of nonhumanitarian terms, Canadian policy was a disaster. But it was also inexcusable in a moral sense—particularly on the part of a country that constantly lectured the rest of the world about its shortcomings.

The Japanese Problem

The Japanese population, mainly in British Columbia, had never been a particularly popular one with most British Columbians, and its position became increasingly difficult as Japan became more aggressive militarily in the later 1930s. The Japanese community was not well prepared to withstand great shocks. Three different sociocultural groups of Japanese people existed in Canada by 1941: the Issei, the Kibei, and the Nisei. The Issei were immigrants from Japan or Hawaii; the Kibei were Canadian-born but Japanese-educated; and the Nisei were both Canadian-born and Canadian-educated, with only 5,000 of their total number of 13,600 being more than twenty years of age. Most of the total Japanese community of 22,000 were scattered in farming communities in the Fraser Valley and in fishing villages and towns along the northern coast. The majority view in the province was hostile to the Japanese community, a combination of fear of economic competition and fear of fifth column activity. British Columbians argued that the Japanese would not assimilate, but the truth was that they were acculturating rapidly. The "Japanese Citizens' League Representing British-Born Subjects of the Japanese Race Residing in the Province of British Columbia" insisted in 1936 that the Japanese nation was great because of its ability to assimilate. It pointed out that among Canadian-born Japanese citizens, more than half were Christian, more than half read English only, and more than 75 percent sought to remain in Canada. More than 70 percent of Canadian-born Japanese people between the ages of five and nineteen were attending school in British Columbia. Indeed, the biggest concern of all in British Columbia was probably that the Japanese were "penetrating" local industry and society in large numbers.

A Board of Review appointed by the Canadian government in 1938 to investigate charges of large-scale illicit immigration of Japanese aliens found that rumors of infiltration were quite untrue. It concluded that there were no more than 120 illegal Japanese immigrants in Canada, most of them in Queen Charlotte Island. Another federal special committee in 1940, appointed about a year after the declaration of war against Germany, concluded that the real problem with the Japanese in the event of war was going to come "from the white population, who with only the slightest additional provocation, might suddenly resort to violence against Japanese individuals or groups" (*Report and Recommendations of the Special Committee on Orientals in British Columbia*, 1940, p. 13). The committee recommended against allowing Japanese Canadians to take military training or serve in the armed forces, chiefly for their own protection in case "racial or national passion be aroused by some untoward incident at home or abroad" (*Report and Recommendations*, 1940, p. 15).

The Japanese attack on Pearl Harbor and the subsequent declaration of war by Canada on Japan came as a considerable surprise to the Japanese Canadians. Not surprisingly, the majority population of British Columbia responded to Pearl Harbor with great anger, made worse by reports of Japanese ill treatment of the Canadian contingent among the British garrison at Hong Kong, which had surrendered in 1940. Ironically, British Columbians were to some extent creatures of their own sense of racial and cultural superiority when the Pearl Harbor attack came. Few residents of British Columbia—if they had been immigrants in Japan—would have supported Japan in this time of war, yet they were quite incapable of appreciating the subtleties of this fact. Like most minorities associated with an enemy during wartime, most of the Japanese wanted to remain neutral. Many British Columbians claimed to be convinced that—as they had preached for years—the Japanese would become part of a fifth column of supporters of Japan. The Canadian military and the Royal

Canadian Mounted Police (RCMP) both agreed that there was no danger from the Japanese on the Pacific Coast. "I cannot see that the Japanese Canadians constitute the slightest menace to national security," wrote Major General Ken Stuart to Ottawa in 1941 (Sunahara, 1981, p. 24).

RCMP investigators were never at the time able to uncover more than a handful of Japanese people even worthy of suspicion, and the passage of time has not uncovered a single Japanese spy in Canada. Nevertheless, the press and many politicians in British Columbia called for action, mainly in the form of the internment of all Japanese people in Canada so as not to miss a few potentially dangerous ones. And although the King government did not believe for a moment that Japanese Canadians represented the slightest military danger, it yielded to local pressure and used the excuse of the need to protect the Japanese from the white majority to evacuate most of them from the west coast. Most were sent to internment camps in the British Columbia interior, but others were scattered across the country, mainly to sugar beet farms in Alberta and Manitoba. Their land was seized, and their property was sold at auction. A few young Japanese men were permitted to serve in special units in the Canadian army in the latter stages of the war, but on grounds of "national emergency" the Canadian government refused to acknowledge any injustice in the treatment meted out to Japanese Canadians as a group. Not until 1990, as upcoming chapters of this book will show, did the Canadian government seek to provide redress for the Japanese citizens victimized during World War II.

The Japanese were not the only internal ethnic group interned during the Second World War by Canada, although they were by far the largest. Less than 1,000 Canadian residents of mainly German origin were also arrested and detained for the duration of the war.

Immigration during World War II

Canada's reluctance to admit large numbers of immigrants continued throughout the Second World War. Canada turned away millions of European refugees, at least partly because of its concern over the possibility of receiving Jews. The flow of immigrants was further reduced by the German U-boat campaign in the Atlantic, which put all passengers at risk. A handful of refugees, well supplied with money and skills, did make their way through the obstacle course of Canadian immigration policy. Some Poles arrived in 1943, for example.

At the start of the war, Canada had agreed to house during the war a number of Germans and Austrians who were held to be "security risks." Some of them were Jews, and almost all had been studying in Britain when the war broke out. Although they were initially housed in maximum-security facilities, the treatment of these internees gradually improved. The last internment camp was closed in 1943. Fewer than 1,000 of these people would choose to remain in Canada, often achieving considerable reputations in their chosen fields. The novelist Henry Kreisel was one of these internees. Their success was perhaps emblematic of the opportunity Canada missed by turning its back on the plight of the Jews.

The Guest Children

Despite the generally negative attitude of Canadian immigration authorities, more than 1,500 young British children were brought to Canada in 1940 to shelter them from the aerial bombardments of the war. In 1939, the Canadian National Council of Women adopted the idea of bringing British children to safety in Canada to provide the "nucleus of a new Britain founded on British stock." The Toronto *Globe and Mail* took up the idea in July 1939, writing that Canada could provide shelter for "Princesses Elizabeth and Margaret Rose and as many British boys and girls as we can make room for . . ." (Bilson, 1988, p. 3). Nothing much more happened officially, but more than 250 children were dispatched privately in 1939, and several public boarding schools in Britain were evacuated as well. But with the surrender of France in 1940, the expectation in Britain of a German invasion, and the opening of a bombing campaign of British cities, Canada House in London was flooded with applications from those who wanted to get their children to Canada. Contemporaries liked to describe such children as "refugees," but the Immigration Branch emphasized that they were evacuees, a distinction that allowed the waiving of policy restrictions that had stonewalled efforts to bring Jewish children to Canada. T. A. Crerar suggested that Canada allow up to 10,000 children between the ages of five and fifteen to be admitted. Britain would pay for their transportation, and volunteer Canadian families would provide care.

A board appointed by the British government received applications, investigated individual cases, and arranged for the successful applicants to be transported to Canada by ship. On 14 September 1940, however, the S.S. *City of Benares* was sunk by a U-boat at sea. Seventy-three evacuated children were lost in this disaster, and it became obvious to proponents of

*Polish immigrants harvesting on their Manitoba farm, ca. 1928
(National Archives of Canada)*

the Guest Children scheme that the youngsters were probably at greater risk in the process of transport than they were in Britain itself. The project was never renewed. As for the relatively small number of children brought to Canada, their experiences varied from good to bad. The biggest problem was the unexpected duration of the war, which meant that most of the evacuated children could not be reunited with their parents until 1945. Five years of separation was a long time.

Conclusion

Perhaps the greatest of many ironies connected with Canadian immigration during World War II was that at the same time that Canada was denying entry to most refugees, including Jews, it was the unwilling host for more than 35,000 German combatant prisoners of war. The British arranged to ship German POWs to the overseas dominions because it feared what might happen in the event of a German invasion of the British Isles. The relatively generous Canadian treatment of POWs during the war was occasionally contrasted with Canadian policy toward refugees, but in fairness to the Canadian government, it had not wanted these prisoners and sought to rid itself of their embarrassing presence as soon as possible after the war. Some of these POWs were held in Canada after the German surrender in 1945 in order to provide agricultural labor for the harvest, however. More than 6,000 of the POWs sought permission to remain in Canada after the war, but their applications were denied by the Canadian cabinet under the terms of the Geneva Convention. Very little that is favorable could be said about Canadian humanitarianism and generosity toward refugees of any description before 1945.

Timeline

1914   Declaration of war by Canada upon Germany; Passage of First War Measures Act.

1917   Disenfranchisement of Ukrainian immigrants; Soldier Settlement Act passed by Canadian Parliament.

1918   Suppression of foreign language press and socialist/anarchist organizations.

1919   Winnipeg General Strike; New Soldier Settlement Act creates a revamped Soldier Settlement Board.

1921   U.S. President Harding signs Emergency Immigration Restriction Act.

1923   Canada agrees to participate in Empire Settlement; New Chinese Immigration Act passed by Canadian Parliament.

1924   United States puts quota system in effect for immigration.

1925   3,000 Families scheme introduced; negotiations opened by Canada with Japan to limit immigration; Railway Agreement of 1925.

1928   Canada turns against assisted emigration; further limitations on Japanese immigration.

1930   Order-in-council suspends European immigration to Canada.

1931   Leaders of Communist Party of Canada arrested; order-in-council P.C. 695 establishes Canadian immigration policy during Depression.

1938   Frederick Blair decides that most Jews admitted to Canada as farmers are not really agriculturalists; Evian Conference convened to discuss international refugee crisis; Canadian Cabinet refuses to change Canadian immigration regulations.

1939   Canada denies admission to passengers of S.S. *St. Louis.*
1940   Guest Children brought to Canada; loss of S.S. *Benares* ends this program.
1941   Pearl Harbor attack.
1942   Canadian government decides to remove Japanese people from west coast "for their own good."
1945   Canadian government refuses to allow 6,000 German POWs to remain in Canada.

Significant People, Places, and Events

BLAIR, FREDERICK CHARLES (b. 1874) Appointed assistant deputy minister of immigration in 1924 and director of the Immigration Branch from 1936 to 1943, he developed and administered immigration regulations designed to keep Jewish refugees out of Canada.

CITY OF BENARES A ship carrying passengers from Britain to Canada, including a number of Guest Children. The ship was torpedoed in September 1940, thus ending the Guest Children program.

COMMUNIST PARTY OF CANADA The most radical political party in Canada, continually persecuted by the Canadian authorities from the 1920s because of its open advocacy of revolution.

EMPIRE SETTLEMENT A series of programs in the 1920s initiated by the British to distribute population, often former soldiers, to the colonies and dominions.

ENEMY ALIENS The label given during the Great War and after to residents of Canada who had been born within the borders of the Enemy Powers.

EVIAN CONFERENCE OF 1938 An international conference held at Evian, France, in 1938 to deal with the growing refugee crisis in Europe. Those nations participating could only agree that they could do nothing to alleviate the problem.

GREAT WAR VETERANS' ASSOCIATION The leading Canadian veterans' association. It was a vocal opponent of immigration to Canada while returning soldiers were still looking for jobs.

GUEST CHILDREN SCHEME A program first proposed in 1938 to allow British children between the ages of five and fifteen to be evacuated to Canada as a means of sheltering them from enemy attack.

INTERNATIONAL WORKERS OF THE WORLD (THE WOBBLIES) A leading radical labor organization in Canada, less associated with the foreign-born than the Communist Party.

Issei Japanese-born residents of Canada.

Jewish Colonization Association An organization founded in Montreal late in the nineteenth century to foster Jewish immigration to, and settlement in, Canada.

Kibei Japanese residents of Canada who were born in Canada but educated in Japan.

Nisei Japanese residents of Canada who born and educated in Canada.

P.C. 695 Order-in-council that in 1931 established Canadian immigration policy for the duration of the Depression, restricting immigrants to Britons and Americans who had the capital to become farmers and to become involved in resource industries.

Picture Brides Female immigrants allowed into Canada in order to marry men whom they had never met and to whom they were known only through photographs.

Railway Agreement of 1925 An understanding reached by the Canadian government with the two major Canadian railways (the Canadian Pacific and the Canadian Northern), which allowed the railroads to recruit agricultural labor from "nonpreferred" parts of Europe.

Red Scare A national hysteria of 1919 and 1920, to a considerable extent encouraged by events in the United States, that had people fearing that the "Bolsheviks" (a term used to refer to all political radicals) in North America would overthrow the democratically elected governments.

S. S. St. Louis A passenger vessel that in 1939 brought European Jewish refugees to Cuba, which refused to receive most of them. When no other North American nation would accept the passengers, they had to return to Europe.

Soldier Settlement A series of programs organized by the Canadian government to provide farms and financing for veterans. The schemes were administered by a series of Soldier Settlement Boards.

3,000 Families Scheme A program introduced by the Canadian government in 1925 to utilize land previously acquired for soldier settlement to place 3,000 British immigrant families on Canadian farms.

Toronto Eight The leaders of the Communist Party of Canada who were arrested and imprisoned by the Canadian government in 1931.

War Measures Act A piece of legislation first introduced in 1914 that allowed the Canadian cabinet to bypass the Canadian constitution in order to respond to emergency conditions. It was invoked over the years in times of crisis.

Winnipeg General Strike An attempt by the workers of Winnipeg in 1919 to close down the city in order to satisfy demands for better wages and working conditions. It led to a confrontation of classes and became the symbol for the political problems of the postwar period.

Documents

A Letter from the Holocaust, 1945

The following letter was sent to a man in Toronto, dated 22 July 1945. Historians know nothing further of the fate of this family. The text has not been corrected for grammar and spelling.

You don't know me and you don't know you are now the only relative from my wife's family to whom I can write. I am the husband of your sister Sonia. We have married 1942. During four years from 1940 till 1944 have we passed through the dark tragic life in the ghetto hand by hand having our love with us, which makes the burden easier to bear. Sonia had always dreamed that our first step after the war will be a journey to you. But all turned in a way we have not expected. In September 1944 when the Russians were near the German Gestapo took all Jews from the getto and send us to the most famous of all concentration camps, to Auschwitz.

We came there all together: Sonia, I, my parents and sister, your sister Rozia with her three children Hesiek, Bela and Salusia (Rozia's husband, Godel, died in ghetto 1941, so as your parents and your brother Herszel.) Belive me that I would like my parents would have died also in getto! In Auschwitz were we separated men and women and then all older people and children till 13–14 years have been burned in crematorium. Can you understand this?! The younger men and women after some selections have been transported to various K.L. in Germany. From our arrival to Auschwitz till to-day I have heard nothing about Sonia. I was transported to Braunschweig and till the end of the war I was in five concentration camps. It's impossible for me to describe and for you to understand what I have survived in the K.L. Enough that when the American troops came and liberated us I was lying so sick and weak that I couldn't already neither move nor speak and when the help would come a few days after it would be too late. From that day I am still lying in hospitals and now I am slowly recovering to health in Sweden. I have in Germany meet several girls and women from Lodz but nobody have heard about Sonia. I get crazy when I think that I can Sonia seen no more. She was delicate and subtle and the life in camps was so hard. I become mad when I think about this all. My last hope is that she is lying in some hospital in Germany where are coming these which seeks their relatives. I am sure that if she is alive her first step will be also to write to you. Oh, it wouldn't be a happier paid in the world as I and Sonia if we can meet again. You cannot imagine how deep and beautiful was our love.

I have you so much to write that I don't know what to write first. I am to be in Sweden for six months. What will be with me after this time—I don't know. I will not go back to Poland. I have there no home anymore and there is no place for Jews. I would—like to emigrate to America. Europe is a damned earthpart. Here there will be still wars.

I must finish my letter because the person who is sending the letter to you is waiting impatiently.

Dear Mortiz?! I mustn't write how impatiently I shall expect an answer from you. I will believe that perhaps you would have a sign of life from Sonia. Oh, when you can come to Europe and help me to find her.

Source: Abella, Irving, and Troper, Harold, *None Is Too Many: Canada and the Jews of Europe 1933–1948* (Toronto: Lester and Orpen Dennys, 1982), pp. 192–193.

A Japanese Woman Recalls Her Evacuation

The following is a transcription of part of an interview with Mrs. Maki Fukishima, conducted by Tomoko Makabe and translated by Kathleen Chisato Merken.

In wartime, all kinds of rumours were circulating. Some people said that if young people were sent to the camps out east, they might have to go to war. At the time, my oldest son had a wife and a baby. I thought it would be too sad if they were separated, and we thought of a place where we could all go together. We didn't have the money to move where we wanted. So we applied for sugar beet growing in Alberta, where we could go as a family.

The people around me didn't have anything good to say about our going to the sugar beet fields. My husband's best friend said "You shouldn't go to work on beets. It's like being a traitor." Making sugar out of beets meant cooperating with the Canadian government that had a policy to produce more sugar. It would be like making bullets for rifles or a sign of loyalty to this country.

I said "We're going to the sugar beet fields, because we decided that's how we can go as a family. The last thing we'd do is aim a rifle at Japan. I've got a Rising Sun flag in my heart," and off we went. We'd never farmed, so that was a worry, but we went because we'd be together. The Japanese all had different ways of thinking, and coping with things, but we were about the only family that went from Fairview to Alberta; I didn't know what else to do.

My husband had died in January [1942] and we left Vancouver in May. My second son was working as a book-keeper in the Fraser Valley Farmers' Association. He sacrificed himself and took everybody along with him to Alberta. He was 22 or 23. At the time I wasn't naturalized, so I was an "Enemy Alien." In the late 1920s, the thinking generally was that there shouldn't be any extra Japanese around, and after it looked like a war was coming, it wasn't easy to get naturalized.

We were in Alberta four years, all during the war, and had a terrible time. When we were on the train leaving New Westminster, a telegram came. It said they didn't need any more Japanese. We'd cleared out our house, so even if we were told to go home, there wasn't any home to go to. So we went off just as we were. We got to Lethbridge in Alberta, after two whole days on the train. Nobody came to meet us, no bosses. They didn't want any Japanese coming. Then it got to be like being sold as slaves. We got taken all across Alberta from west to east, stopping at every station, and family after family got sold off.

We were just five adults and a baby, but we weren't farmers so it was very hard to find a buyer. We were leftover goods, and got sold at the very end. Nowadays, there's oil in Alberta, but then, it was nothing but poor farming villages. The one we went to, I forget its name, but it was a small, poor village. It was a cold place, not good for beets. Right away, we planted seeds, but they didn't grow well. July came, but now it was too hot and the beets grew and grew, it was earth that you couldn't grow daikon radish in, but it was good for leaves. We broke our backs working, but we failed.

The first year we got treated like enemies, and the people hated us. But after that year, they realized that Japanese were hard workers, and honest too, so they took a liking to us, and when you said, "All right, we're leaving the fields," now they wouldn't let us. The bosses just wouldn't sign the papers. Their beet-field labour would dry up, so they wouldn't let us leave the province. There was a sugar shortage in wartime, so they had to get beets grown. There was no work at all besides beet growing, and the young people started wanting to go east. . . .

We lost everything is four years. I didn't get mad. I thought it was no use. Because we were Japanese, we had to go where they said. You can't do anything else, if this isn't the country you were born in; if you're told to get out, that's what you have to do. When we left B.C., I didn't think Japan would lose the war, and I thought it would be over soon, so we left every-thing behind. We left the good things, that is, and only brought the junk. My feeling was to be loyal to this country. But at that time, I hadn't been naturalized, so I was a citizen of an enemy country. I thought I'd go to Japan, because the children could get along by themselves. . . .

After the war, people had all kinds of ideas about what they should do with themselves, and I had trouble deciding, too. Some people kept saying I should go to Japan, and others said: "In Japan, they've got everything ready to welcome us." But other people said, "Even if you go back to Japan, what are you going to do after the war in a small country like that?" I was at my wits' end, I didn't know where to turn, and in the end I went and signed to be repatriated. My second son was shocked at this, and came hurrying back from the east, and applied to the Mounties for a can-cellation. He insisted we were in Canada, and he wouldn't let his mother go back to Japan alone.

He went through all the steps to change the application, and a few months later, I got news that I could stay in Canada, so my problem was solved. But I'd thought that if I was going to be a burden to my children, it would be better to live in Japan. But it isn't good for a family to get split up, no matter what.

Source: Makabe, Tomoko, *Picture Brides: Japanese Women in Canada,* translated by Kathleen Chisato Merken (Toronto: Multicultural History Society of Ontario, 1995), pp. 59–62.]

Bibliography

Abella, Irving, and Harold Troper, *None Is Too Many: Canada and the Jews of Eu-rope 1933–1948,* rev. ed. (Toronto: Lester and Orpen Dennys, 1991).

Avery, Donald, *Reluctant Host: Canada's Response to Immigrant Workers, 1896–1994* (Toronto: McClelland and Stewart, 1995).

Bilson, Geoffrey, *The Guest Children: The Story of the British Child Evacuees Sent to Canada during World War II* (Saskatoon, Saskatchewan: Fifth House, 1988).

Bumsted, J. M., *The Winnipeg General Strike of 1919: An Illustrated History* (Win-nipeg, Manitoba: Watson and Dwyer, 1994).

Constantine, Stephen, ed., *Emigrants and Empire: British Settlement in the*

Dominions between the Wars (Manchester, U.K. and New York: Manchester University Press, 1990).

Fedorowich, Kent, *Unfit for Heroes: Reconstruction and Soldier Settlement in the Empire between the Wars* (Manchester, U.K. and New York: Manchester University Press, 1995).

Harper, Marjory, *Emigration from Scotland between the Wars: Opportunity or Exile?* (Manchester, U.K. and New York: Manchester University Press, 1998).

Kaprielian-Churchill, Isabel, "Armenian Refugees and Their Entry into Canada, 1919–1930," *Canadian Historical Review* 71:1 (1990), 80–108.

Luciuk, Lubomyr, ed., *Righting an Injustice: The Debate over Redress for Canada's First National Internment Operations* (Toronto: Justinian Press, 1994).

Makabe, Tomoko, *Picture Brides: Japanese Women in Canada,* translated by Kathleen Chisato Merken (Toronto: Multicultural History Society of Ontario, 1995).

Report and Recommendations of the Special Committee on Orientals in British Columbia (Ottawa: King's Printer, 1940), p. 13.

Sunahara, Ann Gomer, *The Politics of Racism* (Toronto: James Lorimer and Company, 1981).

Ward, E. Peter, *White Canada Forever: Popular Attitudes and Public Policy Toward Orientals in British Columbia,* 2nd ed. (Montreal, Quebec and Kingston, Ontario: McGill-Queen's University Press, 1990).

CHAPTER EIGHT

An Immigration from Europe, 1946–1962

ANADA ENDED THE SECOND WORLD WAR with neither an immigration policy nor a refugee policy sufficient for dealing with the situations in which it would soon find itself, particularly on the international level. Both the Canadian government and the Canadian people were, by and large, exclusionist, racist, and not terribly humanitarian in their attitudes toward immigration. Over the next few years, this position would change, however. Canada would come to accept millions of immigrants, including both displaced persons and refugees, and by 1962 would overhaul its immigration procedures to bring an official end to racialism.

The War Brides

When the war ended, Canada's first concern was for bringing home its troops and for withdrawing from involvement in Europe as quickly as possible. The Canadian government continued to be persuaded that Europe was a cesspool of trouble. As Prime Minister McKenzie King had put it in 1939, he opposed "the idea that every twenty years this country should automatically and as a matter of course take part in a war overseas, periodically, to fight for a continent that cannot run itself" (Briggs, 1975, p. 131). Canada's eagerness to come home after 1945 was, if anything, only increased by its inability to translate its wartime manpower and resource commitments into any postwar place in the corridors of power that would decide the peace and reconstruct Europe. Canada protested privately about being left out of the surrender agreement, being left out of the drafting of a unilateral statement ending the war, and being left out of the Italian surrender. The final straw may well have been the Allies' decision to admit France (a nation that had allowed itself to be occupied by the Nazis and had fought Germany with only an army in exile) to the ranks of the "occupying Powers" of Berlin.

All of Canada's resources in late 1945 and early 1946 were devoted to transporting home its troops, some of whom had been in Britain since 1939. Partly as a result of the length of the stay abroad, almost 50,000 Canadian soldiers had found wives in Europe, mainly in the United Kingdom, although some soldiers had met and married women on the European continent, especially in Holland. There were 22,000 children from these marriages. Obviously, these dependents would have to be allowed to accompany their soldier fathers and husbands back to Canada, and the Canadian Department of National Defence facilitated matters as expeditiously as possible. The Canadian government not only admitted these dependents without question, but also provided them with transport, documentation, and the transfer of money and possessions as well. The Canadian government, it should be added, did not regard these dependents as immigrants.

Even before the war was over, the war brides were preparing for their departures from their homes to join their husbands. The Salvation Army had formed war brides clubs, in which Canadian military personnel gave crash courses to familiarize the brides with Canadian culture. It helped that many of the brides came from areas around major installations where Canadians had been based. In August 1944, a Canadian Wives' Bureau was set up just off Piccadilly Circus as a branch of the Canadian Military Headquarters. It coordinated orientation for the women, distributing literature and other useful material. When a serviceman filed a claim for a dependent allowance, the Bureau sent the dependent an application form for transportation to Canada and arranged for the dependent to have a medical examination. Dealing successfully with all the paperwork was the war bride's first challenge. Next, the European brides were all collected in London and then sent to Canada on the first available ship. The brides were informed that there would be only a single one-way journey provided for them at government expense. Women who wished to marry after arriving in Canada were assisted, so long as they paid their own passage. Newfoundland made its own similar arrangements for the dependents of its military. The business of being uprooted was not an easy one for many of these women, but by and large they were welcomed enthusiastically by their husbands, new families, and new communities in Canada.

The Refugee Crisis of 1945-1947

As many as 20 million Europeans were displaced by the Second World War. They came in a variety of types and classes. Eight million came from enemy territory. These people were dominated by the *Volksdeutsche*, ethnic Germans from eastern Europe who had fled west ahead of the Russian advance into Germany in 1945 and had been pushed into Allied-occupied Germany, where they joined large numbers of other Germans who had also lost their homes. Nearly 12 million other people came from countries occupied by the Germans. Many of these people had recently been released from prison camps and concentration camps. They joined former slave laborers, resistance fighters, and Nazi collaborators in new camps that were formed for refugees. The Yalta summit had agreed on procedures for the repatriation of refugees, but the Russians were concerned that the eastern European exiles might easily become an anti-Soviet community. Russia demanded their return from Allied-occupied Germany and sent them out of Soviet Germany. By the end of 1945, perhaps 2 million refugees and other displaced persons remained in allied territory, mostly in Germany but also in Austria and Italy. Some lived on the countryside, although most were placed in refugee camps where agencies such as UNRRA (the United Nations Relief and Rehabilitation Administration) could deal with them. Few of these people had proper documentation, and many had been Nazi soldiers and collaborators—even war criminals—who now disguised themselves as innocent victims. Everyone agreed that the criminals needed to be separated out from the "real" refugees and other displaced persons, but this was not easy to do.

For the Allied forces that had to assume responsibility for the screening of the inhabitants of the camps, there were several problems. One was the difficulty of establishing the legitimacy of each refugee, given the absence of documentation and the confusion of the times. Obviously, people would not necessary tell the truth in interrogations, which had to be fairly perfunctory. Despite what were in theory careful background checks and cross-checks, many war criminals, Nazi soldiers, and collaborators slipped through the net, assisted by the scarcity of corroborating evidence, especially for eastern European and Italian refugees. The sheer chaos of the refugee camps, a condition that had persisted since the 1930s, was a major reason why Canada was so unwilling to come to terms with these camps as a source of immigrants. Nevertheless, Canadian officialdom still felt that, as one high-level bureaucrat put it early in 1946 in a classic understatement, "the demands upon Canada to make further contributions to the solution of this problem [of refugees] will probably increase in the near future" (Avery, 1995, p. 152).

Thus, it was necessary to devise a policy. The first step was to admit refugees who had near relatives in Canada willing pay for their transportation and support. These admissions would serve, as one team of scholars later charged, as a "high-profile, low-commitment program to take External Affairs off the hook at international gatherings and split, if not pacify, pro-refugee forces in Canada" (Abella and Troper, 1991, p. 214). The second step, thought the immigration authorities, was to study the problem further. Most of those officials in charge of Canadian immigration had been there since the 1930s, and their understanding was that Canada did not really want to admit refugees at all. An investigation into immigration policy was conducted in May of 1946 by the Senate of Canada's Standing Committee on Immigration and Labour, and to the surprise of immigration officials, it supported immigration. The report emphasized that the witnesses it had heard were unanimous on the principle of immigration into Canada and equally agreed that "Canada, as a humane and Christian nation, should do her share toward the relief of refugees and displaced persons"(Standing Committee on Immigration and Labor, 1946, p. 628). The committee also criticized the government for its failure to produce a proper immigration policy.

Perhaps in reaction to the Senate hearings, the Canadian cabinet in May 1946 amended P.C. 695—the 1931 order-in-council still in effect—with P.C. 2071 to permit the admission of refugees who had close relatives in Canada. This was not intended to represent the opening of any floodgates. All existing immigration regulations were observed, and the definition of a first-degree relative was narrowly conceived. Moreover, the Canadian Parliament was told, "The amending of the regulations does not mean immediate action will be taken to admit immigrants from overseas" (Abella and Troper, 1991, p. 216). The Jewish community was informed that few Jews would be eligible for admission under the revised regulations. The only other small exception to a continued exclusionary policy also came in 1946, when Canada agreed to admit 4,000 Polish veterans from the Polish Second Corps to replace German prisoners of war—who had worked as heavy laborers in Canada during the war. (This "bulk labor" immigration brought howls of protest from the ranks of Canadian laborers.) The Canadian authorities worked hard to keep Jews out of this contingent, and among the first 1,700 Polish arrivals there was only one Jew, who had fought alongside the Poles in Italy. Under this policy, all Polish immigrants had to be less than thirty-five years of age, physically strong, and single. They would be allowed to apply for regular admission to Canada only after their initial three-year labor contracts had expired. A major problem became how to find enough Poles who had no record of collaboration (however coerced) with the Germans. It was eventually decided to bar only Poles who had not fought against the Germans. Later, the *Montreal Standard* would accuse the authorities of having allowed the entry of more than one hundred Nazi collaborators, a charge the government vehemently denied. The new criterion, however, meant that the program was oversubscribed, and an additional 500 men were admitted.

Canadian immigration officials used the absence of inspection facilities as an excuse for not processing first-degree relatives more rapidly, at the same time that the decision was made in principle to screen out "unsatisfactory" immigrants, especially war criminals and suspected Nazi collaborators. The External Affairs office got involved in the refugee business because of its concern that Canadian refugee policy (or the absence thereof) would lead the United Nations to impose an arbitrary quota number on Canada. External Affairs's arguments led to the reestablishment of immigration inspection offices in Europe, but the closest Canada got to action was an inspection tour of the refugee camps by an official from the Canadian High Commission in London. This official thought people from the Baltic region were the best choice as immigrants to Canada, with Jews the least desirable. A Gallup poll in April of 1946 indicated that two-thirds of Canadians opposed immigration from Europe. A subsequent poll in October 1946 asked: if there were to be immigration, what nationalities would the respondent like to keep out of Canada? The Japanese ranked first; the Jews second.

After months of debate in the Canadian press and in the Cabinet, Prime Minister Mackenzie King read a formal statement on immigration policy to the House of Commons on 1 May 1947. King insisted that Canada wanted to encourage immigration, but he introduced into the encouragement the notion of "absorptive capacity," which he did not define and which could be interpreted in a variety of ways. Most Canadians chose to see absorptive capacity as a purely economic issue: Immigration was needed to supply labor but should not disturb the Canadian labor market. Other Canadians thought absorptive capacity was partly a coded term for racism, a definition that gained force from King's spirited defense of the nation's right to pursue a discriminatory immigration policy that would not appreciably alter the makeup of the Canadian population (which, of course, was essentially British, French, and of other European descent). King further emphasized that, although Canada was not obliged by its membership in international organizations to accept specific numbers of refugees and other displaced persons, "We have, nevertheless, a moral obligation to assist in meeting the problem, and this obligation we are prepared to recognize" (Knowles, 1997, p. 132). As the Montreal *Gazette* pointed out in a subsequent editorial, how this statement was implemented depended on the immigration authorities involved in a particular situation.

As a consequence of King's statement, five teams of immigration officials were sent to Germany and Austria over the summer of 1947 to select potential immigrants from the camps. These teams were partly responsible for bringing more than 50,000 displaced persons to Canada in 1947 and 1948. This action was the result of a recommendation from the cabinet in May 1947 for new recruitment from the European camps as per P.C. 2180, which would be modified five times over the next few years to expand the number of refugees involved. A new system of immigration screening was put into effect, and an expansion of the definition of the term *close relatives* was allowed. Those who were selected under the labor selection category were granted visas and transported to a port of embarkation, where they signed labor contracts. On arrival in Canada, each immigrant got money for railway tickets and meals. Most of the security concerns at this time were over potential Communists rather than over ex-Nazis.

Contributing to the new influx of displaced persons were fresh pressures on the Canadian government that changed considerably in 1947. First, rampaging economic prosperity being supervised by C. D. Howe (minister of reconstruction and supply) required fresh supplies of labor. "The speeding up of the immigration movement," he insisted, had to be "treated as a matter of high priority" (Margolian, 2000, p. 77). Second, the objectives and power base of the refugee lobby changed substantially. Symptomatic of this shift was the establishment in June 1947 of the Canadian Christian Council for Resettlement of Refugees (CCCRR). This organization was made up of various German immigrant-aid groups and concentrated on helping refugees from Germany and Austria, especially the *Volksdeutsche*. In November 1947, the CCCRR was officially recognized by the Canadian government as its agent, and the organization negotiated the use of the S.S. *Beaverbrae* to bring immigrants to Canada. The *Beaverbrae* left Bremerhaven on 19 April 1948. At the point of sailing, the ship's loudspeaker system emphasized—in German and Russian—the need to forget old allegiances and to become "future Canadian citizens"

(Abella and Troper, 1991, p. 238). More than 120,000 refugees were ultimately admitted under this CCCRR program, placing Canada behind only the United States, Australia, and Israel as a receiver of refugees in the postwar period.

The Displaced Persons Immigration of 1948–1952

The influx of displaced persons during 1948–1952 was distinguished by several contradictory tendencies beyond its sheer number. One was the inability of the Canadian authorities totally to prevent Jews from becoming part of the flow, however hard they tried. Canada typically put Jews low on the list of desired immigrants, partly for cultural reasons but also partly because of what prospective employers expected of new immigrants, chiefly robust health and considerable strength. Most postwar Jews were still struggling with their concentration camp experiences, both physically and mentally, and could not have coped with a regimen of hard physical labor. Jews' physical condition was of course a catch-22 situation, for what was clearly needed was another program for refugees and other displaced persons and refugees besides the bulk-labor one. Jewish activists were persuaded that it would be easier for war criminals like Martin Bormann (Hitler's private secretary) to get to Canada than for Jews, and, indeed, the refugees of these years may well have included as many as 1,500 war criminals and Nazi collaborators, despite a cabinet order in 1946 that former Nazis or Nazi collaborators were not welcome in Canada. The immigration of these years also saw the arrival of the first "boat people," as several thousand people from the Baltic area made their way independently to Canada aboard small and often unseaworthy vessels. They were usually greeted sympathetically and often allowed to remain by special orders-in-council.

The hard-labor aspect of Canadian criteria for immigrants caused considerable other problems for immigration officials in addition to just keeping Jews out of Canada. Early in 1948, for example, the Communists took over Czechoslovakia, forcing thousands out of the country, including much of its civil service staff. But such people were not eligible under existing immigration programs to enter Canada. One Canadian immigration official commented of the Czech diplomats clamoring for admission to Canada, "As an ex-member of the profession, I may perhaps be forgiven if I suggest that the average diplomat is not likely to be very much use at anything else—particularly at the kind of initial jobs that are commonly available for immigrants" (Avery, 1995, p. 159). Highly trained professionals had been a general problem for nations receiving immigrants since the end of the war. The problem was that local professional organizations and licensing authorities insisted on protecting the public from the unqualified, and it was almost impossible to make any sense out of the credentials offered by a displaced person from a foreign nation. Receiving countries like the United States, Australia, and eventually Canada basically insisted that the professionals, especially the doctors, either take jobs where the receiving country's own nationals would not go—such as the far north in the case of Canada—or else requalify for their profession. Canada was unsympathetic not only to professionals but to intellectuals and artists. An attempt in 1948 by the Ukrainian Canadian Committee to gain special admission for a number of "Ukrainian cultural workers and artists" was ignored by Canadian immigration officials.

By 1949 Canada had come to recognize that its concentration on brawn was biting off its nose to spite its face. A new sponsorship program allowed up to 500 highly trained displaced persons into Canada, although it emphasized that most admitted under this program would not immediately be able to practice their skills. On the other hand, some countries, particularly the United States, had always been quite willing to accept skilled enemy aliens—many of whom had been open Nazis—if they were scientists, particularly those working in weapons research. A few such scientists, no more than fifty, were admitted to Canada before 1950. In a well-reviewed book published in 1951, economist Mabel Timlin actually studied the question of "absorptive capacity," arguing both that Canada was capable of accepting larger numbers of immigrants from an economic standpoint and that such acceptance, by increasing the population, "should mean a higher physical product per capita and hence higher real incomes for Canadian citizens" (Timlin, 1951, p. 122).

The displaced persons who came to Canada in the years immediately after the war shared much in common with one another. In the first place, most of them had suffered many years of emotional difficulties, born partly out of their wartime experiences and partly out of their problems in assimilating in Canada. The sorts of jobs available to most immigrants—most at the very bottom of the occupational chain, working as drawers of water and hewers of wood—tended to be in remoter districts and subject to seasonal unemployment. The Canadian government provided little counseling or financial assistance for the newcomers, and it was left to voluntary organizations to fill the gap as best they could. On the other hand, the postwar newcomers had the great psychological advantage of knowing that they could not return to their former lives—thus providing a sense of finality and permanence to their new situation—and that almost any material conditions were better than those they had suffered in the European camps.

In June 1950 the seeming success of the refugee program led to the passage of P.C. 2856. This order-in-council in effect authorized what had already happened, expanding admissible categories of European immigrants to include any healthy individuals of good character with needed skills and an ability to integrate. It made no mention of the admission of close relatives of Canadian citizens, which had been quietly going on since the war ended. That same year saw the Department of Citizenship and Immigration established to replace the previous administrative structure in which immigration had been one of a number of branches of the Department of Mines and Resources. Canada now had an immigration policy (of sorts) and a separate agency to administer it. In 1951, Canadian immigration policy reached out—oh so tenuously—beyond Europe. The Canadian government agreed with the governments of India, Pakistan, and Ceylon to admit a few additional newcomers from each of those countries beyond the old quotas on Asians.

The Immigration Act of 1952 and Its Implementation

As representatives of many constituencies recognized in 1952, Canada desperately needed to overhaul and rethink its immigration policy. That goal was not achieved in the new immigration act of that year, which was produced after only four days of hearings by a House of Commons subcommittee that heard testimony mainly from the large transportation companies. Most of the other players in immigration, such as the trade unions and the ethnic organizations, received no hearings whatsoever. As a result, the act dealt mainly with administrative procedures rather than new policies. It was subsequently described by the Department of Immigration as legislation that "clarified and simplified immigration procedures and removed certain anomalies which have been brought to light during the continued movement of newcomers to Canada" (Hawkins, 1972, p. 101). It further expanded the discretionary powers of the cabinet and the immigration department (especially the minister of immigration) to select immigrants, even on a case-by-case basis, but did not much alter the criteria used in the selection. The act was mainly concerned with the reasons for keeping people out. These included peculiar customs, unsuitability for Canadian conditions, and "probable inability to become readily assimilated" into full Canadian citizenship. The noisiest complaints about the 1952 act came from the ethnic communities, who set up to lobby for their own particular agendas.

The 1952 act did not have very much to say about refugees and had nothing to say about the United Nations Refugee Convention of 1951. Critics saw several reasons for the silence on refugees. One was the common belief that refugees were looking for temporary asylum rather than permanent resettlement. Another was that not all refugees were necessarily "good guys" who had been driven out of their countries for the wrong reasons. Finally, there was the racial factor. Canada took some token steps toward expanding its refugee policy in 1955, when it decided as a humanitarian gesture to admit some of the 900,000 refugees living in camps in the Middle East. In 1956 a Canadian immigration team visited camps in Lebanon and Jordan, selecting from 575 candidates presented to them by international refugee organizations 98 whom it regarded as potential Canadian citizens. Eventually, thirty-nine heads of families were admitted to Canada in 1956. The fact that this small number attracted little attention from anyone is hardly surprising; its tokenism was manifest.

The 1952 act had little to say about appeals from discretionary decisions involving prospective immigrants. Section 39 of the act specifically denied that courts and judges had jurisdiction "to review, quash, reverse, restrain or otherwise interfere with any proceeding, decision or order of the Minister, Deputy Minister, Director, Immigration Appeal Board, Special Inquiry Officer or immigration officer" acting under the legislation—unless the person involved was a Canadian citizen or had Canadian domicile (Hawkins, 1972, p. 103). J. W. Pickersgill, who became minister of immigration in 1954, probably best expressed the thinking behind the 1952 act when he insisted that the procedures for admission to Canada were not to be compared to a legal trial. "The person concerned is trying to be given a chance to become a citizen of Canada and parliament has enacted that somebody has got to decide whether he is the kind of person we want. It is much more like an applicant for a job. If an employer . . . had to explain to every unsuccessful applicant for a job why he was refused a post . . . it would be perfectly impossible to get anything done at all" (Avery, 1995, p. 174). At the same time, Pickersgill admitted that 90 percent of his time was taken up with individual files that represented "mountains of cases." Not only the minister but also the entire department became constipated by individual cases of admission and deportation. Immigrants admitted to Canada could be deported for mental illness or for becoming a public charge. In 1956 the Supreme Court of Canada ruled that delegating the authority to decide admissions to Special Inquiry Officers exceeded the legal authority of the Governor-in-Council, and the cabinet subsequently spelled out in detail those who were eligible for admission on 24 May 1956.

The Hungarian Refugees of 1956

One of the advantages of discretionary powers was that the immigration system could respond quickly to changing circumstances. This is what happened in 1956 when J. W. Pickersgill, as if to demonstrate the value of discretionary power, acted in response to the Russian suppression, with tanks and armed might, of the Hungarian uprising in November of that year. Canadians had seen the events in Hungary unfold on their television screens, with young student "Freedom Fighters" armed with nothing but stones facing Soviet tanks. The plight of the more than 200,000 refugees who fled to Austria attracted considerable attention. Pickersgill moved quickly, and before November was out he was announcing the government's plan to provide free passage to Canada for every refugee who met

A group of Hungarians en route to Canada, 1957 (Archives of Ontario)

Canadian admissions standards. Although some criticized the Liberals for sticking to the admissions standards—which meant that the whole business was really not about refugees but the recruitment of potential immigrants—most of the world was impressed. In the spring of 1957, Canada brought nearly 20,000 Hungarians to North America on board more than 200 chartered airplane flights, and by the end of the year another 10,000 Hungarians had come to Canada. These refugees were mainly young students, with males outnumbering females. Most had urban backgrounds and were well educated. A substantial number were Jewish.

Organized groups of refugees in this movement included 350 students and faculty from the Forest Engineering Faculty at Sopron University, who were transplanted to the University of British Columbia as the Sopron Division of the Faculty of Forestry; and 150 students and faculty from the Faculty of Mining Engineering at Sopron University, who were brought to the University of Toronto. In general, however, the refugees were widely distributed through various cities across the country rather than settling in one or two centers, although many clustered in Ontario, which today has more than half of all Hungarian-Canadians. The new arrivals were, of course, fervently anti-Communist, which simultaneously made them popular with Cold Warriors—the House of Commons welcomed them enthusiastically almost to a person—and to a certain extent unpopular with some of the older generation of Hungarians in Canada, whose politics leaned toward the left. The enthusiasm of their welcome may have led some of the newcomers to assume that life in Canada would be easier than it later turned out to be, particularly as many suffered from severe postemigration trauma because of the rapidity of their movement from Europe to North America.

The Returning British

Not all postwar immigrants remained in Canada. One specialist in postwar Canadian immigration calculated that about 23 percent of all postwar immigrants to Canada had left the country by 1961, and further estimated "that Canada succeeded in retaining approximately 60 percent of the immigrants who entered the country from the United States, about 70 percent of those from Britain, and 80 percent of those from other countries" (Richmond, 1967, p. 228). For most postwar European immigrants to Canada, their commitment to their new nation was fairly strong. In many cases, immigrants had few family members and sometimes no

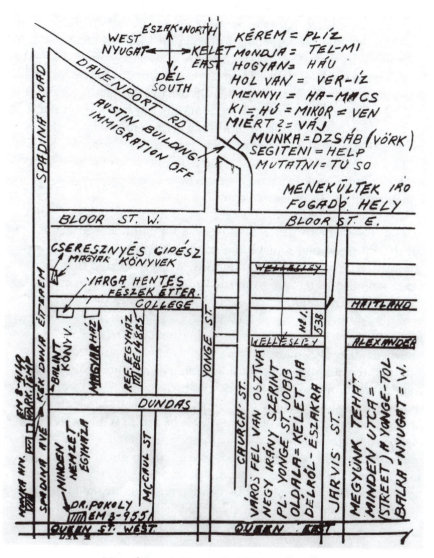

Map of Toronto Drawn for Newcomers, 1956
Source: Polyphony: The Bulletin of the Multicultural History Society
of Ontario 2, *no. 2–3 (1979–1980): 64.*

country to which to return. In other cases, a return to a much less prosperous lifestyle at home was possible but hardly desirable. For the British,
the years immediately after the war were ones of privation, but economic
conditions gradually returned to normal in the United Kingdom, and social conditions under the "Welfare State" may even have improved, particularly for the working classes. In any case, upwards of 100,000 British immigrants to Canada returned to their homeland during the 1950s. Most
had been reasonably successful economically but had not substantially
improved their social standing, remaining in the same occupational status
in Canada as in Britain. Those who had married (and/or had children) in
Canada were more likely to remain there, and single people were far more
likely to return home. The presence of close relatives in Canada was also
important in the decision to remain.

No evidence suggests that the returnees were less socially well adjusted
or that they were returning because of disappointment or disillusion-
ment. So why did they return? In one study in which a questionnaire was
administered to returning immigrants, many indicated that they had
never intended to remove from the United Kingdom permanently and
that they were returning as part of an earlier plan. In short, their original
commitment had never been a total one. Large numbers of females were
in this category. These tended to be young and unmarried. For those who
returned, many also suggested that family obligations (especially toward
parents) were an important consideration. For returnees who listed economic conditions as important, most of them were manual workers who
did not like the uncertainty of seasonal employment, although they admitted that the standard of living they achieved in Canada was higher.
Lack of any close identification with Canada, "manifest in a feeling of
homesickness," this study indicated, was the largest single factor in a decision to return to the United Kingdom (Richmond, 1967, p. 251). The very
ease with which the returnees had emigrated and integrated in Canada
appears to have in part accounted for their lack of commitment.

New Problems and New Solutions, 1957–1962

In 1957 the Liberal government was defeated in a general election. The
Progressive-Conservatives, led by John Diefenbaker, formed first a minority government and then, after an election sweep in 1958, a majority government that lasted until 1962. Diefenbaker's campaign promises with regard to immigration dealt mainly with administrative improvements and

the need for more people in the nation. In 1958 Diefenbaker appointed a woman to the immigration service. Ellen Fairclough (b. 1905) was a Hamilton businesswoman who was the first female appointed to a federal cabinet post. Immigration was not expected by Diefenbaker to be a heavy responsibility, and Fairclough would also be responsible for Indian Affairs as well. But a number of general problems related to immigration had surfaced by the later 1950s. Four were of critical importance. First and foremost was the difficulty with the sponsorship program. Second, there was a need for an expanded and liberalized immigration policy, particularly in terms of attracting non-European immigrants. Third, there was a need for administrative reform. Finally, something would have to be done about a flow of illegal immigrants, mainly Chinese people from Hong Kong, into Canada. Neither Fairclough nor the government had any notion at the outset that the result of grappling with these problems would be a totally new direction in Canadian immigration policy.

The Sponsorship Problem

With the virtual end of the European refugee influx in the early 1950s (except for the Hungarians), one basic way in which immigrants got to Canada was through being sponsored by close relatives already in the country. The sponsorship system, begun in 1946, had some advantages, as it authorized chain migration (by which one immigrant sponsored another) and provided a means of integrating the newcomers quickly into the Canadian community, as well as of preventing them from becoming public charges. The national group that took the greatest advantage of sponsorship after the war was the Italians. More than 240,000 Italian immigrants arrived in Canada between 1946 and 1961. Among immigrants as a whole in these years, less than one-half were sponsored, but among Italian immigrants, more than 90 percent were sponsored by relatives—this was by far the heaviest proportion of sponsored arrivals among any immigrant group.

Most family-sponsored Italians were either dependents (women, children, the elderly) not likely to enter the Canadian labor force, or unskilled males able to work only as laborers on heavy construction sites and thus likely to flood the unskilled job market. More than one-half (60 percent) of these new arrivals were from southern Italy, with the regions of Abruzzi, Molise, and Calabria providing the vast bulk of the immigrants. Most sponsors were male, and, especially before 1956, males predominated in the immigration. But the chains gradually expanded, and by the 1950s whole families and entire villages were migrating to Canada. The new arrivals were typically quite young (average age 22.7 in the 1950s), but as the decade continued, parents (and even grandparents) joined their children in Canada. By the end of the decade, Immigration Department studies indicated that less than 10 percent of these new arrivals would have qualified for admission had they not been sponsored. Because of the volume of Italian immigration in these years, the Italian agents for immigration to Canada committed fraudulent practices, chiefly the misrepresentation of facts on immigration applications. In the early 1950s the department had begun a deliberate bureaucratic slowdown of Italian immigration, as well as introducing an informal quota of 25,000 immigrants per year. The result was a huge backlog of cases, well in excess of 50,000.

Fairclough managed to get cabinet approval for an order-in-council of 1959 (P.C. 59/310), which limited the entry of nondependent relatives into Canada. This limitation immediately affected the Italian flow but also the flow from other Mediterranean countries—such as Portugal and Greece—that featured large extended families and chain migration to Canada. These countries' ethnic communities in Canada raised a wave of protest, and J. W. Pickersgill told the House of Commons that the new limitation was "an unnecessary and inhumane restriction . . . aimed at one community in this country" (Avery, 1995, p. 176). The liberals were regarded as being more supportive of immigration, so most of the new Canadians voted Liberal as a matter of course. Fairclough denied that the revisions were discriminatory, insisting, "well qualified Italians who wished to migrate to this country had little or no chance of having their applications considered unless they were in the sponsored categories"(Avery, 1995, p. 176). She insisted that over the long term the limitation on sponsorship would produce a more diversified Italian immigration. But she was soon forced to back down, stating that she was asking the cabinet to withdraw the order-in-council and would propose new regulations shortly. She was later transferred in 1962 to the post office, at that time a totally innocuous post, and was later defeated in the 1963 election by an Italian-Canadian Liberal candidate. The Fairclough initiative had failed partly because it was not well explained, and partly because the government had not taken ethnic politics sufficiently into account.

Despite her defeat over sponsorship in 1962, Fairclough persisted with immigration reform. In 1962 she tabled in the House of Commons new immigration regulations, which removed racial discrimination and introduced skill as the major criterion for unsponsored immigration. Such a policy was consistent with Prime Minister Diefenbaker's 1960 Bill of Rights, which rejected discrimination based upon race, color, national origin, religion, or gender. With this change to immigration policy, sponsored immigration—which was continuing—almost immediately became by definition part of the old discriminatory system favoring European over non-European immigrants, as there were many more Canadians of European descent to sponsor new arrivals. According to the deputy minister of immigration,

> Our prime objective in the proposed revision is to eliminate all discrimination based on colour, race or creed. This means that, if we continue to allow Greeks, Poles, Italians, Portuguese and other Europeans to bring in the wide range of relatives presently admissible, we will have to do the same for Japanese, Chinese, Indians, Pakistanis, Africans, persons from the Arab world, the West Indies and so forth. The only possible result of this would be a substantially larger number of unskilled close relatives from these parts of the world to add to the influx of unskilled close relatives from Europe (Hawkins, 1972, p. 112).

To avoid this result, he added reluctantly that it was going to be necessary to close the door to close relatives from all parts of the world, and to reduce somehow the flow of European close relatives. However, Section 31(d) of the new regulations did not open the sponsorship door to non-Europeans.

The new regulations also provided for an Immigration Board semi-independent of the Immigration Department to hear appeals, except in sponsorship cases. With regard to the matter of illegal Chinese immigration, the government decided to declare an "amnesty" to all Chinese immigrants who had arrived illegally in Canada before 1 July 1960. This was the first of a long series of amnesties that would be declared to deal with illegal immigration to Canada. The Liberals complained in Parliament that this cosmic shift in Canadian policy had occurred without any public debate, which was true. Whether Canadian public opinion would have sustained such a nonracial policy in 1962 is, of course, quite doubtful. The new nonracial policy did not have an immediate impact upon Canada, though, because of the low level of immigration in the early 1960s. These low levels were a result of budget cutbacks to the Department of Immigration under the Diefenbaker government, caused by financial considerations rather than policy ones. At the same time, it must be admitted that the Diefenbaker cabinet saw immigration as an unpleasant and necessary evil upon which as little money as possible should be spent.

Conclusion

By 1962, Canadian immigration and immigration policy had come a long way from the restrictive and constrictive policies of the immediate post-war period. Canada had admitted large numbers of refugees and displaced persons, and sponsorship had allowed 1 million more people to enter the country. Almost all the immigration had come from Europe, although under the sponsorship program the source of the immigrants had shifted from western to southern Europe. In 1962, Canada was clearly poised on the cusp of a new era of immigration, one that would begin to change the racial composition of the nation.

Timeline

1945	Canada supports UNICEF (United Nations International Children's Emergency Fund) and UNRRA; Canadian troops and war brides brought home.
1946	Demands for a Canadian immigration policy that responds to the refugee situation in Europe.
May 1946	P.C. 2071 passed by cabinet, allowing Canadian residents to sponsor admission of first-degree relations and nieces and nephews under age of sixteen.
July 1946	Cabinet provides that displaced persons can be accepted without passports; cabinet also approves a resettlement program (paid for by the British) for Polish refugees.
7 November 1946	Mackenzie King announces in Parliament emergency measures to aid refugees and displaced persons in collaboration with refugee agencies.
spring 1947	Growing criticism of bulk labor programs.
1 May 1947	Landmark statement on immigration read by King in House of Commons.
6 June 1947	Canada begins admitting displaced persons before international agreement is reached.
June 1947–1948	Thousands of unsponsored displaced persons admitted.
summer 1948	U.S. Congress passes Displaced Persons Act, which makes United States preferred destination for displaced persons.

9 June 1950   Passage of P.C. 2856: Expanded admissible categories of European immigrants to include anyone healthy of good character with needed skills and ability to integrate.

1950   Department of Citizenship and Immigration established; opening up further of admissible classes of Asians; expanded openings for Germanic peoples.

1951   Agreements with governments of India, Pakistan, and Ceylon; Mabel Timlin writes book on immigration.

1 June 1952   New immigration act takes effect.

1954   Poll suggests only 45 percent of Canadians favor immigration.

1955   Pickersgill initiates process of admitting a few Arabs from the Middle East.

November 1956   Hungarian uprising leads to emergency admission of refugees, on top of a spurt of British immigration caused by Suez crisis.

1957   "Air Bridge to Canada" scheme started; highest yearly total of immigrants since 1913–1914 (282,000 people); Diefenbaker promises a more humane immigration policy.

May 1958   Ellen Fairclough appointed minister of immigration.

March 1959   Government attempts to control sponsorship movement (largely from Italy); P.C. 1959/310 limits admissible classes of close relatives.

22 April 1959   Sponsorship regulation rescinded.

1960   Evidence of immigration abuses grows.

1962   Fairclough tables new regulations that abolish racial discrimination.

1 February 1962   New regulations come into effect, abolishing the White Canada policy of previous governments.

Significant People, Places, and Events

ABSORPTIVE CAPACITY A term first used by Prime Minister W. L. Mackenzie King in 1947 to refer to the capability of the Canadian economy to accommodate new immigrants to Canada.

BEAVERBRAE A vessel that, in 1948, brought to Canada immigrants of mainly German origin recruited by the Canadian Christian Council for the Resettlement of Refugees.

BILL OF RIGHTS Canadian federal charter, passed into law in 1960 at the instigation of John Diefenbaker, that recognized the entitlement of individuals to various human rights and that banned discrimination based on race, color, national origin, religion, or gender.

BULK-LABOR PROGRAM Canadian program created in 1946 to allow European refugees into Canada to provide unskilled and semiskilled labor to the Canadian economy.

CANADIAN CHRISTIAN COUNCIL FOR RESETTLEMENT OF REFUGEES (CC-CRR) Umbrella organization of mainly German ethnic groups founded in 1947 to lobby for and facilitate German immigration to Canada.

CANADIAN WIVES' BUREAU Organization founded in Britain in 1945 to assist Canadian war brides in being reunited with their husbands in Canada.

CHINESE AMNESTY OF 1960 A federal government declaration that illegal Chinese immigrants to Canada would be allowed to remain in the country and qualify for legal status.

DISPLACED PERSONS A term used to describe individuals who have been forced to leave their homes and have been uprooted by political upheavals. It was initially applied to Europeans during and after World War II.

FAIRCLOUGH, ELLEN (b. 1905) Minister of immigration 1958–1962, she attempted to reform and liberalize Canadian immigration policy and procedures.

HUNGARIAN REFUGEES OF 1956 More than 200,000 people who fled Hungary in 1956 after the brutal invasion of Hungary by the Soviet Union. A substantial proportion (about 40,000) of these refugees was admitted to Canada as a humanitarian gesture outside the normal Canadian immigration procedures.

IMMIGRATION ACT OF 1952 Canadian legislation that "clarified and simplified immigration procedures and removed certain anomalies which have been brought to light during the continued movement of newcomers to Canada."

P[RIVY] C[OUNCIL] 695 The Canadian order-in-council that served as the basis for immigration policy from 1931 to 1946. It focused on the immigration of farmers.

P[RIVY]C[COUNCIL] 2071 An order-in-council amending P.C. 695 and allowing for the admission of immigrants from Europe who were sponsored by immediate relatives.

P[RIVY] C[OUNCIL] 2180 A 1947 order-in-council that authorized the immigration authorities to recruit selected immigrants from European refugee camps.

P[RIVY] C[OUNCIL] 59/310 A 1959 order-in-council that attempted to limit the number of sponsored immigrants allowed to enter Canada.

PICKERSGILL, J. W. (1905–1997) Minister of immigration in the St. Laurent government, he was responsible for bringing Hungarian refugees to Canada in 1956. He was an advocate of a flexible immigration policy.

POLISH SECOND CORPS A military unit formed in 1941 out of Polish POWs by Stalin for use against the German invaders. Led by General Wladyslaw Anders, it served in Iran and Italy and added recruits of all nationalities and credentials over the years. Four thousand men from this unit would be admitted to Canada in 1946 as laborers.

REFUGEES A term used to describe individuals who have fled their homes for political or military reasons.

SPONSORSHIP PROGRAM An immigration program begun in 1946 whereby Canadian citizens could sponsor close relatives for admission to Canada. In the 1950s it became the major vehicle for immigration to Canada.

STANDING COMMITTEE OF THE CANADIAN SENATE ON IMMIGRATION AND LABOUR A legislative committee of the Canadian Senate that held lengthy hearings into Canadian immigration policy in 1946. They recommended a generous policy toward displaced persons and refugees.

UKRAINIAN CANADIAN COMMITTEE (UCC) An ethnic organization created to help Ukrainian immigrants and to lobby for their welfare. It advocated the admission of Ukrainian intellectuals to Canada in 1948.

UNITED NATIONS REFUGEE CONVENTION OF 1951 An international agreement of 1951 dealing with refugee rights.

UNITED NATIONS RELIEF AND REHABILITATION ADMINISTRATION (UN-RRA) An organization created by the Allies in November 1943 to plan for and deal with the chaos of war-torn Europe. It had a particular responsibility to deal with refugees and displaced persons.

VOLKSDEUTSCHE Ethnic Germans from central Europe who had been displaced and driven west into Austria, Italy, and Germany by the Soviet Army in 1945.

WAR BRIDES European (mainly British) wives of Canadian soldiers, who were brought to Canada with their children to be reunited with their husbands in 1945 and 1946.

Documents

Testimony of Mr. Jolliffe, 1946

In 1946, Mr. A. L. Jolliffe, Director of Immigration, Department of Mines and Resources, testified before the Senate of Canada Standing Committee on Immigration and Labour. He began by describing the organization of his department.

Mr. Jolliffe: Mr. Chairman, I shall be very glad to furnish any information I possibly can to assist you in your studies of immigration. The Immigration Branch is one of four or five branches of the Department of Mines and Resources, and it operates under a Director, who is responsible to the Deputy Minister and the Minister. The branch for administration purposes is divided into three divisions: Headquarters Division, Field Service, Canada, and Field Service, Overseas. The Headquarters Division deals with all administrative matters. It is composed of various subdivisions, such as central registry for correspondence, manifest division for recording immigration, a statistical division, a juvenile division for dealing with juvenile immigrants, a staff division, and a general division, which deals particularly with the administration of the law in Canada, under a Commissioner.

The second division is the field and inspectional division in Canada, and for purposes of administration it is divided into four districts: the Atlantic District, which takes in the Province of Quebec and the Maritime Provinces; the Eastern District, which takes in that part of Ontario from the Quebec border up to but not including Port Arthur; the Western District, from Port Arthur west to and including Kingsgate, British Columbia; and the Pacific District, all territory west of Kingsgate, including the Yukon Territory. Each of these districts is under the direction of a district superintendent and staff at district headquarters. The district headquarters of the Atlantic and Eastern Divisions are at Ottawa; of the Western District, at Winnipeg; of the Pacific District, at Vancouver. In the districts are ports of entry, both boundary ports and ocean ports and some inland agencies. The ports are under the direction of an Inspector in Charge. Some of them have as many as fifty inspectors, and one or two, such as Windsor and Niagara Falls, have more than that. The inland agencies are for the purpose of dealing with investigation work in the interior of Canada. The overseas organization is in Europe, the headquarters in London, under the direction of a Commissioner. Under normal conditions there are agencies in the United Kingdom and inspectional points on the continent. At the present time there are no inspectional points or agencies overseas, apart from the London Office, and I shall comment on that in a few moments. Under normal conditions there is also one inspectional point in Hong Kong, which deals with a particular phase of our work, relating particularly to Chinese immigration, under a special immigration officer. That office is not open at the present time.

There are 40 inspectional points at seaports in Canada, and there are 203 international boundary ports. The year before last, on the international boundary, officers of the department examined over 21 million persons coming into Canada. That does not mean that 21 million different people were examined; it means that 21 million persons passed inspection. To illustrate what I mean: at Windsor, for instance, there are a lot of people who commute, and they will come over from Detroit and go back once or twice a week, some of them daily. But the actual number of persons that passed inspection on the international boundary in the year ending March 1945 was over 21 million. I mention that to show the amount of inspectional work that is performed by the service.

Thus the ports of entry are primarily engaged in the inspection of immigrants coming to Canada. Each person is required to be examined to ascertain whether admissible under the law. If he is not admissable he is rejected and has the right of appeal to the minister. The rejection with the appeal procedure frequently involves investigation in the interior, with officers who can conduct a quick investigation and also prevent the unnecessary or lengthy delay of persons at the border who have been refused admission. Our overseas inspection service operates similarly to the inspection service at the international boundary ports. There is an inspector in charge, and the immigrant coming from Europe is required to obtain an immigration visa at the port to establish his admissibility to Canada. In normal times we have inspectional points at Paris, Antwerp, Rotterdam, Hamburg—which includes Bremen—Danzig, Gdynia, and Riga. At these points we also have medical officers who are required to examine all persons coming from the continent to Canada.

Source: Proceedings of the Senate of Canada Standing Committee on Immigration and Labour, 21 May 1946.

David Fulton on Canadian Immigration, 1954

Mr. [E. Davie] Fulton [opposition critic on immigration]
Saturday, June 26, 1954

In 1951 we had a good year in immigration. There were some 100,000 immigrants admitted to Canada. The totals admitted during the next three years declined substantially from that level, so that not only have we a decline in the numbers being admitted but it is my view that the policy laid out by the government in 1947 by the prime minister, and since that time subscribed to and reiterated by the present minister, is not being fulfilled. I have reference particularly to the situation regarding the maintenance of the ethnic balance of this country. If one looks at the figures put on the record again by the minister last night, and I have them in detail before me in a release from the statistical unit of the department [of immigration], it will be seen that when you have 47,077 from the United Kingdom plus 9,000 from the United States, making a total of 56,000 of that category admitted in the year, and in the same year you have 63,675 north Europeans, including 35,105 Germans and you have 43,737 others, including 24,219 from Italy, it is not possible to agree with the minister when he says the policy of preserving the ethnic balance within the country is being followed.

From time to time we on this side of the house have made perfectly clear we do not ask for any special preference being given to one country as a source of origin of immigration or that we should concentrate exclusively on bringing in immigrants from that country. I want to reiterate that position here this morning. We subscribed to the view that Canada should take immigrants who are capable of being absorbed into both our economic and cultural background from any country where suitable immigrants offer. But we do say that should be tempered, if you like, to fit in with this policy of maintaining the ethnic balance and not distorting the cultural or economic situation in Canada. . . .

We have also, from time to time, criticized the government for apparent inability to work out an intelligent and vigorous application of the assisted passage loan scheme as applied to the United Kingdom, so that we may encourage more immigration from there. I have been given information as to the countries in which that scheme was applied, and the number of immigrants brought forward under that scheme since February, 1951, up to December 31, 1952, which I was given to understand was the last day for which figures were available. . . . Up to that time, out of a total of 78,403 admitted, there were 4,361 from the United Kingdom, 22,224 from Germany and Austria, and a very small number, something in the neighbourhood of 1,700 or 1,800 from other European countries. The proportion between those countries from which immigrants have come under this scheme working out at approximately 15.4 per cent from the United Kingdom, 78.2 per cent from Germany and Austria and 6.3 per cent from elsewhere. Once again the figures show that with respect to pre-serving the ethnic balance of this country, the assisted passage loan scheme is not being equitably applied to the different countries of Europe, in that the United Kingdom has a disproportionately low number of immigrants coming out under that scheme.

Now, there are other matters which are causing concern in connection with the immigration policy of the government. One of these is the picture with respect to the fact that, of the large number of immigrants coming from Italy, practically none came from the north. I draw the attention of the committee to a series of articles appearing recently in the Vancouver *Sun* and written by Stanley Burke. He pointed out that last year Canada had taken more immigrants from Italy than any other country had taken. He obtained figures from the Italian government which showed that 24,000 went to Canada, and only 400 returned. Out of 10,000 who went to the United States, 2,400 returned. Immigrants to the Argentine totalled 13,000, and almost that many made the "disillusioned" trip home.... The suggestion has been made that in our policy of soliciting immigrants from Italy we should pay more attention than we do to those in northern Italy. Experience has shown that the latter make excellent Canadian citizens with background of industrial and technical training. These people would be easier to fit into the Canadian scene than those drawn exclusively from southern Italy.

Source: House of Commons Debates, 1954 session, pp. 6787–6789.

Bibliography

Abella, Irving, and Harold Troper, *None Is Too Many: Canada and the Jews of Europe 1933–1948*, rev. ed. (Toronto: Lester and Orpen Dennys, 1991).

Avery, Donald H., *Reluctant Host: Canada's Response to Immigrant Workers, 1896–1994* (Toronto: McClelland and Stewart, 1995).

Briggs, Susan, *The Home Front: War Years in Britain 1939–1945* (London, U.K.: Weidenfeld and Nicolson, 1975).

Corbett, David C., *Canada's Immigration Policy: A Critique* (Toronto: University of Toronto Press, 1957).

Fairclough, Ellen, *Saturday's Child: Memoirs of Canada's First Female Cabinet Minister* (Toronto: University of Toronto Press, 1995).

Hawkins, Freda, *Canada and Immigration: Public Policy and Public Concern* (Montreal, Quebec and London, U.K.: McGill-Queen's University Press, 1972).

Iacovetta, Franca, *Such Hardworking People: Italian Immigrants in Postwar Toronto* (Montreal, Quebec and Kingston, Ontario: McGill-Queen's University Press, 1992).

Keyserlingk, Robert H., ed., *Breaking Ground: The 1956 Hungarian Refugee Movement to Canada* (Toronto: York Lanes Press, 1993).

Knowles, Valerie, *Strangers at Our Gates: Canadian Immigration and Immigration Policy, 1540–1997* (Toronto: Dundurn Press, 1997).

Margolian, John, *Unauthorized Entry: The Truth about Nazi War Criminals in Canada, 1946–1956* (Toronto: University of Toronto Press, 2000).

Richmond, Anthony, *Post-War Immigrants in Canada* (Toronto: University of Toronto Press, 1967).

Standing Committee [of the Canadian Senate] on Immigration and Labour, *Senate Report no. 6* (Ottawa: King's Printer, 1946).

Timlin, Mabel F., *Does Canada Need More People?* (Toronto: Oxford University Press, 1951).

Wicks, Ben, *Promise You'll Take Care of My Daughter: The Remarkable War Brides of World War II* (Toronto: Stoddart, 1992).

CHAPTER NINE

Redefining Immigration and Ethnic/Cultural Policy, 1960–1975

U P UNTIL ABOUT 1960 Canada had been a very traditional nation. Its population was not very welcoming of mass immigration. There were large pockets of racism and considerable hostility to cultural diversity. Much of the country was dominated by highly conservative rural values. Canadian international attitudes tended to be relatively isolationist as well. Between 1960 and 1975, a major change occurred in Canada regarding all its attitudes, both on the official level and the unofficial one. The process by which Canada became a cosmopolitan country was a complex one that is, even today, not very well understood. A number of factors stand out in the cosmic shift, however.

Factors Altering Canada's Attitude to Immigration and Cultural Diversity

The conversion, within the space of a single generation, from a very insular and parochial nation to one that was relatively sophisticated and cosmopolitan and much more capable of toleration of ethnic differences, was one of the most remarkable public changes in Canadian history. One factor in the change of attitude was World War II, in which more than 1million Canadians served in the military, more than one-half of them overseas. Unlike World War I, which most Canadian soldiers spent residing in disgusting trenches on the continent of Europe, World War II actually gave Canadians some foreign experience. More than one-quarter million troops spent up to four years in Great Britain, waiting for the big show of D-Day to begin and, at least sometimes, playing at being tourists. Canadian soldiers fought in Italy and through France, the Low Countries, and Germany. Such fighting was not pleasant, but it was considerably more broadening than life in a muddy trench. The fact that more than 50,000

Hutterite children at school, Alberta 1971 (National Archives of Canada)

Canadians met foreign girls and got to know them well enough to pro-pose marriage suggests some of the possibilities. The American popular song of World War I had queried, "How you gonna keep 'em, down on the farm, after they've seen Paree?" That question was really much more rele-vant for Canada in 1945 than in 1918.

A second factor was the postwar immigration itself. Between 1946 and 1972 more than 3.5 million "New Canadians" entered the country, an av-erage of about 135,000 per year. Even after emigration to other nations from Canada is subtracted (as people, especially recent arrivals, also *left* the country in substantial numbers during that period), the net gain was well in excess of 2 million. By 1971, one in every four Canadians claimed an ethnic origin other than British, French, or aboriginal. The changes are detailed in Table 9.1.

Taken in proportion to the total population, the post–World War II fig-ures for immigration were not as significant as the earlier influxes of im-migration to Canada before Confederation and before the Great War. However, the postwar immigration was different. Unlike earlier arrivals, many of whom ended up on isolated farmsteads on the frontier, this pop-ulation settled almost exclusively in the cities, especially those in Ontario and Quebec, transforming them enormously in the process. Toronto, for example, had before 1945 been a predominantly Anglo-Saxon city, in

TABLE 9.1   POPULATION BY ETHNIC ORIGIN, 1951, 1961, 1971

Ethnic Group	1951	1961	1971
British Isles	6,709,685	7,996,669	9,624,115*
English	3,630,344	4,195,175	
Irish	1,439,635	1,753,351	
Scots	1,547,470	1,902,302	
Welsh	92,236	145,841	
French	4,319,167	5,540,346	6,180,120
Other European	2,553,722	4,116,849	4,959,680
Asiatic	72,827	121,753	285,540
Other**	354,028	462,630	518,850***

SOURCE: Statistics Canada.

*By 1971 Statistics Canada had decided to no longer separate the British into national groups.

**Including Eskimo, Native Indian, Negro, West Indian, and not stated.

***Americans are not included in this table because Statistics Canada did not regard the people of the United States as an ethnic group; Americans are listed under their national origins.

which only in certain areas could any language other than English be heard. By 1961, one observer wrote of the Toronto scene:

> Near Toronto's downtown area can be found the great unassimilated for-
> eign communities, towns within a town, the bustling Jewish markets with
> their Kosher stores and Hebrew signs, the women in their shawls and
> aprons of eastern Europe, the Italian quarter with its pasta shops and
> multi-tudinous children; the Germans driving most of the cabs in Toronto;
> and most recently the sad faced Hungarians huddled together in disap-
> pointment, often despair. . . . Its new polyglot life is what gives Toronto a
> colour and fascination which it would not otherwise possess; but it is also
> what causes the native born (those outnumbered few) to exclaim in dis-
> gust, "One never hears English on Yonge Street these days." (Richmond,
> 1967, p. 4.)

Although Montreal had always been bilingual rather than unilingual, the same sense of a polyglot city was present in it by the 1960s, as it was in almost all of the larger cities of Canada west of the Atlantic region. The urban concentration of the postwar immigration made for the emergence of ethnic cities.

A third factor in the new acceptance of cultural diversity was the rapid transformation into modern times of the rural communities of Canada between 1945 and 1960. In 1945 most rural Canadians lived in virtual isolation in a world of unpaved roads, horse-powered vehicles, cash shortages, and an absence of telephones and electricity. By 1960 the roads had been paved. The horse had been replaced by the tractor and the automobile. Farm families now had cash, from the monthly mothers' allowance check (a payment to every mother in the nation, based on the number of children she has) from the federal government, if from no other source. Virtually every family had a telephone, and the world of electricity meant milking machines, electric stoves and refrigerators, radios, television sets, and stereos. Rural and farm families had become plugged into the larger industrial economy rather than isolated from it, and there would be no going back.

Both the urban preferences of postwar immigrants and the rural transformation helped contribute to a fourth factor in the change, which was the overall extent to which Canada became an urban nation in the years after 1945, especially in the provinces of Ontario and Quebec. This new wave of urbanization was based on a transportation shift to automobiles and trucks, the change from an industrial to a service-based economy, suburban development, and on the influx of immigrants and rural Canadians into the urban centers. In 1941 only 55 percent of Canada's people lived in cities. That figure grew to 62.9 percent in 1951 and 69.7 percent in 1961. By 1971 more than three-fourths of the Canadian population lived in an urban environment. Cities have usually been responsible for breaking down the old traditionalism of a society, and for longtime residents of Canada in the postwar period, they did their job. It must be added that for many new arrivals, large cities and the resultant concentration of ethnics in complete communities meant that Canadian cities could actually slow the acculturation process rather than speed it up.

A fifth factor, related in part to this rural transformation but also involving the entire society, was the rapid modernization of Quebec. Previously a traditional society with its values based on Catholicism, between 1939 and 1960 Quebec experienced substantial industrialization and urbanization and came more into tune socially and economically with English-speaking Canada. (It is worth noting as an illustration of this change that the birth rate in Quebec during these years dropped from one of the highest in Canada to one of the lowest.) This socioeconomic transformation was accompanied by a series of profound ideological shifts within Quebec society that shook it to its foundations. The patterns of that development were relatively easy to understand for anyone familiar with what was happening elsewhere in developing societies. Traditional forms of defensive nationalism designed to protect the status quo, including the power and authority of the Catholic Church, were being swept away by a powerful new secular form of nationalism that had already become fully articulated in the years before 1960. The main opposition to the new nationalism came less from the old nationalism than from a renewed current of nineteenth-century liberalism adapted to twentieth-century Quebec conditions.

In the 1960s, these two competing ideological currents—the new nationalism and the renewed liberalism—would find popular labels in Quebec as "separatism" and "federalism." Quebec's new internal nationalism meant both that the province no longer served as a brake on Canadian federal policies of liberalization and that the province's demands indeed helped contribute to change. The "Quiet Revolution" of the 1960s would be a major impetus to a number of new Canadian policies. Most Quebeckers, for example, were quite happy to accept ethnic minorities so long as they were prepared to speak French and associate themselves with the aspirations of Quebec. In the process of dealing with the new Quebec, a succession of Canadian governments would remake policy toward immigration and ethnic culture.

Finally, the new communications media, particularly the general expansion of television across Canada after 1950, increasingly plugged Canadians into the world. The very speed of the spread of television told its own story. The Canadian Broadcasting Corporation opened its first two television stations in Montreal and Toronto in September 1952. At the time of the introduction of Canadian television broadcasting, only 146,000 Canadians owned television receivers, tuning to American border stations and using increasingly elaborate antenna systems to draw in distant signals. By December 1954 there were 9 stations and 1,200,000 sets; by June 1955 there were 26 stations and 1,400,000 sets; and by December 1957 there were 44 stations and nearly 3 million sets. The rate of proliferation of television sets in Canada had been almost twice that of the United States, and the market for new sets was virtually saturated within five years. By the early 1960s virtually the only sign of life in entire blocks of residential urban and suburban neighborhoods—or on rural roads with their periodically scattered farmhouses—was the dull, flickering glow of black-and-white television screens within otherwise darkened dwellings. Paradoxically, while television put Canadians back into their homes, it also helped force them out of their narrow insularity, not so much into their local communities as into the international world previously beyond their ken.

A New Immigration Policy

Although there had been some shift in country of origin of immigrants to Canada after 1945, in 1965 Britain still provided nearly 30 percent of the newcomers, Europe nearly one-half, and the United States 10 percent, leaving only a little more than 10 percent of immigrants originating in the remainder of the world. All of the top ten "nations of origin" except the United States were still European in 1965. In 1966 the Liberal government of Lester B. Pearson epitomized much of the official Canadian philosophy of immigration when it put immigration under the same minister as manpower in the Department of Manpower and Immigration. The opposition in Parliament criticized the melding of immigration policy into the labor portfolio, preferring instead that Canada should form a department of citizenship and immigration. The deputy minister of the new Department of Manpower and Immigration found his task no easy one, reporting in his memoirs:

> Politicians were understandably chary of defining immigration policy at all precisely. On one hand, there was a broad public sentiment in favour of easy immigration; so many Canadians, if not immigrants themselves, had known parents or grandparents who were. There was also strong humanitarian sentiment on behalf of the oppressed and the deprived. And behind these general attitudes were powerful special interests: business wanting both skilled professionals and cheap labour; expanding universities wanting professors with doctorates not available in Canada; richer people wanting domestic servants. And, of course, recent immigrants wanted their relatives and friends to join them, and ethnic organizations had strong interests in the growth of their particular communities. (Kent, 1988, p. 407)

The new ministry sounded out public opinion in 1966 through the publication of a White Paper on Immigration Policy. This document argued for the recruitment of workers with high degrees of skills, regardless "of race, colour or religion." It also insisted that the government should not hesitate to keep out misfits and criminals. Public hearings on the White Paper by the Special Joint Committee of the Senate and House of Commons on Immigration began in November of 1966.

The Joint Committee heard a full spectrum of opinion from what Tom Kent had called the "special interests." The Confederation of National Trade Unions (CNTU) in Quebec opposed an emphasis on skills, insisting that such a policy would represent an international brain drain in which Canada would weaken Third World nations by taking their professionals. The Canadian Labour Congress agreed, adding that unskilled immigrant workers were needed to carry out "tasks which native born or already established immigrants refuse to perform because of their better training." The Mining Association of Canada definitely wanted at least 4,000 semiskilled workers admitted per year, noting, "The type of immigrant we have in mind has been the backbone of the labour force of the mining industry in the past. . . . a man has to be physically fit; but his education is not too important, so long as he can read or write." Canadians would not work in mines, reported one witness from the mining interests, because "there are no roads, no TV's, no cars, few girls, little or no liquor and most people recoil from the idea of working underground" (Avery, 1995, p. 181). No mention was made by this witness of the danger or relatively low pay experienced by mine workers. Most Canadian industrialists advocated the admission of the unskilled into the nation, although the Canadian Manufacturing Association and the Canadian Medical Association both stressed the need for those who were technologically prepared. The Canadian Jewish Congress emphasized humanitarian concerns, "the need for people to find asylum." Many ethnic organizations applauded the new emphasis on skills, but most also insisted on the maintenance of the sponsorship category.

Having listened to the interest groups, the ministry moved quickly to implement a major reform of immigration policy, instituting in 1968 a major new mechanism for immigration selection, the "points system." According to Tom Kent, "If we could identify and define the various factors affecting a person's ability to settle in Canada, and attach relative weights to them, then immigration officers would have a consistent basis on which to assess potential immigrants" (Kent, 1988, p. 410). Thus, education, employment opportunities, skills, age, and the immigration officer's assessment of potential were all to be awarded points adding up to a maximum total of one hundred. The points system was put in place as a separate program apart from sponsorship, which was continued (although with reduced categories) because of its support from corporate Canada, trade unions, and ethnic groups. The idea of implementing a skills-based program had only limited support from the hearing.

A new procedure allowing a person to apply for immigrant status from within the country was also introduced and would ultimately become one of the most controversial parts of the new immigration law. This last policy was prompted chiefly by the appearance as visitors in Canada of American draft evaders. In the late 1960s, as many as 100,000 Americans seeking to avoid service in the Vietnam War had come to Canada and were sheltered by Canadians and the Canadian government. The policy of allowing people to apply for status after already arriving in Canada was intended to regularize requests for landed immigrant status from this particular group of refugees. The points system officially eliminated discrimination on the grounds of race or class but managed to perpetuate several traditional features of Canadian policy. By awarding large numbers of points on the basis of occupation, education, language skills, and age, it continued both the economic rationale for immigration and the selectivity of the process.

Bilingualism and Biculturalism

The profound socioeconomic changes in Quebec led in 1960 to the "Quiet Revolution," in which a new spirit of French Canadian nationalism took control of the province of Quebec and its institutions. Quebec began demanding its own social and economic programs apart from those of English-speaking Canada. A small group of radical organizations began taking violent action, such as putting bombs in mailboxes, while a somewhat larger group of radicals began talking about independence from Canada. One of Quebec's major concerns was the erosion of its language and culture in the face of the anglophone majority across not only Canada but North America in general. Part of that erosion was being caused by immigration. The new arrivals in Quebec often spoke neither English nor French, and they preferred to see their children educated in English, which would make them far more mobile outside Quebec than would an education in French. The whole question of mobility, economic and geographic, was yet another issue. French Canadians insisted that they were discriminated against in the large multinational corporations within Quebec, partly because they spoke French, and partly because they were of French Canadian descent. An increasing sense of militancy within Quebec led anglophone Canadians to ask almost in chorus, "What does Quebec really want?"

The Liberal government of Lester B. Pearson, which came to power without a majority in 1963, sought to respond to Quebec with three strategies. One was called cooperative federalism, a program by which Ottawa allowed Quebec to opt out of increasing numbers of national social insurance programs in favor of its own program. Cooperative federalism could only achieve so much, however, before Ottawa began to fear that there would be nothing left of Canada, and so Ottawa lost interest in the concept. A second program dealt with the symbols of the nation. Canada had neither an official flag nor an official national anthem. By common usage, Canada's flag was the red ensign of British origin (which contained a union jack in the top left corner), and its anthem was "God Save the Queen." In 1963 Canada began talking in Parliament and outside it about changing its flag, ultimately to the present maple leaf design, and adopting as the national anthem "O Canada," originally written by a French Canadian with original words in French. These new symbols were in large measure designed to be less offensive to the French majority in Quebec, who had never been completely enthusiastic about the British imperial ties reflected in the old flag and anthem. But they also served to please new Canadians who were not of British origin. Moreover, the search for new national symbols fit well into new spirit of Canadian nationalism of the 1960s, particularly prevalent among the young. The debate over the new flag in Parliament was particularly emotional and bitter, however, with the opposition claiming that the replacement of the union jack and red ensign, under which Canadian soldiers had fought in two wars, was particularly disrespectful of veterans, as well as of the monarchy and the entire British connection. The new symbols won out, though, and as the government had intended, the new symbols were in place for Centennial Year in 1967. Canadian youngsters took instantly to the new flag, although learning the words to "O Canada" took many older Canadians a little longer.

A final policy initiative of the Pearson Liberals was the concept of "equal partnership," the right of both French-speaking and English-speaking Canadians to participate equally in the institutions that controlled their present and future. This concept, along with the notions of cultural dualism and "two founding peoples," was enshrined in the Order-in-Council that in 1963 set up the Royal Commission on Bilingualism and Biculturalism. The Commission's terms of reference, written into the order, called for it "to enquire into and report upon the existing state of bilingualism and biculturalism in Canada and to recommend what steps should be taken to develop the Canadian Confederation on the basis of an equal partnership between the two founding races, taking into account the contribution made by the other ethnic groups to the cultural enrichment of Canada and the measures that should be taken to safeguard that contribution" (quoted in Appendix I, *Report of the Royal Commission on Bilingualism and Biculturalism*, IV). Chaired by André Laurendeau and Davidson Dunton (1912–1987), president of Carleton University, the Commission was plainly a response to the growing problems of Quebec. It was instructed to recommend ways of facilitating Canada's cultural dualism.

Two obvious points about the work of the Commission and its eventual recommendations must be emphasized. The first is that its terms of reference (the directions given it by the order that created it) stated almost all the conclusions that it reached, the Commission simply legitimizing them in appropriate academic language. Second, the Commission neither disputed those terms of reference nor attempted to widen them. More than most royal commissions, therefore, it served as a facilitator of articulated public policy rather than as an instrument for the thorough examination and analysis of cherished beliefs. This distinction is important, for the B and B (or Bi and Bi) Commission discovered in the course of its hearings and investigations a good deal of evidence that might have suggested the very real limitations of its original terms of reference. If it had paid more attention to that evidence in formulating its eventual recommendations, it might well have saved the nation a good deal of subsequent agony.

The major problem, of course, was that a cultural dualism based on the concept of two founding peoples flew in the face of much of the nation's history. In its final report the Commission evaded the fact that its designated founding peoples did not include Canada's indigenous peoples. In its "General Introduction" to "Key Words of the Terms of Reference," the Commission alluded to the problem of the native peoples, stating that it would not examine it because "Our terms of reference contain no allusion to Canada's native populations." It appreciated that native peoples were not included among either the "founding races" or the "other ethnic groups," but did not draw the logical conclusion. In its volume on "Other Ethnic Groups," the Commission offered a brief and unsophisticated history of settlement that opened with the statement: "Canada, a vast territory inhabited in the beginning by Indians and Eskimos, was first colonized by the French, beginning early in the 17th century, and then by the British" (the use of the term *British* in this context was, of course, incorrect, as Great Britain did not exist before 1707) (Ibid., p. 4). In a footnote after the word *Eskimos*, the Commission added, "Since the terms of reference contain no mention of Indians and Eskimos, we have not studied the question of Canada's native population." Instead it contented itself with an introductory "reminder" to "the proper authorities that everything possible must be done to help the native populations preserve their cultural heritage, which is part of the patrimony of all Canadians."

When the Commission moved its public hearings outside the central Canadian corridor, it heard from hundreds of groups and thousands of individual Canadians, many of whom expressed doubts about its terms of reference. Most of the criticism came from spokespeople for ethnic communities that were not part of the cultural duality. The Commission was forced to devote an entire volume of its report to "The Cultural Contribution of the Other Ethnic Groups." The "embarrassments" caused by native peoples may have been avoided through bureaucratic sleight of hand, but those caused by other ethnic groups were more complicated. The Commission dealt with them by denying ethnic validity as a "third force" in Canadian society. Other ethnic groups were too disparate, it argued, and it was clear

That this "third force" does not exist in Canada in any political sense, and is simply based on statistical compilations. All the available evidence indicates that those of other languages and cultures are more or less integrated with the francophone and anglophone communities, where they should find opportunities for self-fulfillment and equality of status. It is within these two societies that their cultural distinctiveness should find a climate of respect and encouragement to survive. (Royal Commission on Bilingualism and Biculturalism, 1969, p. 10)

Other ethnic communities were to be seen as cultural groups, argued the Commission, rather than as a basic structural element of Canadian society equal to the French or the British. As more than one scholar pointed out in essays submitted to the Commission at the time, however, there were serious doubts about the existence of an English Canadian culture equivalent to that of French Canada.

In the end—as the Commission recognized both in its opening remarks and in its recommendations—its principal concerns had to be language and bilingualism rather than culture. Most Canadians were prepared to accept that the nation should implement equality for the two languages it declared official, and it was perhaps unfortunate that the Commission strayed into other areas (such as culture) while failing to challenge more directly some of the assumptions underlying its terms of reference. Its first recommendation was implemented by the Official Languages Act of 1969, which declared French and English to be the official languages with equal status in all institutions under federal jurisdiction. This did not resolve the question about the usage of language in Canada, but the federal government could do no more. Most other recommendations, particularly those about language education, involved provincial cooperation and were more difficult to bring about, although many were subsequently implemented in whole or in part. Bilingualism and biculturalism were very limited concepts that did not really address the cultural complexity of Canada. They did reflect, however, a growing realization on the part of many Canadians that the nation was in no sense homogeneous.

The Major New Postwar Ethnic Groups

Volume IV of the report of the Royal Commission on Bilingualism and Biculturalism, which dealt with non-British and non-French ethnic groups, was not designed as a history of Canadian ethnicity, but rather as an analysis of the cultural contributions of ethnic groups to the nation. Except in some detailed charts and tables, it did not treat ethnic groups as particular entities or focus on their history. The postwar immigration was considered in four pages, focusing mainly on residential patterns. The commission did note that most of the immigration between 1945 and 1971 was of European origin, broken essentially into northern European, eastern European (described as "refugees displaced by political disruptions in their homeland") and southern European (described as "immigrants from the less economically advanced countries"). From each of these geographic divisions originated a large number of ethnic groups.

A more detailed examination of representative groups from each of these divisions can suggest the major complexities and new patterns that were developing. Three patterns were important. One was the postimmigration behavior of people like the Dutch and most of the British, who were quite willing to meld into the Canadian population without many ethnic pretensions. The British and Dutch newcomers were not particularly interested in ethnic retention, and they affected ethnicity in Canada more by their volume than by the new directions they introduced into the situation. The second pattern was for the immigration, chiefly from southern Europe, of people with a traditional family-oriented society, who came to Canada and quickly reproduced culturally complete ethnic communities within Canada's largest cities that were fairly resistant to assimilation. The third pattern was for immigrants from eastern Europe (which had its ethnicity greatly confused by the great political changes of the first half of the twentieth century); they needed either to rediscover their ethnic roots in the pre–World War I ethnic communities of Canada or to create new ethnic identities. The Jews among the eastern Europeans had their Jewish identities imprinted upon them by the Holocaust and were able to find acceptance in Jewish communities in Canada.

The Dutch

Although there had always been a substantial Dutch presence in Canada for many years—and although more than 15,000 Dutch immigrants had arrived in Canada between 1915 and 1930—the major Dutch movement to Canada occurred in the two decades after 1945. The Netherlands had been occupied and both badly damaged and badly exploited by the Nazis during the war, and large numbers of Dutch citizens were eager to leave the nation and its ruined economy after the war. The facts that the United States was virtually closed to the Dutch because of its quota system and that Canadian troops had liberated the Netherlands were both contributory factors in the attraction of Canada for Dutch immigrants, who numbered more than 200,000 between 1945 and 1965. Traditionally, the Dutch coming to Canada had been farmers or farm laborers, and Canada in the years immediately after 1945 concentrated on recruiting this agricultural element. Many of the new arrivals went to Ontario, Alberta, and British Columbia, but the Dutch dispersed to all provinces, with perhaps some underrepresentation in Quebec. Particularly in the Pacific province, the newcomers were active in drainage and irrigation projects in the Fraser Valley and in the British Columbian interior. They acquired substantial numbers of farms in all provinces in the years after the war.

After 1950, the Dutch people who came to Canada were predominantly urban and industrial in origin, immigrating on their own rather than as part of reunited families. They began to congregate in Canadian cities, where they dispersed among the population rather than congregating in their own ethnic neighborhoods. The Dutch often spoke some English before their arrival, and after immigration they often displayed a very low interest in retention of their native language. Less than 10 percent of the second generation after the immigration and less than 5 percent of the third retained any knowledge of the Dutch language. The Dutch also showed little interest in the retention of Dutch culture, and even less interest in their homeland. They did not create national churches nor engage in ethnic politics, and they were among the least visible ethnic groups in Canada, so invisible that many observers doubted that they really were an ethnic group at all, although they were treated as one by Statistics Canada. Full assimilation into Canadian society was the goal for almost all Dutch arrivals. In this ambition the Dutch joined the newcomers from the British Isles, who were the largest single group of immigrants between 1945 and 1971.

The reasons for this extreme assimilability on the part of the Dutch have not been carefully studied and thus are not well understood. The Dutch were clearly disenchanted with their country's performance in the Second World War. Dutch immigrants had always fit in well in Canada, and their tendency to migrate as single immigrants or in small families without much cultural baggage militated against much cultural retention. The Dutch were also one of the few European populations after World War II that produced a substantial movement to Canada coming from a highly industrialized and highly urbanized nation. None of the Scandinavian countries produced such large numbers of immigrants to Canada, and so historians do not know what the response of immigrants from these lands to Canada would have been. In any case, a large proportion of the postwar Dutch (and British) arrivals were culturally compatible with the existing Canadian population and merged into it quite easily.

The Portuguese

If the Dutch and British were easily assimilable, the newcomers from southern Europe were quite another matter. The Italians have been discussed in chapter 6; another significant group was the Portuguese. Between 1900 and 1949, less than one thousand Portuguese immigrants entered Canada, most illegally. Most emigrants from Portugal went to Brazil during those years, but Portugal's economy stagnated during that time, and Brazil became a less attractive option. In the 1950s more than 17,000 Portuguese immigrants arrived in Canada, mainly as laborers. As has usually occurred with peoples from the Mediterranean, strong traditional family ties led to much sponsorship and family reunification, and 56,677 more Portuguese came in the 1960s, with another 79,891 arriving in the 1970s. Most of the newcomers originated in the Azores Islands, one of the poorest regions of Portugal. They congregated in Canadian urban centers from coast to coast, establishing strong ethnic neighborhoods in some of

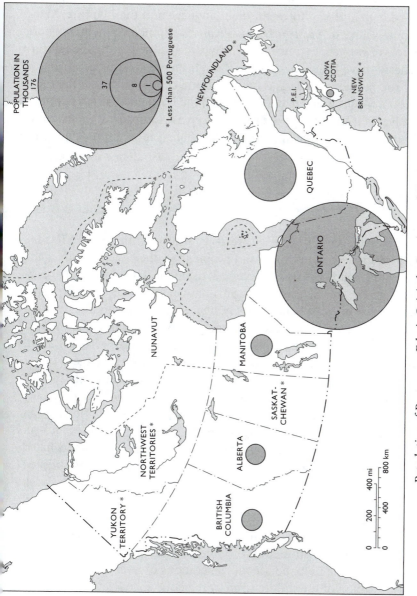

POPULATION IN THOUSANDS
176
37
8

* Less than 500 Portuguese

NEWFOUNDLAND *

QUEBEC

ONTARIO

P.E.I.

NOVA SCOTIA

NEW BRUNSWICK *

MANITOBA

NUNAVUT

SASKAT- CHEWAN *

ALBERTA

NORTHWEST TERRITORIES *

BRITISH COLUMBIA

YUKON TERRITORY *

0   200   400 mi
0   400   800 km

Population of Portuguese Ethnic Origin by Province and Territory, 1991

Source: Teixeira, Carlos. "The Suburbanization of Portuguese Communities in Toronto and Montreal: From Isolation to Residential Integration?" Pp. 181–202 in *Immigration and Ethnicity in Canada,* ed. Anna Laperrière, Varpu Lindström, and Tamara Palmer Seiler. *(Montreal: Association for Canadian Studies, 1996).*

the poorest slum districts of the inner cities. By the 1960s the Portuguese had replicated a large number of their native social, cultural, and business services in Canada and were remarkably slow to assimilate into Canadian society outside their neighborhoods. Unlike the Dutch, the Portuguese displayed a great desire to retain their language and their culture. Many traditional values of *Portuguesismo*—from the Roman Catholic religion, to the role of women, to music and cuisine, to an absence of political consciousness—have been preserved, although there was considerable erosion of the mother tongue and other cultural characteristics in the third generation. Most observers have explained the Portuguese's lack of political involvement in terms of their lack of experience in the mother country. A similar pattern was followed by the Italian immigrants, especially those from southern Italy and Sicily.

The Greeks

The Greek experience in Canada was very similar to that of the Italians and the Portuguese. A few thousand people from the Greek islands made their way to Canada before the Second World War. There were 9,450 persons of Greek origin in Canada in 1931. But Greece was greatly disrupted during the war by both Italian and German occupation and then by a series of bitter internal conflicts. Unemployment was high. From 1945 to 1971, more than 107,000 Greeks came to Canada. Most were unskilled, undereducated, and sponsored by friends and relations. A large number of single young Greek women (10,500) arrived during these years as domestic servants. A number of Greek Cypriots would come later, especially after the Turkish occupation of Cyprus in 1974. The Greeks clustered in Canada's largest cities, establishing communities on Jean Talon Avenue in Montreal and Danforth Avenue in Toronto. Most of the newcomers hated farming, which was associated with poverty in Greece. They established the Greek Orthodox Church in their new communities, along with Greek taverns and nightclubs. Like other Mediterranean peoples, the Greeks had a strong family orientation, both patriarchal and authoritarian. The extent of ethnic retention was quite high and marriages quite endogamous in a search for the continuation of Greek culture, although there were strains between the first and second generations caused by the increased level of education of the children and by religious liberalization. As late as 2002, out-marriage was quite unusual in Canadian Greek families, forming the basis for the popular movie *My Big Fat Greek Wedding* (which, although set in Chicago, was originally written about the Greek community in Winnipeg).

The Ukrainians

People from the Ukraine were part of the postwar refugee population that constituted a mélange of 6 million people in Europe. The refugees included former inmates of concentration campus, conscripted workers for German industry, prisoners of war, and displaced civilians. Many of these people had been forced to change their nationality three or four times in the period between 1918 and 1940. A large number had come from the Soviet Union and had been pushed westward in attempts to stay ahead of Russian armies invading Germany. A substantial proportion of these people were forcibly repatriated to the USSR immediately after the war, although more than 1 million of the remaining refugees, including several hundred thousand Ukrainians, made clear that they did not want to be returned to countries that were now under Communist domination. Reestablished in refugee camps under the International Refugee Organization (IRO), 34,000 of this population, including many Ukrainians, were allowed to come to Canada.

Many of this considerable refugee population were confused about their ethnic identity, and although the typical immigrant experience was for the newcomers to lose some of their ethnicity, in the case of some postwar displaced persons who emigrated to Canada, they were enabled to rediscover their ethnic roots. Other Ukrainians discovered their national roots in the prison and concentration camps, and many of these people only reluctantly immigrated to Canada, as they had hoped to be able to reestablish a nation in the Ukraine. Like all the displaced persons admitted to Canada after 1945, those of Ukrainian origin were theoretically able to become part of an existing ethnic community, although the new immigrants' tendency to right-wing politics distinguished them politically from existing Ukrainian groups. The refugee camp experience also led the post-1945 Ukrainian newcomers to join in various cultural organizations composed of displaced persons of various European nations. Although they were a relatively well-educated group of immigrants (particularly in comparison with those Ukrainians who had gone before), most of the post-1945 Ukrainians were sent to the Canadian frontier as semiskilled workers. But after fulfilling their contracts these people moved south into the larger cities of Ontario and Quebec, where they were able to take greater advantage of their education and skills and to contribute to a resurgence of Ukrainian history and culture in those provinces.

The Curious Case of the Visible Americans

The relatively uncontroversial pattern of American immigration to Canada changed markedly for a few years after 1965. Americans had been among the most invisible immigrants to Canada for many years, representing one of the larger national streams of newcomers into the nation, which went almost totally unheralded because Americans were able to fit so easily into Canadian society. Documenting the numbers of arrivals in the late 1960s is virtually impossible, because so many were not included in official data. One obvious reason for the change was the Vietnam War, which produced a wave of refugee immigrants to Canada from the United States. But the war resisters were not the only new American immigrants, nor even the most controversial.

The mid-1960s also saw a major expansion of Canadian higher education, with a number of new universities constructed. Unable to staff its burgeoning universities with its own nationals, Canada turned abroad, particularly to Britain and the United States, to recruit a professoriat. In 1963, there were 390 university teachers who immigrated to Canada, 24.4 percent from Britain and 44.6 percent from the United States. By the peak year of 1969, that immigration number had risen to 2,398 (with the percentages of Britons and Americans virtually identical to those of 1963). After 1969 the percentage of Americans increased to approximately one-half of the influx. Between 1965 and 1975, a total of more than 16,000 university teachers arrived in Canada from abroad, nearly 50 percent of them American in origin. Although the immigrants specialized in all academic fields, many worked in the social sciences, relatively new fields for expansion in Canadian universities. Unfortunately, most of the newcomers were almost totally ignorant about Canada and taught their courses (in sociology or anthropology or economics) from American textbooks and employing American examples. Thus, by 1970 there was a growing groundswell of concern in the Canadian academic community about the absence of "Canadian content" in the offerings of many departments. The problem would gradually disappear as those Americans who stayed in Canada became Canadianized.

As for the American war resisters, they could be divided into three categories: draft dodgers who left the United States rather than face selective service; deserters; and—a group that was difficult to analyze—immigrants who were not formally escaping the military system but were nevertheless alienated from current American foreign and domestic policy. The draft dodgers were for the most part middle-class young men who were welcomed in Canada. The deserters, also young men but less well educated and less demonstrably middle class (reflecting the class bias of the American draft system), received a more mixed reception, partly because they were less qualified for work in Canada and partly because Canadians themselves had mixed feelings about desertion from duty. The political and social radicalism of many of the resisters (particularly the "hippies") led to some negative reactions as well.

Jews were overrepresented among the dodgers, and Catholics among the deserters. Both dodgers and deserters tended to congregate in large Canadian cities, especially Toronto, Montreal, and Vancouver. Mark Satin's *Manual for Draft-Age Immigrants to Canada* (1968) sold more than 100,000 copies in eight editions. Though some war resisters eventually returned to the United States after amnesties were declared, many others remained in Canada, often becoming Canadian citizens. Canada's acceptance of and protection for American war resisters was a policy of some courage, as the United States could well have been more difficult than it was about the Canadian policy. By and large, young Canadians (who were the most militant Canadian nationalists) were pleased to have an opportunity to support those dissenting from American policy. Canadian headcounters never quite knew how to deal with the Americans, as Statistics Canada resolutely refused to recognize "American" as an ethnic origin until the late 1990s, insisting that American immigrants had to declare a national origin previous to their American one.

The Recognition of Other Minorities in the 1960s

Not only ethnics but other groups of Canadians also gained a new recognition in the 1960s. The typically Canadian solution is to list such people as "Others" rather than as "Ethnics."

The Blacks

By the mid-1960s, there were an estimated 60,000 to 100,000 blacks in Canada. Nobody knew for certain, as accurate numbers would require a racial/color question on the census form, and such a question did not exist. Many of those blacks were descendants of the major strands of early black immigration to Canada, including the Loyalists of Nova Scotia and the Underground Railway in southwestern Ontario—both described earlier in this book—although increasing numbers of Caribbean blacks were entering Canada by the end of the decade. Canadian blacks faced a variety of discriminatory realities, both subtle and open, that often located them on the margins of their society. Segregated seating in movie theatres and restaurants was quite routine up to the 1950s, for example, and the courts were quite reluctant to intervene. A test case in Alberta was filed over the refusal of a motel to provide accommodation to a black guest; the case ended in 1961 with the Supreme Court of Alberta deciding that such denial was not illegal; the Alberta government had to amend its Innkeepers' Act. Ontario blacks, learning from experience about the courts, turned instead to legislative solutions, pushing for a comprehensive Human Rights Code that was finally adopted in 1962.

Canadian blacks had learned over the years to survive partly by stoic endurance of their lot with little complaint and protest, and partly by merging with the white community wherever possible, although the black community was becoming more vocal after World War II. Except for a history of discreet oppression and their support of their churches, which tended to provide local leadership, there seemed little in their lives that could be identified as a distinctive heritage. Neither the blacks nor the larger society recognized a distinctive black heritage. When the city of Halifax decided in the mid-1960s to relocate the working-class black community of Africville—which was at that time on the shores of the Bedford Basin—on the grounds that it was a disgraceful slum, the 400 inhabitants protested but were unable to stop the clearance of the community, which was carried out by the city between 1964 and 1970. When residents tried to remain in their homes, the city cut off their water and electricity and paid very little for the expropriation. The people of Africville were forced into public housing, which they found very constricting. Not until July 2002 was Africville declared a national historic site.

During the 1960s, Canadian blacks, like other minority groups, underwent a transformation. The various black rights movements in the United States had a considerable impact in raising black consciousness in Canada. The very use of the designations *black* or *African* to replace the more traditional and highly charged term *Negro* was significant and was accompanied by an increasing sense of racial pride and identity. In Halifax, Burnley ("Rocky") Jones led a public campaign to raise the white mainstream's consciousness about racism and to give blacks a helping hand through self-help programs. By the early 1970s, the destruction of Africville had become a symbol of mainstream neglect and ignorance, and the history of Africville and other black communities began to be systematically recovered, lest they all suffer the same fate. Some black militancy came from the United States, but probably more important in the increased willingness to protest discrimination were the Canadian immigration trends of the 1960s, when substantial numbers of decolonized Caribbean and African blacks settled in Canada. Many of these new arrivals were highly skilled and educated professionals whose professional qualifications had been downgraded and who were not accustomed to racism, however subtle.

The most publicized incident of protest occurred in late January and early February 1969, when the computer center at Sir George Williams University (now Concordia University) in Montreal was occupied by a group of students and others for two weeks to protest racial intolerance and "the military, imperialist ambitions of Canada in the West Indies" (Forsythe, 1971, p. 9). The student protestors ended their occupation on 11 February by smashing the computers and causing damage to the university's equipment and records that was estimated in the millions of dollars, thus attracting the attention of Canadians everywhere. Ninety "occupiers" were arrested, including forty-one blacks, many of whom were from the Caribbean. The episode was a classic example of student radicalism, but it also publicized racial tensions in the larger cities. To a considerable extent, the problems of West Indian immigration deflected attention away from the difficulties of Canada's traditional black community, a situation that many black leaders resented.

The Aboriginal Peoples

As with so many other long-standing issues in Canada, that of Canada's native peoples moved into a new activist phase in the 1960s. Native activism built on its own accumulated traditions of constructing organizations to speak for aboriginal concerns, but it was also able to take advantage of American models and Canadian federal policy, such as the 1960 Canadian Bill of Rights. Just as critically, the search for new sources of raw materials for exploitation in the Canadian north threatened indigenous peoples' way of life and forced them into the political mainstream in an attempt to protect land that they often claimed was theirs by right. By the end of the 1960s, an emerging native militancy met head-on a government reevaluation of both the situation of natives and their relationship to the federal government.

Before 1960, regional and provincial organizations had gradually developed across Canada to represent the interests of the native peoples, often in response to particular situations or to organized investigations and commissions on either the provincial or federal level. Thus, the Depression called into existence the Native Brotherhood of British Columbia in 1931, and a strike gave rise to the Pacific Coast Native Fisherman's Association in 1936, which merged with the former in 1941. A number of Saskatchewan native groups merged into the Federation of Saskatchewan Indians at the end of the 1950s. National organizations were slower to take hold. An effort originating in British Columbia in 1943 to create a national organization called the North American Indian Brotherhood was not successful, partly because Andrew Paull (1892–1959), the organization's founder, was seen to be linked too closely with the Roman Catholic Church. Finally, in 1961, the National Indian Council was formed "to promote unity among Indian people, the betterment of people of Indian ancestry in Canada, and to create a better understanding of Indian and non-Indian relationship" (Patterson, 1972, p. 177).

The National Indian Council was organized chiefly by urbanized natives who hoped to combine the concerns of "status Indians" (those under the protection of the federal government as a result of treaties signed between Canada and the aboriginal people) and "nonstatus Indians," including Métis. In 1968 political incompatibility led to the dissolution of the National Indian Council and the formation of two new groups: the Canadian Métis Society, which in 1970 renamed itself the National Council of Canada—representing Métis and nonstatus Indians—and the National Indian Brotherhood, which would become the Assembly of First Nations, representing status Indians, that is, those who were directly under the protection of the Department of Indian Affairs.

Before the late 1960s, the process of consciousness-raising with regard to native issues was slow. Then a sudden shift occurred, particularly among the native peoples themselves, one that is still ongoing. In 1966, one government report complained of the difficulty of ascertaining native opinion. As late as 1971, a study, "The Indian in Canadian Historical Writing," found that aboriginals, particularly in textbook surveys, were regarded as inferior beings who deserved what they got from Europeans and generally were treated more as "obstacles to be overcome in Canada" than as integral parts of historical development (Walker, 1971, p. 23). The real explosion of Canadian academic interest in native peoples would not come until the 1970s, though, and Canadian popular awareness of natives would occur at the same time, less because of the academics than because the natives themselves had discovered political and legal ways to fight for their rights that drew attention to their situation. "Aboriginal rights" existed as a concept in the 1960s but had not yet produced the landmark court actions of later periods.

One of the real catalysts for native consciousness was the publication in 1969 of a "White Paper" on federal policy under Indian Affairs Minister Jean Chrétien. One native leader of the time observed, "No single action by any Government since Confederation has aroused such a violent reaction from Indian people" (Patterson, 1972, p. 178). The White Paper dealt with all aspects of Indian policy, but its principal recommendations were threefold: the abolition of the Indian Act (and the Department of Indian Affairs), which would mean an end to status Indians; the transfer of native lands out of Crown trust into the hands of the aboriginal peoples; and the devolution of responsibility for natives to the provinces. The White Paper touched off bitter criticism in all quarters, and it produced the first popular manifesto for Canadian natives in Harold Cardinal's *The Unjust Society: The Tragedy of Canada's Indians* (1969), which argued for the reestablishment of special native rights within the strengthened contexts of treaties and the Indian Act.

The *White Paper on Immigration,* in broad outline, was consistent with federal policy toward all minorities, including French Canadians, at the end of the 1960s. It called for the advancement of the individual rights of natives rather than the collective rights of native peoples:

> The Government believes that its policies must lead to the full, free and non-discriminatory participation of the Indian people in Canadian society. Such a goal requires a break with the past. It requires that the Indian people's role of dependence be replaced by a role of equal status, opportunity and responsibility, a role they can share with all other Canadians. (Government of Canada, 1969, p. 5)

The liberal philosophy of Pierre Trudeau (Canada's prime minister at the time) can be heard echoing in this statement. The White Paper insisted that treaties between the Crown and natives only produced "limited and minimal promises" that had been greatly exceeded in terms of the "economic, educational health and welfare needs of the Indian people" by subsequent government policies. Allowing natives full access to Canadian

social services (many of which were provincially administered, especially
in Quebec) would mark an advance over existing paternalism. The government seemed surprised that natives responded so negatively to the
White Paper, conveniently ignoring its implications for the concepts of
treaty and aboriginal rights. The government was proposing that natives
should be treated like everyone else rather than possessing special rights
based upon their primacy of residence and subsequent treaties with European incomers. Prime Minister Trudeau defended the policy as an en-
lightened one, noting, "the time is now to decide whether the Indians will
be a race apart in Canada or whether they will be Canadians of full status." He added: "It's inconceivable, I think, that in a given society one section of the society have a treaty with the other section of society. We must
all be equal under the law." (Cumming and Mickenberg, 1970, p. 331)

Harold Cardinal, a member of Alberta's Sucker Creek band (a nation
group), had been elected president of the Indian Association of Alberta in
1968—and had read widely from the American rhetorical literature of the
1960s. He condemned the 1969 White Paper as a "thinly disguised programme of extermination through assimilation," adding that the federal
government, "instead of acknowledging its legal and moral responsibilities to the Indians of Canada and honouring the treaties that the Indians
had signed in good faith, now proposes to wash its hands of Indians entirely passing the buck to the provincial governments" (Cardinal, 1969, p.
170). Cardinal coined the term *the Buckskin Curtain* to refer to the separation between Europeans and aboriginals in Canada, noting that "while
Canadian urbanites have walked blisters on their feet and fat off their
rumps to raise money for underdeveloped countries outside Canada,"
Canadians generally did not "give a damn" about the plight of their own
native people. He criticized "Uncle Tomahawks" among his own people
who continually apologized for being natives, and he noted with some
irony that natives who wore their traditional clothing ran the risk of being
confused with hippies. Cardinal also complained of the Canadian government's "two founding peoples" concept, which did not recognize "the role
played by the Indian even before the founding of a nation-state known as
Canada." He pointedly denied that Indians were separatists, arguing that
they merely wanted their treaty and aboriginal rights recognized so that
they could take their place "with the other cultural identities of Canada."
As Cardinal and other native spokespersons made quite plain in 1969, Indians did not want to be abandoned to the provinces. And they were less
critical of Quebec's position of separatism than insistent that they needed
what Cardinal called "a valid, lasting Indian identity."

The Introduction of Multiculturalism

"Non-charter" ethnic groups had vociferously informed the Royal Commission on Bilingualism and Biculturalism of their unhappiness with the concept of having two languages and two cultures in Canada, insisting that such a policy offended those not part of the "charter" communities. The Commission had devoted a separate book of its final report to the "other ethnic groups" and seemed to be suggesting that there was more to Canada than simply two cultures. Indeed, in 1971, as we have seen in this book, more than one in every four Canadians was not a member of either of the two charter communities. On 8 October 1971, Prime Minister Pierre Trudeau declared in the House of Commons a federal government policy of "multiculturalism within a bilingual framework." The policy would involve, he said, assistance to all Canadian cultural groups to continue to grow, to "overcome cultural barriers to full participation in Canadian society," to interact with other cultural groups, and to become conversant in one of Canada's two official languages (Canada Parliament, 1971, pp. 8485–8486). The reaction from Quebec was immediate and negative. French Canadians, probably quite accurately, saw the emphasis on multiculturalism as a way to deflect the aspirations of Quebec by demonstrating that its linguistic and cultural aspirations were not unique and could not be considered apart from the needs of other communities in Canada. Rene Levesque described multiculturalism as a "red herring" designed "to give the impression that we are all ethnics and do not have to worry about special status for Quebec." Many French Canadians were incensed that Trudeau had chosen to link multiculturalism with language as well as culture. According to more than one commentator in Quebec, multiculturalism had reduced Quebec distinctiveness to an ethnic phenomenon.

The government embodied this new multiculturalism in a Canadian Consultative Council on Multiculturalism, created in 1973, and in a separate section of the Department of the Secretary of State (the Multiculturalism Directorate), which was given funds to support multicultural activities of various sorts. Much of the funding was devoted to the support of ethnic research and scholarship, contributing to an explosion of ethnic studies, although money was also made available to ethnic organizations for various purposes, a practice that subject to considerable criticism. The ethnic community was not united in its response to the funding for multiculturalism. Some members of the ethnic community itself complained that the funds were "miniscule," and others pointed to the waste of money on meaningless projects. In the wake of the federal policy, various provincial governments also proclaimed policies of multiculturalism and began funding ethnic organizations and ethnic studies. The concept of multiculturalism was introduced into most provincial educational curricula to socialize school children to the new complexities of Canadian society, although not much was done about providing education in ethnic languages.

Although multiculturalism was introduced as a highly politicized policy by a prime minister who did not really take minority ethnic causes very seriously, it struck a respondent chord with many Canadians. For Pierre Trudeau, multiculturalism was probably part of a Quebec-related strategy that may also have been important as part of a conscious elimination of ethnic and racial discrimination. For many Canadians, however, it would become part of a new definition of national identity, a statement of the Canadian "mosaic" in contradistinction from the American "melting pot." The mythology of the mosaic would become even more powerful after the introduction of the Canadian Charter of Rights (again by Trudeau) in 1982. Before long, many Canadians had quite forgotten the prime minister's contextualization of multiculturalism as being "within a bilingual framework." It would eventually become such a potent metaphor that many Canadians felt that their behavior had to live up to its ideal.

Timeline

1952   Introduction of television broadcasting into Canada.

1960   Beginning of Quebec's "Quiet Revolution."

1961   National Indian Council formed.

1963   Flag debate; new Canadian flag adopted; Royal Commission on Bilingualism and Biculturalism appointed.

1964   City of Halifax begins clearing Africville.

1966   Creation of Department of Manpower and Immigration, Tom Kent appointed deputy-minister; White Paper on Immigration released.

November 1966   Hearings on White Paper on Immigration begun by joint committee of House of Commons and Senate.

1967   Centennial Year; report of royal commission on bilingualism released; points system and new immigration policy receives approval in principle from joint House of Commons and Senate committee.

1968   National Indian Council reorganized as Canadian Métis Society and National Indian Brotherhood; Mark Satin's *Manual for Draft-Age Immigrants to Canada* is published.

February 1969   Computer center at Sir George Williams University is occupied; White Paper on Indian policy is released; Harold Cardinal's *The Unjust Society* is published.

1970   Africville clearance completed.

October 1971   Trudeau declares multicultural policy in House of Commons.

1973   Canadian Consultative Council on Multiculturalism and a Multiculturalism Directorate are established.

Significant People, Places, and Events

ABORIGINAL RIGHTS Rights acquired by aboriginals as a general consequence of their occupation of Canada prior to the Europeans. These were often distinguished from treaty rights, which were the rights acquired by aboriginals as a result of specific treaty negotiations between aboriginals and the Canadian government.

AFRICVILLE A black community established in the nineteenth century, which the city of Halifax began tearing down in 1964—without consultation with the inhabitants—as a slum clearance project. The destruction of Africville became the symbol for blacks in Canada of racist ignorance among the majority.

CARDINAL, HAROLD The First Nations activist who led the opposition to the 1969 White Paper on Indian Policy.

CENTENNIAL YEAR The year 1967, in which Canada celebrated the one hundredth anniversary of Confederation.

CONFEDERATION OF NATIONAL TRADE UNIONS (CNTU) A francophone labor organization that led the opposition in 1966 to a new immigration policy based on skills.

DEPARTMENT OF MANPOWER AND IMMIGRATION New name for the Canadian department responsible for immigration, reorganized in 1966.

DRAFT DODGERS Also called draft evaders, these were young Americans who crossed the border to Canada in the late 1960s rather than serve in the American armed forces in Vietnam.

FLAG DEBATE A parliamentary debate in 1963 over the choice of a new Canadian flag. Opposition to the new flag was led by those who wanted to keep Canada British in flavor and culture.

KENT, TOM A former Liberal party advisor appointed deputy-minister of Manpower and Immigration in 1966 with instructions to reform immigration policy.

MANUAL FOR DRAFT-AGE IMMIGRANTS TO CANADA A reference work published in Vancouver by Mark Satin in 1968 to provide information for American draft-dodgers; it went through many editions and sold more than 100,000 copies.

MULTICULTURALISM An official policy adopted by the Canadian government in 1971 by which, within a bilingual framework, ethnic pluralism was declared to be a feature of Canadian society that was worthy of protection and development.

NATIONAL INDIAN COUNCIL An umbrella organization formed in 1961 to look after the interests of aboriginal people in Canada.

OFFICIAL LANGUAGES ACT Legislation passed by the Canadian Parliament in 1969 to make Canada an officially bilingual nation.

PEARSON, LESTER B. Canadian prime minister from 1963–1968, who was responsible for a new Canadian flag, a new national anthem, and the creation of the Royal Commission on Bilingualism and Biculturalism.

POINTS SYSTEM A new system adopted by Parliament in 1967 for selecting admissible immigrants to Canada.

QUIET REVOLUTION Term used to refer to the political awakening of Quebec in the 1960s.

ROYAL COMMISSION ON BILINGUALISM AND BICULTURALISM Royal commission established in 1963 to deal with the questions of bilingualism and biculturalism; it would produce a report in 1967.

SIR GEORGE WILLIAMS UNIVERSITY Site of a famous student occupation in January and February 1969 to protest racist policies.

SPECIAL COMMITTEE OF THE SENATE AND THE HOUSE OF COMMONS ON IMMIGRATION Parliamentary committee that held hearings on immigration policy beginning in November 1966.

STATUS INDIANS Those aboriginals in Canada who are under the protection of the federal government as a result of treaties signed between Canada and the aboriginal people.

THIRD FORCE A term used in 1967 to refer to those Canadians who did not belong to either the Anglo majority or the French minority.

TRUDEAU, PIERRE ELLIOTT Canadian prime minister 1968–1979, who was responsible for many important policy shifts, including the introduction of multiculturalism in 1971.

WHITE PAPER ON IMMIGRATION POLICY A public policy document released for discussion by the Department of Manpower and Immigration in 1966.

WHITE PAPER ON INDIAN POLICY A public policy document released for discussion by the Department of Indian Affairs in 1969. It provoked a tremendous negative reaction from the aboriginal community.

Documents

Prime Minister Trudeau's Speech on Aboriginal and Treaty Rights, 1969

In August of 1969, Prime Minister Pierre Elliott Trudeau delivered a speech in Vancouver on aboriginal rights, which offers a clear statement of his position both on those rights and on other questions of ethnicity in Canada.

I think Canadians are not too proud about their past in the way in which they treated the Indian population of Canada and I don't think we have very great cause to be proud.

We have set the Indians apart as a race. We've set them apart in our laws. We've set them apart in the ways the governments will deal with them. They're not citizens of the province as the rest of us are. They are wards of the federal government. They get their services from the federal government rather than from the provincial or municipal governments. They have been set apart in law. They have been set apart in the relations with government and they've been set apart socially too.

So this year we came up with a proposal. It's a policy paper on the Indian problem. It proposes a set of solutions. It doesn't impose them on anybody. It proposes them—not only to the Indians but to all Canadians—not only to their federal representatives but to the provincial representatives too and it says we're at the crossroads. We can go on treating the Indians as having a special status. We can go on adding bricks of discrimination around the ghetto in which they live and at the same time perhaps helping them preserve certain cultural traits and certain ancestral rights. Or we can say you're at a crossroads—the time is now to decide whether the Indians will be a race apart in Canada or whether they will be Canadians of full status. And this is a difficult choice. It must be a very agonizing choice to the Indian peoples themselves because, on the one hand, they realize that if they come into the society as total citizens they will be equal under the law but they risk losing certain of their traditions, certain aspects of a culture and perhaps even certain of their basic rights and this is a very difficult choice for them to make and I don't think we want to try and force the pace on them any more than we can force it on the rest of Canadians but here again is a choice which is in our minds whether Canadians as a whole want to continue treating the Indian population as something outside, a group of Canadians with which we have treaties, a group of Canadians who have as the Indians, many of them claim, aboriginal rights or whether we will say well forget the past and begin today and this is a tremendously difficult choice because, if—well one of the things the Indian bands often refer to are their aboriginal rights and in our policy, the way we propose it, we say we won't recognize aboriginal rights. We will recognize treaty rights. We will recognize forms of contract which have been made with the Indian people by the Crown and we will try to bring justice in that area and this will mean that perhaps the treaties shouldn't go on forever. It's inconceivable, I think, that in a given society one section of the society have a treaty with the other section of the society. We must be all equal under the laws and we must not sign treaties amongst ourselves and many of these treaties, indeed, would have less and less significance in the future anyhow but things that in the past were covered by the treaties like things like so much twine or so much gun powder and which haven't been paid this must be paid. But I don't think that we should encourage the Indians to feel that their treaties should last forever within Canada so that they be able to receive their twine or their gun powder. They should become Canadians as all other Canadians and if they are prosperous and wealthy they will be treated like the prosperous and wealthy and they will be paying taxes for the other Canadians who are not so prosperous and not so wealthy whether they be Indians or English Canadians or French or Maritimers and this is the only basis on which I see our society can develop as equals. But aboriginal rights, this really means saying, "We were here before you. You came and you took the land from us and perhaps you cheated us by giving us some worthless things in return for vast expanses of land and we want to reopen this question. We want you to preserve our aboriginal rights and to restore them to us." And our answer—it may not be the right one and may not be one which is accepted but it will be up to all of your people to make your minds up and to choose for or against it and to discuss with the Indians—our answer is "no."

Source: Cumming, Peter A., and Mickenberg, Neil H., eds. *Native Rights in Canada,* 2nd ed. (Toronto: Indian-Eskimo Association of Canada, in association with General Publishing, 1970), Apx. 8.

Tom Kent on the Genesis of the Points System, 1967

In his memoirs, deputy minister of Manpower and Immigration Tom Kent recalled hearings on the government White Paper on Immigration in 1967.

The [parliamentary] committee had a considerable influence on policy. Its proceedings soon made it clear that the White Paper did not stand up well to informed criticism. We would have to do better. Under the impetus provided by the committee, we at last developed a solution to the problem. Who, if anyone, gave me the basic idea, I cannot now remember. It was the kind of idea that, once had, was so obvious that one wondered how it could have been missed for so long.

The need was for selection procedures that would result, to the greatest possible extent, in immigrants being those who could best settle down as useful and satisfied citizens. The problem was not unlike, in principle, that involved in the comparative evaluation of jobs. Why not try similar methods? If we could identify and define the various factors affecting a person's ability to settle successfully in Canada, and attach relative weights to them, then immigration officers would have a consistent basis on which to assess potential immigrants.

Boris Celovsky undertook the heavy task of examining how our tentative criteria and weights might have been applied to a sample, drawn from the files, of both accepted and rejected applicants. (Dr. Celovsky . . . was one of the able public servants who came to the new department from the economics and research branch of the Department of Labour, led by Jack Francis.) We satisfied ourselves that the evaluation process would work a good deal better than the rule of thumb of eleven years' schooling plus highly arbitrary other judgments.

Education was still given significant weight: one unit of assessment (out of a hundred total) for each year of successfully completed education and training (professional, vocational, or trades), to a maximum weight of twenty. Thus eleven years of schooling, instead of being a *sine qua non*, counted for eleven percent in the total evaluation. From zero to fifteen units were assigned according to employment opportunities in the occupation that the applicant was likely to follow in Canada; his or her present occupation—not necessarily the same—was given a weight between one (for the unskilled) to ten (for the professional). Youth and middle age were favoured by giving ten units of assessment to applicants between eighteen and thirty-five, with one unit less for each year of age over thirty-five. Finally, among the major factors, a maximum weight of fifteen was assigned for the immigration officer's assessment of the applicant's relevant personal qualities of adaptability, motivation, initiative, and resourcefulness.

The minor weights were: ten if the applicant had arranged employment in Canada with reasonable prospects of continuity; up to ten for his or her competence in English and French; up to five according to the general level of employment in the area of Canada to which the applicant wanted to go; and up to five if he or she had a relative (not, formally, a sponsor) in Canada.

An independent immigrant would be admissible if he or she scored at least fifty out of the maximum hundred units of assessment on all the above factors.

Source: Kent, Tom, *A Public Purpose: An Experience of Liberal Opposition and Canadian Government* (Montreal, Quebec and Kingston, Ontario: McGill-Queen's University Press, 1988), pp. 410–411.

Bibliography

Avery, Donald H., *Reluctant Host: Canada's Response to Immigrant Workers, 1896–1994* (Toronto: McClelland and Stewart, 1995).

Canada, Government of, *A Statement of the Government of Canada on Indian Policy* (Ottawa: Queen's Printer, 1969).

Canada, Minister of Manpower and Immigration, *White Paper on Immigration* (Ottawa: Queen's Printer, 1966).

Canada Parliament, *House of Commons Debates, 28th Parliament, 4th Session* [Hansard] (Ottawa: Queen's Printer, 1971).

Cardinal, Harold, *The Unjust Society: The Tragedy of Canada's Indians* (Edmonton, Alberta: M. G. Hurtig, 1969).

Clairmont, Donald, and Magill, Dennis, *Africville: The Life and Death of a Canadian Black Community* (Toronto: McClelland and Stewart, 1974).

Cumming, Peter A., and Mickenberg, Neil H., eds. *Native Rights in Canada,* 2nd ed. (Toronto: Indian-Eskimo Association of Canada, in association with General Publishing, 1970), Apx. 8.

Forsythe, Dennis, ed., *Let the Niggers Burn: The Sir George Williams University Affair and Its Caribbean Aftermath* (Montreal: Our Generation Press, 1971).

Kent, Tom, *A Public Purpose: An Experience of Liberal Opposition and Canadian Government* (Montreal, Quebec and Kingston, Ontario: McGill-Queen's University Press, 1988).

Goldsmith, Renee Kasinsky, *Refugees from Militarism: Draft-Age Americans in Canada* (Totowa, NJ: Littlefield, Adams, and Company, 1976).

Patterson, E. Palmer, *The Canadian Indian: A History since 1500* (Toronto: Collier-Macmillan Canada, 1972).

Richmond, Anthony, *Immigrants and Ethnic Groups in Metropolitan Toronto* (Toronto: York University Ethnic Research Programme, Institute for Behavioural Research, 1967).

Royal Commission on Bilingualism and Biculturalism, *Report,* 4 vols. (Ottawa: Queen's Printer, 1969).

Satin, Mark, *Manual for Draft-Age Immigrants to Canada,* 2nd. ed. (Toronto: House of Anansi, 1968).

Stanley, George F. G., *The Story of Canada's Flag: A Historical Sketch* (Toronto: Ryerson Press, 1965).

Walker, James, "The Indian in Canadian Historical Writing," *CHA Historical Papers,* (1971), 23.

Weaver, Sally M., *Making Indian Policy: The Hidden Agenda 1968–70* (Toronto: University of Toronto Press, 1981).

Since 1975

I N   T H E   P A S T   T W E N T Y - F I V E   Y E A R S a number of important changes have occurred within Canada with regard to ethnicity. The nation has survived, at least for the moment, the movement within Quebec to become independent, but it has done so by permitting francophone Quebec to provide large measures of protection for its language and culture, as well as allowing it virtual domestic autonomy. The Quebec situation helped influence the repatriation of the Canadian constitution and the entrenchment within it of the Canadian Charter of Rights and Freedoms, which has provided both legal guarantees of equality for many of the nation's collectivities (including ethnics) and a mechanism for enforcing that equality. In turn, the Charter of Rights and Freedoms has contributed to a legal expansion of the concept of aboriginal rights. For many Canadians, the First Nations have become, because of their history, a special case among Canada's peoples. The Charter of Rights and Freedoms and the expansion of aboriginal rights have also provided in turn a climate better disposed to the redress of historic grievances by Canada's peoples. And, finally, Canada's almost total reliance on Third World immigration in recent decades, particularly from Asia, has begun to remake not only the ethnic but the racial makeup of the nation. Multiculturalism has provided a vision and a metaphor for the changing racial composition of Canada, although it has not succeeded in eradicating racism.

Quebec Separatism and the Constitution

In 1976 the Parti Québécois (PQ) came to power in the province of Quebec. The PQ was best known for its advocacy of constitutional reform, particularly for what it called "sovereignty association," an ill-defined arrangement by which a totally autonomous Quebec would remain under

Rene Levesque (1922–1987), premier of Quebec, Canada, fought for the separation of Quebec from the rest of Canada. Along with the Parti Québécois, a separatist group he formed, Levesque campaigned for a sovereignty-association agreement with Canada. (Corbis)

the Canadian economic and international umbrella. The Péquistes (supporters of the PQ) had insisted that they would not act unilaterally on separation, and so voters were able to support the social-democratic reformism of the PQ without necessarily favoring constitutional radicalism. Nevertheless, the PQ victory came as a shock to English Canadians, who immediately responded by debating new ways to save the nation. Once in office, the PQ pursued a policy of linguistic and cultural nationalism. In 1977, Bill 101 turned Quebec into an indisputably francophone province. Most Quebeckers, regardless of their history or preference, would under Bill 101 be educated in French-language schools. Only those temporarily resident in Quebec or those whose parents had been educated in English-speaking schools in Quebec were exempted. The bill also insisted that French was the only legal language of business and government in the province. This language policy upset not only the old anglophones in the province, but also many of the new immigrants, who preferred to keep their options open by sending their children to English-language schools.

On 20 May 1980, the PQ held a referendum on sovereignty association, which it defined in a 1979 White Paper as "a free, proud, and adult national existence" in which an independent Quebec would still have access to Canada, its courts, and its economy. The nonfrancophone population in Quebec, both the 600,000 of British origin and the 600,000 of other ethnic origins, voted No, and in the end more than 52 percent of the province's francophones also voted Non. Quebec had publicly rejected separation, and the nation both breathed a sigh of relief and called for a new constitution.

The New Constitution and the Genesis of the Charter of Rights

Constitutional reform, especially constitutional repatriation, had been discussed between Ottawa and the provinces since the 1960s, always sticking on Quebec's insistence on a veto over any proposed changes. In 1971 the Trudeau government made another attempt, offering to the newly elected Quebec premier Robert Bourassa a package of reforms that included the writing of some constitutional rights into the document itself (called "entrenching"), and an amending formula that allowed perpetual vetoes to both Quebec and Ontario. Bourassa wanted the provinces to control social policy as well, and no agreement was reached. Throughout the 1970s, the issue of constitutional reform surfaced from time to time, always involving an entrenched bill of rights. By 1978 the bill of rights had become labeled "The Charter of Rights and Freedoms," and the listing of the rights and freedoms had taken on a ritualistic formula that included most of the final ingredients. Only "mental or physical disability" would later be added to the formula, which called for equality before the law for those facing discrimination "based on race, national or ethnic origin, colour, religion, sex, age." Many legal commentators objected to an entrenched charter as being too "American." The Americans wrote these things down, it was said, but the British tradition was to leave such matters unspecified, counting on Parliament and the courts to protect rights in a more flexible way. Although the act of spelling out the rights involved may have been American, the rights themselves did not so much protect the individual (as did the Whiggish American eighteenth-century Bill of Rights) as they protected collectivities and communities (a very Tory concept). The Canadian Charter was quite different from the American Bill of Rights. What was perhaps more American than either the writing down of the rights or the rights that were written down was the specifying of the Supreme Court of Canada to enforce them. The British tradition was for Parliament to be supreme, to have virtually untrammeled power, and to protect rights itself.

A number of factors account for most Canadians' ready acceptance of the innovations of entrenchment and judicial protection. Probably the most important was that the major goal of constitutional reform was repatriation, the process by which the Canadian constitution would no longer be the creature of the British Parliament but could be amended right at home in Canada. But repatriation involved eliminating the possibility that the British Parliament would serve as a final check against the abuse of power, and so some alternate mechanism had to be developed to protect what everyone regarded as fundamental rights. The Charter's popularity also reflected in part a growing enthusiasm for breaking with British tradition in this as in so many other matters. And, of course, the concept of writing down and protecting fundamental human rights had become more popular during World War II, when the Allies had begun attempting to explain why the Nazis were war criminals, and continued after the war in a series of declarations of human rights by a variety of international agencies.

The defeat of the Quebec referendum in 1980 offered Prime Minister Trudeau an opportunity to reintroduce constitutional reform, and he called a first ministers' conference for early June 1980. Politically, the federal constitutional package that Trudeau brought to the conference was carefully calculated. As an ardent federalist, a trained constitutional lawyer, and an avowed exponent of realpolitik, Trudeau was in his element. The new proposal called for the elimination of recourse to the British Parliament for amendment of the British North America Act (that is, "repatriation"). It contained a charter of rights, including rights for a variety of minorities, to prevent the French Canadians from being treated as a distinctive case in having their language rights entrenched. A new means of amendment was introduced in the institution of the national referendum, to be initiated in particular instances in Ottawa, in case of provincial obstructionism. Discussions on the new provisions broke down in September 1980, and as Trudeau had threatened, he proceeded to move unilaterally toward reform anyway. He prepared to pass the package in the Federal Parliament and send it to Britain for approval without recourse to either the Supreme Court of Canada or the provinces, although this procedure clearly infringed on the customary "rights" of the provinces to consent to constitutional change. Trudeau had brilliantly placed two groups of rights in opposition: one the human rights protected by the charter and the other the provincial rights ignored in both the amending process and in the charter itself. Most of the provinces objected to Trudeau's process, but he had much support from at least the citizens of English-speaking Canada. But it is important to recognize that to some extent the Charter of Rights was, on a variety of levels, a political weapon in the federal approach to constitutional reform.

Trudeau was unable to avoid the Supreme Court of Canada, as several constitutional opinions from provincial courts had gone there on appeal. The Supreme Court in its turn handed down a political ruling. By a vote of 7 to 2 it declared that the federal repatriation process was legal, as the provincial right of approval was only a customary one that was nowhere written down. The Court then opined, by a vote of 6 to 3, that federal repatriation was "unconventional." Trudeau took this decision as a brake on his unilateral process, and in the end the nine English-speaking premiers worked out a deal with him on 5 November 1981. The prime minister made considerable concessions. He dropped the provision for a referendum and agreed to a "notwithstanding" clause that allowed any province to opt out of clauses in the Charter of Rights covering fundamental freedoms and legal and equality rights, although not out of other categories of rights, including those of language. In theory the provinces certainly gained through this "notwithstanding" clause, which helps explain why many civil rights groups and collectivities (including aboriginal rights advocates and feminists) opposed the new constitution, which passed the British Parliament early in 1982.

The new constitution was in many ways not a fundamental overhaul of the British North America Act of 1867. Reform had instead focused on repatriation and on the amending process. The most radical new feature was the Charter of Rights and Freedoms. It not only provided for equality before the law for those facing discrimination "based on race, national or ethnic origin, colour, religion, sex, age or mental or physical disability," (section 15.1), but it also permitted in section 15.2 "any law, program or activity that has as its object the amelioration of conditions of disadvantaged individuals or groups," including (but not limited to) those disadvantaged by the factors of discrimination mentioned in section 15.1. In addition, aboriginal and treaty rights of the First Nations—although not spelled out—were entrenched, as were sexual equality and multiculturalism. The result was, at least potentially, the introduction of a new level of collective rights, as well as a new mechanism for enforcing them.

Contemporary commentators understood full well that the profundity and impact of the changes wrought by the Charter of Rights would depend on two factors: first, the extent to which the provinces invoked the "notwithstanding" clause to negate charter provisions, and second, the way in which the charter was interpreted by the Supreme Court of Canada. Over the past twenty years, as it turns out, the "notwithstanding" clause has not often been employed. Only two provinces—Quebec and Saskatchewan—have ever utilized the clause, and then very gingerly. Most Canadians seem to support both the charter and the courts, leading governments to see the "notwithstanding" clause as an overkill solution likely to draw public attention to an issue. Some scholars have argued that the erosion of the "notwithstanding" clause has helped strengthen judicial power. As for the Supreme Court, it is still building up a body of cases and

precedents in charter matters after a fairly slow start. Since the first char-
ter-related case in 1984, the Supreme Court had issued more than 350
judgments concerning charter provisions by 2001.

As we shall see, the Court's clearest direction has perhaps been in terms
of the affirmation of aboriginal rights, although it is increasingly pro-
nouncing on other issues as well, particularly in areas of the charter in
which the government has been hesitant to act, such as equality rights and
democratic rights. The Supreme Court appears to have taken a middle
road on most charter issues, especially those on which public opinion has
polarized on both sides of a contentious issue. Many opponents of
pornography, for example, regard the Court's support of freedom of expression as favorable to hard-core pornographers, and it has been argued
that Mormon bigamy not only persists but flourishes in parts of Canada
because of the difficulty of convicting bigamists under the charter. It is
not yet clear how far the Supreme Court will go to protect unpopular ethnic practices that are justified in either cultural or religious terms. At the
same time, there is no doubt that the court has expanded judicial supremacy, and there is considerable opposition within the legal (and political) community to judicial social engineering

The Charlottetown Accord

In 1987 the Progressive-Conservative government of Brian Mulroney fas-
tened on one of the loose ends of the 1982 constitutional process, the refusal of Quebec to accept the 1982 Constitutional Act. By this time, René
Lévesque had retired, and the Liberals were back in power in Quebec.
Mulroney summoned the provincial premiers to a resort hotel at Meech
Lake, Quebec on 30 April 1987, and a new deal was struck. Quebec gained
recognition as a "distinct society" and was allowed a veto over most constitutional amendments, as were the other provinces. Further discussion
of Senate reform would follow; all provinces could opt out of federal programs and receive federal compensation instead. Meech Lake failed in
1990, however, when it was not adopted by all the Canadian provinces.

Prime Minister Mulroney made a last cast at the Canadian constitution
in the Charlottetown Accord in August 1992. Another series of closed-
door meetings between Ottawa, the anglophone provinces, and representatives of First Nations groups—joined at the end by Quebec at Charlottetown—produced a revised package. This one offered Quebec a distinct
society, each of the provinces a veto, and the aboriginal peoples an

acknowledgement that First Nations government was a distinct third level of government alongside Parliament and the provincial assemblies. Charlottetown was thus a much more profound constitutional revision than the 1982 package, and it was put to a national referendum on 26 October 1992. Six provinces (including Quebec) voted No. The national totals were 44.8 percent in favor and 54.2 percent against. Opposition to various parts of the agreement existed in different regions of the nation, although there was a general suspicion of aboriginal self-government and of the process of decentralization that was implicit in the Agreement. Most of those who voted No believed that their vote would not have negative consequences for the nation. As a region, the four western provinces cast the most decisive negative votes.

Any hope that the referendum defeat of the Charlottetown Accord had put a lid on constitutional matters was ended by the 1994 PQ victory in Quebec. Led by Jacques Parizeau, the PQ moved inexorably toward another Quebec referendum on sovereignty. The vote was set for 30 October 1995. The official question was, "Do you agree that Quebec should become sovereign, after having made a formal offer to Canada for a new Economic and Political Partnership, within the scope of the Bill respecting the future of Quebec and of the agreement signed on June 12, 1995?"

The vote turned into a real cliff-hanger, as virtually every eligible resident of Quebec cast his or her ballot. The final turnout—more than 94 percent of the total electorate—was seldom matched except in police states with compulsory elections. Millions of Canadians remained tuned to their television sets until late in the evening, waiting for the definitive result. Finally, it became clear that the "Non" forces had won a narrow victory. In the end, 2,362,355 Quebeckers (or 50.6 percent of the total) voted Non, and 2,308,054 (or 49.4 percent) voted Oui. The young, the francophone, and the Quebecker outside Montreal led the way in supporting sovereignty. There were many informal complaints about voting irregularities, but the vote was allowed to stand. Premier (or almost Prime Minister) Parizeau had prepared a gracious speech to present in case of a sovereigntist victory, a speech full of conciliation to those who opposed Quebec's independence, but the result meant he had to tear it up. In his off-the-cuff and bitter acknowledgment of failure on national radio and television, he blamed the anglophones and the "ethnics" for thwarting the aspirations of francophone Quebec. Although such a statement was impolitic, it was true that immigrants and new Canadians were as overwhelmingly federalist in their political views as were anglophone Quebeckers. As a result, an adversarial relationship had earlier developed between Quebec's immigrant/ethnic community—which consisted of a large array of recent arrivals to the province—and the sovereigntists in the province, which was reflected in Parizeau's comments. As Parizeau spoke, the cameras panned across the crowd of people gathered at *Oui* headquarters. Many were in tears. Parizeau's impulsive attack turned much public opinion against him, even within his own party; within hours he announced his resignation.

In February 1996 Parizeau was officially replaced by Lucien Bouchard. In more recent discussions on the size of the public majority required for separation, the Quebec government has argued that to require a substantial majority would give too much weight to the anglophones and especially the ethnics living in Quebec. In effect, the government has maintained that if a massive francophone majority was not regarded as sufficient for independence, the francophones would be held hostage to the newcomers.

In the wake of the 1995 Quebec referendum, the Chrétien government passed a unilateral declaration in the Canadian Parliament that recognized Quebec as a distinct society. As almost everyone had come to appreciate, this gesture was too little too late. French Canadians in Quebec had made clear their desire for a new constitutional relationship with Canada. Virtually the only remaining questions were, when would a sovereign Quebec finally emerge from its chrysalis, and would it remain within some sort of Canadian Confederation? Postreferendum polls continued to emphasize that Quebeckers wanted to remain within Canada but not under Canada's present constitution. Canadians turned to debate the next step in the ongoing constitutional process. One of the most difficult parts of this discussion would be the need to figure out a process for generating a new constitutional arrangement, as most of the previous ones employed appeared to have been totally discredited. As the century ended, economic problems in Quebec took the bloom off of the prospect of separatism, and the PQ put the issue very low on its agenda. But the question remained in the wings, ready to reemerge at any moment.

Aboriginal Rights

The first Europeans to arrive in North America found an existing, long-established population already inhabiting the land. Today in Canada these First Nations represent a population of more than 1 million, including "status" Indians (those registered under the Indian Act), nonstatus

Indians, Inuit, and Métis (who are very difficult to count because Canada does not ask racial questions on its census). These native people now live in every section of Canada and are divided into a number of broad linguistic and culture groups that can be further separated into a large number of distinct tribes. The broad groupings are:

1. *The Algonquians*, further divided into Woodland, Plains, and Subarctic groups. The Woodland Algonquians live south of the Gulf of St. Lawrence and the Atlantic region, as well as in Ontario and the other provinces. The Plains Algonquians reside in Saskatchewan and Alberta. The Subarctic Algonquians live in the north from Labrador through Peace River, Alberta.
2. *The Inuit* live in the region straddling the North American Arctic.
3. *The Iroquoians* inhabit Ontario and Quebec.
4. *The Ktunaxa* inhabit the region of the Kootenay River in British Columbia.
5. *The Na-Dene* are speakers of the Athabaskan language residing in Western Canada.
6. *The Salish* live in the coastal region of British Columbia.
7. *The Siouans* inhabit the central and western plains.
8. *The Tsimshian* reside in northwestern British Columbia.
9. *The Wakashans* live in the central mainland coast of British Columbia and Vancouver Island.
10. *The Métis* are formally recognized as an aboriginal people in section 35 of the Constitution Act of 1982 but have never been exactly defined. Perhaps 400,000 Métis live in Canada, most of them in the prairie provinces, but others are scattered across the country.

These aboriginal peoples have a very high birth rate and represent the most rapidly growing sector of the Canadian population. Since Confederation, most First Nations have been paternally governed under the Indian Act. Beginning in the 1970s, the First Nations have increasingly widened the meaning of aboriginal rights. These rights fall into two categories. The first are those rights that aboriginals have as a result of having been the first inhabitants of North America and are usually called "aboriginal rights." These include rights to land that the First Nations have occupied since before European intrusion, and a right to self-government. There are also "treaty rights," which are those rights resulting from specific written arrangements between European governments—especially the British

TABLE 10.1   ABORIGINAL AND MÉTIS PEOPLES IN CANADA, 1991, BY PROVINCE

Province	Aboriginals	Métis
Newfoundland	5,846	1,600
Prince Edward Island	1,665	185
Nova Scotia	19,950	1,590
New Brunswick	11,835	980
Quebec	112,590	19,475
Ontario	220,140	26,905
Manitoba	76,375	45,580
Saskatchewan	69,390	32,840
Alberta	99,655	56,305
British Columbia	140,570	22,290
Yukon	5,875	565
Northwest Territories	11,095	4,320
Total	783,980	212,650*

SOURCE: Statistics Canada, 1991 Census.

*This official figure probably underrepresents the total by as much as 200,000.

government and its Canadian successor—and First Nations peoples. Since the first arrival of the Europeans, treaties have been negotiated, chiefly to extinguish native title to much of the land of North America. Aboriginal and treaty rights were entrenched without specifics in the Constitution Act of 1982 and in the Charter of Rights and Freedoms. This entrenchment has led the Canadian courts to become much more aggressive in defining and defending aboriginal rights, especially in comparison with the American courts. The Canadian public has had great difficulty in understanding the concept of aboriginal rights, although the ongoing saga is regularly reported in the media.

Aboriginal Title

In 1969 Frank Calder of the Nisga'a people brought a court action before the British Columbia court, claiming aboriginal title to 1,000 square miles in northwestern British Columbia. The case eventually reached the Supreme Court of Canada, which upheld a British Columbia finding against Calder on a technicality. But despite the seeming defeat, the Supreme Court had agreed with Calder that there were such things as aboriginal rights and title. As one of the judges wrote in his decision, "The fact is that when the settlers came the Indians were there, organized in societies and occupying the land as their forefathers had done for centuries. This is what Indian title means" (Dickason, 1997, p. 325). Aboriginal title came up again in *Guerin v. the Queen* (1985), in which the Supreme Court insisted that aboriginal title predated European occupation and thus served as a check on the Crown's right to deal with lands.

The recognition of aboriginal title was temporarily set back by a decision of the British Columbia Supreme Court in 1991 in the Gitksan (*Delgamuuku v. the Queen*, B.C. Supreme Court, 1991) case. Here, Justice McEachern rejected the claim to title, partly on the grounds of the absence of proper evidence. The judge did not regard native oral history as sufficient, although he ruled that the plaintiffs had "unextinguished non-exclusive aboriginal rights, other than right of ownership" (Dickason, 1997, p. 330). As a result of this case, the First Nations and the government of British Columbia agreed to a treaty-making process. The plaintiffs in the Delgamuukw case appealed, however, and were rejected again on their major points in 1993. Another appeal was heard by the Supreme Court of Canada, with a decision handed down on 11 December 1997. In this Delgamuukw case (*Delgamuukw v. British Columbia*, Supreme Court of Canada, 1997), the Supreme Court did not rule on title, indicating that the case would be better resolved through negotiations. But it did indicate that the courts must "come to terms with the oral histories of Aboriginal societies, which for many Aboriginal Nations, are the only record of their past." On 16 July 1998, the federal and British Columbia governments signed a final agreement with the Nisga'a people, which granted them 1,930 kilometers of land, self-government, and a large amount of cash. The extent to which aboriginal title equates with ownership remains unclear.

Other Rights

Other aboriginal rights, such as the right to hunt, fish, and trap, have been consistently upheld by the courts since the 1950s. The courts in Manitoba have upheld Métis rights to hunt and fish for food at all times. In 1990 the Supreme Court in *Sparrow v. the Queen* insisted that a member of the British Columbia Musqueam band had an aboriginal right to fish. The court ruled that such aboriginal rights could be restricted only under certain conditions. The limitation had to be for valid reasons, usually conser-

Jim Sinclair (left), president of the Saskatchewan Métis society, meets with Prime Minister Pierre Trudeau (right) to discuss Métis problems concerning allocation of land and settlement of old treaties, August 1972 (Bettmann/Corbis)

vation; it had to be minimal; and the government had to have acted consistently in the restriction. The court also insisted that the government had a duty to consult with aboriginal peoples about matters affecting their rights. Subsequent cases, including that of Donald Marshall Jr. in 1997, have confirmed this judgment. In one case, a former Chief Justice of Canada wrote:

> In my view, the doctrine of aboriginal rights exists, and is recognized and affirmed by [the Constitution] because of one simple fact: when Europeans arrived in North America, aboriginal peoples were already here, living in communities on the land and participating in distinctive cultures, as they had done for centuries. It is this fact, and this fact above all others, which separates aboriginal people from all other minority groups in Canadian society and which mandates their special legal, and now constitutional, status. (McDonald and McDonald, 2000, p. 20)

Despite several court rulings to the contrary, however, the federal government still persists in attempting to limit native fishing rights on both coasts.

Self-Government

Before the arrival of the Europeans, the First Nations had their own governments. After the Europeans had imposed their sovereignty over what is now Canada, both the French and the English allowed the First Nations to continue to operate their own governments without any attempt at control. Aboriginals governed themselves politically and legally in their own territory and were subject to European law and authority only when they visited or resided in territory under European control. This gradually changed in the nineteenth century, with First Nations being brought under the supervision of the Department of Indian Affairs. In modern times, the First Nations have long demanded their own governments. A number of successful negotiations have occurred on this matter of autonomous government in recent years. In 1984 the band councils of the Cree-Naskapi of Quebec were given substantial political authority as a consequence of the James Bay and Northern Quebec Agreement of 1975. The Sechelt band of British Columbia received municipal-style government in 1986 by agreement between the province of British Columbia and the band. In 1998 the Nisga'a Nation of British Columbia negotiated with the province a treaty that provided for local self-government, to come into effect in 2000. In 1999, after twenty years of negotiation, the territory of Nunavet was officially separated off from the Northwest Territories by the federal government, in response to the needs of its Inuit residents. The new territory is not technically under an aboriginal government, but 85 percent of its population is Inuit, and aboriginal control is guaranteed in the final agreement.

The question of aboriginal self-government remains an extremely controversial one. The Constitution Act of 1982, while entrenching the existing aboriginal and treaty rights of the natives, had not really come to terms with native self-government, chiefly because the First Nations and Ottawa were so far apart on the subject. The aboriginals have insisted that their government should be based on inherent jurisdiction as a historic right. For many native peoples, this involves sovereign jurisdiction and the independent right to make laws and institutions for their people and their territory, as these rights were not surrendered with treaties.

The militants among the natives object to the federal authorities' concept of native self-government as a mere equivalent of municipal government that was delegated to the First Nations by those jurisdictions (Ottawa and the provinces) claiming sovereignty under the Crown and constitution of Canada. If they were sovereign entities, native governments would deal as equals with Ottawa, which the native peoples insist still owes them a heavy debt of financial responsibility. As municipal governments, native nations would become the agents of the senior governments and would have only those powers allowed to them by those governments. The Charlottetown Accord of 1992 acknowledged aboriginal government as a distinct third level of government alongside the federal Parliament and the provincial legislatures. To recognize the First Nations (with their more than 600 bands) as sovereign would certainly be more possible in a constitution that also accepted Quebec. For many Canadians, however, this recognition would not only further balkanize the country but would also create independent jurisdictions within Canada that benefited from their Canadian affiliation but held no concurrent responsibilities under it.

Settlement of Land Claims

First Nations land claims come in two types: comprehensive claims and specific claims. Comprehensive claims are based on history. Ten comprehensive claims, involving large expanses of territory, have been settled to date, and others are in the process of negotiation. Specific claims are concerned with the failure of the Crown to live up to its legal obligations under treaties or the Indian Act. More than 200 such claims have been dealt with, and more than 100 more are in the process of negotiation.

The British Columbia Reaction to First Nations Negotiations

No province has been more involved with aboriginal rights negotiations than British Columbia, where few treaties existed between First Nations and the Crown. On 4 July 2002, the results of a British Columbia referendum of aboriginal negotiations were announced in the nation's newspapers. The referendum had been held on the basis of new legislation passed in the British Columbia legislature in the spring of 2002. The legislation stated that a legitimate vote of more than 50 percent of those voting on any referendum question would be binding on the province. In April 2002, Elections British Columbia mailed out 2,127,829 referendum packages to its citizens. The questions were phrased in such a way that affirmative answers considerably limited the province's flexibility—and its ability to make a generous settlement—in its negotiations with its First Nations (for the questions, see the end of this chapter). The province's churches and other organizations had counseled the electorate to spoil their ballots as a protest against the legitimacy of the process, but only 26,702 voters returned improper material, which indicated that the protest campaign was a failure. In the end, 763,480 ballots were returned. This figure represented 35.83 percent of those eligible to vote, a very low figure by comparison with the referendum results of the constitutional referendum of 1992 or the Quebec referendum of 1995. But very large majorities of those who did cast their ballots voted in favor of the referendum questions, which meant that these majorities were binding on the province. Whether such referenda will become more common, both to deal with First Nations negotiations and other public issues that require negotiation, is not clear at the time of this writing.

Aboriginal Justice

A series of public inquiries between 1987 and 1994 consistently established that First Nations were treated badly by the criminal justice and court systems of Canada. Perhaps the best-known individual case of mistreatment was that of Donald Marshall Jr. of Nova Scotia. On 28 May 1971, a seventeen-year-old black teenager named Sandford (Sandy) Seale left a church hall dance in Sydney, Nova Scotia, to make his way home before a midnight curfew. Walking through Wentworth Park at about 11:40 P.M., he met another seventeen-year-old, Donald Marshall Jr. Sometime between then and midnight, Sandy Seale was fatally stabbed, dying in a hospital about twenty hours later. Although Donald Marshall Jr. had called the ambulance and reported to police that he and Seale had been assaulted by two older men (whom he described in considerable detail), the police investigation quickly focused on Marshall himself, who had a reputation as being an aboriginal "troublemaker." Witnesses were persuaded that Marshall had been the assailant, alternative evidence was ignored, and the young Micmac was arrested and charged with murder on 4 June. Like the Sydney police, the Crown prosecutor ignored a file full of conflicting evidence and testimony. Defense counsel, although they were well-paid and competent criminal lawyers, did not bother to ask the Crown to disclose its case and the contradictions in it. Compounding matters, the trial judge limited the cross-examination of important witnesses and refused to permit other important testimony in Marshall's favor to be heard. Not surprisingly, Donald Marshall Jr. was convicted and sentenced to life imprisonment.

Marshall remained in prison for 11 years, although another man was soon found to be the killer. Marshall was released in 1982, and his lawyer insisted on an acquittal. Although in 1983 the Nova Scotia Court of Appeal acquitted him, it insisted that Marshall was partially responsible for his own fate. After years of public agitation, the Nova Scotia government appointed a royal commission to examine the handling of the Marshall case. The final report of the commission, released late in 1989, concluded:

> The criminal justice system failed Donald Marshall Jr. at virtually every turn from his arrest and wrongful conviction for murder in 1971 up to, and even beyond, his acquittal by the Court of Appeal in 1983. The tragedy of the failure is compounded by evidence that this miscarriage of justice could—and should—have been prevented, or at least corrected quickly, if those involved in the system had carried out their duties in a professional and/or competent manner. That they did not is due, in part at least, to the fact that Donald Marshall Jr. is a Native. (*Royal Commission on the Donald Marshall Jr. Prosecution*, 1989, p. 119)

The "Marshall case" had dragged on for nearly twenty years. It did not end even with the royal commission report of 1989, which was criticized for pulling its punches about the extent of the "cover-up" by provincial police officials and civil servants Above all, the Marshall case demonstrated that the judicial system of Nova Scotia both discriminated against visible minorities and was entirely capable of ignoring abuse until evidence of its existence became overwhelming. The sadly consistent findings of other public inquiries across the nation—including an Aboriginal Justice Inquiry in Manitoba in 1991—suggested that the Canadian judicial system itself had become abusive in general but was particularly stacked against First Nations people.

Redressing Historical Mistreatment

The history of Canada is strewn with raw deals for various peoples. Beginning in the 1960s, various collectivities began to mutter about possible redress in the form either of apologies or even compensation. The First Nations were in the forefront of these concerns. The Liberal government of Pierre Elliott Trudeau refused to deal with any of these collective grievances. As Trudeau told an audience in Vancouver in 1969 in a speech (transcribed as given orally):

> If we think of restoring aboriginal rights to the Indians well what about the French who were defeated at the Plains of Abraham? Shouldn't we restore rights to them? And what about though the Acadians who were deported— shouldn't we compensate for this? And what about the other Canadians,

the immigrants? What about the Japanese Canadians who were so badly treated at the end or during the last war? What can we do to redeem the past? I can only say as President Kennedy said when he was asked about what he would do to compensate for the injustices that the Negroes had received in American society. We will be just in our time. This is all we can do. We must be just today. (quoted in Cumming and Mickenberg, 1970)

Trudeau not only made clear that he did not believe in "restoring" aboriginal rights, but also that he did not believe in historical redress either. The situation changed somewhat for aboriginals when the courts began to recognize the existence of aboriginal rights, and Trudeau himself admitted in 1973 that the First Nations might have had more rights than he had previously believed. Those interested in redress had two routes: They could pressure government, or they could go to court. The two most successful redress cases were those of the First Nations people abused in residential schools and the Japanese Canadians mistreated during World War II.

The Court Route: Native Residential Schools

The beginnings of the residential school system long predated Confederation and were usually part of the missionary activities of the churches, designed both to educate aboriginal people and especially to assimilate them into European society. Residential schools came in a variety of forms, although in the twentieth century the most common were the so-called "industrial schools." They were located in almost every province and territory. The government of Canada shared in the administration of these schools from at least 1874. By the end of the nineteenth century, the schools had shifted from being church institutions partly funded by the government to being government institutions operated by the churches. Their purpose also shifted from an effort to assimilate aboriginals into European society to one that prepared aboriginals for life on controlled reserves. From an early date there was an undercurrent of abuse and intimidation connected with the schools, as their very nature was based upon the (often) forcible removal of children from their families in order to "civilize" them and "convert" them to Christianity. Such schooling had, of course, begun in the seventeenth century. In most of the schools, the process of education involved rules against speaking native languages and practicing native religious beliefs, rules that were typically enforced with denigration of native culture and use of corporal punishment.

In 1969, the government of Canada took over complete administration of these schools, and they gradually disappeared, the last closing in 1996. Both churches and government were slow to respond formally to the rising tide of complaints from the aboriginal community about their treatment in the residential schools, although stories of abuse were recounted before every commission that investigated the treatment of aboriginal people in Canada (including the Royal Commission on Aboriginal Peoples, which was created in 1991 and made its report in 1996). The Anglican Church did not formally apologize to the aboriginal community for its part in the schools until 1993, and the federal government and the United Church did not do so until 1998.

Beginning in the 1990s, aboriginal victims of the residential schools began taking the federal government to court over their treatment. These cases were not, strictly speaking, aboriginal rights cases but rather historic abuse cases. The government in its turn insisted on involving as codefendants the various churches that had served as government agents, in the process virtually bankrupting at least the Anglican Church of Canada and a number of its dioceses. By the end of the decade there were more than 8,000 such cases pending. Early in January of 1998, the government of Canada announced a program ("Gathering Strength—Canada's Aboriginal Action Plan") for dealing with past injustices, based on reconciliation and concrete action for the future.

As part of the program, the government issued a statement of reconciliation acknowledging its part in the residential schools and apologizing for its actions. It offered $350 million to help heal the injuries but was not able to come to terms with the litigants. As of this writing the federal government has admitted that it had not intended to destroy the churches by involving them in the lawsuits, but it has not offered any solution to the problem, and it has reached a tentative agreement with the Anglican Church on the matter. In the meantime, many churches, dioceses, and religious orders have been bankrupted by legal fees. Some native spokespeople have maintained that the churches caused their own problems by attempting to use the courts to protect themselves from liability.

The Government Route: The Japanese Canadians

Early in 1990, thousands of Canadians received a letter from the Minister of State Multiculturalism and Citizenship that enclosed a substantial check and an "acknowledgement signed by the Prime Minister" (see "The Canadian Government Acknowledgment to the Japanese Canadians,

1990"). The acknowledgment was not quite an apology. The recipients of this material were Japanese Canadians who had been uprooted from their homes in 1942 by the Canadian government. The check was for "redress" (or compensation, as it was usually called), and the document from the prime minister acknowledged "that the treatment of Japanese Canadians during and after World War II was unjust and violated principles of human rights as they are understood today." Japanese Canadians had first organized to seek redress in 1977, at the time of the centennial of the first arrival of Japanese immigrants in Canada. The government of Pierre Trudeau had refused to consider action on this issue, but the leader of the opposition, Brian Mulroney, was more sympathetic. After Mulroney's Progressive-Conservatives swept to power in 1984, the Japanese renewed their efforts, which, finally, on 22 September 1988, led to the signature of the prime minister on a Redress Agreement between the National Association of Japanese Canadians and the Canadian government.

The success of the Japanese with their cause for redress in Canada was undoubtedly facilitated by a parallel movement for redress in the United States, which had led to the passage of compensation legislation under the Reagan administration on 10 August 1988, only weeks before Canada's action. Unlike the Japanese Americans, however, the Japanese in Canada did not have to wait very long for their compensation checks. According to the Redress Agreement, negotiated on 26 August 1988, each eligible person of Japanese ancestry would be paid a tax-free lump sum of $21,000. In addition, the Japanese Canadian community would get $12 million for community improvement, and another $12 million (matched by the government of Canada) would be used to create a Canadian Race Relations Foundation. Those of Japanese ancestry convicted of violations under the War Measures Act or the National Emergency Transition Powers Act had their names cleared, and Canadian citizenship was conferred on persons of Japanese ancestry who had been expelled from Canada or who had their citizenship revoked (Miki and Kobayashi, 1991, pp. 138–139). By 1993, more than 18,000 compensation checks had been issued to those who applied for them. Such an agreement symbolized the changed attitude both to ethnicity and to redress at the end of the twentieth century.

Other Efforts at Redress

A number of other campaigns for redress have occurred since the late 1980s, usually without much success. Attempting to take advantage of what appeared to be the potentially successful Japanese Canadian campaign for redress, the Civil Liberties Commission of the Ukrainian Canadian Committee presented a brief to the Standing Committee on Multiculturalism of the House of Commons in December 1987 that called for Parliament to "officially acknowledge the mistreatment suffered by Ukrainians in Canada during and after the First World War and that the government undertake negotiations with the Ukrainian Canadian Committee to redress these injustices" (Luciuk, 1988, p. 28). There was media debate over this question through the early 1990s, but nothing was ever done. In 1992 the Manitoba Métis Federation went to court to attempt to recover lands promised to the Métis by the federal government, which the Métis claimed they had never received because of government manipulation. This case fell into the redress category rather than under aboriginal rights because Canada had never recognized the legitimacy of the Métis as aboriginals. The Métis also introduced several private members' bills (not sponsored by the government) into Parliament in an effort to clear Louis Riel. In 2002, the Acadians hoped that Queen Elizabeth II would issue an apology for British removal of the Acadians from the Maritime provinces in 1755. And finally, in June 2002 a class action suit was entered in a London (England) court on behalf of those young British immigrants who had been transported to Canada by the philanthropy of Dr. Barnardo's Homes at the turn of the century. The suit claimed that the young men had been kidnapped and sold into slavery and that they deserved to be compensated for their mistreatment.

Immigration

While the Canadian population continued to drift off the farms, westward, and into the cities and surrounding suburbs, because of declining birth rates it also became increasingly dependent on immigration for its growth. That inflow increased its shift away from the highly industrialized and formerly preferred nations of western Europe and North America that had once been Canada's main sources of newcomers. Canada was no longer a special land of opportunity for citizens of the European Community. The new immigrants were largely from third world countries in Africa, the Caribbean, Latin America, and Asia. Table 10.2 graphically illustrates the changes in the origins of immigrants between 1972 and the end of the century. The figures for the Americas are a bit misleading, as a large influx from Spanish-speaking nations had occurred in the late 1960s and early 1970s.

TABLE 10.2 IMMIGRANT ARRIVALS BY REGION OF LAST RESIDENCE,
1972 AND 1999-2000

Region	1972	1999-2000
Europe	51,293	39,915
Africa	8,308	16,753
Australasia	2,148	867
North and Central America (including Caribbean)	31,836	15,905
South America	11,057	5,932
Asia	23,325	125,903
Oceania	787	774
Total	122,006	205,469*

SOURCE: Statistics Canada.

In 1975 Immigrant Minister Robert Andras tabled another government discussion document in the House of Commons, the so-called Green Paper. A special joint committee of the House of Commons and Senate held almost fifty public hearings across Canada on the Green Paper. The hearings seemed to confirm that Canadians wanted to continue accepting relatively large numbers of new immigrants but not to open the nation's doors to unrestricted admissions. The result of the national discussion was another major Immigration Act, that of 1976, which stated Canadian goals regarding immigration and insisted on the need to plan for the future. The Act recognized three classes of immigrants: the family class (relatives of current Canadian residents), the humanitarian class (refugees and displaced persons), and an independent class.

In 1978 immigration regulations were revised to alter the points system by placing greater importance on practical experience and to alter the refugee situation by creating a new program of refugee sponsorship. Most of the Vietnam boat people, about 50,000, entered Canada under this plan between 1979 and 1984. Quebec was the only province to take full advantage of federal opportunities built into the legislation of 1976 and 1978 to assume new provincial powers in immigration matters. As a result, Quebec could now in practice select its own immigrants. Ontario and Nova Scotia also signed more limited immigration agreements with Ottawa. Whether or not Quebec could attract and hold its share of the immigration total was another matter entirely. Many immigrants were not enthusiastic about education in French for their children. Tough language legislation led to considerable outward migration, and fewer francophones came to Quebec.

By the mid-1980s the traditional sources for Canadian immigrants were producing only about 30 percent of the total, and their share continued to drop. Moreover, the pattern was shifting simultaneously in other ways as well. Asia continued to be the principal supplier of immigrants. But the number of people from the Caribbean area increased, and those from Central and South America continued to come, as did those coming from the Middle East and Africa. The 1980s also witnessed another rise of the refugee question, both internationally and in Canada. Between the end of World War II and the new Immigration Act of 1978, more than 300,000 refugees—mainly European but including 7,000 Ugandan Africans in 1971 and 7,000 Chileans in 1973—had been admitted to Canada under the relaxation of formal regulations. Those fleeing strife and disasters came to Canada in increasing numbers, occasionally by unusual means, such as the lifeboat loads of Tamils who were picked up off the Atlantic coast of Canada in 1986. Debate over Canada's refugee admission policy after 1978 revolved around both overseas selection by visa and the question of individuals already in Canada claiming for refugee status without any previous processing or documentation. (Dirks, 1995)

The visa question was an old one. The Canadian government has long tried to insist on proper visas for those entering the country. This policy forms a preliminary screen for identifying arrivals (immigrants or not) undesirable on medical or security grounds. When people applying for entry into Canada have visas issued by Canadian officials at foreign posts, the Canadian immigration officers know they have been prescreened. Demand for visas for all visitors grew after the increased number of terrorist activities around the world beginning in the 1960s. The crash of an Air India airliner in 1985, on which Canadian authorities suspected that a bomb had been planted in the Vancouver airport, reminded Canada of the problem.

Despite its obvious advantages, however, insistence on visas has always been a point of contention in Canada for several reasons. For one, political refugees may not have proper documentation and may be unable to get it. Humanitarian organizations in Canada vehemently opposed insisting on proper documentation for all visitors and immigrants. Also, visas may be hard to obtain in countries in which the Canadian presence is fairly limited. To get a visa may require lengthy travel to a national capital, for example, or even outside the country. As was well known, Canada used an absence of official presence as one way to reduce applications for immigration from some places. This was certainly the case for a country like Guyana. As a result, Canada in the 1980s did not insist on a strictly enforced visa policy. One of the most serious problems was caused by visitors who outstayed their permitted period for visits. Some suspected that these overstays were a way for people to get around the screening mechanisms. Nationals from some countries for which Canada did not require visas, chiefly India, Portugal, and Guyana, were particularly likely to overstay. It should be emphasized that potential immigrants who were able to afford to come to Canada as visitors and then remain in the country claiming refugee status were not usually impoverished peasants but rather highly skilled professionals. Their entrance into their professions in Canada was hampered both by their use of the refugee route and by the typical reluctance of Canadian professional organizations to recognize foreign education and experience.

A related question was whether people would be allowed to apply for permanent residence (that is, formally become "landed immigrants") from inside the country. This issue again criss-crossed the problem of controlling immigration and the related problem of determining refugee status. By the early 1970s there was a substantial backlog of appeals from rejected applicants both within and without the country for landed status, and in 1972 the regulation permitting application from within was rescinded. But it continued to be possible to remain in the country by special minister's permit, a procedure employed mainly by family members of residents for compassionate reasons. Moreover, the practice of allowing a determination of refugee status from within, made possible by the 1976 and 1978 Immigration Acts, later became increasingly common. The machinery of refugee status determination had not been intended as a way for avoiding routine admission procedures, but this was what it became in the later 1970s and early 1980s. The number of refugee claimants totally clogged the immigration system. Altered American regulations in 1986 granting amnesty to illegal immigrants in the United States before 1982 subjected those arriving after 1982 to the threat of deportation. Many of those threatened hoped to come to Canada, placing an additional burden on the Canadian system. An "amnesty" was declared in 1986, allowing almost all refugees currently resident in Canada—some 63,000—to remain in the country as residents. In 1987 the Mulroney government introduced new legislation to deal with the refugee situation, but by the time the revised system went into operation there was already another major backlog, with more than 122,000 residents claiming refugee status. Many of these claims were regarded by the authorities as patently improper. However, those whose cases had not been heard could not legally work, and their families often went on provincial and municipal welfare. Ultimately, clearing the backlog took more than three years.

Although it was claimed that Canada's record with refugees was one of the best in the world—the nation allowed more refugees relative to its own population to immigrate than any other nation—many critics insisted that it needed to do far more. Canada's behavior toward refugees was increasingly contrasted with its policy toward rich businesspeople. Beginning in 1986 individuals with substantial amounts of capital (initially $250,000; later reduced to $150,000) could invest this money in projects approved by provincial governments and thereby gain admission to Canada. This scheme was heavily criticized in many quarters on a variety of grounds, including the charge that the imported capital helped drive up the real estate markets in a few Canadian cities, such as Vancouver and Toronto.

By the 1990s many Canadians had become concerned about the new patterns of immigration, most of which could be seen as finally confirming popular fears and paranoia of inundation by non-European immigrants expressed over many years. In 1991, the European share of Canadian immigration was down to 20.2 percent. Even with the addition of those immigrating to Canada from the United States, newcomers of European origin represented less than one-quarter of the total of 230,781. In 1991 Africa sent 7.2 percent of the total, Asia 53 percent, the Caribbean area 8.2 percent, and South America 4.5 percent. The top ten sources for immigrants to Canada between 1981 and 1991 had been, in order, Hong Kong, Poland, the People's Republic of China, India, the United Kingdom, Vietnam, the Philippines, the United States, Portugal, and Lebanon. As these statistics indicate, the number of people in the underdeveloped nations of the world seeking admission to Canada had increased and doubtless would continue to increase.

Most people from the underdeveloped nations were visibly different from the majority of the host population in Canada. Many of the newcomers represented racial, religious, and cultural backgrounds considerably unlike those of the traditional Canadian population, potentially producing considerable strains on Canadian society. People of Third World origin, who had represented less than 1 percent of the Canadian population in 1967, by 1986 represented 4.6 percent, and those from the Third World totaled 30 percent of all foreign-born people in Canada. Between 1981 and 1991, the number of followers of Islam in Canada grew from

98,165 to 253,260, the number of Buddhists from 51,955 to 163,415, and the number of Sikhs from 67,715 to 147,440.

In a Canada of high permanent unemployment (close to 10 percent even in times of "prosperity"), the newcomers might take jobs away from Canadians, a continued public fear no matter how often researchers and immigration experts insisted that it was a myth. Moreover, for better or worse, in terms of locating themselves geographically, the new immigrants behaved in many ways little different from earlier ones. They flocked to a few large Canadian cities, mainly in English-speaking Canada, eschewing rural areas, Atlantic Canada, and Quebec. In the 1993 federal election, at least one political party, the Reform Party, began to talk openly of closing the door to immigration. Few Canadians were prepared to go that far, but many were worried about how a fair and just immigration policy could be developed.

In 1993 the Liberal government of Jean Chrétien announced that it would maintain a Canadian immigration intake at about 1 percent of the total Canadian population. The resulting annual immigration figures since that date have been more than 200,000, up from the figures of the 1970s and 1980s. Such an intake did not begin to satisfy the demands of people from around the world who wanted to immigrate to Canada. But it did mean that Canadian society would never be suddenly overwhelmed by people of different backgrounds. Nevertheless, over a protracted period, these sorts of numbers—especially if they continued to come from the Third World—would have a profound cumulative effect on the makeup of the Canadian population.

Timeline

1969   Frank Calder brings court action on aboriginal title to British Columbia Supreme Court.

1971   Trudeau government offers constitutional deal to Quebec, which is refused; Donald Marshall Jr. found guilty of murder.

1973   Supreme Court of Canada finds against Calder on appeal, but affirms existence of aboriginal rights.

1975   "Green Paper" on immigration tabled in the House of Commons.

1976   Parti Québécois comes to power in Quebec; Immigration Act of 1976 revises Immigration policy and procedures.

1977   Bill 101 passed by Quebec legislature; Japanese Canadians begin to seek redress for treatment during World War II.

1980   Quebec referendum on sovereignty association; Prime Minister Trudeau calls first ministers' conference and presents it with a constitutional package; Supreme Court rules on federal repatriation process.

1982   Canada Constitution Act, including the Charter of Rights and Freedoms, passes British Parliament and becomes law; Donald Marshall Jr. is released and acquitted of murder.

1984   Canadian Supreme Court hears first Charter of Rights case.

1985   Guerin (*R. v. Guerin*, 1985) case confirms existence of aboriginal title.

1987   Prime Minister Mulroney calls Meech Lake Conference; Ukrainian Canadians call for Parliament to redress mistreatment suffered by Ukrainians 1914–1920.

1989   Royal Commission reports on Marshall case.

1990   Japanese Canadians receive an "acknowledgment" and a check from the Canadian government for their treatment during World War II; Meech Lake Agreement fails to gain approval; Supreme Court rules on aboriginal right to fish.

1991   Gitskan (*Delgamuukw v. British Columbia*, 1997) case calls oral history into question in native rights cases; Aboriginal Justice Inquiry reports in Manitoba.

1992   Prime Minister Mulroney calls conference at Charlottetown, which produces Charlottetown Accord; the Accord is defeated in a national referendum in October.

1995   Quebec referendum on sovereignty; Non vote barely wins.

1998   Nisga'a Treaty negotiated with British Columbia; federal government announces a program for residential school injustices.

1999   Nunavet becomes a territory; more than half of Canada's immigrants come from Asia, and less than one-quarter from Europe and North America.

2002   British Columbia referendum on aboriginal rights negotiations.

Significant People, Places, and Events

ABORIGINAL JUSTICE INQUIRY A commission of inquiry in Manitoba, headed by an aboriginal judge, which reported in 1991 that the justice system in the province was rife with discrimination and prejudice against aboriginal peoples.

ABORIGINAL RIGHTS The concept that First Nations in Canada have rights to land and other matters, including self-government, as a result of their occupation of North America before the arrival of the Europeans.

ABORIGINAL SELF-GOVERNMENT The concept that as a result of their occupation of North America before the arrival of Europeans, the First Nations have a right to retain their customary law and the right to self-government. In 1992 the Charlottetown Accord tried unsuccessfully to entrench such self-government as one of the three levels of government in Canada, along with the federal and provincial legislatures.

ABORIGINAL TITLE The contention-ridden question of whether the First Nations have actual ownership of their traditional lands.

BILL 101 Legislation in Quebec in 1977 that required almost all residents of the province to attend French-language schools.

BRITISH COLUMBIA REFERENDUM ON ABORIGINAL NEGOTIATIONS A provincial referendum held in British Columbia in the spring of 2002 that asked citizens of the province to vote on eight propositions relating to First Nations negotiations; if the Yes vote on any proposition was more than 50 percent of those voting, it would be regarded as binding on the government.

CHARLOTTETOWN ACCORD An agreement in 1992 in which the federal government made substantial concessions to the provinces and to the First Nations. It was defeated in a national referendum in October 1992.

CHARTER OF RIGHTS AND FREEDOMS A Canadian bill of rights written into the Canadian constitution in 1982. It provided for the protection of individual and collective rights by the Supreme Court of Canada.

CONSTITUTION ACT OF 1982 The act of the British Parliament that amended the Canadian Constitution so that it was no longer dependent on the British Parliament. The act provided a future amending procedure and included the Canadian Charter of Rights and Freedoms.

DISTINCT SOCIETY A term used in the 1987 Meech Lake agreement to refer to the recognition that in a variety of ways—linguistic, cultural, religious—Quebec was different from the other provinces of Canada and was to be treated differently within the Confederation.

ENTRENCHMENT The process of establishing something so strongly that it is virtually impossible to dislodge. In Canadian constitutional terms, it refers to safeguarding matters, particularly rights, by specifically writing them into the constitution.

GREEN PAPER ON IMMIGRATION A Green Paper is a government statement of a proposed policy put before the public for discussion, usually at an early point in the policymaking process. The Green Paper on Immigration of 1975 was issued after legislation on immigration and population had been drafted but before it was passed into law.

Indian Act The parliamentary legislation that governs the relationship between "status Indians" and the Canadian government.

Marshall, Donald Jr. (b. 1953) A Micmac aboriginal whose improper conviction in Nova Scotia in 1971 for murder—and his subsequent mistreatment—provoked a searching examination of the Canadian justice system.

Meech Lake Agreement A constitutional agreement of 1987 that was intended to allow Quebec to agree to the constitutional reforms of 1982. It established Quebec as a "distinct society" and provided for various powers to the provinces. Meech Lake failed to become law in 1990.

Notwithstanding Clause A clause in the Canadian Constitution Act of 1982 that allows provinces to opt out of many aspects of the Charter of Rights and Freedoms. It has not often been invoked.

Nunavet The eastern part of the old Northwest Territories, established as a separate territory dominated by the Inuit in 1999.

Parti Québécois A social democratic political party formed in 1968 and committed to a program of Quebec nationalism culminating in a new independent relationship between Quebec and Canada.

Patriation (Also Called Repatriation) In Canadian constitutional terms, the process by which a constitution is brought under the sole authority of the nation to which it applies by being removed from the control of its previous mother country.

Quebec Referendum of 1980 A provincial referendum on the question of sovereignty association, in which voters rejected that principle.

Quebec Referendum of 1995 A provincial referendum on sovereignty association; voters again rejected that principle by a very narrow margin.

Residential Schools Government-supported schools, usually administered by religious denominations, in which First Nations children were housed and educated, usually in assimilative ways and often involving brutality and even sexual abuse by teachers.

Sovereignty Association A constitutional proposal in Quebec by which the province would be given political independence but would still maintain a formal—mostly economic—association with Canada.

Status Indians Those First Nations people who fall directly under the protection and jurisdiction of the Indian Act, usually because of treaties made between Canada or its predecessors and the aboriginals.

Document

The Canadian Government Acknowledgment to the Japanese Canadians, 1990

In January of 1990, more than 17,000 Canadians of Japanese origin received the following in letters enclosing compensation checks.

ACKNOWLEDGMENT

As a people, Canadians commit themselves to the creation of a society that ensures equality and justice for all, regardless of race or ethnic origin.

During and after World War II, Canadians of Japanese ancestry, the majority of whom were citizens, suffered unprecedented actions taken by the Government of Canada against their community.

Despite perceived military necessities at the time, the forced removal or internment of Japanese Canadians during World War II and their deportation and expulsion following the war, was unjust. In retrospect, government policies of disenfranchisement, detention, confiscation and sale of private and community property, expulsion, deportation and restriction of movement, which continued after the war, were influenced by discriminatory attitudes. Japanese Canadians who were interned had their property liquidated and the proceeds of sale were used to pay for their own internment.

The acknowledgement of these injustices serves notice to all Canadians that the excesses of the past are condemned and that the principles of justice and equality in Canada are reaffirmed.

Therefore, the Government of Canada, on behalf of all Canadians, does hereby:

1. acknowledge that the treatment of Japanese Canadians during and after World War II was unjust and violated principles of human rights as they are understood today.
2. pledge to ensure, to the full extent that its powers allow, that such events will not happen again; and
3. recognize, with great respect, the fortitude and determination of Japanese Canadians who, despite great stress and hardship, retain their commitment and loyalty to Canada and contribute so richly to the development of the Canadian nation.

Brian Mulroney
Prime Minister of Canada

Source: Miki, Roy, and Kobayashi, Cassandra, *Justice in Our Time: The Japanese Canadian Redress Settlement* (Vancouver, British Columbia: Talonbooks, 1991), frontispiece.

TABLE 10.3   CANADA POPULATION BY RELIGION, 1991 CENSUS

Total Population	26,994.0
Catholic	12,335.3
Protestant	9,780.7
Eastern Non-Xian	747.5
Eastern Orthodox	387.4
Jewish	318.1
Para-religious	28.2
No religious affiliation	3,386.4
Other religions	10.6

SOURCE: Statistics Canada, 1991 Census, Catalog no. 93-319-XPB.

TABLE 10.4   CANADIAN POPULATION BY ETHNIC ORIGIN, 1996

Ethnic Origin	Population
British Isles	3,267,520
French	2,683,840
European	3,742,890
Western European	1,126,095
Northern European	167,285
Eastern European	867,055
Southern European	1,376,935
Other European	205,525
Arab	188,435
West Asian	106,870
South Asian	590,145
East and Southeast Asian	1,271,450
African	137,315
Pacific Islands	5,765
Latin, Central, and South American	118,640
Caribbean	305,290
Aboriginal	477,630
Canadian	5,326,995
Other origins	80,840
Single origins	18,303,265
Multiple origins	10,224,495
Total Population	28,528,125

SOURCE: Statistics Canada, 1996 Census *Nation* tables.

TABLE 10.5   CANADA, VISIBLE MINORITY POPULATION, 1996

Minority Group	Population
Black	573,860
South Asian	670,590
Chinese	860,150
Korean	64,840
Japanese	68,135
Southeast Asian	172,765
Filipino	235,195
West Asian	244,665
Latin American	176,975
Visible minority	69,745
Multiple visible minority	61,575
Total visible minorities	3,197,480
Total Population	28,528,125

SOURCE: Statistics Canada, 1996 Census *Nation* tables.

TABLE 10.6   CANADA, POPULATION BY ABORIGINAL GROUP, 1996 CENSUS

Place	Population	Aboriginal Population Total	N.A. Indian	Métis	Inuit
Canada	28,528,125	99,010	554,290	210,190	41,080
Newfoundland	547,155	14,200	5,340	4,685	4,265
Prince Edward Island	132,855	950	825	120	15
Nova Scotia	899,965	12,380	11,340	860	210
New Brunswick	729,630	10,250	9,180	975	120
Quebec	7,045,080	71,415	47,600	16,075	8,300
Ontario	10,642,795	141,520	118,830	22,790	1,300
Manitoba	1,100,295	128,680	82,990	46,195	360
Saskatchewan	976,615	111,245	73,205	36,535	190
Alberta	2,669,195	122,835	72,645	50,745	795
British Columbia	3,689,755	139,655	113,315	26,750	815
Yukon	30,650	6,175	5,530	565	110
Northwest Territories	39,460	39,690	3,895	24,600	24,430

SOURCE: Statistics Canada, 1996 Census.

TABLE 10.7   CANADA, IMMIGRANT POPULATION BY PLACE OF BIRTH, 1996

Place of Birth	Population
United States	244,690
Central and South America	273,820
Caribbean and Bermuda	279,400
Europe	2,332,060
United Kingdom	655,535
Northern and Western Europe	514,310
Eastern Europe	447,830
Southern Europe	714,380
Africa	229,300
Asia	1,562,770
West Central Asia and Middle East	210,850
Eastern Asia	589,420
Southeast Asia	408,985
Southern Asia	353,515
Oceania and Other	49,020

SOURCE: Statistics Canada, 1996 Census *Nation* tables.

TABLE 10.8   CANADA POPULATION BY MOTHER TONGUE, 1996 CENSUS

Mother Tongue	Population
Single responses	28,125,560
English	16,890,615
French	6,636,660
Nonofficial languages	4,598,290
Chinese	715,640
Italian	484,500
German	450,140
Polish	213,410
Spanish	212,890
Portuguese	211,290
Punjabi	201,785
Ukrainian	162,695
Arabic	148,555
Dutch	133,805

(continues)

TABLE 10.8 (continued)

Mother Tongue	Population
Tagalog	133,215
Greek	121,180
Vietnamese	106,515
Cree	78,840
Inuktitut	26,960
Other nonofficial languages	1,198,870
Multiple responses	402,560
English and French	107,945
English and nonofficial languages	249,545
French and nonofficial languages	35,845
English French and nonofficial languages	9,225
Total Population	28,528,125

SOURCE: Statistics Canada, 1996 Census *Nation* tables.

Bibliography

Cairns, Alan C., *Charter versus Federalism: The Dilemmas of Constitutional Reform* (Montreal, Quebec and Kingston, Ontario: McGill-Queen's University Press, 1992).

Cheffins, Ronald, and Johnson, Patricia, *The Revised Canadian Constitution: Politics as Law* (Toronto: McGraw-Hill Ryerson, 1986).

Cumming, Peter A., and Mickenberg, Neil H., *Native Rights in Canada,* 2nd ed. (Toronto: Indian-Eskimo Association of Canada, in association with General Publishing, 1970).

Dickason, Olive Patricia, *Canada's First Nations: A History of Founding Peoples from Earliest Times,* 2nd ed. (Don Mills, Ontario: Oxford University Press, 1997).

Dirks, Gerald E., *Controversy and Complexity: Canadian Immigration Policy during the 1980s* (Montreal, Quebec and Kingston, Ontario: McGill-Queen's University Press, 1995).

Halli, Shiva S., and Driedger, Leo, *Immigrant Canada: Demographic, Economic, and Social Changes* (Toronto: University of Toronto Press, 1999).

Korden, Baldan, *Righting Historical Wrongs: Internment, Acknowledgement, and Redress* (Saskatoon, Saskatchewan: Ukrainian Canadian Congress, 1993).

Luciuk, Lubomyr, *Time for Atonement: Canada's First National Internment Operations and the Ukrainian Canadians 1914–1920* (Kingston, Ontario: Limestone Press, 1988).

Manfredi, Christopher P., *Judicial Power and the Charter: Canada and the Paradox of Liberal Constitutionalism*, 2nd ed., (Don Mills, Ontario: Oxford University Press, 2001).

McDonald, Neil, and McDonald, Trever, *Aboriginal Peoples: Past and Present: Summary of the History, Rights, and Issues Relating to Aboriginal Peoples in Canada* (n.p., Cross Cultural Consulting, 2000).

Miki, Roy, and Kabayashi, Cassandra, *Justice in Our Time: The Japanese Canadian Redress Settlement* (Vancouver, British Columbia: Talonbooks, 1991).

Romanow, Roy, Whyte, John, and Leeson, Howard, *Canada Notwithstanding: The Making of the Constitution 1976–1982* (Toronto: Methuen, 1984).

Royal Commission in the Donald Marshall Jr. Prosecution, *Summary of Findings and Recommendations* (Halifax, Nova Scotia: Queen's Printer, 1989)

CHAPTER ELEVEN

The New Ethnic Groups in Canada since 1967

LTHOUGH THE NEWCOMERS to Canada over the final third of the twentieth century have come chiefly from the Third World, their various situations before immigration and their subsequent experiences in Canada have been quite different. Particular ethnic groups have had histories quite different from one another, and there has often been considerable variation within both the backgrounds and the immigration patterns of any one ethnic group. Generalizations about treatment within Canada and the success of these Third World groups are often hard to make, as groups are not at all homogeneous. Many Third World immigrants have met with quite favorable receptions, particularly if they bring capital and professional skills, although employing their professional skills may prove more than a bit of a problem. Other immigrants have many difficulties in Canada, especially if they are refugees, speak neither of Canada's official languages, and bring no capital and little in the way of specific skills and education.

These realities produce a number of potential dilemmas for some people in Canada. Canadian immigration policy does attempt to select the most highly trained people from the Third World, thus producing a brain drain that tends to extract from developing nations exactly the people those nations most need in order to progress. On the other hand, impoverished refugees brought to Canada straight from refugee camps often have great difficulty in adjusting (and succeeding) in the Canadian environment, producing considerable social problems along the way. Placing the new immigrants into tidy geographic or ethnic boxes is often not easy, as there has historically been considerable movement of peoples from one country (or colony) to another as workers, especially within the old British Empire, in the modern Middle East, and in South Asia.

From the cover of Polyphmy: The Bulletin of the Multicultural Society of
Ontario, *1979–1980 (Courtesy of the Multicultural History Society of Ontario)*

Many of the recent Third World immigrants are political refugees from highly repressive regimes, and their situation in Canada is often dominated by that previous experience. There are bad memories, and guilt about loved ones left behind. Many newcomers to Canada suffer from depression and require extensive psychological assistance in order to manage from day to day. Those among the poor who became caught in the refugee backlog of the 1980s—which meant they were unable legally to work until their status had been formally determined—were obviously often seriously disadvantaged. These visible minorities from the Third World have also been likely to be the targets of racial hostility, both from the general population and from law enforcement agencies. Most immigrant groups are eager to insist that their members are not and have not been illegals. The refugees are often ill-served by public assistance programs and rely heavily on community organizations, including churches, for aid both economic and emotional. On the other hand, what refugee status also produces is a relative inability to return to the country of origin, which in the long run can forcibly assist in making adjustments to the new environment.

Canadian immigration policy has increasingly come to insist on the need for skilled and highly educated immigrants, concentrated in scientific and technological occupations. According to one recent study, "the landed immigrant cohort of 2000 was dominated by one single occupational group: professional occupations in natural and applied sciences" (Couton, 2002, p. 116). This cohort was led by engineers. The policy of emphasizing skills is, frankly, designed to assist the Canadian economy, although at least in theory it should assist new immigrants (typically from the underdeveloped world) to make a successful transition to life in Canada. It comes up against an interesting long-term phenomenon in Canada: the "deskilling" of new immigrants. Canadian employers and professional bodies (usually governed by provincial jurisdictions) have traditionally insisted on their employees having Canadian work experience and have looked with suspicion on foreign credentials. Two general explanations exist for the failure to recognize non-Canadian credentials. First, the credentials really are nontransferrable because of quality issues or, at least, because of the difficulty in certifying them. Second, there is discrimination for various reasons, including both racial prejudice and efforts to limit the numbers in professions in order to keep demand and income high. In the modern world of high technology, deskilling is a serious problem, particularly for visible minority groups, who are understandably sometimes unable to distinguish between racial and nonracial reasons for the discrimination. The extent and duration of deskilling depends on a variety of factors, headed by inability to communicate in one of Canada's two official languages. As most observers realize, the younger immigrants adjust more easily to the problems of deskilling.

The new Canadian immigrants come mainly from six vastly different regions of the world: Africa, the Caribbean, Latin America, the Middle East, and three regions of Asia—South Asia, Southeast Asia, and Asia proper. An examination of some of the major immigrant groups from each of these regions suggests both the complexities and similarities of their backgrounds and experiences. The divisions employed here are strictly geographical rather than cultural.

Africa

The African continent has been in a state of upheaval since the 1950s. The process of decolonization was an extremely painful one for many nations. Immigration to Canada has not been generally distributed across the African continent. Instead, until very recent years, substantial numbers have come from only a small handful of nations, notably Ethiopia, Egypt, Somalia, and South Africa. It is difficult to know in which category to place the refugees expelled from Uganda in 1972, as almost without exception they were people of Asian origin rather than African. Also, it should be noted that few of the African nations supplying large number of immigrants to Canada are part of black Africa. The increase in immigration from Africa in the 1990s has been so recent that there are not good statistics on or studies of the newcomers. African experience in Canada has ranged from acceptance and acculturation (in the case of the Egyptians and South Africans) to only limited economic success in an environment perceived to be highly racist.

The Egyptians

Immigrants from Egypt began arriving in Canada in the late 1950s. They have come in three phases. In the first phase—the years up until 1966—a number of non-Egyptians resident in Egypt (Jews, Europeans, and Armenians, for example) left the nation in response to the increase in Egyptian nationalism beginning in 1954 under General Gamal Abdul Nasser. These emigrants preferred Canada above all other destinations. In the second phase, from 1967–1975, native Egyptians predominated in the African arrivals to Canada, but the numbers were small. Since 1975 the immigration of native Egyptians has increased in number. Most immigrants from Egypt have come with either capital or skills, or both, and by Canadian standards they are an extremely highly educated people.

Unlike most immigrants, a majority of Egyptians have preferred Quebec as a destination, especially before the mid-1970s. Egyptian immigrants brought with them a polyglot culture and adhered to several different religions, including Coptic Christianity, Catholicism, and Islam. Most spoke either English or French, and often both, as well as Arabic. Egyptians have been subject to little discrimination in Canada, partly because of their previous acculturation to English and French and partly because of their skills and social background. Moreover, because of their bilingualism or multilingualism, , they have been much in demand in Quebec. Most Egyptians, especially those in Quebec, have shown little interest in politics. To the extent they are politicized, it has been in opposition to Quebec nationalism, which probably seems to them all too similar to the Egyptian nationalism from which many escaped. Those that the 1991 Canadian census labeled as Egyptians numbered 25,425.

The Ethiopians

Ethiopia, formerly known as Abyssinia, first came to the attention of Canadians in the 1930s, when the Italian dictator Mussolini decided to invade the country and add it to his overseas empire. It is a vast country in northeastern Africa, much of it semiarid. Since liberation from the Italians in 1940, Ethiopia has experienced racial tensions, including a war with Eritrea that led to that nation's independence from Ethiopia in 1993, as well as serious famine caused by endemic drought. The struggle with Eritrea was not only racial but also political, as the liberation movement was led by Marxist nationalists.

The western world has been supplying aid to Ethiopia for many years, sometimes as a result of high-profile fund-raising by rock stars, but much of the aid has never reached its intended targets. In fact, Ethiopian aid has become a notorious example of how not to give it. War and famine have produced more than 2 million refugees, who have spread into refugee camps outside Ethiopia's boundaries. Most Ethiopian immigrants to Canada have come from the camps or at least from exile, rather than from Ethiopia itself. They come as (at least unofficial) refugees, although some students who came to Canada in the 1960s and chose to remain constituted the first Ethiopian presence in Canada. The immigrants have been mainly males. The later appearance of females has come in the context of considerable struggle over the place of women in their culture, and some females still suffer the effects of traditional cultural practices such as female circumcision and infibulation (the fastening of the sexual organs with a clasp).

Because of screening by Canadian officials, some of the Ethiopian immigrants spoke English and were well-educated members of the country's upper classes. In Canada the Ethiopian immigrants have flocked to Toronto. Close to half of the 11,000 people who identified themselves as born in Ethiopia in the 1991 Canadian census actually came from Eritrea in the 1970s. Although they, too, have been drawn to Toronto, they are also located in communities in Winnipeg and in Quebec. Almost without exception, Ethiopians and Eritreans reside in Canada's largest cities. Numbers are small, with perhaps a total of 15,000 entering the country by the 1990s.

The Ethiopians and Eritreans have not had an easy time in Canada. Many spoke neither of Canada's official languages. Some have not had marketable job skills, and those with education and training have suffered from the Canadian phenomenon of deskilling, in which foreign credentials are not accepted because of the difficulties of assessing and confirming them and because of employers' insistence on Canadian experience. Lacking capital, most of the newcomers have ended up in low-skill employment, although a few have become small-scale entrepreneurs, particularly in the restaurant business. Most of these people have experienced some form of racial discrimination as well. Some of the immigrants have formed community organizations, although such formations are hampered by the ethnic history of Ethiopia and the tendency of some of the Eritreans to hope to return home. Although Ethiopia has been known as a Christian state (with Coptic rites), more than half of the Ethiopian newcomers to Canada are Muslims, and the Ethiopian Orthodox Church in Canada has not been able to serve as a basis for cohesion.

The Somalis

Somalia is a small, relatively homogeneous country on the Horn of Africa, between the Gulf of Aden and the Indian Ocean, more a part of the Arab world than of the black African one. An extremely poor country, Somalia achieved international notoriety in the 1970s because of drought and later because of fierce internal clan warfare that eventually (in the early 1990s) resulted in United Nations intervention from American and Canadian troops. The Canadian presence in Somalia, which included some racist behavior by the Canadian Airborne Regiment, paradoxically appears to have produced a rush of immigrants, and Somalia was one of the major sources of refugee claimants in Canada in the 1990s. Many of the immigrants had little or no documentation, few employable skills—although some professionals have also fled Somalia for Canada as well—and most had little facility in either French or English. Many of the newcomers flocked to one small district of Toronto, where they crowded together and produced complaints from neighbors about their living conditions that the Somalis regarded as racist in nature; there were some riots. Because of both their refugee status and their lack of skills, a large percentage of Somalis are or have been on welfare rolls. Many Somali women have been victims of genital mutilation, a practice that is still widely practiced in their homeland, and it is a sensitive topic in Somali communities. Most Somalis are Muslims, and many feel extremely disadvantaged in Canada because of the general reputation of Somalis in Canada.

The South Africans

South Africa is a large nation covering most of the extreme southern part of the continent. For many years after World War II, the government fought a desperate battle to enforce strict racial segregation, the policy known as apartheid. Most South African immigrants to Canada have been whites. In earlier years the vast majority were of British background, often leaving their homeland because of its racial policies, although after 1970 many have also been Jews as well. Many of these people have kept a low profile about their background because of the common hostility in Canada to the South African white regime. The South African government long prohibited blacks from emigrating, and there are very few black South Africans in Canada. In recent years, however, there has been a substantial increase in the numbers of South Africans of mixed origin (the "Coloreds") or of other racial origin, chiefly of East Indian descent. The whites have vanished into British society, the Asians into the various Asian communities, and only the "Coloreds," who have no ethnic origin to give the Canadian census-takers, have been left behind. The vast majority of the "Colored" South Africans have been drawn to Toronto, where they numbered about 4,000 people by the early 1980s, when they began to form a distinctive community there.

The Caribbean

The Caribbean region, also known as the West Indies, includes fifty different territories located on islands and on parts of the mainland of Central and South America. The region was once almost completely under colonial guardianship, although most countries are now independent. The first inhabitants were Amerindians, soon largely replaced by African slaves supervised by a handful of Europeans. In the nineteenth century, Asian Indians were imported as indentured labor in some places, and small groups of traders (Syrians and Portuguese, for example) have also established themselves. Some cultural elements, such as language, religion, and the memories of slavery, go back to the colonial period. Canada has long maintained an economic relationship with the region, and Canadian banks are some of the biggest investors there. The region continues to be economically underdeveloped and generally impoverished.

The British Caribbeans

The chief sources of immigration to Canada are the ex-British colonial countries. Barbados, Guyana, Jamaica, and Trinidad and Tobago have provided most of the immigrants (chiefly but not solely blacks) who have been attracted to Canada. Before the 1960s, these blacks had headed chiefly for the British Isles, but a combination of new liberal Canadian immigration practices and new British exclusionist ones produced a shift after 1967. Many of these newcomers took advantage of the regulations between 1968 and 1973 that allowed admitted visitors to Canada to apply for immigrant status, and there has also been a remigration in recent years from Britain that is officially of "British" immigrants. There is much pressure for family reunification, considerable claims of refugee status (particularly by the Guyanese), and much illegal immigration. Overall, there is a distinct sense among the experts that official statistics routinely undercount the total numbers of people from the British Caribbean area actually resident in Canada. The vast majority of British Caribbeans in Canada (more than 80 percent) live in Ontario, where they are concentrated mainly in Toronto in a number of distinct ethnic neighborhoods. Many immigrants leave their young children behind when they first come to Canada, bringing their children to join them later. As a result, the children can sometimes be late entrants into the educational system, contributing to their dropping out of school and sometimes turning to petty crime. Although most Caribbeans value education, the experiences of some of the young in the school system of Ontario have been difficult, with a racist system confronting students who are seen as having "attitude."

The most common pattern of Caribbean immigration to Canada has been that of the young single woman, often initially attracted by domestic labor arrangements. Most British Caribbeans work, but mainly in manual labor positions. They tend to experience much higher levels of racial discrimination in Canada than they did in their homeland, an experience made more difficult to accept because of the oft-repeated mythology that Canada was relatively free of virulent racism. Finding it difficult to maintain traditional extended families in Canada, Caribbean women have great trouble finding child care, particularly as many families do not have resident fathers for reasons connected with Caribbean cultural practices. Many Caribbeans feel unwelcome in the traditional churches of Canada and have moved into fundamentalist churches of their own making. In recent years, the Caribbean community has developed a number of mechanisms for improving solidarity and visibility, including midsummer carnivals in many Canadian cities. A number of Canada's leading track and field athletes in recent years were born in the West Indies.

The Guyanese

Guyana is a small country on the northeast tip of South America, formerly known as British Guiana. It is an ethnically complex place, with its largest single population component being not blacks but people of Asian Indian descent brought there as indentured servants in the nineteenth century. Decolonization there was accompanied by political conflict, which pitted racial groupings against each other. The People's Progressive Party, which governed in the 1960s, became dominated by Asian Indians and Communists. The British authorities responded by helping Linden Forbes Burnham, a black man, to organize the competing People's National Congress, which took the country to independence in 1966. In the 1980s, the Burnham government began persecuting the East Indian population on racial grounds, and many East Indians responded by coming to

Canada. The newcomers often took advantage of Canada's policy of permitting political refugees to be identified from within the country (see chapter 10) and helped create the enormous backlog of refugee claims of the 1980s. The Guyanese refugees tended to be highly skilled professionals, who could afford to buy airplane tickets to Canada and who found their way fairly readily into the work force, despite considerable deskilling in the early years. Most Guyanese were attracted to metropolitan Toronto, where their common political experiences led to the rapid establishment of a community there. Many of the Guyanese of Indian ancestry, curiously enough, were Christians. Despite considerable obstacles to overcome, the Guyanese have been one of the most successful Third World immigration groups in Canada.

The Haitians

Haiti is an independent republic on the western third of the island of Hispaniola. It experienced a revolution against French colonialism in the 1790s and set up a new nation in 1804. The country was occupied by the United States between 1915 and 1934, and after the American withdrawal Haiti was left in considerable chaos. Out of the disorder the Duvalier family rose to power in the 1950s, governing with the aid of a terrorist body of secret police called the Toutons-Macoutes. This political system produced substantial emigration by people who considered themselves refugees. The bulk of the Haitian population was black and Roman Catholic. Most Haitians spoke Creole, a mixture of French, English, and other languages, but a minority spoke pure French, and many believed in—if they did not actually practice—voodoo. Haitians have been leaving the island in large numbers for most of the twentieth century. Perhaps 200,000 immigrated to the United States between 1950 and 1970. As the Americans narrowed their immigration gateway, the Haitians turned increasingly to Canada. Most of those who came to Canada settled in Quebec.

The first Haitians to arrive in Canada, refugees from the Duvalier regime, consisted mainly of professionals, particularly female teachers and nurses, who immigrated independently. They found ready employment in prosperous Quebec. Later arrivals under "sponsored" and "designated" categories have tended to be less skilled and less well educated, and they have also experienced considerable economic and social discrimination. As with British Caribbeans in Toronto, the problems young Haitians experienced in the school system have led to much dropping out, juvenile delinquency, and the formation of gangs. Especially in Montreal, Haitians have been greatly overrepresented among those complaining of racism before the human rights commission, generating 60 percent of the complaints although representing only 25 percent of the blacks in the city. A number of well-publicized eruptions of violence have occurred between Haitians and the authorities. At the same time, Haitians in Quebec have achieved considerable success as athletes and performers.

Latin America

Latin America is a designation for nearly all of the Americas south of the United States, with the exception of a few small countries (Guyana, Belize) on the northeast coast, which were colonized by the traditional imperial powers of the Caribbean area rather than the Spanish or Portuguese and which are therefore best considered as Caribbean. Most of Latin America speaks Spanish and is Roman Catholic. The largest and most populous nation, Brazil, speaks Portuguese, although it is Roman Catholic in religion. In most areas of Latin America it is the ruling elites who tend to be the most Europeanized; however in some nations there has been considerable political backlash against the Europeans from the majority population, which consists of indigenous Indians and mixed-bloods. Canada has received significant (rather than truly large) numbers of Latin Americans from eight nations: one in North America (Mexico), three in Central America (Guatemala, Nicaragua, and El Salvador), and four in South America (Argentina, Brazil, Chile, and Peru). In most cases the immigration has been relatively recent.

There is a larger overall pattern to most Latin American immigration to Canada: Small initial numbers come from the European elements, who have considerable education, skill, and sometimes even capital. Larger numbers follow as refugees, often illegal arrivals escaping from the political turmoil (either civil war or repressive governments or both) that has occurred in nearly every nation of the region. The refugees are typically less skilled and less European and experience considerable trouble in Canada, partly because of racism, partly because of their refugee history.

The Argentineans

The first significant immigrant arrivals from Argentina were Welsh settlers from Patagonia in 1902. After World War II, small numbers of European professionals from Argentina came to Canada almost every year, often fleeing the Perón regime in Argentina, which became more repressive in the 1970s. By 1991, just more than 11,000 Canadians were listed in the census as Argentinean-born. The bulk of the Argentineans have settled in Ontario (mainly the Toronto area) and Quebec (mainly the Montreal area). Because of their small numbers, wide geographical distribution, and economic integration into Canadian society, the Argentineans do not have a very cohesive or culturally complete community anywhere in Canada. They have generally been well received in Canada.

The Brazilians

Brazil is a vast nation of more than 150 million people. Its population is mostly of mixed racial origin, representing various combinations of Europeans (both the Portuguese, who settled there long ago, and more recent immigrants from every corner of the world), indigenous people, and imported slaves. Brazil was historically not an exporter of immigrants but rather an importer. The poor who might have wanted to emigrate lacked the resources, both capital and documentation. Brazil and Canada have also had few connections, with the possible exception of capitalist investment from Canada in Brazilian transportation and power generation, which for many years made Canada the second leading investor in Brazil, exceeded only by the United States. Much of Canadian investment was involved in the Brazilian Traction Light and Power Company (Brascan), although Alcan Aluminum and Massey-Ferguson have also been heavy investees.

Few immigrants from Brazil came to Canada until the 1960s. Those who did immigrate were usually well-to-do and well-connected Europeans. Since that time, and especially since 1986, a constant trickle of 300–500 immigrants per year have immigrated, often as illegal entrants. Many, especially from the state of Minas Gerais, arrived penniless in Toronto airport on the strength of fraudulent promises made by immigrant recruiters back in Brazil. Thus, Brazilians in Canada are divided into the elite and the poor. Many of the illegal entrants suffered during the 1980s, and a number were eventually expelled or gave up to return home. As with many other national groups in Canada, one of the few unifying cultural factors has been support for the Brazilian team in World Cup soccer competition. Another distinctive feature of Brazilians, of course, is the Portuguese language, which they share in Canada only with the Portuguese and which sets them apart from other Latin Americans.

The Chileans

Chile is another large South American nation with a population of Europeans, mestizos (persons of mixed European/American Indian ancestry), and indigenous natives. About two-thirds are mixed-bloods. As with the rest of Latin America, Europeans are among the elite, and those mestizos closest to the indigenous population are extremely poor. Immigration abroad began under the Allende government, which attempted socialist reforms regarded as hostile by the upper classes; immigration continued under the military dictatorship that overthrew Allende in 1973. Violations of human rights have led many Chileans to flee the country. Canada developed a special program for Chilean refugees in the 1970s. Because of the nature of the Chilean diaspora in the 1960s and 1970s, it is difficult to calculate the total number of Chileans in Canada, although it is generally agreed to be much larger than official statistics would suggest. Chilean immigrants tended to be young but equally divided between males and females. The number of immigrants per year persistently declined from the 1970s to the late 1980s, when it again increased. After the initial refugee stream, most of whom regarded their Canadian residence as temporary, most Chileans coming to Canada sought economic improvement and hence have settled in successfully. Unlike many recent immigrant groups, the Chileans began in Ontario but have left that province. More Chileans are now in urban Quebec and urban Alberta than in Ontario. Chileans have experienced little overt discrimination in Canada, and the extent of their integration in Canadian society depends as much on their own attitudes as on those of the host society.

The Guatemalans

Guatemala is a small country in Central America with a population of about 9 million people, more than half of them indigenous natives, descendants of the Mayas. The indigenous people speak their native languages, and the remainder of the population, mostly mixed-bloods of various origins called ladinos, speak Spanish. Most of the population is Roman Catholic in religion, although Protestant missionaries began making inroads beginning in the 1970s. In the late nineteenth century, land became concentrated in the hands of a small elite. Attempts at land reform by the government of Colonel Jacobo Guzman led to his overthrow, with American assistance, in 1954. The subsequent history of the nation has been one of military dictators defending the large landholders. In the 1970s a left-wing popular movement emerged; it lasted for twenty years, until a form of peace was established in 1996.

Guatemalans began immigrating to Canada in the early 1980s, along with people from El Salvador. About half of the immigrants have regarded themselves as political refugees. Most are young ladinos relatively prosperous by Guatemalan standards, with some education and white-collar experience. Although Guatemalan immigrants on the whole are evenly divided by gender, refugees are heavily skewed toward men, perhaps because of screening processes by Canadian officials in the refugee camps. Guatemalans were among the refugees who sought admission to Canada after arriving in the country, and Guatemala has been on a small list of nations whose people are regarded as impossible to deport because of the dangers to dissenters in their homeland. Immigration from Guatemala has increased annually since its beginning, partly because the United States does not routinely admit many refugees from Central American dictatorships it has favored. Quebec has been favored over Ontario as a destination for Guatemalan immigrants to Canada, and existing studies suggest that most Guatemalans work in unskilled and semiskilled employment in Canada. Women, often without access to education, have some difficulty in finding work because of their lack of skills in Canada's official languages.

The Mexicans

Although Mexico is a North American country that has more than twice the population of Canada—composed of mestizos, indigenous people, and Europeans, in that order numerically—there are relatively few Mexicans in Canada. Spanish-speaking and Roman Catholic, most Mexicans have migrated, legally or illegally, to the United States, with which Mexico shares a lengthy border. A number of Mexicans, though, perhaps 5,000 per year, enter Canada as migrant workers in the summer. Those Mexicans who have officially immigrated in recent years tend to be well off and highly skilled, quickly integrating into the host society. Some of the least well-educated Mexicans to come to Canada have been Mennonites, who have not been treated by Canadian authorities as Mexicans and have tended to blend into existing Canadian Mennonite communities. As with other immigrants, most Mexicans have gravitated to the cities in Ontario and Quebec. There are a few Mexican organizations, but the immigrants are not politically very active and are well dispersed. There has been some professional and occupational deskilling, but most Mexican Canadians are quite successful in their new homeland.

The Nicaraguans

Another small republic in Central America, Nicaragua experienced a Marxist resistance (the Sandinista National Liberation Front) to its military dictatorship beginning in 1963. The success of the Sandinistas in seizing power in 1979 led the United States to refuse to recognize the new government and even to organize a competing guerrilla army (the contras), which produced a bloody civil war that lasted throughout the 1980s. The civil war forced large numbers of Nicaraguans into exile as political refugees. Most Nicaraguans are of mixed blood, speak Spanish, and are Roman Catholics. They began immigrating to Canada in 1984. Official statistics are thought to significantly underestimate the numbers of people from Nicaragua in Canada. Most Nicaraguans reside in Ontario and Alberta, where they have experienced not only the usual deskilling, but also a very high rate of unemployment.

The Peruvians

Peru is another large (in area) country in South America, with a population made up of Europeans, mestizos, and indigenous people. In the 1970s the emergence of two leftist terrorist organizations executing regular violence met with extreme responses from the government, and many Peruvians fled the resultant civil war, which lasted all through the 1980s. Many early Peruvian immigrants had entered Canada illegally between 1957 and 1971. Their status was regularized by an amnesty in 1973, and they began to sponsor family members. Thus, few of the new immigrants from Peru actually entered as refugees. By 1991, the Peruvians officially counted in the Canadian census represented the fourth largest group of Spanish speakers in the country. Most live in Ontario, Quebec, and British Columbia, residing in Toronto, Montreal, and Vancouver. Like most such groups, Peruvians have suffered considerably from deskilling. On the whole, Peruvian Canadians keep a low profile and are seldom in the news.

The Salvadorans

El Salvador is a small Central American republic with a small indigenous population (of Mayan descent) and a larger group of Spanish and mixed-blood people. Land is in the hands of an elite. The Spanish language predominates, and the country is largely Roman Catholic. The country is dominated by coffee cultivation and has experienced considerable displacement of peasants for agricultural purposes, a process that has produced much poverty and discontent. Many Salvadorans joined a guerrilla resistance (the Faribundo Marti National Liberation, or FMLN), causing a civil war. El Salvador's civil war created a large refugee population (one-fourth of the country's 5 million people), many of whom came to Canada under special refugee provisions when the United States closed its doors. Eventually, fear of Salvadorans without documentation led Canada to clamp down on illegal entrants. Estimates are that a much larger number of Salvadorans are in Canada than are counted in official statistics. Most refugees entering Canada were relatively prosperous by Salvadoran standards, due to Canadian selection preferences, and yet they were systematically if unintentionally deskilled in Canada, ending up in low-skilled manual employment—particularly in Toronto, where most immigrants have headed. Like most recent ethnic groups in Canada, the Salvadorans have not been studied much, and there is little detailed information available on their adjustment to Canada.

The Middle East and the Arabs

The Middle East is a vast territory, dominated by Arabic-speaking people and stretching from the Arabian Sea in the east to the Red Sea in the west and beyond. There are twenty-one countries in the Arab world, some of them in North Africa and others in Africa proper. Until the terrorist bombings of 11 September 2001, which placed a spotlight on Arab communities in both the United States and Canada, few Canadians realized how many people of Arab origin resided in Canada—today 1.2 out of every 100 Canadians. Most are clustered in Toronto and Montreal. Of the more than 200,000 Arab immigrants to Canada, less than 10 percent arrived before 1961. Official statistics have difficulty coping with the ethnopolitical complexities of the Arab arrivals. But it is clear that the earlier comers are quite different from the later ones in a variety of ways. The early Arab immigrants were chiefly young males of Eastern Orthodox Christian religion, mainly from Lebanon, and were widely distributed across Canada. The more recent wave is considerably more diverse, headed by Arabs from Lebanon and Egypt but including those of many other countries. The largest number are Palestinians who have entered on passports from Egypt, Israel, Lebanon, Jordan, and the countries of the Persian Gulf (where many Palestinians had moved to work during the conflicts with Israel).

Two categories of immigrants have predominated: entrepreneurs and refugees. The refugees have tried to escape the conflicts in the Holy Land (which date back to the 1940s), the Lebanon wars of the 1970s and 1980s, and more recently, the conflicts in the Persian Gulf region. Despite their diversity, however, most of the recent Arabic immigration, especially since 1981, has been Muslim, with a considerable sense of increasing identification as Arabs, which can be seen in their community organizations. Many are well-educated but have been forced to take menial employment in Canada because of deskilling. The Gulf War produced many negative reactions to the Arab community in Canada, including some violence and intimidation in Toronto and Montreal. Of course, "9–11" has generated even more hostility toward Arabic people. Arabs have not only been associated with terrorism but with illegal immigration and border-crossing as well.

South Asia

South Asia is a region that includes the nations of India, Pakistan, Bangladesh, Sri Lanka, and Nepal. As many as one-half million people residing in Canada have originated from this region, which presently contains a population of more than 1 billion. The South Asians come, at least originally, from an area governed for many centuries by the British Raj, which has a number of consequences for them. It means that they are usually familiar with the English language and with British political traditions. It also means that many have immigrated to Canada only after a previous migration or even migrations to other places in Africa, Asia, the Caribbean region, and even to Europe, all facilitated by the international trade and communications of the British Empire. Despite their diaspora, these people managed over the years before their arrival in Canada to maintain significant aspects of their separate identities as Sikhs or Goans or Bengalis or Pakistanis or Tamils, and have continued the process in

Canada as well. Their history in South Asia was often one of internal conflict, which has sometimes been imported to Canada as well.

The South Asians have come to Canada in three stages. The early stage consisted chiefly of males from the Punjab who came to British Columbia before World War I (see chapter 6). The second stage came in the 1950s and 1960s, when small numbers of South Asian immigrants came chiefly to Toronto. The third stage has occurred since the 1960s. It has included much larger numbers—chiefly of businesspeople, professionals, and entrepreneurs—who have settled in Canada's larger cities, mainly, although not exclusively, in the eastern part of the country. Although the South Asians are typically highly skilled and familiar with English, many have experienced occupational downgrading. They do not share a common religion but are chiefly adherents of non-Christian religions that fall outside the common value systems of Canadians. Many South Asian religions have roots in Hinduism, such as Buddhism, Sikhism, and Jainism. Others have roots in Islam.

The sheer volume of this South Asian migration means that it is both visible and vocal. Unlike most Third World newcomers to Canada, the South Asians have contended for political office, and some have been successful. A premier of British Columbia and several federal cabinet ministers have been members of the larger South Asian community. The members of Parliament who are of South Asian origins have typically been elected by block voting (in which an ethnic group votes *en masse* for a candidate) in constituencies in which their compatriots are numerous. A number of South Asians in Canada, notably Neil Bissoondath, Michael Ondaatje, and Rohinton Mistry, have also become best-selling and award-winning Canadian authors. They are virtually the only representatives of the communities of new immigrants who have established wider literary reputations. In their varying backgrounds, moreover, Bissoondath (born in Trinidad of South Asian parentage), Ondaatje (born in Sri Lanka), and Mistry (born in Bombay) suggest the complexities of the South Asian diaspora.

Southeast Asia

Much of Southeast Asia was originally called Indochina. It consists mainly of the modern states of Vietnam, Burma, Cambodia, Laos, Malaysia, Singapore, and Thailand (previously known as Siam). Much of Southeast Asia has seen large-scale immigration from China and India, and, in recent years, equally substantial emigration, often of those same Chinese and Indian newcomers. Virtually all the Malaysians and Singaporeans in Canada, for example, are ethnically Chinese, living mainly in the greater Toronto area. The region became well known to North Americans during the Vietnam War. Much of the Indochinese part of Southeast Asia was destabilized after World War II when the French were driven out, subsequently becoming involved in civil wars and American intrusion during the 1960s and 1970s. Most of the people from Southeast Asia who came to Canada arrived as refugees; they have experienced deskilling and unemployment but have met their problems stoically. The largest contingents of Southeast Asians came from Cambodia, Laos, and Vietnam, arriving mainly before 1990.

The Cambodians

Cambodia suffered a major holocaust during the mid-1970s when Communist-backed military forces (the Khmer Rouge) occupied the nation and systematically persecuted and evacuated much of the existing population. The Khmer Rouge tried to produce a radical Communist state by force, killing large numbers of Cambodians and forcing millions of others into exile. When neighboring Thailand could no longer absorb more refugees, the refugees ended up in border camps, exposed to military action between the warring factions. Cambodians came to Canada mainly from the refugee camps as "designated class refugees" after 1979. They were sponsored by both the Canadian government and private agencies and became distributed across the cities of the provinces, although most settled in Toronto and Montreal. Most refugees spoke Khmer and practiced various forms of Buddhism. As agricultural peasants, they had few marketable skills, and adjustment to life in Canada was understandably very difficult for these people, complicated by various forms of psychological problems caused by their wartime experiences.

The Laotians

People from Laos began fleeing political turmoil in the 1970s, particularly fearing persecution by a Communist-led nationalistic movement, the Pathet Lao, which set up the Lao People's Democratic Republic in 1975. Most refugees went initially to Thailand, where they joined millions of other displaced persons. Many ultimately found refuge in the United States, although Canada was a popular destination in the period between 1975 and 1984, when western nations attempted to deal with the refugee problems caused by the Vietnam conflict. Many of the best educated Laotians speak French, which drew them to Quebec, where they typically entered unskilled employment. Religion has been an issue for the Laotian community, as reestablishing Theravada Buddhism—the principal religion of the Laotians—in Canada has not been easy, not least because of the need for monks.

The Vietnamese

Vietnamese people began immigrating to Canada in large numbers only after the end of the Vietnam War, although a few Vietnamese students had arrived in Canada earlier and attended various francophone universities. Postwar Vietnamese immigrants have arrived in Canada in two waves. The first, between 1975 and 1978, consisted almost entirely of ethnic Vietnamese of middle-class or professional standing. As francophones, many went to Quebec. These newcomers hold well-paid skilled jobs in Canada and have integrated quite well.

Beginning in 1978, many Vietnamese citizens left their country illegally. These "boat people," many of whom were Sino-Vietnamese (that is, Chinese-Vietnamese), often ended up in refugee camps from which they were resettled by a few Western nations, including Canada. The post-1978 immigrants from Vietnam, including the boat people, were not well equipped to integrate into Canadian life. They were ethni-

A young Vietnamese refugee waves a Canadian flag as he waits to be processed with his family at an immigration center in Montreal. (Owen Franken/Corbis)

cally Chinese, worshipped non-Christian gods, typically spoke neither English nor French, were not well educated, and tended to have few relatives in Canada. These people were attracted to large cities outside the Atlantic region, usually found employment in less well-paid semiskilled occupations, and have had trouble integrating into the labor force. They have experienced considerable racial discrimination in Canada, and many have suffered professional declassification. A number of the Sino-Vietnamese were tradespeople in Vietnam and have opened small businesses in Canada, usually to serve the Vietnamese community. Most Vietnamese immigrants still speak their own tongue most of the time, although parents are concerned about the rapid loss of the language and its replacement by English and French among the young. The second-wave Vietnamese are usually Taoists (a branch of Buddhism), although there is a Christian minority. Like many Southeast Asians, the typical Vietnamese immigrant still does not think of himself or herself as a full-fledged integrated Canadian but is cautiously optimistic about the future of the younger generation. According to the 1991 Canadian census, there were almost 95,000 people of Vietnamese ancestry in Canada.

Asia

Asia is a huge region of the world consisting of a number of nations and territories, including Tibet, China, Korea, Hong Kong, and the island nations of Taiwan, the Philippines, Indonesia, and Japan. Japan, Indonesia, and Tibet have all sent relatively small numbers, between 10,000 and 15,000 immigrants each, to Canada since the 1960s; most Japanese immigrants are associated with Japanese corporations operating in Canada. The principal Asian ethnic groups recently immigrating to Canada in substantial numbers are the Chinese, the Koreans, and the Filipinos.

The Chinese

Chinese people began immigrating to Canada in the 1850s and have in recent years arrived from a number of countries as well as from the two Chinas (mainland China and Taiwan). Before the 1960s, the Chinese were under the same restrictions for admission as other people from Asia. A few were admitted after 1947, but between 1968 and 1984, 170,000 ethnic

*Immigrants from Hong Kong share a music class with other residents of Vancouver,
British Columbia. (Annie Griffiths Belt/Corbis)*

Chinese immigrants came to Canada, principally from mainland China,
Taiwan, Indochina, and particularly Hong Kong. Between 1984 and the
early 1990s, another 176,000 immigrants from that part of the world entered the country. Many of the immigrants from Hong Kong brought
large amounts of capital with them after 1985, under a government program that admitted as immigrants without other tests those who could
invest at least $250,000 in Canadian business ventures. Most of these peo-
ple invested in Canada in order to shelter money and guarantee themselves asylum after the British agreement in 1984 to allow Hong Kong to
become reunited with China in 1997. These rich businesspeople were
deeply resented by many Canadians.

Many of the other Chinese newcomers were highly educated and in
professional occupations, although they typically earned less than Canadians in comparable jobs. Most first-generation Chinese immigrants
speak Chinese at home, but there has been a substantial language loss and
a major shift to English in the second generation. The size of the Chinese
community in several Canadian cities, especially Vancouver and Toronto,
has made possible a substantial cultural life and many institutions, such
as newspapers, radio stations, and banks, to help maintain it.

The Filipinos

People from the Philippines began arriving in Canada in large numbers only after the introduction of Canada's points system in 1967, and the number of Filipinos in Canada now totals nearly 200,000. They have come in two waves. The first, during the 1970s, was mostly composed of young female professionals (mainly in health care), migrating as individuals and taking advantage of the point system. The second, beginning in the late 1970s and continuing ever since, has reflected a more balanced immigrant intake that has relied heavily on sponsorship and family reunification. Many recent Filipino immigrants have been women older than sixty. Filipinos have tended to be attracted to metropolitan Toronto, which has since the 1960s taken in about one-half of the Filipino newcomers each year. British Columbia and Manitoba have also been popular. Quebec and the Atlantic region have received few Filipinos.

Because most postsecondary education in the Philippines is conducted in English (as the common educational language of the nation), most immigrants to Canada have had enough familiarity with English to adjust fairly easily to Canadian culture. In their familiarity with English the Filipinos share much with immigrants from the Indian subcontinent. Filipinos have experienced some discrimination, more in employment than in housing. The problem has usually taken the form of refusal of Canadian employers to recognize educational qualifications acquired in the Philippines. Moreover, although Filipinos rank high among ethnic groups in educational achievement, they rank fairly low in average income, suggesting that there is a general level of discrimination at work. The absence of overt discrimination in housing is a result of the tendency of the immigrants to congregate in Filipino neighborhoods. Filipinos are overwhelmingly Roman Catholic, and their religion has not only helped maintain group solidarity in Canada but also contributed to their acceptance in Canadian society. On the whole, the Filipino experience in Canada has been a positive one.

The Koreans

After World War II, the peninsula of Korea found itself partitioned along the thirty-eighth parallel between the Communist-held portion in the north and the American-occupied portion in the south. Each part set up its own government. In 1950 the Communist Democratic People's Republic of Korea (that is, North Korea) invaded the Republic of Korea (that is, South Korea), touching off a three-year conflict known as the Korean War. At its end, the two countries remained divided and had been virtually destroyed. Both Koreas recovered, and the south gradually experienced a transforming industrial revolution. In the meantime, many Koreans left their war-torn countries and moved to the West, including Canada. By 1991 there were nearly 50,000 people of Korean origin living in Canada. They had come either as independent immigrants or as relatives of those already in the country; few were regarded as refugees. Not many Koreans spoke one of the two official languages of Canada, which slowed down Koreans' integration, but many of the newcomers—who had been professionals at home—opened small businesses across Canada. Many Korean immigrants to Canada were Christians before arrival, and many others have found membership in Christian churches to be a good means to make their way in their new communities. There is an active Korean language press in Canada, as well.

Conclusion

The recent reception of Third World immigrants in Canada, often members of visible minorities, suggests a much more complex pattern than mere racist reaction on the part of the host society. On the whole, the new immigrants have made as satisfactory an adjustment to life in Canada as could realistically be expected. Their experiences in most respects have been little different from those of earlier generations of immigrants to Canada, although the hostile reactions they have suffered from the majority society may in some cases have been more intense or more prolonged because of considerations of skin color. Moreover, for those who came as refugees, those experiences have been much the same as those of any minority refugee group coming to a host nation dominated by a white society. And almost without exception, contemporary members of these various ethnic groups of newcomers have expressed considerable satisfaction with the improvement that has occurred in their situations.

Timeline

1950   Communist Democratic People's Republic of Korea invades Republic of Korea, starts Korean War.

1954   Gamal Abdul Nasser rides wave of nationalism to power in Egypt; Colonel Jacobo Guzman overthrown in Guatemala.
1962   Vietnam War escalates.
1966   Linden Forbes Burnham leads People's National Congress to independence in Guyana.
1967   New guidelines for immigration admissions to Canada.
1972   South Asians expelled from Uganda.
1973   Allende government overthrown in Chile.
1974   Khmer Rouge occupy Cambodia.
1975   Pathet Lao set up Lao People's Democratic Republic.
1979   Sandinistas seize power in Nicaragua.
1985   Hong Kong millionaires bring their capital to Canada.
1986   Penniless refugees come to Toronto from Minas Gerais in Brazil.
1991   United States and Canada intervene in Somalia.
1992   Peace accord between the government of El Salvador and the FMLN.
1993   Eritrea becomes independent from Ethiopia.
1994   Election of Nelson Mandela ends South African apartheid regime.
1999   Adrienne Clarkson, born in Hong Kong in 1939, becomes first immigrant to be chosen as Governor-General in Canada.
2000   Ujjahl Dosanjh becomes first Indo-Canadian chosen as a provincial premier (in British Columbia).

Significant People, Places, and Events

APARTHEID A policy of national racial segregation in all aspects of life, practiced by the government of South Africa from the end of World War II to 1994.

BOAT PEOPLE A reference to any refugee group that has used boats to make their way to freedom. In Canada it is particularly used to refer to South Vietnamese refugees in the 1970s and to Tamil refugees who tried to land in Nova Scotia in the 1980s.

BRAIN DRAIN The tendency for immigration policy from the wealthier nations to lure the most well-educated and the professional citizens away from developing nations.

BRASCAN The Brazilian Traction Light and Power Company, which for many years was one of the largest corporations in Brazil, largely owned by Canadian investors.

BUDDHISM A religious faith that was founded by Buddha in the fifth century B.C.

COPTIC CHRISTIANITY A variety of Christianity practiced in northern Africa among people belonging to the Jacobite sect of Monophysites.

"COLORED PEOPLE" OF SOUTH AFRICA An official designation in South Africa used to refer to people of mixed blood.

DESKILLING The practice of refusing to accept an immigrant's work experience and educational credentials from his or her home nation, thus forcing the newcomers to take employment at a much less skilled level than they had enjoyed in their home countries.

FAMILY REUNIFICATION The process by which other family members—usually females and children—are brought to a new country to join family members already residing there. In Canada this process has turned into formal policies and programs.

FARIBUNDI MARTI NATIONAL LIBERATION (FMLN) The left-wing revolutionary guerrilla movement in El Salvador.

GULF WAR The war in the Middle East against Saddam Hussein and Iraq in the early 1990s.

ISLAM The religious faith practiced by the Muslim followers of Mohammed.

JAINISM An East Indian religion holding doctrines resembling those of Buddhism.

KHMER ROUGE The Communist-backed military group that occupied Cambodia and persecuted millions of people there in the mid-1970s.

LADINOS A term used to refer to the mixed-blood people of Guatemala.

MESTIZOS A Spanish word meaning "mixed blood" and used to refer to mixed-blood people in Latin America.

MISTRY, ROHINTON A prize-winning Canadian author born in Bombay, India.

ONDAATJE, MICHAEL A prize-winning Canadian author born in Sri Lanka.

PATHET LAO The Communist-led nationalist movement in Laos.

SANDINISTA NATIONAL LIBERATION FRONT The Communist-inspired revolutionary movement in Nicaragua.

SIKHISM The religious beliefs of the Sikhs, originally a military-type community founded in sixteenth-century Bengal.

TAOISM One of the main systems of religion in China, founded by the ancient philosopher Lao-Tsze.

TOUTONS-MACOUTES The terrorist police force of the Duvalier regime in Haiti.

Voodoo Traditional magical practices still practiced in twentieth-century Haiti.

Documents

Somalis in Canada: Faduma Abdi Speaks

We are Muslims, we believe in the Islamic religion, and we practised it in our country. People from all over the world, every continent, every country maybe, come to Canada, so all the religions are here. We go to mosque on Fridays instead of Sunday like the Christians. On Saturday and Sunday, there are certain religious classes, but sometimes it is difficult to get transportation. The nearest mosque is on Dundas [Street, in Toronto]. It's too far away, so sometimes it is difficult to get there. I'm Muslim, but I'm not a very religious person. We have our own clothes and our own culture. We like and are very proud to wear our traditional dresses in the summertime. Whether you are very religious or not, winter is your master because you have to wear what the other people wear. But in the summertime, we are very comfortable wearing our dresses, our style. If you are married, you have to cover your hair. That's for religious purposes. We have different *sheekh* (religious leaders). Those are in the top ranks of the religion. In some circles, if you are a woman, whether you are married or not, you have to cover your body except for maybe your eyes, your face. Our tradition is the Somali tradition. We cover our hair and our body. We are all Muslim, but some wear short dresses the way that they like. They pray five times a day, but they wear whatever they like, and others have some restrictions, but it depends, just like Catholicism.

We pray five times a day. Sometimes we pray as a family, but it is not compulsory to do it together. Amina prays on her own and the others do so as well, but on the weekend, if we are all together, we pray together in the morning *(Subah)*, at noon *(Duhur)*, evening *(Asar)*, *(Macrib)* and the final prayers *(Isha)*. That's five prayers. We pray before sunrise, after two o'clock, at six, at nine, and at ten we pray the last one before we go to bed. If it is not possible for them to pray during the day, when they come home, they have a late prayer.

My children socialize with the people at school and maybe they make conversation, but we are different from Canadian girls who want boyfriends. This is prohibited in our culture and our religion. When a girl is ready to be married, then maybe she will talk or make some conversation in order to know the boy before she gets married. But they don't have boyfriends. So my two eldest daughters go to school together, they come home together, they are friends and they walk together. When they come back from school, one of them may go to the kitchen and do her chores and one does her homework and so on, but they don't go out on dates. My son is more active than my daughters. He has some friends, but not girlfriends. I don't know whether he's hiding them from me. He goes with his Canadian friends to the school, then he comes back and usually I don't allow him to go out at night.

Source: Elizabeth McLuhan, ed., *Safe Haven: The Refugee Experience of Five Families* (Toronto: Multicultural History Society of Ontario, 1995), pp. 192–194.

Voices of South Asians in Canada

1. One of the things which most people in Fiji don't appreciate about immigration is how different will be their family and social life in Canada. Immigration changes everything before you even realize it's happening. At least now immigrants can learn from the successes and mistakes of those who came earlier. When I arrived there were only a handful of people from Fiji here, and most of them hadn't arrived so very much earlier than me. Fortunately, I travelled with a few friends, and we stuck together until we got settled. Even so, in looking back we had to overcome really big difficulties. We didn't know a thing about Canada—how to find work, where to live, what a good wage was. We didn't have many people to turn to in order to find out, and had no relatives here to help us in the meantime. If we had brought our families over when we first arrived I don't know how we would have made it financially. Perhaps the worst thing was the loneliness. You can't imagine how strange it was for us, living away from family and friends. It was something that we were not prepared for and could do little to change. In Fiji we were pretty poor by Canadian standards, but we certainly were rich in other ways. Until we got established we shared the worst of both worlds.

2. In Punjab, I and other women had little control over our own affairs. Our responsibilities did not extend beyond everyday household decisions. Most of us had nowhere near the freedom of movement of our husbands. We spent almost all of our time at home; this wasn't too bad, because there were usually other women living in the household and we all visited a lot with other families.

From what I had heard about life in Canada before we came I knew things would be different, but not in the way it turned out. Once we had settled into our own house I found myself terribly alone. My husband worked long hours and spent a lot of time after work visiting with his men friends. We could afford only one car, and I never learned to drive. This meant that all day I usually stayed home—I even had to wait for my husband to drive me to the store. Most other women that I knew were in the same situation. Although no one had intended it, we were all prisoners in our own homes. Some jealous husbands even locked up the telephone when they were away from the house. Maybe Canadian women can stand that kind of isolation, but we just weren't used to it. We all waited for the weekend, when we could at least visit with each other. It's been only in the last few years that some have had their own cars.

3. One of the Five Pillars of Islam that we used to always follow before we came to Canada was to pray five times daily and to attend the mosque on Fridays. Generally speaking, the places from which we came and their style of life was organized in such a way that neither of these posed any real difficulties. What are we to do here, when the work day is so closely regulated by the clock? Some people bring prayer rugs to work and then use their breaks and part of their lunch time for their prayers. Others have had to give up some of their daily prayers. Almost no one has been able to get time off from work on Fridays, so working people generally attend mosque very early in the morning or after work. Ramadan also poses some difficulties, but of a different kind. During the month of Ramadan [the ninth month of the Islamic year] we are supposed to refrain from all food and drink from dawn to dusk. Again, where we come from the days and nights are about equal, so that with practice this fast goes smoothly. But try it in Edmonton, where the late summer days are almost eighteen hours long!

Source: Buchignani, Norman, and Indra, Doreen M., with Srivastiva, Ram, *Continuous Journey: A Social History of South Asians in Canada* (Toronto: McClelland and Stewart, 1985), pp. 149, 156, 188–189.

Bibliography

Abu-Laban, Baha, *An Olive Branch on the Family Tree: The Arabs in Canada* (Toronto: McClelland and Stewart, 1980).

Adelman, Howard, ed., *The Indochinese Refugee Movement: The Canadian Experience* (Toronto: Operation Lifeline, 1979).

Adelman, Howard et al., eds., *Immigration and Refugee Policy: Australia and Canada Compared*, 2 vols. (Toronto: Centre for Refugee Studies, York University, 1994).

Barrier, N. Gerald, and Dusenbery, Verne A., *The Sikh Diaspora: Migration and the Experience Beyond Punjab* (Delhi: Chanakya Publications, 1989).

Basran, H., and Zong, Li, "Devaluation of Foreign Credentials as Perceived by Visible Minority Profession Immigrants," *Canadian Ethnic Studies* 30 (1998), 6–23.

Buchignani, Norman, and Indra, Doreen M., with Srivastiva, Ram, *Continuous Journey: A Social History of South Asians in Canada* (Toronto: McClelland and Stewart, 1985).

Chan, Kwok B., and Indra, Doreen Marie, eds., *Uprooting, Loss and Adaptation: The Resettlement of Indochinese Refugees in Canada* (Ottawa: Canadian Public Health Association, 1987).

Chantavanich, Supang, and Reynolds, E. Bruce, eds., *Indochinese Refugees: Asylum and Resettlement* (Bangkok: Chulalongkorn University, 1988).

Couton, Philippe, "Highly Skilled Immigrants: Recent Trends and Issues," *Isuma: Canadian Journal of Policy Research* 3:2 (fall 2002).

Dorais, Louis-Jacques, Chan, Kwok B., and Indra, Doreen M., eds., *Ten Years Later: Indochinese Communities in Canada* (Montreal: Canadian Asian Studies Association, 1988).

Henry, Frances, *The Caribbean Diaspora in Toronto: Learning to Live with Racism* (Toronto: University of Toronto Press, 1994).

Kurian, George, and Srivastava, Ram P., *Overseas Indians: A Study in Adaptation* (New Delhi: Vikas, 1983).

Magosci, Paul Robert, ed., *Encyclopedia of Canada's Peoples* (Toronto: University of Toronto Press, 1999).

McLellan, Janet, *Many Petals of the Lotus: Five Asian Buddhist Communities in Toronto* (Toronto: University of Toronto Press, 1999).

Moeno, Sylvia Ntlantla, "The 'Non-White' South Africans in Toronto: A Study of the Effects of 'Institutionalized' Apartheid in a Multicultural Society," unpublished Ph.D. dissertation, York University, 1981.

Richmond, Anthony, *Immigration and Ethnic Conflict* (New York: St. Martin's Press, 1988).

Waugh, Earle H., Abu-Laban, Sharon McIrvin, and Qureshi, Regular Burckhardt, eds., *Muslim Families in North America* (Edmonton, Alberta: University of Alberta Press, 1991).

CHAPTER TWELVE

The Future

ROM THE VERY BEGINNING, the land that became Canada was a multiracial place, the destination of a constant flow of new immigrants of varying ethnicities. First came the aboriginal people from Asia. Then came European settlers. In the nineteenth century, immigrants in small numbers began arriving from Asia and were joined in the twentieth century by new arrivals from Africa, Asia, Latin America, and the Caribbean. For most of its history, Canada had an extremely racist dominant society, European in origin and especially hostile to aboriginals and newcomers of visibly different racial origins and cultures. Not until late in the twentieth century, when it adopted both a nondiscriminatory immigration policy and official multiculturalism, did Canada become officially welcoming to visible minorities. The official embracing of multiculturalism and multiracialism does not, of course, necessarily mean that these policies have been translated into action at the grassroots level. As Canada moves into the twenty-first century, its ethnic future remains unclear and uncertain. The trends of the past twenty-five years have to some extent been contradictory ones, and it is not at all certain which ones will prevail in the future.

Canada's current immigration policy provides several important dilemmas for the Canadian government and people. One involves the speed with which the racial and religious makeup of the Canadian population is changing. If the change comes too fast and is not greeted positively by the Canadian public, racist reaction is likely to increase. A second dilemma is the question of whether ethnic customs that infringe on human rights (such as female genital mutilation, blood feuds, or the jihad) are to be protected under the guise of multiculturalism. A third dilemma revolves around the extent to which international gangsters and terrorists have been able to enter Canada as immigrants—sometimes as political refugees—and find shelter. Canadians were distressed both before and after the 11 September 2001 attack on the World Trade Center to discover that many terrorists had been living in Canada as ordinary citizens. What effect the threats of international terrorism will have on Canadian immigration policy and practice remains to be seen.

Immigration

The 2001 Canadian decennial census reaffirmed the future importance of immigration to Canada. Data for all Canadian provinces indicated that the Canadian birth rate had fallen well below replacement level, at less than 1.5 children per female inhabitant. Such a birth rate means that Canada cannot maintain its existing population much longer through natural increase, much less grow its population. A continued immigration of several hundred thousand newcomers per year will be necessary to sustain even the slowest of population growth. Such an intake, according to Statistics Canada, would allow the Canadian population to grow to about 37 million in 2040 and then to stabilize. More, or even continued, growth will obviously require either increased birth rates or a higher intake of immigrants.

Determining how many new immigrants to admit each year remains a basic problem for Canada. Although Canada ranks very high on all unofficial surveys of the best nations in the world in which to live, it can no longer expect to attract large numbers of newcomers from the highly industrialized world and will have to continue to obtain its new immigrants from the underdeveloped portions of the world, as it has been doing for the past thirty years. There are thus only limited options for choosing those parts of the

West Indian Canadian writer Neil Bissoondath, author of the best-selling book Selling Illusions: The Cult of Multiculturalism in Canada, *photographed in 1999. Bissoondath is a critic of Canada's multiculturalism legislation. (Bassouls Sophie/Corbis)*

world from which immigrants will be drawn; immigrants will inevitably come from the Third World, often as refugees. They are likely to be more difficult to assimilate than earlier immigrants because of their cultural differences from the majority of Canadian society—as well as because of their racial origins—and are likely to require increasing amounts of racial, religious, and ethnic tolerance as time goes on. The difficulties of dealing successfully with this sort of intake are likely to prevent the nation from opening its doors to numbers much larger than are being admitted at present. All available evidence suggests that race, religion, and color are not as important as was once thought. On the other hand, social class and educational level are clearly key determinants in the successful integration of newcomers into Canadian society. At the same time, immigration policy must come to terms with both domestic and international trends.

Probably the most important problem for Canada in dealing with its new immigrants is attempting to determine whether or how to prevent them from continuing to congregate in a handful of the nation's largest cities and how to distribute them better across the country. Geographically, Canada remains a vast nation of relatively empty space, with most of its population clustered within a few miles of the American border. Even along that border there are large areas of very low population density.

The exploitation of natural resources is still very important to Canada, which faces a serious internal problem of development because of the relative lack of attractiveness of the nonurban areas, particularly in the more remote regions. Natural-born Canadians continue to be drawn to urban centers by the availability both of economic opportunity and of amenities, including health care, shopping, and culture. It is true that the resource sector of the Canadian economy has displayed many weaknesses in recent years. Agriculture, especially the family farm, is in serious disarray, and fishing off the coasts suffers from a decline in fish stocks. The most serious problem remains that most Canadians simply find nonurban residence to be a relatively unattractive proposition, and new immigrants are not drawn to the countryside either. Not only do these realities limit resource development, but they also mean that rapid—almost uncontrolled—urbanization has produced a large number of social problems, especially for such larger Canadian cities as Toronto, Montreal, and Vancouver.

Some debate has occurred over the question of how to direct new immigrants to areas where their economic and social contribution can be more rather than less functional. There are those who regard any attempt to direct the destination of new immigrants as coercive, but it appears likely that only some policy of coercion, such as a requirement that new arrivals reside in certain regions for specified periods of time or a policy that ties benefits to nonurban locations, will have much effect.

A related problem in distributing immigrants is the tendency for the newcomers to gather in the largest cities in certain regions. Ontario and British Columbia attract a disproportionate number of immigrants, and the Atlantic region very few. As for Quebec, it takes in fewer newcomers than its geographic position and economic situation might suggest. In large part, this is because relatively few of the current wave of immigrants are francophones. Few are anglophones either, but given the choice of learning one or the other of the official languages of Canada, many immigrants prefer to learn English, which has utility across the continent, rather than French, which is of value only in Quebec. Whether Quebec's long-term strategy of insisting on education and French language usage to guarantee the preservation of a core culture will work—at least with immigrants—is still not entirely clear.

If the most important internal problem with immigration policy is achieving a better distribution in residency of new immigrants, the most important external problem has been the increasing evidence that certain worldwide political and religious beliefs can produce undesirable candidates for immigration. There appear to be some newcomers who positively conspire while residing in the country. This is an extremely contention-laden question that has appeared in recent years, especially with the spread of international terrorist activities among certain religio-political groups. Canada has in recent years been relatively welcoming to members of these groups, and some leaders in the United States have gone so far as to claim that Canada has actually harbored and protected terrorists. The solution usually advocated for this problem is a perimeter security zone around North America that would be jointly policed with the intent of keeping terrorists out of the zone. The Canadian government has quietly resisted implementing such a plan, chiefly on the grounds that the nation would in the process lose control over its immigration policy and perhaps lose its welcoming attitudes. It is certainly true that most Canadians regard much of the American reaction to the World Trade Center terrorist attack of 11 September 2001 as overstated. But, at the very least, it would appear that Canada will have to monitor much more carefully the religious and political beliefs of those it admits into the country, both as visitors and as immigrants.

Toronto Blue Jays mascot "Diamond" stands with fifty new Canadian citizens prior to a Toronto Blue Jays game in 2003. The new citizens participated in throwing out the ceremonial first pitch. (REUTERS/Mike Cassese)

Ethnicity

By the year 2000 it was abundantly clear that Canada had won its campaign to impose the concept of multiculturalism upon the nation. Indeed, most Canadians had by the new millennium quite forgotten that multiculturalism had been originally intended to exist only in a bilingual and bicultural framework. What has happened instead is that multiculturalism itself has become the principal framework within which biculturalism operates. To a considerable extent, this victory—mainly at the level of national mythology—has been encouraged by the idea that multiculturalism distinguishes Canada from the United States in ways desired by the Canadian people. Most Canadians still see the United States as a melting pot, however outdated such a notion has become, and Canada as a mosaic or rainbow in which ethnic or racial groups are treated less coercively by the state or other forces of assimilationism.

But if multiculturalism has become an integral part of Canada's national mythology, it is still not clear what its long-term impact will be on

Canadian society and Canadian culture. The most detailed and fully articulated critique, now almost two decades old, has come from the writer Neil
Bissoondath in a best-selling book entitled *Selling Illusions: The Cult of
Multiculturalism in Canada,* originally published in 1984. In this book, Bissoondath pointed out that Canadian multiculturalism legislation lacked
any clear definitions. He went on to insist that multiculturalism assumed
that immigrants did not wish to assimilate into Canadian society and that
their cultures could be frozen in time. The policy encouraged racial tolerance, Bissoondath claimed, but it discouraged racial acceptance, thus producing a mild form of cultural apartheid. Like many Canadians at the
time, Bissoondath was incensed by a conference of writers held in Vancouver, which attempted to limit attendance to members of visible racial minorities, including native people, and he thought about apartheid in these
terms. Perhaps most significantly, he maintained, multiculturalism did not
come to terms with either ethnic intermixing or the possibilities for a new
multiracial society emerging from the Canadian experience.

   We still do not know what the long-term implications of multiculturalism will be, especially in terms of how the schools will deal with the concept. From Quebec's standpoint, schools in the province are intended to
educate all Quebeckers into a core French culture. To a considerable extent, there is a comparable anglophone core culture outside Quebec. As
for multiculturalism, it continues to emphasize the ceremonial vestiges of
the immigrant past. But there is also increasing evidence that recent immigrants desire to be educated in their own languages and culture and
now often have the population concentrations to make such separate
schools work. If new Canadians come to insist on ethnic schooling rather
than core-culture schooling, the nation could become culturally balka-
nized relatively rapidly. What versions of Canadian history or the Canadian literary canon, for example, would be taught in separate schools?
Moreover, should the emphasis be placed not on the old issues of the past
but on the creation, as Bissoondath suggests, of a new multiracial society
in Canada? Despite the extent and cogency of the critique of multiculturalism, however, it remains a popular policy in most quarters outside Quebec and has become, for better or worse, part of Canadian thinking.

Quebec

To a considerable extent, Quebec still controls the constitutional agenda
for Canada. Although Quebec separatism is relatively quiet at this writing,

few experts could be found to argue that it could not spring to life again very quickly. A resurgent separatism, if successful in gaining a majority within Quebec, might produce two possible outcomes. One would involve, through some form of negotiated sovereignty association, a major revision of the very nature of the Canadian nation. Certainly in theoretical terms, sovereignty association for Quebec could be achieved, however differently the resultant nation might function. The model would likely be the European community, with Canadian provinces standing in for European nation-states. One of the consequences of such a new constitution might well be the possibility of finding a better fit for aboriginal self-government.

The other possible outcome of renewed separatist agitation could be a unilateral declaration of independence by Quebec. Total Quebec independence would, in the short run, probably produce fewer changes for the Canadian constitution than sovereignty association, but in the long run it would have profound effects on the nation. Whether the new Canada without Quebec would become a multicultural nation within a unilingual and unicultural framework—or something entirely different—is an interesting question. Whether Canada would survive as a nation without Quebec, or whether the various provinces and/or regions would scramble to relocate themselves within North America and thus destroy Canada, is equally unclear. Although it is impossible in a brief space to discuss all the possible permutations of a resurgent and successful Quebec separatism movement, it is clear that the implications for Canada could be quite profound.

Aboriginal Rights

Canadian aboriginals are easily the fastest-growing segment of the Canadian population. The First Nations have considerably higher birth rates—often described as resembling those in the Third World—and their overall increase in numbers will have considerable influence on the future of Canada. Aboriginal populations are hardly equally distributed across the nation, and increases will be felt only from Quebec westward. One of the most important current policy debates within Canada is over the question of how best to move the First Nations out of their Third World demographic status. The traditional answer of the Canadian government has been that aboriginals need to become assimilated into Canadian society. The traditional response of the First Nations has been to refuse such assimilation, which in recent years has been resisted with the aid of insistence on aboriginal rights, including the right of self-government.

As of this writing, the Canadian government is attempting another major overhaul of the federal Indian Act, so far on a unilateral basis because the First Nations have resolutely refused to cooperate. The government wants to eliminate most of the present paternalisms of the Indian Act, but the First Nations insist that Canada owes them a certain level of positive treatment and that, in any event, it could remove paternalism only by negotiating an entirely different structure of relationships. Canadians still do not have any clear idea of how the aboriginal rights claims of the First Nations will play out, especially in British Columbia, which is the province with the largest number of native peoples and the largest number of rights cases in the courts.

The recent plebiscite strategy of the British Columbia government, if it continues, could make negotiated settlements virtually impossible. No province has been more involved with aboriginal rights negotiations than British Columbia, where few treaties existed between First Nations and the Crown. On 4 July 2002, the results of a British Columbia referendum on aboriginal negotiations were announced in the nation's newspapers. The referendum had been organized on the basis of new legislation passed in the British Columbia legislature in the spring of 2002. The legislation stated that a legitimate vote of more than 50 percent on any question would be binding on the province. In April of 2002, Elections British Columbia mailed out 2,127,829 referendum packages to its citizens. The questions were phrased in such a way that affirmative answers considerably limited the province's flexibility—and its ability to make a generous settlement—in its negotiations with its First Nations. (For the questions and responses, see the end of this chapter). The province's churches and other organizations had counseled the electorate to spoil their ballots as a protest against the illegitimacy of the process, but only 26,702 voters returned improperly completed material, which indicated that the protest campaign was a failure. In the end, 763,480 ballots were returned. This figure represented 35.83 percent of those eligible to vote, a very low figure by comparison with the results of the constitutional referendum of 1992 or the Quebec referendum of 1995. Whether such referenda will become more common, both for dealing with First Nations negotiations and for dealing with other public issues that require negotiation, is not clear at this time.

A number of collateral questions also confuse and complicate the First Nations agenda. The residential schools question, although not, strictly speaking, an aboriginal rights issue, remains before the courts. And the federal government consistently refuses to recognize either the aboriginal rights of, or any official aboriginal status for, the Métis, who are one of the most rapidly growing segments of the aboriginal community across the nation. Not only are the Métis growing in number, but any recognition of their status could also instantly increase their numbers substantially, as many Métis do not declare their origins so long as it is not a official or legal status. First Nations spokespeople continue to insist that aboriginals are not simply another ethnic group in Canada but one with a special claim upon the government and the nation. At the same time, it might well be difficult for the government to grant real concessions to aboriginal rights because of the constitutional implications. So far no ethnic community has come forward to insist on complete self-government, and such a demand is probably unlikely. But ethnic communities often do ally with aboriginal communities on educational matters, particularly on the right of such communities to opt out of the core educational system in favor of the teaching of their own language and culture.

Life with Uncle Sam

The question of immigration screening and continental security represents the most immediate manifestation of the problems immigration and ethnicity pose for the Canadian-American relationship. But there are really much larger matters at stake. Even before the creation of Canada as a distinct nation in North America, many observers north of the forty-ninth parallel had begun to appreciate that those resident there could remain out of the American orbit only if they were able to maintain a separate culture and a separate identity. Over the years, much of the insistence on the maintenance of a core culture or cultures and the assimilation of immigrants into those core cultures has come from those seeking to distinguish Canadians from Americans.

Although the myth of multiculturalism may on one level help maintain Canada's distinctiveness from the United States, it is a frail weapon in several senses. In the first place, the United States is a much more multicultural place than most Canadians realize. More importantly, one of the consequences of multiculturalism could be the gradual erosion of the core cultures of Canada, especially outside Quebec, and thus the disappearance of the so-called Canadian Identity, most aspects of which are based upon European inheritances. The battlefield in these matters will be in the various classrooms across the nation. At the moment, Quebec history and Quebec literature are prominent in the curricula of the Quebec schools, and Canadian history and Canadian literature are equally prominent in the curricula of schools outside Quebec. There is virtually no overlap. Whether this would continue to be the case in the future is another matter.

A number of scenarios are possible; four seem most likely. In one, reshaping of Canadian ethnicity through immigration could well produce a majority population that does not share (and even rejects) the European heritage and core cultures of earlier generations. In another, a non-European population could well continue to accept and adhere to the core cultures as the gradual acculturation of newcomers proceeds. The American example suggests that core cultures can survive, providing that the addition of new populations is sufficiently small, but the Australian experience indicates that some core values—such as the monarchy—may have to be sacrificed along the way. A third possibility would be to maintain both the core culture and elements of (or respect for) minority ethnic cultures. In a final scenario, those defending the core cultures may well decide that only the termination of substantial immigration will permit the retention of core values.

Documents

British Columbia Referendum on Aboriginal Land Title Settlement

The following questions were included on a ballot sent on 2 April 2002 to all registered voters in the province of British Columbia by its government as part of a provincial referendum on the Nisga'a Final Agreement. The percentage of Yes votes is in parentheses.

1. Do you agree that the Provincial Government should adopt the principle that private property should not be expropriated for treaty settlement? (84.52 percent voted Yes)
2. Do you agree that the Provincial Government should adopt the principle that the terms and conditions of leases and licenses should be respected; and fair compensation for unavoidable disruption of commercial interests should be ensured? (92.12 percent voted Yes)
3. Do you agree that the Provincial Government should adopt the

principle that hunting, fishing, and recreational opportunities on Crown land should be ensured for all British Columbians? (93.14 percent voted Yes)

4. Do you agree that the Provincial Government should adopt the principle that parks and protected areas should be maintained for the use and benefit of all British Columbians? (94.50 percent voted Yes)

5. Do you agree that the Provincial Government should adopt the principle that province-wide standards of resource management and environmental protection should continue to apply? (93.63 percent voted Yes)

6. Do you agree that the Provincial Government should adopt the principle that aboriginal self-government should have the characteristics of local government, with powers delegated from Canada and British Columbia? (87.25 percent voted Yes)

7. Do you agree that the Provincial Government should adopt the principle that treaties should include mechanisms for harmonizing land use planning between aboriginal governments and neighbouring local governments? (91.79 percent voted Yes)

8. Do you agree that the Provincial Government should adopt the principle that the existing tax exemptions for aboriginal people should be phased out? (90.31 percent voted Yes)

Multiculturalists Are the Real Racists

The following editorial by Mark Steyn appeared in the National Post, *one of Canada's national newspapers, on 19 August 2002.*

As I understand it, the benefits of multiculturalism are that the sterile white-bread cultures of Australia, Canada and Britain get some great ethnic restaurants and a Commonwealth Games opening ceremony that lasts until two in the morning. But, in the case of those Muslim ghettoes in Sydney, in Oslo, in Paris, in Copenhagen and in Manchester, multiculturalism means that the worst attributes of Muslim culture—the subjugation of women—combined with the worst attributes of Western culture—licence and self-gratification. Tattooed, pierced Pakistani skinhead gangs swaggering down the streets of Northern England are as much a product of multiculturalism as the turban-wearing Sikh Mountie in the vice-regal escort at Rideau Hall. Yet even in the face of the crudest assaults on its most cherished causes—women's rights, gay rights—the political class turns squeamishly away.

Once upon a time we knew what to do. A British district officer, coming upon a scene of suttee, was told by the locals that in Hindu culture it was the custom to cremate a widow on her husband's funeral pyre. He replied that in British culture it was the custom to hang chaps who did that sort of thing. There are many great things about India—curry, pyjamas, sitars, software engineers—but suttee was not one of them. What a pity we're no longer capable of being "judgmental" and "discriminating." We're told that the old-school imperialists were racists, that they thought of the wogs as inferior. But, if so, they at least considered them capable of improvement. The multiculturalists are just as racist. The only difference is that they think the wogs can never reform. Good heavens, you can't expect a Muslim in Norway not to go about raping the womenfolk! Much better just to get used to it.

As one is always obliged to explain when tiptoeing around this territory, I'm not a racist, only a culturist. I believe Western culture—rule of law, universal suffrage, etc.—is preferable to Arab culture: that's why there are millions of Muslims in Scandinavia, and four Scandinavians in Syria. Follow the traffic. I support immigration, but with assimilation. Without it, like a Hindu widow, we're slowly climbing on the funeral pyre of our lost empires. You see it in European foreign policy already: they're scared of their mysterious, swelling, unstoppable Muslim population.

Islam For All reported the other day that, at present demographic rates, in 20 years' time the majority of Holland's children (the population under 18) will be Muslim. It will be the first Islamic country in western Europe since the loss of Spain. Europe is the colony now—Mark Steyn

Source: National Post, 19 August 2002, p. A14.

Bibliography

Abu-Laban, Yasmee, *Selling Diversity: Immigration, Multiculturalism in Canada* (Toronto: Broadview Press, 2002).

Asch, Michael, *Home and Native Land: Aboriginal Rights and the Canadian Constitution* (Vancouver: University of British Columbia Press, 1993).

Bissoondath, Neil, *Selling Illusions: The Cult of Multiculturalism in Canada* (1984).

Fieras, Augie, *Engaging Diversity: Multiculturalism in Canada,* 2nd ed. (Scarborough, Ontario: Nelson Thomson Learning, 2001).

Foster, Lorne, *Turnstile Immigration: Multiculturalism, Social Order, and Social Justice in Canada* (Toronto: Thompson Educational Publishing, 1998).

Isajiw, Vsevolod, *Understanding Diversity: Ethnicity and Race in the Canadian Context* (Toronto: Thompson Educational Publishing, 1999).

Kallan, Evelyn, *Ethnicity and Human Rights in Canada*, 2nd ed. (Toronto: Oxford University Press, 1995).

Kazarian, Shahe, *Diversity Issues in Law Enforcement*, 2nd ed. (Toronto: Emond Montgomery, 2001).

Lenihan, Donald, *Leveraging over Diversity: Canada as a Learning Society* (Ottawa: Centre for Collaborative Government, 2001).

Li, Peter, *Destination Canada: Immigration Debates and Issues* (Toronto: Oxford University Press, 2002).

Index

About the Author

J. M. Bumsted is professor of history at the University of Manitoba, Winnipeg, Canada, and the author of numerous books and articles on Canadian history.